ONCE INTREPID WARRIORS

258-69
243-49.
32-33, 66-67, 92

ONCE
INTREPID
WARRIORS

INDIANA UNIVERSITY PRESS
BLOOMINGTON AND INDIANAPOLIS

GENDER, ETHNICITY, AND THE CULTURAL POLITICS OF MAASAI DEVELOPMENT

Dorothy L. Hodgson

This book is a publication of

Indiana University Press
601 North Morton Street
Bloomington, IN 47404-3797 USA

http: //www.indiana.edu/~iupress

Telephone orders   800-842-6796
Fax orders   812-855-7931
Orders by e-mail   iuporder@indiana.edu

First Indiana University Press
paperback edition 2004

© 2001 by Dorothy L. Hodgson

The paper used in this publication meets the minimum
requirements of American National Standard for
Information Sciences—Permanence of Paper for
Printed Library Materials, ANSI Z39.48-1984.

Manufactured in the United States of America

Library of Congress Cataloging-in-Publication Data

Hodgson, Dorothy Louise.
   Once intrepid warriors : gender, ethnicity, and the
cultural politics of Maasai development / Dorothy L.
Hodgson.
      p.   cm.
   Includes bibliographical references and index.
   ISBN 0-253-33909-X (cl : alk. paper) —
   ISBN 0-253-21451-3 (pa : alk. paper)
      1. Masai (African people)—Social conditions.
   2. Masai (African people)—Ethnic identity. 3. Rural
development—Tanzania. 4. Women, Masai.
   I. Title.

DT443.3.M37 H63 2001
305.89650678—dc21
                                              00-050640

2 3 4 5   06 05 04

For my parents
Sigrid and Gordon Graves and Hutch and Jan Hodgson

CONTENTS

Contents

Acknowledgments

This book, although promoted as an individual accomplishment, would have been an impossible task without the support, advice, and contributions of family, friends and colleagues. First and foremost, I would like to thank the many people in Tanzania who for over fifteen years have welcomed me into their homes and lives, answered my endless questions, and made Tanzania a place where I must always return, as it now occupies *nusu ya moyo yangu* (half of my heart). My debts to the residents of Emairete, Embopong' and Mti Mmoja for their patience and insights are tremendous, and I only hope that this book in some small way meets their expectations. Others who have been part of the broad and varied networks that have supported my work in Tanzania include the Peterson "clan," Stan and Marie Benson, Trish McCauley and Kees Terhell, Dick Bakker, Jo Driessen and Judith Jackson, Leo Fortes, Marian Fortes; Bishop Dennis Durning, Pat Patten, Gerry Kohler, Ned Marchessault, Joe Herzstein, Elfreide Steffen, and other members of the Spiritan community; Saning'o Milliary, Alais Morindat, Josephine Kashe and other friends from my days with the Arusha Diocesan Development Office; Francis Ikayo, Peter Toima, the late Saruni Ngulay, and other Maasai activists; and my first research assistant, Christopher ole Ndangoya. I am grateful to the late Henry Fosbrooke, Gerry Kohler, Reuben Kunei, the Congregation of the Holy Ghost and various district officers in Monduli for allowing me access to their files and libraries. Visits with Majorie Mbilinyi while I was in Dar always refreshed and revived me intellectually and emotionally. Morani Poyoni's friendship, intelligence, sense of humor, and companionship made my research not only possible but enjoyable.

My research and writing has been generously supported at various stages by the following sources: an International Doctoral Research Fellowship funded by the Joint Committee on African Studies of the Social Science Research Council and the American Council of Learned Societies with funds provided by the Rockefeller Foundation, a Fulbright-Hays Doctoral Dissertation Abroad Award, a National Science Foundation Doctoral Dissertation Improvement Grant (BNS #9114350), an Andrew W. Mellon Candidacy Fellowship, an Andrew W. Mellon Dissertation Fellowship, a Rackham Predoctoral Fellowship, a Margaret Wray French Foundation Grant, a Center for Afroamerican and African Studies—Ford Foundation Grant, several Rackham Travel Grants from the University of Michigan, a Jacob J. Javits Fellowship from the U.S. Department of Education, a Richard Carley Hunt Memorial Postdoctoral Fellowship from the Wenner-Gren Foundation for Anthropological Research, and Faculty Research Grants and research allowances from the Research Council and Faculty of Arts and Sciences at Rutgers University. I am grateful to the Tanzanian Commission for Science and Technology for permission to carry out this research (especially to Mr. Nguli and Ms. Gideon for their patience and assistance), to Professor C. K. Omari, who has served as my local sponsor since 1991, and to the Department of Sociology and Anthropology at the University of Dar es Salaam for research affiliation in 1991–1993. The staff at the Tanzanian National Archives in both Dar es Salaam and Arusha graciously assisted me in locating files and making endless photocopies.

This book began as a dissertation at the University of Michigan and reflects the intellectual guidance of Gracia Clark and Ray Kelly, my co-chairs, as well as Fred Cooper, Roger Rouse, and David William Cohen. In particular Fred Cooper, although officially an "outside" member, was extremely influential in shaping the direction of first the thesis, then the book. His encyclopedic knowledge of African history, theoretical incisiveness, and minute attention to detail has helped me to be a better historian. Other faculty members at Michigan who shaped my intellectual development include Maxwell Owusu, Paul Dresch, Tom Fricke, Nick Dirks, the late Skip Rappaport, and Sherry Ortner.

Numerous colleagues have read all or parts of the manuscript at different stages of development. I would especially like to thank the following for their critical comments, advice, and encouragement: Richard Schroeder, Elliot Fratkin, Jane Parpart, Tom Spear, Rod Neumann, Neil Smith, Cindi Katz, Maria Grosz-Ngate, Sheryl McCurdy, Pam Scully, Lisa Lindsay, Vigdis Broch-Due, Aud Talle, David Anderson, Dan Brockington, Pete Brosius, Clifton Crais, Gudrun Dahl, Arturo Escobar, Akhil Gupta, Susan Geiger, Robert Gordon, Jean Hay, Sharon Hutchinson, Jim Igoe, Alan Jacobs, Alice Kessler-Harris, Monica van Beusekom, and Eric Worby. Richard Waller carefully read the manuscript at a critical point and has been consistently generous in his sharing of ideas and sources.

At Rutgers, I have benefited tremendously from intellectual and social engagements with my colleagues in anthropology, African studies, and women's studies. Special thanks to Abena Busia, Barbara Balliet, Carolyn Brown, Peter Guarnnacia, Jack Harris, Allen Howard, Walton Johnson, Bonnie McCay, Michael Moffat, Pat Roos, and Meredeth Turshen, who, each in their own way, have advised and encouraged me in the sometimes strange world of academia. A number of graduate students at Rutgers and elsewhere have influenced my thinking in this book, including Belinda Blinkoff, Becca Etz, Paige West, Andy Bickford, Johnelle Lamarque, Jessica Libove, Nia Parson, Rob Marlin, Wanda Mills, Beth Pratt, and Waranee Pokapanichwong. Robyn Stone, Belinda Blinkoff, Andy Bickford, Lisa Vanderlinden, Nia Parson, and Nelly Hala served as research assistants for various stages of this manuscript; their contributions included typing tape transcripts, re-entering census data, verifying German translations, and making endless trips to the library to find books and copy articles. The computer wizardry of my mother, Sigrid Graves, rescued my census data from oblivion, and first Cindi Katz then Jesse Barron exorcised the evil spirits who were hexing my computer and printer.

Research and writing require emotional as well as intellectual support, and I would like to thank those who have kept me going, and even laughing, through this long process: Abena Busia, Pete Brosius, Barbara Cooper, Clifton Crais, Joe Cronley, Janet Finn, Tamara Giles-Vernick, Sheila Grant, Jim Hagen, Deb Judy, Catherine Macdonald, Monica Marciczkiewicz, Leslie McCall, Sheryl McCurdy, Richard Miller, Jan Opdyke, Adela Pinch, Maaria Seppanen, Pam Scully, John Stiles, Noel Sturgeon, Ken Vernick, Geri Waksler, and Anne Waters. Cindi Katz and Neil Smith have been the best of friends, with bottles of champagne, gourmet feasts, and soothing irreverence at the ready to celebrate every step of the way. Karen Goldstein's loving care of my son, Luke, made it possible for me to focus on my work and helped teach me to be a parent.

But without my family, none of this would have been achieved. Visits and conversations with my siblings and their children provided much-needed respite from theoretical tangles and grammatical knots. My grandmother, Nana, offered financial and moral support at critical junctures. My husband and partner in life, Rick Schroeder, helped shape the thesis and now the book with his intellectual insight, gift for writing, and consistent companionship and support. I fear many of my sentences and thoughts don't measure up to his exacting standards, but I tried. Our son Luke arrived between the thesis and book and quickly made both of us rethink our priorities. Life (and book-writing) slowed down a bit, as I vowed to never be one of those authors who thank their family for doing without them for a few years. He is a delight in every way.

But my parents, Sigrid and Gordon Graves and Hutch and Jan Hodgson, made me what I am today with their love, support, and sacrifices. It is to them, therefore, that I dedicate this book, in hopes that it might help them understand why I became an anthropologist and historian.

Kind thanks to the following publishers for permission to republish selections, often revised, from the following: "Pastoralism, Patriarchy and History: Changing Gender Relations among Maasai in Tanganyika," *Journal of African History* 40, no. 1 (1999): 41–65 and "Taking Stock: State Control, Ethnic Identity and Pastoralist Development in Tanganyika, 1948–1958," *Journal of African History* 41, no. 1 (2000): 55–78, both reprinted with the permission of Cambridge University Press; "Once Intrepid Warriors: Modernity and the Production of Maasai Masculinities," *Ethnology* 38, no. 2 (1999): 121–150, reprinted with the permission of the University of Pittsburgh; "Critical Interventions: Dilemmas of Accountability in Contemporary Ethnographic Research," *Identities* 6, nos. 2/3 (1999): 201–224, reprinted with the permission of *Identities: Global Studies in Culture and Power;* "Embodying the Contradictions of Modernity: Gender and Spirit Possession among Maasai in Tanzania," in *Gendered Encounters: Challenging Cultural Boundaries and Social Hierarchies in Africa,* ed. Maria Grosz-Ngate and Omari Kokole, pp. 111–129, reprinted with the permission of Routledge Press; "Women as Children: Culture, Political Economy and Gender Inequality among Kisongo Maasai," *Nomadic Peoples* n. s. 3, no. 2 (1999): 115–130, reprinted with the permission of Bergahn Books; and "Images and Interventions: The Problems of Pastoralist Development," in *The Poor Are Not Us: Poverty and Pastoralism in Eastern Africa,* ed. David M. Anderson and Vigdis Broch-Due, pp. 221–239, reprinted with the permission of James Currey Publishers.

Abbreviations

AD	Arusha District
ADB	Arusha District Book
ADO	Assistant District Officer
ADDO	Arusha Diocesan Development Office
AO	Administrative Officer
AR	Annual Reports
ARB	Arusha Region Book
ARG	Arusha Region
BB	Blue Books
BPP	Bovine pleuropneumonia
CCM	Chama Cha Mapinduzi (Revolutionary Party)
CDA	Colonial Development Act, 1929
CDWA	Colonial Development and Welfare Act, 1940
CHG	Congregation of the Holy Ghost
CO	Colonial Office series, Public Records Office
CS	Chief Secretary
CVO	Chief Veterinary Officer
Dar	Dar es Salaam
DC	District Commissioner
DO	District Officer
DPO	District Political Officer
EAC	East Africana Collection
EARC	East African Royal Commission
ECF	East Coast fever
FAO	Food and Agriculture Organization
HCP	Hans Cory Papers
IBRD	International Bank for Reconstruction and Development
IDO	indigenous development organization
IIED	International Institute for Environment and Development

Abbreviations

IMF	International Monetary Fund
KIPOC	Korongoro Integrated People Oriented to Conservation
KPS	Kisongo Pilot Scheme
MaD	Masai District
MC	Masai Council (variously called Masai District Council, Masai Local Council, Masai Federal Council)
MCR	Masailand Comprehensive Report
MD	Monduli District
MDB	Masai District Book
MDP	Maasai Development Plan, 1951–1955
MLDRMP	Maasai Livestock Development and Range Management Project (USAID)
MLDRMPA	Maasai Livestock Development and Range Management Project Archives
MMJ	Monduli Mission Journal, Volumes I & II
NA	Native Authority, Native Administration
NGO	non-governmental organization
NP	Northern Province
NPWS	Northern Province Wheat Scheme
PANET	Pastoralist Network in Tanzania
PC	Provincial Commissioner
PRO	Public Records Office
RC	Regional Commissioner
RHL	Rhodes House Library
SAP	Structural Adjustment Policy
SC	Senior Commissioner
SI	Stock Inspector
SIDO	Small Industries Development Organization
SOAS	School of Oriental and African Studies
SVO	Senior Veterinary Officer
SW	Swahili
TANU	Tanganyika African National Union
TGNP	Tanzania Gender Networking Programme
TNA	Tanzania National Archives
UPE	Universal Primary Education
USAID	United States Agency for International Development
UWT	Umoja wa Wanawake
VD	Veterinary Department
WID	women in development

ONCE INTREPID WARRIORS

INTRODUCTION:
SEEING MAASAI

In a 1989 letter to the *New York Times*, Susan Scharfman lamented the fate of Maasai in Tanzania, as described in a recent article by Jane Perlez (1989):

> After reading your [article] from Tanzania, which asks if the fate of the semi-nomadic Masai people is at last to be fenced in, I was horrified to learn that Tanzania is encouraging subjugation and ultimate obliteration of some of its oldest and noblest inhabitants, the once free and beautiful Masai.
>
> Now they are supposed to be farmers. They know nothing of farming. They are nomadic herdsmen and once intrepid warriors. The herdsmen have become the herded. Your photo, showing Masai languishing around a mud hut, is a loathsome and grim reminder of what can happen to the cultural integrity of any people. (Scharfman 1989)

Scharfman's letter elicited a lengthy reply from another reader:

> Scharfman seem[s] to have fallen victim to the common fallacy that all undeveloped and indigenous cultures are superior to the attempts by governmental forces to change them.
>
> Every culture, whether "primitive" or "sophisticated," has its good and bad features, and admiration for the good aspects should not blind one to the undesirable practices or attitudes that might be perfectly legitimate targets for modification.
>
> It is surprising that a professional woman such as Ms. Scharfman, a retired Foreign Service Officer who lived in Nairobi in the 1960's [is] so quick to defend the Masai, whose culture considers women to be completely valueless.
>
> A Masai woman derives her only status from the production of sons, and a barren woman or widow with daughters is treated as much less than the cattle from whom the Masai derive their wealth. Further, the Masai practice universal female circumcision, a practice that is brutal, painful and often leads to severe health problems, which may end in early female mortality through complications of reproductive function.
>
> The Masai, who believe that cattle are wealth and that the whole world (as they know it) is their domain, do not practice responsible animal husbandry—

they are interested in quantity, not quality. The vast herds that result from such views are a severe drain on a fragile ecological system.

While the Government of Tanzania may not have the best-thought-out approach to solving the problems engendered by the Masai way of life, it is attempting to change cultural attitudes that Ms. Scharfman might [not] wish [her] own daughters to suffer under.

Masai men may well bitterly resent the loss of a freedom that made them the undisputed kings of their own world. In several generations, however, Masai women may well rejoice in the opportunities for education, advancement and free choice that are now as alien to their culture as farming is. (Akhtar 1989)[1]

The contradictory images invoked by the letters are shared by wider audiences: the essential linkage of Maasai[2] ethnic identity to pastoralism prompts either a romantic vision of Maasai and other pastoralists as "once free and beautiful" but now "languishing" or the impression that Maasai, interested "in quantity, not quality," hold vast, destructive herds. These images are also gendered: the belief that pastoralism as a mode of production is an inherently male pursuit; the obsessive fascination with young men, the "once intrepid warrior"; the subsequent notion that Maasai culture "considers women to be completely valueless"; and the contention that Maasai women lack "opportunities for education, advancement, and free choice." Reinforced by emotion, bolstered by common usage and lush coffee-table books (e.g., Saitoti and Beckwith 1980; Amin, Willetts, and Eames 1987), expressed in letters full of moral indignation and outrage, these images become realities, become "facts," for many and all too often become the assumptions shaping policies and practices.

Both the gendered images and the contradictory positions Scharfman and Akhtar espouse have been shared by many Westerners, from the first explorers and missionaries in the nineteenth century to the tourists taking their pictures today. To mention "the Maasai," as I have discovered in conversation after conversation about my research, is to invoke for most people images of warriors, of men herding cattle, of proud patriarchs. But it also evokes comments on their "cultural conservatism," "unwillingness to change"—Maasai are icons of "primitive," "prehistoric," "traditional" Africa. As an article in the *East African Annual* of 1956–1957 exclaimed:

> The most picturesque people in East Africa are those of a tribe which has changed little of its ways since the advent of the White Man—the Masai. The tourist, when he spots a Masai herding his beloved cattle, or leaning gracefully on the haft of his long bladed spear, cannot but feel the spirit of Africa of yesterday. ("Kilusu" 1956–1957: 135)

Even today, for certain Tanzanians and other Africans, "the Maasai" represent embarrassing reminders of a lifestyle now despised and denigrated.

But these caricatures have little resemblance to the Maasai men and women I have come to know since I first began living and working with them in 1985. The first Maasai I met were young men studying at the Oldonyo Sambu Secondary School, where I lived and briefly taught from March 1985 through December 1987. Sponsored by the local Catholic diocese, the school was originally started for Maasai boys, who were often rejected or ignored by other secondary schools. Some, such as Thomas, thrived on the opportunity to study and learn science, history, English, and geography. Others, such as Alex, yearned for the holidays when they could return to their homes, their parents, and their fellow *ilmurran* age-mates. At the Arusha Diocesan Development Office (ADDO), where I wrote proposals and coordinated women's development projects and, as of March 1996, served as the diocesan coordinator of development, I came to know a range of Maasai: from my hard-working colleagues and friends on the development team to the men and women I met during my travels, community meetings, and development work throughout Maasai areas in Ngorongoro, Kiteto, Monduli, and Arusha Districts.[3] I listened carefully as people discussed their problems, debated their development priorities (a new road or borehole?), challenged my preconceptions about their needs and desires, and taught me to think anew about the meanings of terms such as poverty, progress, and power. Throughout, I was touched by the generous hospitality of even the most destitute women, the insistent teasing and laughter of young and old, and a remarkable ability to endure almost daily slights and depredations by those non-Maasai they called "Waswahili."

During my three years as a development practitioner, I was intrigued by the deep ambivalence many Maasai expressed toward development and the Tanzanian government. "So the government is finally asking us what we want!" one older man exclaimed at the beginning of a village meeting. Others refused to meet with us, claiming they had no time to waste on empty promises. Many were eager to share their development goals with us, but only because we were affiliated with the Catholic church, *not* the government. "Every year we pay a 'development tax,' but where does that money go? Into the bellies of the government workers!" Their array of feelings and responses to our initiatives—resentment, hope, betrayal, mistrust, cautious optimism, effusive gratitude—made me wonder about their prior experiences with the government and development.

I was also troubled by the strained relationships I witnessed between men and women of all ages. In Simanjiro, as in other places, women such as Nanyorie complained bitterly about how their husbands treated them "like donkeys": demanding labor, ignoring their rights to cattle and smallstock, beating them on occasion, and generally treating them without *enkanyit*, or respect. Some men I spoke to mocked the capacity of women to design, implement, and manage their own development projects, such as maize-grinding machines or small cooperative stores. Women were mere "children" in the eyes of these men and thus needed male guidance and control. In Loliondo, women berated men for being impotent relics of another age, hopelessly and helplessly attached to their cattle and resistant to change of any kind. These women saw themselves on the forefront of development, eager to experiment with and adopt new practices and ways of being. In Kijungu, at the instigation of an American Maryknoll sister, women responded to the attempts by their menfolk to usurp their transportation project by refusing to cook for them or sleep with them. A few days later, a group of beleaguered men arrived on our doorstep at ADDO, pleading with us to intervene as mediators in the situation.

Similarly, development efforts affected relationships between the generations. Many older men and women bewailed the selfishness and sassiness of their adult children. Elder men, in particular, denounced their children for ignoring, if not challenging, their authority. "He doesn't listen to me anymore," explained one old man in Simanjiro about his adult son. "He just does as he pleases, regardless of what I tell him." Several older women accused their sons of neglecting them, of failing to adequately care for them in their old age.

Of course not all relationships between men and women were troubled or tense. In Engarenaibor, a junior male elder enthusiastically encouraged a gathering of women to voice their complaints and express their needs. Many women had fond relationships with their sons and warm interactions with their lovers (usually *ilmurran*) and their husbands' age-mates (their classificatory husbands). Some spouses treated each other with respect and care. But the main tensions seemed to be within households: between husbands and wives and between older parents (especially fathers) and their young adult children. Almost everyone spoke of these familial tensions in terms of an increasing lack of respect (*enkanyit*), a key principle of Maasai social relations.

These experiences prompted many questions: Was development helping or hurting people? Why were some Maasai so distrustful of development, while others were eager to embrace it? Why had relationships between and among men and women changed so drastically? Why were relationships strained within so many households? What was the role of "outsiders" such as myself, other ADDO workers, and the Tanzanian state in provoking such tensions? Traveling through Maasai areas, I read the layered, complicated history of development and change in these relationships and in the landscape—the schools without books, health clinics without medicine, demolished water taps, corrugated iron roofs over empty rectangular buildings, bicycles, eroded plains, cattle dips and more. Searching for answers led me to cultural anthropology and, eventually, to history.

My initial assumptions were that the problems and tensions I had witnessed during my work among Maasai were the products of a lack of development initiatives. As a result, people struggled to access and control the meager resources made available for development projects, debating and negotiating their differing priorities. I recall one meeting in Engarenaibor, where after a series of separate meetings with men and women we asked everyone to convene together. In response to our question about how best to use development funds which had been contributed by the villagers, man after man stood up and argued that the money should be spent to improve the road to the village. The women, seated quietly together at the back of the meeting, muttered among themselves. Finally, a respected elderly woman stood up and denounced the men: "What do you men know about the needs of this village! As women, we do all of the work, and we know best. Will a road feed our children and cattle? What we need is clean water close to our homes so that we women don't have to walk long distances every day, and so we no longer get sick from dirty water. A road, hmphh!" As she sat down, another woman stood and repeated the demand for a nearby domestic water source, then another woman, and yet another. Stunned, the men talked among themselves, then several spoke in favor of the women's demands: "The women know best and we have listened. Without this meeting we wouldn't have heard them, but we agree with their demands. Let us use the money to build a borehole."

This story about competing visions of development highlights the centrality of gender to such differences and debates and the possibilities for reconciling contrasting demands. But, like most development anecdotes, it masks a crucial element of the story—the long history of development interventions among Maasai. Imagine my surprise when I discovered through archival research and interviews that Maasai, in Engarenaibor and elsewhere, had been the focus of development interventions for over eighty years. Instead of the short, erratic history that I had presumed, I discovered wave after wave of development efforts, ranging from small-scale "self-help" water projects to large, integrated schemes encompassing animal husbandry, water development, and range management.

My research has therefore been driven, in part, by a desire to explore and explain a compelling paradox: "the Maasai" in Tanzania, particularly male Maasai, have been the focus of almost eighty years of "development" interventions, from efforts by the British in the early colonial period to build more water sources and reduce the incidence of certain livestock diseases to a huge multimillion-dollar, ten-year USAID-sponsored project in the 1970s to convert Maasai areas into "ranching associations" and Maasai men into "modern ranchers." Rather than producing food security, collective empowerment vis-à-vis the nation-state, or adequate health and education opportunities, these development interventions increased stratification, limited food production and income strategies, and facilitated the economic and political disenfranchisement of women. Furthermore, despite these years of development, Maasai are still viewed as "culturally conservative," stubbornly persistent in their pursuit of pastoralism and rejection of farming, sedentarization, education, and other more "modern" ways of being.

Similar "problems" of "pastoralists" and "development" have been documented throughout eastern Africa (see, e.g., Galaty, Aronson, and Salzman 1981; Galaty and Salzman 1981; Raikes 1981; Evangelou 1984; Fratkin 1991; Hogg 1992; Anderson and Broch-Due 1999); they include lack of participation by pastoralists in state-sponsored development projects, declining livestock production, failure to repair and maintain water projects and other infrastructures, limited offtake[4] for beef sales, and lack of interest in income-earning opportunities. My purpose is not to deny the importance of addressing these concerns, but to argue that part of the "problem" is the formulation of "the problem" itself. Using the Maasai case as an example of the dilemma of many pastoralist groups throughout East Africa, this book argues that it is not Maasai (and other pastoralists) who have persevered unchanged by history, but the cultural images which shape how state administrators, nongovernmental organizations, and other development agents perceive "pastoralists," particularly "the Maasai." In other words, it is the ways of "seeing Maasai," not "being Maasai," which have persisted.[5] That development projects that have consistently failed to meet their own objectives are repeatedly implemented in almost identical versions has less to do with any inherent Maasai "conservatism" and more to do with the fixed images which produce invariable definitions of the problem, and therefore similar measures to solve it.[6]

To disentangle this paradox, I combine anthropological and historical data, methods, and theories[7] to look at the discourses, practices, and effects of "development" among Maasai in Tanzania: the historical and spatial location of "development" as a global discourse, focusing on how the legacies and experiences of development in the colonial period have shaped contemporary attitudes, interventions, and experiences; the relationship between the "politics of representation" and the "politics of intervention" (Castells 1997), especially in terms of the role of "development" in constituting and reinforcing certain "categories of control," particularly ethnic identity; and the gendered ways in which "development," "ethnicity," and other categories of control have been constituted and their subsequent effects on local gendered relations of power. In what follows, I want to assess how key aspects of culture, power, history, and space contribute, together, to an understanding of the relationship between development as a transnational process and the lived experience of development.

Defining and Locating "Development"

Anthropologists have long had an "ambiguous engagement" (Bennett 1988) with development as policymakers, practitioners, consultants, or critics. Because most believe in the "doctrine of local self-determination" ("the right of local people to make their own decisions about change"), anthropologists confront moral, theoretical, and political dilemmas about whether or not (and if so, how) to participate in the seemingly inevitable development process (Bennett 1988). Many of their studies reluctantly take development for granted and explore how to "improve" it by incorporating "better" understandings of local culture and social structure (see Hoben 1982 for an overview), while others decry "development" for "destroying traditional culture" (e.g., Harman 1988; Bodley 1975).

Many would sympathize with the frustrated ambivalence of one elderly Maasai man who told me in 1992 that "really, I don't want our culture to be changed, because if we change our culture we will all be stupid. But I also don't want development to be lost. Because if it is lost we will all go to the bush." Or as another male elder complained: "I don't want our Maasai culture to be changed at all; I don't want our children to be changed; I don't want our cattle to be changed so that we don't have them anymore. . . . I don't want this area to be cultivated even though I want a farm, but I don't want it to be farmed so that the cattle have to be fenced in." Like the opinions of anthropologists and other scholars of development, the opinions of these elders were shaped by their beliefs and assumptions about the meaning of and relationship between development and culture.

As many have noted, the marvelous ambiguity of the term "development"—its multiple, often contradictory meanings and uses for different peoples in different places and times—allows for its appropriation as a justification for or objective of innumerable interests and agendas (e.g., Sachs 1992; Cowen and Shenton 1996; Crush 1995; Grillo and Stirrat 1997; Cooper and Packard 1997; Watts 1993). Thus, while "development" could mean something as abstract as "social progress," an equally vague concept open to varied visions of the route and destination of such a journey, it can also be applied to narrower, supposedly technical agendas, such as water development or livestock development. These ambiguities of meaning enable related mystification over the purpose, objectives, and effects of development: Development for whom? By whom? Toward what goals? Whose goals?

Moreover, development is a site for struggles over meaning as well as struggles over practice. Implicit in the multiple uses of the term are assumptions about the proper nature of progress and the content and criteria of prosperity and poverty. Dominant explanatory paradigms such as modernization theory (e.g., Rostow 1960), underdevelopment theory (e.g., Gunder Frank 1970 [1966]), and world systems theory (e.g., Wallerstein 1974) all privilege economic categories such as markets, production, exchange, industrialization, profit, and consumption. Yet these categories themselves entail cultural assumptions and convey cultural, even moral, messages. Poverty, for example, is reconceptualized in terms of material deficits, ignoring other modes such as spiritual poverty, while progress is defined as economic growth rather than, say, social justice. Every invocation of development implies a vision about a particular ordering of the world, promotes specific processes of change, and privileges certain objectives over others. To analyze and understand development, we must therefore integrate political-economic analysis with cultural analysis: How do struggles over the meaning of progress, prosperity, and poverty inform the policies and practices of development, and vice versa? How do certain cultural assumptions and images shape the form and content of development interventions, or, to use the terms of Castells (1997), what is the relationship between the "politics of representation" and the "politics of intervention"?

To address the cultural politics of development, this book seeks to define and locate "development" both historically and spatially. Chapters 2 through 5 explore the consequences of development interventions from the colonial period to contemporary times. What is this structure/process/paradigm called "development"? How and why has it become the dominant process structuring contemporary political-economic relationships between nation-states, recasting the political geography of "metropoles" and "colonies" into that of the "first" world and "third" world"? In his incisive book, Escobar (1995) noted how the "discovery" of mass "poverty" in Asia, Africa, and Latin America in the post–World War II era led to the emergence of "development," a vague term which encompassed and justified a range of interventions to "manage" and "reduce" poverty. Influenced, as I am, by Foucault's work on the relationships of power and knowledge and their articulation through discursive practices (see, e.g., Foucault 1972, 1978 [1976], 1979), Escobar demonstrated convincingly the pervasive effects of development discourse as a "hegemonic form of representation":

> the construction of the poor and underdeveloped as universal, preconstituted subjects, based on the privilege of the representers; the exercise of power over the Third World made possible by this discursive homogenization (which entails erasure of the complexity and diversity of Third World peoples, so that a squatter in Mexico City, a Nepalese peasant, and a Tuareg nomad become equivalent to each other as poor and underdeveloped); and the colonization and domination of the natural and human ecologies and economies of the Third World. (Escobar 1995: 53)

Yet, as Escobar recognizes, however totalizing the production and effects of development discourse may seem at a global level, development is always mediated, reshaped, and even resisted at local levels when policies are translated into practices. He calls, therefore, for

> local-level ethnographic studies that focus on development discourses and practices—how they are introduced in community settings, their modes of operation, the ways in which they are transformed or utilized, their effects on community identity formation and structures, and so on. (1995: 48)

My book is just that—a local-level, ethnohistorical study of the discourses, practices, and effects of "development" as it has emerged, shifted, and persisted among Maasai in Tanzania in the colonial and post-colonial periods.[8]

Although primarily "local" in focus, I situate the particular development discourses and practices I examine in terms of the shifting national and transnational imperatives and objectives which partly produce them. Local people, however "marginal" and "out of the way" they may be, are still a people living in our common world of power and knowledge, "of expanding capitalisms, ever-militarizing nation-states, and contested cultural politics" (Tsing 1993: x). Vested with the cultural assumptions and political agendas of its practitioners, "development" is a significant medium for the national and transnational dissemination of cultural ideas and practices. Development policies and practices therefore interact with and reconfigure local political, economic, and cultural relations and ideas in important, although often unintended and unexpected, ways. Furthermore, development operates simultaneously on multiple scales, at once producing and reinforcing certain spatial and symbolic boundaries (such as "the community" or the "nation-state") while working across them (cf. Gupta and Ferguson 1997). As in the Maasai case, many problems and conflicts arise because of disputes over or contradictions inherent in scale: What is the appropriate unit of development—an individual, a community, a village, an ethnic group, or a state? Who defines and monitors the boundaries of these units? Whose goals take precedence, a community's or a government's? How do international donors, non-governmental organizations, and others who operate across these boundaries and scales mediate and inform such debates?

The primary relationship I examine is that between development and the exercise of state power. Development, as I demonstrate, was never a peripheral project of the colonial or post-colonial state but was central to the expansion and maintenance of state power (cf. Berman and Lonsdale 1992; Little 1992). While Cooper (1997), Escobar (1995), and others date the emergence of what we know as "development" to the post–World War II period, I believe that interventions we would call "development" emerged earlier, at least in Tanzania.[9] Certain types of interventions, such as the construction of additional water supplies or measures to reduce stock diseases and "improve" animal husbandry methods, were instituted in tandem with the establishment and expansion of colonial rule and control. Although not called "development" at the time, these same measures were repeatedly instituted under the name "development" at later dates. What did change were the bureaucratic structures and administrative rationales for development: from itinerant district officers and veterinary experts working (tensely) together in the early colonial period to the professionalization of development into a formalized, heavily bureaucratized division of labor between managers, planners, and technical experts today. Yet the earlier, haphazard efforts closely resemble recent development projects organized around the tropes of "self-help" and "grassroots." Broadening the definition of "development" to include the early pre–World War II efforts in the historiography of development enables us to understand development as central to the establishment, exercise, and expansion of state power from the moment when what we call "states" first began.

Another central issue of this book is the relationship between development in the colonial and post-colonial periods.[10] What are the continuities and changes in the form and content of development policies and practices over time? How have the legacies of development efforts by the colonial state shaped development in the post-colonial period? Development practitioners, whether employed by international donors, state governments, or indigenous NGOs, often suffer from what I call "historical amnesia." Although many planners rely on the past in the form of "baseline" surveys in order to evaluate the progress of their projects, few consider the actual history of development itself in the places in which they work. Intent on working for change in the future, they ignore the transformations that have occurred in the past, especially in terms of prior development projects. In the Maasai case, state administrators repeatedly implemented similar projects, which inevitably failed, yet again, for similar reasons. When projects were evaluated, administrators could understand their failures only in narrow terms as problems of administration or technical expertise rather than as symptoms of broader social, economic, and political problems.

The planners may have historical amnesia, but those who are the "targets" of repeated development efforts remember the struggles, successes, and failures all too well. Memories of prior interventions into their lives shape their attitudes and involvement with new initiatives. Each new project leaves a legacy for the next, a layered history of success and failure often visible in the landscape. But the memories and lived experience of development resonate far beyond particular projects. Social changes in gender relations, political authority, or economic rights are usually gradual, impossible to trace to a specific time or project. They only become visible in greater time depths, such as decades or generations. Thus, while Ferguson (1990), in his influential and important ethnography of a World Bank project in Lesotho, seeks to analyze "the apparatus that is to do the 'developing'" rather than "the people to be 'developed'" (1990: 17), I include both "the apparatus" and "the people" in my field of analysis. Attention to the ways people reshape, negotiate, avoid, and even resist development reveals how development never determines but only structures their lives. Expanding the field of analysis to include the multiple local relations of power of gender, ethnicity, age, and class shows that while development, as Ferguson argues, may well operate as an "anti-politics" machine by deflecting and silencing political activism against "the state," it nevertheless has profoundly political effects in terms of local and regional power relations.

Constituting Categories of Control: "Ethnicity"

A second, overlapping concern is how first the colonial state then the post-colonial state used "development" to facilitate the formation of certain "identities," or what I call "categories of control," to signify the power implicit in the construction, negotiation, assertion, or denial of "identities" (cf. Friedman 1994; Gewertz and Errington 1991). Ethnic identity, or "being Maasai," is first and foremost among the categories, but there are others, including livestock "owner," native "authority," household "head," and even a territorial identity, "Maasailand."

Ethnicity, of course, has long been a topic of study for anthropologists, historians, and other scholars. After the radical critique launched by Mafeje (1971) and others accusing European colonizers of reconstructing African reality in terms of their perceptions that African societies were particularly tribal, Iliffe (1979), Ranger (1983), and others built on similar insights. They presented substantive analyses of the invention of tradition during the colonial period, especially the invention of "tribes" and "chiefs" crucial to facilitating the implementation of indirect rule. Similarly, Ranger (1983) showed how Europeans froze certain flexible laws and rights into "tradition" by codifying them: "Once the 'traditions' relating to community, identity and land-rights were written down in court records and exposed to the criteria of the invented customary model, a new and unchanging body of tradition had been created" (1983: 251). In other words, "what were called customary law, customary land-rights, customary political structure and so on, were in fact *all* invented by colonial codification" (1983: 250).

But this creation of tradition required active participation and collaboration by some Africans (see also Vail 1991; Ambler 1988). As Iliffe states, while the colonizers in Tanganyika "had the power and created a new political geography [of tribes], . . . many Africans had strong personal motives for creating new units which they could lead. Europeans believed Africans belonged to tribes; Africans built tribes to belong to" (Iliffe 1979: 324). Ranger, aware that "codified and reified custom was manipulated by such vested interests as a means of asserting or increasing control" (1983: 254), identified four sets of power dynamics in which such manipulation of "custom" took place: relationships between elders and youths, men and women, chiefs and subjects, and indigenous populations and migrants (1983: 254–260).

Ethnic identity, however, did not disappear with colonialism but took on new meanings and political roles vis-à-vis nationalist politics (see, e.g., Saul 1979; Van Binsbergen 1981). The invocation of ethnic identity by contemporary Africans, and its ongoing construction, negotiation, and saliency, cannot be dismissed as "false consciousness" (Mafeje 1971: 259), nor can it be discounted by some Marxists as residual or reduced to mere class consciousness (Saul 1979). Van Binsbergen's experience, as my own fieldwork confirms, is not unique: the people with whom he was working kept emphasizing their distinct "Nkoya-ness" to him, despite the lack of any distinguishing features from their neighbors: "How did the Nkoya, against so many odds, manage to convince me that they were 'a tribe'?" (1981: 67). For Maasai, as for Nkoya, their sense of ethnic identity is not a primordial attachment but a product of shared historical experience. However exaggerated or incongruous it may be, *"this does not make it less real"* (Van Binsbergen 1981: 68, my emphasis).[11]

How did a certain configuration of characteristics come to be defined as "being Maasai"? I do not think that Maasai ethnicity was merely an imposed, colonially constructed identity. Instead, a certain representation of "Maasai-ness" came to dominate colonial imaginations, shape colonial policies, and eventually, with the collaboration of some Maasai themselves, shape Maasai realities. The British did not "invent" Maasai identity so much as they manipulated and heightened distinctions among categories of relationality that were already present and provided the means for certain factions of Maasai to articulate and strengthen their hegemonic notions of ethnic and gender identity (cf. Waller 1993b). Development interventions were central to reinforcing and perpetuating this image of "Maasai-ness." Simply put, since "being Maasai" meant being a pastoralist, most development initiatives were designed to sustain Maasai as pastoralists, as "Maasai." But most important, "being Maasai" was configured as a masculine category—"real" Maasai were pastoralists, warriors, and nomads, all of which were perceived as male pursuits. This static, androcentric image of Maasai ethnic identity persists today, continuing to shape the content and form of post-colonial development interventions.

The Politics of Gender

Gender is another category of analysis, especially in terms of the interconstruction of gender and ethnicity. The study of gender has received increasing theoretical attention in the past two decades. As distinguished from the "anthropology of women" school, which seeks to recover and represent the experiences of women as central to their studies and texts (e.g., Shostak 1981; Rosaldo and Lamphere 1974),[12] the anthropology of gender shifts the focus from just women to study the cultural construction of gender, patterns of gender relations, and gender as an organizing force in societies (see, e.g., Mac-Cormack and Strathern 1980; Ortner and Whitehead 1981; Collier and Yanagisako 1987; Moore 1988; Collier 1988). Key to this shift has been the realization that the actions of and ideas about women can never fully be understood unless they are examined in relationship to those of men in the same society (Rosaldo 1980; Scott 1988).

Gender, I argue, is produced, maintained, and transformed through the cultural and social relations of power between women and men (but also among women and men) (cf. Connell 1987; di Leonardo 1991). At a given time and place, a particular configuration of gender ideas and practices prevails that is the historical product of certain power relations. Power is central to the maintenance, reproduction, and transformation of such a configuration and to the relations between its elements. As such, gender inequality is never merely a matter of economic, political, or religious prestige or other power differences but a complicated, tenuous interaction between these and other relations. Furthermore, since these multiple terrains of power are embedded in regional, national, and global landscapes, any configuration of gender shapes and is shaped by these broader sets of structures and relations (cf. Grosz-Ngate and Kokole 1997). Merging ethnographic and historical methods and theories provides the analytic capacity to unravel and analyze key dimensions of these interwoven relations, revealing how shifts, however slight, in one domain reverberate through the network, undermining or reinforcing other relations of power (cf. Scott 1988; di Leonardo 1991; Imam, Mama, and Sow 1997).

To me, the interconstruction of gender and ethnicity is particularly fruitful for the study of development among Maasai. In the past, most studies which considered both gender and ethnicity held one term constant: if gender was the focus of analysis, then women and men were assumed to experience and express ethnicity in similar ways (see, e.g., Etienne and Leacock 1980; Stichter and Parpart 1988); if studies of ethnicity examined the practices and ideas of men, they assumed that the same was true for women (see most chapters in Spear and Waller 1993 for "the Maasai"). But gender and ethnicity are interconstructed (e.g., Greene 1996; Davison 1997); that is, these axes of difference interact over time to produce, reproduce, and transform one another. Gender and ethnicity are both dynamic, historical categories that mutually constitute one another, along with other social differences such as age, class, and citizenship.

Specifically, I explore the gendered ways in which the paradox of male Maasai as icons of tradition was produced and perpetuated: the historical origins of the prevalent masculine imagery of "being Maasai"; its rigid enforcement through development interventions by both the colonial and postcolonial states; and the ways such gendered images and interventions shaped and were shaped by the ideas and practices of Maasai women and men. Today, what it means to be a Maasai in general, and a Maasai man or woman in particular, is significantly different from what it meant even twenty years ago. The ethnic signifier "Maasai" has itself become gendered, at least in dominant representations of the state; many scholars, and most Maasai men, see their world as primarily male. Yet both men and women actively define, monitor, and redefine the boundaries of what it means to be a Maasai, such that ethnicity, in this case, serves as a vehicle for negotiating gendered relations of power.

This book offers a challenge to androcentric assumptions and accounts of pastoralist gender relations.[13] In part because of the enduring influence of structural-functional accounts of the "cattle complex" of pastoralist peoples (Herskovits 1926; Evans-Pritchard 1940; Schneider 1979), most descriptions of African pastoralists presume that men dominate and have always dominated virtually every domain of life, including economic resources, political decision-making, and cultural production (cf. Hodgson 2000c). In fact, despite work which has demonstrated the complexities of trying to determine the "status" of East African pastoralist women,[14] pastoralist gender relations seem to exist outside of history and be immune to change. Harold Schneider, for example, contended in 1979 that among East African pastoralists, men's control of livestock gave them control of women, who were "usually thoroughly subordinated to men and thus unable to establish independent identity as a production force" (1979: 82). In his rich 1979 ethnography of Matapato Maasai, Paul Spencer claimed that both male and female Maasai believe in "the undisputed right of men to own women as 'possessions'" (1979: 198). Marriage, in his view, was therefore "the transfer of a woman as a possession from her father who reared her to her husband who rules her" (1979: 25). Melissa Llewelyn-Davies's (1981) study of Loita Maasai women in Kenya corroborated Spencer's findings. Loita Maasai women perceived themselves and were perceived as "property" to be bought and sold by men with bridewealth. Llewelyn-Davies argued that the "elder patriarchs" used their control of property rights in women, children, and livestock to control the production and reproduction of both livestock and human beings. Similarly, in his symbolic analysis of pastoral Maasai ideology, John Galaty (1979) contended that Maasai men were the "real" pastoralists, while Maasai men negatively equated Maasai women with lower-status hunters, providing an ideological explanation for their lower status. Thus, whether they attributed their findings to material or ideological sources (or some combination of the two), few anthropologists questioned the "undisputed right" of contemporary male pastoralists "to own women as possessions."

But, one should ask, how do women come to be thought of as "property," as "possessions" that are "owned" and controlled by men? Contemporary gender relations among pastoralists, which many scholars (myself included) have described as "patriarchal" because of men's political and economic domination of women, are not inherent to pastoralism as a mode of production or an ideology but are the result of a historically particular constellation of interactions involving both British and Maasai ideas and practices.[15] Specifically, it was during the colonial period of state formation that the parameters of male Maasai power expanded to embrace new modes of control and authority, becoming something that might be called "patriarchal."[16] Although the term "patriarchy" is ambiguous in that it can name a range of context-specific gendered power relations, I use it here to refer to situations as described above, where men dominate women politically and economically. Such control is relational, never thorough; often contradictory and inconsistent; and maintained through extended negotiations and struggles. In other words, patriarchy, like gender, is produced, maintained, and transformed not only through the cultural and social relations of power between women and men but also among women and among men. These relations are therefore historically produced at the intersection and through the interplay of local and translocal cultural, social, and political-economic forces, including crosscutting relationships of age, race, nationality, ethnicity, and class.[17]

So, in this book, I also trace the emergence of "patriarchy" among Maasai as it is related to colonial development interventions and state formation; specifically, the division of the complementary, interconnected responsibilities of men and women into the spatially separated, hierarchically gendered domains of "domestic" and "public/political," and the consolidation of male control over cattle through the commodification of livestock, the monetization of the Maasai economy, and the targeting of men for development interventions. Incorporation into the state system reinforced and enhanced male political authority and economic control by expanding the bases for political power, introducing new forms of property relations and circumscribing female autonomy and mobility. Together, these processes shifted the contours of male-female power relations, resulting in the material disenfranchisement and conceptual devaluation of Maasai women as both women and pastoralists.

Research Methodologies

This book is based on almost six years of field experience in Tanzania, including two years of field and archival work (1991–1993), several shorter research stints (1990, 1995, 1997–1998), and three years of community development work with Maasai throughout the Arusha Region (1985–1987). Maasai, who live in both Kenya and Tanzania, are divided into sections (*iloshon*) that differ slightly as to dialect, customs, rituals, and so forth. Kisongo Maasai are the largest Maasai section and the biggest section in Tanzania. Most of the historical chapters of this book discuss Maasai of various sections throughout Tanzania, while the ethnographic portions focus primarily on Kisongo Maasai. From 1991 to 1993, I conducted an intensive study of three Maasai communities—Embopong', Mti Mmoja, and Emairete—located within the same political ward which differed historically in the intensity and duration of their interaction with processes of "development," including education, commoditization, extent of cultivation, integration into the market economy, and involvement with government and non-governmental development projects. Data was collected using a multi-pronged methodological approach including a census, semi-structured interviews, participant observation, life histories, and oral and archival historical research.

To provide a systematic basis for the comparison of gender practices and ideas, I collected basic social and economic data through a census of all the households (454) and individuals (1,974) in the three communities. Then, to elicit ideas and images of gender, ethnicity, development, power, and other concepts and determine the degree of similarity and variance in these ideas, I held semi-structured interviews with a random sample of five people within each gender/age category[18] in each community (150 interviews). These interviews were taped and transcribed (with sections translated into Swahili) for detailed textual analysis and comparison.

To assess the correspondence between these ideas and everyday practices, I was a constant participant-observer of the daily life and interactions of men and women of different ages, collecting basic ethnographic information such as the social organization of production and exchange, descriptions of ceremonial life-course events, genealogies, migration histories, and kinship terms. I shifted regularly between each of the three communities to observe different phases of the agricultural and pastoral cycles in the wet and dry seasons. Approximately half of my time in the field, however, was spent in Emairete, since it was the largest study community and served, until August 1992,[19] as my "home base," where I did most of my computer and administrative work in a rented room.

I also collected oral histories from several key figures in the communities. I reviewed documents in relevant government, missionary, and private archives and interviewed key government, missionary, and development personnel who have worked in the villages. From August to October 1991, I reviewed primary and secondary historical documents on the colonial period in Tanzania available from the Cooperative Africana Microfilm Project (CAMP) and the Library of Congress. I completed extensive archival work in the Tanzania National Archives in Dar es Salaam and Arusha and reviewed the Hans Cory collection and other documents in the East Africana Collection at the University of Dar es Salaam. May 1993 was spent in England, reading archival files at the Rhodes House Institute in Oxford, the Public Records Office in Kew Gardens, and the School for Oriental and African Studies (SOAS) document room.

Language, as always, is an important research issue. I am completely fluent in Swahili, the national language of Tanzania, but still only speak and comprehend Maa at a basic level, despite two months of intensive language school and extensive use while I was in the field. During my research, I worked with a full-time Maa-speaking assistant. Christopher ole Ndangoya, a former student of mine, assisted me briefly from January to March of 1992, when he resigned because of the pressure of other obligations. Morani ole Poyoni, a former head teacher of a primary school and a lifelong resident of Emairete, then became my assistant. With two exceptions,[20] we collected all the census information and conducted the open-ended interviews together in Maa. During the census, Morani asked the questions and I recorded the answers on the coding form, carefully asking for clarification or repetition of answers as needed. During the open-ended interviews, Morani was the main interviewer, working from our list of questions, but we both shared the job of encouraging people to elaborate on or clarify answers. While staying at homesteads, attending ceremonies and celebrations, or just "hanging out," we would often split up and rendezvous later to share what we had seen, heard, or learned. Inevitably, I would circulate more with the women and Morani with the men, but we would both "cross over" frequently.

Given the centrality of gender and age categories to Maasai social organization (and to this book) it is important to briefly explain the benefits—of which I was initially unaware—of my gender and age relationship with Morani. Morani's age-grade (Ilmakaa, junior elders at this time) and my ascribed age-grade (wife of an Ilmakaa) ensured us both great freedom in interacting with men and women of all ages and in traveling and working together constantly. As a junior elder, it was only the daughters of his age-mates who had to treat him and be treated by him with "respect," and few of them were old enough to be interviewed as adults for this study.[21] Since he was not an *olmurrani*, he represented no direct sexual threat to the women, and since he was not a senior elder or older, they were not required to "respect" him. He was free to enter houses and talk to almost all the women without the constraints on conversation and behavior entailed by proper "respect." As a classificatory "daughter" and even "granddaughter" to many men, I was always properly respectful in my greetings and behavior, and my respectfulness encouraged rather than constrained their conversation. Furthermore, as a classificatory wife of Morani, our constant togetherness was never a problem, merely fuel for teasing and rumors.

* * *

This book combines cultural, historical, and political-economic approaches to explore the intersection and interconstruction of gender and ethnicity and to demonstrate how they shaped and were shaped by the shifting meanings, uses, and effects of "development." By examining the political-economic objectives and cultural images which shaped the development interventions of first the British and then the Tanzanian state and NGOs, I demonstrate how these interventions valorized particular masculine constructions of Maasai ethnicity. I then explore the lived experience of "development," gender, and ethnicity through detailed ethnographic data from three Maasai communities with different historical experiences of "development." Interspersed throughout the book are Maasai Portraits, brief profiles of certain Maasai men and women whose lives and perspectives illuminate and complicate the discussion of development contained within the more analytic chapters. The portraits at once comment on and foreshadow issues explored in the chapters.

This book illustrates the importance of "ethnicity" and "ethnic identities" to the colonial and post-colonial projects of "development" and the constitution of the nation-state. It also shows how all of these interrelated projects are profoundly gendered and, accordingly, interact in significant ways with local relations of power. The myth of the male herder becomes a factor in this history, shaping the perspectives of colonial and state administrators and, therefore, the content of their interventions. In turn, these representations and interventions influence Maasai men and women's perceptions of their own possibilities, resulting in a contemporary situation whereby Maasai men who conformed most closely to the idealized, rigid notion of Maasai ethnicity are in fact paralyzed by this notion, while categories of Maasai historically constructed as marginal to this conception, such as women and educated men, find themselves freer to maneuver and make other choices.

I believe my work contributes to current scholarly efforts to understand the relationship between "development" as a transnational process and the lived experience of "development" in local communities. It also enhances feminist approaches to history and anthropology by showing how the inclusion of gender as a central category of analysis reconfigures understandings of processes such as development, colonialism, and nationalism; "domestic" and "political" structures; institutions such as marriage and "tradition"; and broader theoretical concepts such as "culture," "power," and "social inequality." Finally, as a product of the growing convergence between anthropology and history in African studies, it suggests the power and insight that can be provided by such an interdisciplinary approach.

GENDER, GENERATION, AND ETHNICITY: BEING MAASAI MEN AND WOMEN

1

Long ago wild animals used to be women's cattle. Then, one morning before the cattle were taken out to graze, a cow was slaughtered. Soon the cattle started moving away to graze by themselves and wandered off. One woman told one of the children to go and drive the cattle back before they went too far. When the child's mother heard this she said: "Oh, no, my child is not going until he has eaten the kidney." It followed that whenever a child was asked to go, his mother forbade him to go until he had a bite of the meat. This went on until all the cattle, sheep and goats wandered away into the bush and got lost. When all the children had eaten the meat, they tried to bring the cattle back, but they found that they had all gone wild. And so that is how it came about that women lost their cattle. They then went and lived with the men who had all along taken good care of their cattle. This is why up to this very day, all the cattle belong to the men and women simply wait for the men to provide for them.

(Kipuri 1983: 32)

Like all such stories, this Maasai myth recorded by Naomi Kipuri in the 1980s in southern Kenya expresses a clear ideological position: Maasai men care for and therefore control the cattle, while women attend to their children and depend on men for their subsistence. As I argue elsewhere (Hodgson 2000c: 1): "Similar myths pervade most popular beliefs and much of the scholarship on pastoralists in sub-Saharan Africa, of which the primary and most debilitating one is the assumption that pastoral women are subordinate to pastoral men because of the (supposedly) inherently androcentric nature of pastoralism as a mode of production and an ideology: 'pastoralists' are men, and 'pastoralism' is an essentially patriarchal system." Such perspectives ignore the dynamism, complexity, and historicity of pastoralist gender relations and ideologies, as well as the centrality of gender to the production of culture and history in pastoral societies. Attention to such issues as economic activities, political power, ritual practice, moral authority, environmental knowledge, social organization, cultural identity, life cycles, and household domestic cycles, set within their shifting historical and political-economic contexts, complicates any easy understanding of the experience and expression of gendered power among Maasai, as well as in other pastoralist and agro-pastoralist societies (Hodgson 2000b).

The notion, therefore, that "all the cattle belong to the men and the women simply wait for the men to provide for them" (Kipuri 1983: 32), which is repeated in other myths and sayings (e.g., Kipuri 1983; Llewelyn-Davies 1978), masks complex cultural and historical realities among Maasai. The presumed gendered division of labor and control is neither as clear nor as stable as the myth suggests. Maasai gender relations, as everywhere, are dynamic and historical and are crosscut and complicated by other distinctions such as age and wealth. As discussed in detail below, Maasai women are the primary caretakers of their children, but they have also long been central to livestock production. Furthermore, the rights and responsibilities of both men and women vary by age and have changed through generations in response to internal dynamics and colonial and post-colonial interventions in their lives. Moreover, the symbolic inference of the myth, that women lack a sense of identity as pastoralists, masks the historical processes that gradually disenfranchised Maasai women from not only their rights over livestock but their ethnic and cultural identity as well.

To understand these changes in Maasai ethnic and gender relations, we must first examine them on the eve of the colonial encounter when these processes were just beginning to take place. My main sources for this earlier period are the findings of archaeologists and linguists, archival sources such as travelers' reports and early ethnographies, semi-structured interviews with numerous Maasai men and women, and life history interviews with three elderly Maasai.

Ethnicity and Gender among Maasai in the 1890s

Historians, archaeologists, linguists, and others are still exploring, reconstructing, and debating the pre-colonial history of the Maasai. Central to their findings and ensuing debates and disagreements are their very definitions of Maasai identity: Who are "the Maasai"? Were they Maa-speaking peoples? Peoples living in the Rift Valley whose artifacts reveal evidence of pastoralism and/or raiding? How should the current versions of origin myths and oral traditions recounted by Maasai elders be understood? Contemporary definitions of Maasai ethnicity structure investigations into their past: Are "the Maasai" distinguished by their language, their economic mode(s) of production, certain social institutions, cultural beliefs, political systems, and leaders? Or perhaps certain combinations of these, shifting through time? While these alternative definitions of "identity" are partly shaped by differences in disciplinary foci, they also reveal fundamental differences in understandings of ethnic identity.

Although the details of Maasai origin myths vary, one contemporary rendition, told to me by Wanga (Maasai Portrait 2), explains their history as follows:[1]

The first person was Maa (sometimes known as Maasindat), who lived at Kerrio and had three wives: Naiterokop, Nasotua, and Nainyiti. Maa gave birth to all Maasai. The first child of his wife Naiterekop was a son named Nagol, who had only one tooth. He was a bit of an outsider, and didn't get along well with others. His parents tried to pull out his one tooth, as he was laughed at, but it was too hard. He moved away, and started the tribe (*entipat*) called "Ilogol lala" (hard teeth). They are still around these days in Kenya and Tanzania (Morogoro and Ruvu), sometimes called "Likikoine" or "Lumbwa." Naiterekop's second child, Maasai, fathered the Maasai, Purko, Arusha and Irkaputie. Maa's second wife, Nasotua, gave birth to a girl named Simal, who later left and was taken by Somali Dorobos. She gave birth to twins, a boy and a girl, in Somalia. The name "Somalia" comes from her name, "Simal," and is the reason the Somalis speak like Maasai. Finally, Maa's third wife, Nainyiti, gave birth to the Iltengwal, Samburr (Samburu), Ilaikipiak, Iluasinkishu.

Wanga's version, like others, describes the complicated relationship between Maasai and other ethnic groups (as well as clans within Maasai) in terms of kinship relationships from an apical ancestor, Maa. Some versions foreground Naiterekop, a woman, as the apical ancestor (her name means "she who gave birth to the land") (Mol 1996: 271; Kipuri 1983: 27; Hollis 1905: 270, although Hollis, relying on Krapf, insists on identifying her as male); others discuss how Eng'ai (God) gave Maasai the right to control all the cattle in the world (e.g., Kipuri 1983: 30–31).

The stories of scholars describe an equally complicated history of the origins of Maasai as an ethnic group and their relationship with other ethnic groups. The ancestors of contemporary Maa speakers began to migrate from an ancient community of proto-Eastern Nilotes in southern Sudan during the first millennium A.D.[2] By the latter part of the first millennium, Maa-speaking peoples were living in the Rift Valley of present-day Kenya. People came together and separated, stayed in place or moved, shaping and shifting

Table 1.1 Age-Set Names and Approximate Period during
Which Members Were *Ilmurran*

Age-Set	Years Members Were *Ilmurran*
Iltalala	1881–1905
Iltuati	1896–1917
Iltareto	1911–1929
Ilterito	1926–1948
Ilnyangusi	1942–1959
Seuri	1957–1975
Ilmakaa (later called Ilkitoip)	1973–1985
Landiss	1983–1996

Source: Adapted from Frans Mol, *Maasai Language and Culture
Dictionary* (Narok: Maasai Centre Lemek).

their own senses of community and identity. Numerous groups of people migrated from the central group to outlying areas both north and south, eventually developing separate dialects of Maa and, in time, separate but related identities, such as Samburu, Chamus (Njemps), and Parakuyo. Sometime during the fifteenth century a large group of Maa-speakers left those living in the Kenyan Rift Valley and moved southward into present-day Tanzania, expanding their areas of occupation in northern and central Tanzania between the mid-sixteenth and early nineteenth centuries.

Most scholars agree that while the majority of Maa-speakers were originally agro-pastoralists, cultivating sorghum and millet and raising cattle and smallstock, in time a group emerged with an increasing specialization in pastoralism and a heightened sense of their self-identity as pastoralists (Sutton 1993; Galaty 1993a). Material, political, social, cultural, and ecological changes enabled increasing specialization: the discovery and mastery of iron-forging techniques for spears; the development of age-grades for the horizontal organization of men, especially as *ilmurran* (sing. *olmurrani;* young, circumcised men of the "warrior" age-grade; see Table 1.1 for list of age-grades); and the emergence of prophets (*oloiboni/iloibonok*) as religious and political rallying points for the vertical organization of people into opposing groups. These age-grades and prophets also encouraged the emergence of self-conscious collective identities other than clan between different age-sets or followers of different *iloibonok*. Some scholars have debated whether the "Maasai expansion" (as their move southward through the Rift Valley is often called) had more to do with the spread of a hegemonic identity than with the physical movement of people themselves (e.g., Galaty 1993a: 61–62). Pastoral Maasai were known for their willingness to assimilate non-Maasai through marriage, child adoption, and direct incorporation of individuals and even entire communities who were willing to adopt their dress, cultural practices, and social allegiances. To "become" Maasai was for some a desired goal, for others it was probably easier than fighting over territory and livestock.

By the early nineteenth century, communities of Maa-speakers existed with different economic specialties: as pastoralists, agro-pastoralists, farmers, and hunter-gathers. At issue is whether they were all considered equally "Maasai," or if some—pastoralists—were more "Maasai" than others. Here the scholarship becomes murky, as the perceptions of traders, travelers, missionaries, and scholars cloud and confuse the fragmentary evidence of how these groups of Maasai perceived themselves. Part of the confusion and debate has arisen around the meanings and uses of the terms "Maasai," "Iloikop," and "Kwavi" (or "Wakwavi") in the accounts of early travelers and in the later reports of European administrators and scholars.[3] According to Bernsten (1980), these terms were used in the early accounts of the 1840s–1870s to indicate territorial differences among Maa-speakers (with Maasai living in certain areas, Iloikop/Kwavi in others), with a shift in meaning by the late 1870s to indicate economic differences (Maasai as pastoralists, Iloikop/Kwavi as agriculturalists or agro-pastoralists).[4] The ambiguity about which terms were used by Swahili traders and other non-Maasai to describe Maasai groups and which terms were used by Maasai themselves only furthers the confusion and possibility for multiple interpretations. Did groups of Maasai distinguish themselves by economic occupation, clan, territorial affiliation—or various combinations of these, shifting according to context and through time?

Based on the coast, the early missionary travelers heard most of their reports and descriptions of Maasai from the Swahili traders whose caravans passed through Maasai areas. Farler's Swahili trader informants "spoke of the Masai as being treacherous and unprincipled" and insisted that encampments in "the Masai country proper" had to be fenced and carefully guarded against surprise attacks at night (Farler 1882: 731). Reports of "attacks" and "massacres" by Maasai circulated freely. But those European travelers who actually ventured through Maasai areas noted the discrepancies between their encounters with Maasai and the tales of the traders. As Sir Frederick Jackson, who traveled through Maasailand in the late 1880s, wrote: "I began to suspect that the terrors and dangers of entering Maasailand were very grossly and purposely exaggerated by a small clique of traders" (1969 [1930]: 190–191, cited in Jacobs 1968: 28; cf. Thomson 1968 [1885]: 198; Last 1882: 225). While some believed that the traders had a vested interest in exaggerating stories about Maasai savagery to protect their caravan routes from competition, Johnston (1902: 227) argued that the "real explanation" of the "supposed ferocity" of Maasai was

> that the Swahili caravans . . . never hesitated to plunder the natives when they thought themselves strong enough. They had received several well-merited and drastic punishments at the hands of the Masai for these attempts to rob and rape, therefore they had circulated reports about Masai ferocity, which for a long time caused Europeans to regard this lordly tribe with quite exaggerated dread.

Being Maasai in the 1890s

Describing social relations during this era, especially gender relations, is an enduring difficulty in African history. Fortunately, although Maasai sources are almost non-existent, we do have the rich ethnographic account of Moritz Merker, a German military officer who lived and traveled among Maasai in German East Africa (later Tanganyika) from 1895 to 1903,[5] as well as numerous reports from travelers, missionaries, and others.[6] Although not ideal sources, these documents can be critically read against one another to compile a provisional, if incomplete, portrait of Maasai lives and livelihoods in this period.

Together, the accounts reveal that age and gender were the key axes of social organization which distinguished categories of persons and structured their roles, rights, and responsibilities. To ensure minimal ambiguity, each category of person was visibly marked by distinct clothing, hairstyles, and ornamentation and was linguistically differentiated in greetings and other nomenclature.[7] For men, differences in age were marked formally by their designated age-grade (*olaji/ilajijik*), a set of life stages that men moved through as part of their age-set, or group of men, known by a unique name, who were circumcised during the same time period. Although women were not formally divided by age-grades,[8] their progression from young girls (*endito/intoyie*) to old grandmothers (*koko*) was marked linguistically and often ritually.

Relationships between men and women varied by their age, kinship, clan, and age-set affiliations, but they were generally based on mutual respect (*enkanyit*) and relative autonomy. For example, Merker produced two detailed tables listing the proper forms of address among females, among males, and between males and females of different ages, reflecting degrees of familiarity and formality (most of which are still used today). Improper greetings (implying disrespect) could elicit sharp rebukes: "The word *esiangiki* sometimes means legal wife; I have more than once heard a young wife answer someone not entitled to use the phrase by shouting in annoyance: 'I am not your *esiangiki!*'" (Merker 1910 [1904]: 71). But "improper" behavior, especially of a wife to her husband, could elicit more than a verbal rebuke: "light" wife-beating was prevalent (Merker 1910 [1904]: 120). Unhappily married men and women had some recourse, however; "divorce" was possible, although it was more common for a wife and husband to live in permanent separation, even within the same homestead (Merker 1910 [1904]: 49). Although they shared common objectives, men and women granted each other autonomy, premised on mutual respect, to pursue and manage their own affairs. Merker (1910 [1904]: 30) commented on women's freedom and mobility as traders (discussed further below): "In this she is in no way supervised by her husband. It is beneath his dignity to concern himself with such matters."

Gender and age prescribed whether one lived in an *emanyata*, or "warrior's village" as Merker calls it, or *enkang'*, a "family village" (which I call a homestead). *Ilmurran* lived in the *emanyata*, accompanied by their mothers and their "girlfriends," the *intoyie*. Married men and women and children lived in the *enkang'*. Neither men nor women, however, were confined to the *enkang'*. Men traveled to neighboring homesteads to visit members of their age-set, fellow clan elders, and other friends, relatives, and stock partners to discuss clan and locality affairs, exchange news and information, and arrange livestock grazing and watering matters.[9] Women traveled to markets and trading settlements or to visit friends and relatives at neighboring homesteads.

Within each gender, Maasai men and women were crosscut by differences other than just age. Both men and women garnered more or less prestige according to their homestead's wealth in stock, number of children, and overall reputation for successful management of their domestic affairs. Individual men earned respect according to their speaking abilities, their generosity, and other valued traits. Women achieved varying degrees of respect and authority according to their position in the order of wives (a first wife having authority over other wives) and their ability to manage their household property (including livestock) and affairs. "The head wife," according to Merker,

> is the best off, for her husband hands over to her a large part of his cattle for all her needs, and also marks her out from amongst the other wives by gifts of clothing and ornaments, and by treating her with greater consideration. Her eldest son has privileges of inheritance [of the father's auxiliary herd]. The head wife exercises control over the other wives and keeps them to their work when they are neglectful. (Merker 1910 [1904]: 27–28)

1.1 A Maasai homestead, ca. 1900. Reproduced from Merker (1910 [1904]: 23).

1.2 Maasai women and a man outside a house, ca. 1900. Reproduced from Merker (1910 [1904]: 25).

As families, Maasai were also stratified by relative wealth. Merker describes the average number of wives of married men as five to six, then adds that "rich men" had even more (Merker 1910 [1904]: 27). The discrepancy in wealth had its redistributive consequences, however; boys from poorer families worked as herders for wealthier families until they had earned a small herd of cattle for themselves, and rich men often paid up to four cattle more in bridewealth than others (Merker 1910 [1904]: 45, 60).

According to Merker and the other accounts, age and gender also structured the production system for those Maasai who were predominantly pastoralist. Maasai men and women held separate roles and responsibilities in the care and management of cattle and smallstock (sheep and goats). Adult women cared for calves, smallstock, and sick animals. They milked cattle (and sometimes smallstock) in the morning and evening and controlled the distribution of milk to household members and visitors. They maintained the right to trade any surplus milk. Women also processed animal skins and either made clothing or sleeping skins from the hides or traded them. Young boys usually herded livestock; *ilmurran* guarded people and livestock from raids, attacks, and wild animals; and elder men made the broad management decisions about the timing and location of grazing and watering the herds.

In addition to women's rights to cattle products such as milk and hides, wives sometimes shared overlapping rights in livestock with their husbands, depending in part on how, from whom, and by whom an animal was first obtained. Cattle were given for bridewealth and wedding ceremonies, loaned or exchanged to build relations between patrons and clients or stock partners, and contributed for ceremonies, fine payments, and feasts. Goats and sheep were circulated even more constantly for the above reasons; they were also traded for food, beads, wire, and other necessities. Husbands and wives conferred about and agreed on decisions to slaughter, trade, or give an animal away. Although men were the primary exchangers of livestock, women also gave livestock (usually smallstock, but occasionally cattle) to one another and to men. A man's first wife, for example, gave his new second or third wife a calf, "after which they called one another *paashe*, i.e. the giver and receiver of a calf" (Hollis 1905: 303). As for smallstock, oral evidence suggests that men and women shared rights in some animals and held individual rights to others. When a woman married, her husband transferred a certain amount of cattle to her as "house-property" to be managed by her for her household's immediate benefit in terms of milk and hides but also to be kept in custody for her sons' inheritance.

The ability of Maasai to sustain their specialized production system depended in great part on women's roles as traders. Although Maasai depended on the milk and blood of their cattle for subsistence, as well as the meat of smallstock, most Maasai (other than *ilmurran,* who had strict dietary restrictions) supplemented their diet with grains and other foodstuffs, especially during the dry season. Women created and maintained links with neighboring agricultural groups, trading surplus milk, hides, smallstock, and even donkeys for the needed grain and foodstuffs. Their trade took two forms: they either traveled alone or in small groups to markets or the large permanent trading settlements such as Taveta and Moshi to barter their wares, or they traded with groups of old non-Maasai women who passed through their homestead every three to six days laden with maize, bananas, and sweet potatoes (Merker 1910 [1904]: 30; Thomson 1968 [1885]: 259–260; Baumann 1894: 242; Johnston 1886: 404; Spear 1997: 41; Kjekshus 1977: 112–126). Thomson (1968 [1885]: 93) described one such Maasai woman, "well dressed in bullock's hide and loaded with wire, beads and chains, [who] appear[ed] driving a donkey before her as she wend[ed] her way fearlessly towards Kibonoto to buy the vegetable food eaten by married people and children." Besides foodstuffs, Maasai traded for tobacco, cloth, glass beads, and copper wire from Swahili traders who traveled in large armed trade caravans through their areas or at the permanent trading settlements (Farler 1882: 736; Krapf 1968 [1860]: 364; Merker 1910 [1904]: 212–213; Johnston 1886: 404).[10] Tobacco, for example, was popular with Maasai men and women, who would trade one goatskin for about two half-pound packets of tobacco. In addition, although Maasai still preferred to wear leather prepared by women instead of the cloth offered by ivory traders, a few had discovered one item they liked—umbrellas—which they used to shelter themselves from the heat of the sun (Merker 1910 [1904]: 136). In the nineteenth century, Maasai women were therefore crucial intermediaries in the extensive and active trade networks which enabled Maasai to sustain their specialized production strategy by linking them to the commodities of regional and global commerce.

Like production, political power was also structured by gender and age. As men grew older, their political power as arbitrators of community and clan disputes increased as well, peaking when they were elders/senior elders. As they grew even older and more feeble, however, the venerable elders still attracted great respect but management of the affairs of the *enkang'* (homestead) shifted to more junior elders. Women followed a similar trajectory of increasing respect and power through their lives. As young uncircumcised girls (*endito/intoyie*), they worked hard helping their mothers in child care, collecting wood and water, and other household chores, but they also played hard, flirt-

1.3 Maasai women with backloads, presumably preparing for a trading trip. Reproduced from Merker (1910 [1904]: 39).

ing, dancing, singing, and sleeping with their lovers, the *ilmurran*. Once circumcised, the girls became adult women and were soon married. As married women, they carried out many of the duties described above. As they grew older, and their children grew older, they gained respect, especially once their sons became *ilmurran*. When their sons began to marry and they became mothers-in-law, their authority increased and their workload decreased as they managed their daughters-in-law. These same sons and daughters-in-law would in turn care for these women when they became elderly and feeble *koko*.

Politically, men and women were responsible for different spheres of interaction. Men occupied certain recognized leadership positions (*olaigwenan/ilaigwenak, olaunoni*) as representatives of their age-grades, sections, and clans and were responsible for consulting each other, making decisions, and settling disputes about matters between homesteads, clans, and communities. Women had varying degrees of involvement in these decisions: they could initiate, attend, and testify at judicial proceedings (Merker 1910 [1904]: 220); encourage their adult sons to advocate certain positions; lobby and confer with their hus-

1.4 Young girls (*intoyie*) and young men (*ilmurran*) dancing together, ca. 1900. Reproduced from Merker (1910 [1904]: 89).

bands; or directly speak their minds when men gathered in their homes to discuss their affairs over milk or alcohol. For their part, adult women, especially elder women and senior wives, were responsible for settling disputes and controlling the behavior of younger women and children in order to ensure a peaceful life within their households and homesteads. They were also central players in negotiating the marriage alliances and arrangements of their sons and daughters (Merker 1910 [1904]: 44).

Although there were distinctions of behavior, attitude, and dress between the more "domestic" spaces of home and homestead and the "public" spaces outside their borders, neither domain was gendered as primarily male or female or reflected significant differences of power or access between men and women; both men and women occupied sections of the domestic sphere and traversed and congregated in the more communal "public" spaces beyond the homestead. Furthermore, the domestic/public distinction does not adequately express either the range of zones of intimacy and informality or their complex intersections. For example, each house was spatially divided into several zones (see Figure 1.5). The most "private" spaces were the separate, enclosed wife's bed (*erruat kiti*, lit. "small bed") and husband's bed (*erruat kitok*, lit. "large bed"). A woman slept with her children in her bed, while a man (or visiting age-mate) slept in the larger bed. A less intimate, but still private, space was the inner room of the house surrounding the hearth, in which a woman cooked, stored her household belongings, and penned young smallstock and calves at night. Only men and women with whom the woman was familiar had access to this space: her husband, family members (although her father and other senior male relatives had to maintain their distance to demonstrate respect, and therefore usually sat in the outer foyer), age-mates of her husband, co-wives, and other women friends. More formal guests sat to greet and converse with the woman (who stayed in the inner room) in the "public" outer foyer, or just outside the entrance to the house. More public still was the outside perimeter of the house, in which groups of men or women would sit together in the daytime (Merker 1910 [1904]: 25). Thus the private/public spatial distinction was not equivalent to a domestic/political distinction of power, nor was it clearly gendered or hierarchical.[11]

Finally, although men certainly exercised greater power and authority in the realm of the political, women were central to the ritual sphere. Men would pray on occasion, and the *iloibonok* (spiritual leaders and diviners) were male, but it was women who were responsible for constantly mediating the relationship between Maasai and their God (Eng'ai). Women prayed at least twice a day, in the morning and evening, to Eng'ai "for having protected her and hers, and entreat[ed] him further to protect, preserve and increase the stock, and also to send her many children" (Merker 1910 [1904]: 207).[12] Women also played central roles in the numerous rituals that marked transitions in life stages, such as the birth of children, naming ceremonies, circumcision rites, and the passage of groups of men from one set of age-grade statuses to another (Merker 1910 [1904]: 52, 56, 59, 104, 208–209). Although not specifically "political," women's religious and ritual activities were laden with power in that they reflected and expressed their moral authority.

Merker's descriptions provide a rich picture of gender relations during this period. He is, however, fixated on only seeing Maasai women as wives. He continually asserts that Maasai wives were subordinate in status to their husbands but admits that "[n]aturally Maasai wives do not recognize their menial position as such, for they do not know otherwise, and fortunately, unknown amenities cannot be missed" (Merker 1910 [1904]: 120). This statement speaks to women's contentment with their roles and responsibilities and

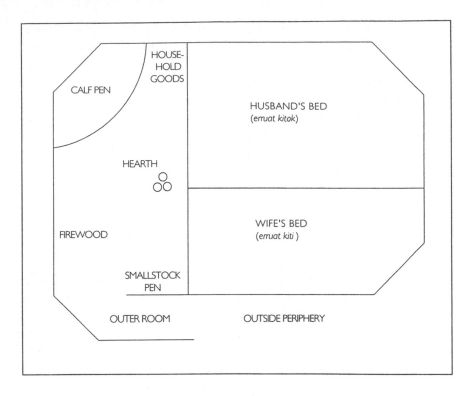

1.5 Interior spatial arrangement of Maasai house, ca. 1900. Based on Merker (1910 [1904]: 24).

to the gendered assumptions which informed the perspectives of outsiders such as Merker as they tried to evaluate Maasai gender relations. Merker himself clearly documents women's powers as pastoralists, mothers, sisters, and mothers-in-law through their involvement in the care and management of milk and livestock, marriage, bridewealth transactions, active prayer life, relationships with sons and brothers, and control over daughters and daughters-in-law. Women were also central to several ceremonies described in his book, including *eunoto* (marking the transition of men from *ilmurran* to junior elders), the naming of children, the circumcision of daughters, and "peacemaking" ceremonies with neighboring groups.[13] While women may in fact have been subordinate as wives, his own evidence demonstrates the many ways in which they did exercise power and authority.[14]

Although men, especially elder men, served as the primary leaders and arbitrators for their communities, the responsibilities and interactions of men and women were complementary and interdependent. Like the spokes of a wheel, each category of person, whether young boys or old women, was required to fulfill her or his responsibilities for livestock and for each other to ensure the survival and progress of Maasai households, homesteads, and communities. Merker presents substantial evidence of the autonomy and mutual respect of women and men, the pride of women in their identity as pastoralists, and their deep satisfaction with their lives and relationships. If anything, adult married women were the centralized node around which other people—"the spokes"—revolved and joined together. As the builders and "owners" of their homes, women provided the spaces for men, children, and guests to sleep, eat, and congregate.[15] Their spatial centrality was paralleled by their centrality to ritual relationships with Eng'ai as daily mediators through song and prayer on behalf of themselves and their families.

Women's autonomy and mobility in this period is further demonstrated by reports of their free and fearless interactions with European travelers. For instance, in 1883, after a brief visit by a Maasai "chief," the traveler Joseph Thomson described how the next group of Maasai to visit him was a delegation of Maasai women returning from a trip to trade for food with Chagga farmers. The women entered the camp carrying grass (a sign of peaceful intentions). They greeted and chatted with the men in the camp, looked at and touched Thomson with great curiosity, and eventually informed him that after a great debate, a deputation of men would visit "to interview" him the following day (Thomson 1968 [1885]: 89). Other travelers described similarly free and relaxed encounters with Maasai women at the time, with some even hinting that women's freedom of movement included the sexual freedom to spend the night in camp with the porters. Baumann (1894: 165), for example, wrote of "the easy approachability of the caravan members and other indigenous peoples to the Maasai women, [which] leads to a large influx of foreign blood into the Maasai."[16] After describing the relative sexual freedom of *intoyie* and even married women, Johnston concluded in disgust that "one way and another, by custom and by disposition, it must, I think, be stated that the Masai women are very immoral" (1902: 825). Later, he reported that "venereal diseases were unknown amongst [the Masai] until the Swahili traders and porters came on the scene, and even yet, despite the immorality of their women, they are not seriously affected" (1902: 829).

Maasai ethnic and gender identities and relations in this period were thus premised on interaction and complementarity—between Maasai pastoralists and their cultivating neighbors, between Maasai men and women, and across generations. Such interaction was accomplished spatially by their dispersed homesteads intermingled with non-Maasai, by women's mobility as traders and wives, and by the flexibility of the very category of "Maasai" itself, which could accommodate a diverse array of peoples and productive strategies. Gender relationships of power varied within and between groups, according to age, marital status, kinship relationship, and other social differences and individual circumstances. Moreover, there was no clear, gendered distinction between the "domestic" and "public/political" domains, or among social, economic, and political activities.

Furthermore, it is important to note that intentional, planned change—what we might call "development"—also occurred during this time: technological innovations such as the digging of wells and construction of leather sacs to carry water; advances in identifying and treating human and livestock diseases (Waller and Homewood 1997); adoption of certain useful commodities such as umbrellas, metal bowls and cups, blankets and cotton cloth; even social changes such as the creation of male age-sets and the adoption of pastoralism. Whether Maasai considered these social and material changes "development" or even "progress" is another matter.

In the Shadow of the Colonial State

Maasai life, as described by Merker, was radically disrupted on the eve of the colonial encounter. In the last two decades of the nineteenth century, Maasai peoples and herds, like others in East Africa, were struck by a series of disasters, including bovine pleuropneumonia (BPP) in 1883, rinderpest in 1891, then smallpox in 1892.[17] Large numbers of Maasai people and cattle died during the epidemics and the ensuing famines and wars between Maasai sections (Waller 1988: 101–105, cf. Jacobs 1965: 96; Iliffe 1979: 124–125; Koponen 1996: 593; see also Merker 1910 [1904]: 271). Although the impact of these epidemics had a disparate impact in Maasai areas, the direct consequences of these crises for social organization in general and gender relations in particular were dramatic. Men (and perhaps some women) encouraged female kin to marry Arusha and other cultivators in exchange for cattle to rebuild their herds, older boys left their families to work as herders and laborers for more fortunate neighbors and relatives, children were offered to passing caravans in exchange for food[18] or just left by the wayside for sympathetic strangers to adopt, and Maasai warriors intensified their raiding to replenish their lost herds (Waller 1988: 94–97). Nkoije, a wizened but wise midwife in Emairete, who identified herself as a "Dorobo" (a common name for Maasai hunter-gatherers, but also a term for "poor Maasai"), told me that her father "sold" one of his daughters to an Arusha family for three days' worth of food then stole her back. He encouraged her to "sell" herself to another family then run away. Married and unmarried women returned to their families, allied themselves with relatively prosperous cultivators, or fled to Nairobi and other towns to work as traders and prostitutes.[19] Many families dispersed to the more fertile coastal areas in search of food. Some families became hunter-gatherers, with faint hopes of returning to pastoralism in the future, while others requested land from Arusha relatives or stock friends and settled down as cultivators (Merker 1910 [1904]: 10, 30). Koko, another elder woman (see Maasai Portrait 1), recalls her father's stories of the disasters, which occurred when he was a warrior:[20]

People ate donkey meat . . . and fathers tried to convince their children the meat was good. . . . People dispersed to far away places with their children. They went to the Arusha, to Machame, everywhere, every place. Iltareto [men of the Iltareto age-set] put themselves out to work, to a place called Imbokeshi. . . . While they were still ilayioni, they worked to get cattle. They were hired by the Germans to herd, as well as to do other work as laborers.

Nkoije remembers the period in even starker, metaphorical terms: her mother died, so her father had to nurse her at his breast. This dramatic inversion of gender roles conveys some of the magnitude of the disruptions to Maasai social and economic life. As Koko remarked, "no person ever returned to the old way of life, as before."

These crises in social organization and reproduction of Maasai life coincided with the beginning of colonial rule. Formalized by the Anglo-German agreement of 1890, German rule of Tanganyika was very uneven, concentrating on a few accessible, productive regions, and had limited sustained involvement in peripheral areas such as Maasailand.[21] The period of German rule is not my focus here, in part because of the scarcity of evidence, but more because of the limited long-term impact. The Germans did, however, introduce Maasai to some of the procedures and practices of state rule, many of which were continued and expanded by the British. These included the creation of a mediating administrative apparatus with the appointment of three *jumbes,* or headmen, to implement and supervise German directives (the small number is in itself a testament to their inability to effectively carry out their duties), efforts to control Maasai raiding and "illegal" movement through the presence of German military stations and punitive raids by German soldiers with African auxiliaries, and the formation of a Masai Reserve in order to alienate their land for European settlement (Merker 1910 [1904]: 271; Great Britain Admiralty ca. 1915; Koponen 1994: 648–649).

Maasai responses to the disasters and to German administration culminated in several long-term changes to Maasai social organization. The social changes that Merker reported for the post-disaster period included shifts in residence patterns so that several families lived together, a relaxation of clan endogamous marriage prohibitions, sharply reduced bridewealth payments, and increased intermarriage of Maasai with neighboring cultivators. Elopement was also fairly common at this time (Merker 1910 [1904]: 10, 32, 45, 46–47). The claims by his Maasai informants that venereal diseases were virtually unknown before the cattle plague pointed to severe social disruption (cf. Johnston 1902: 829).

The implication that the dispersion and intermingling (even sexually) of Maasai with other non-Maa speaking peoples caused contagion is echoed in similar accounts about the origins of *orpeko,* or spirit possession, at the time. Maasai report that the first cases of *orpeko* began with their dispersal in the late 1800s and early 1900s as a result of the "disasters" (Hurskainen 1989). Nanoto, an elderly woman interviewed by David Peterson in 1971, claims that she was first possessed between 1900 and 1910, when she was living (as a result of the dispersal) along the Tanzanian coast (Peterson 1971). After a spate of occurrences during this period, *orpeko* seems to have moved northward in waves, recurring during other times of extreme stress in the 1930s, 1950s, and 1980s. As I discuss in Chapter 6, the symptoms and spread of *orpeko* marked the disruptions in gender rights and relations experienced by Maasai women but also served to strengthen relationships among women, who cared for and consoled one another when sick.

Despite the sometimes violent social dislocations produced by the disasters (as evidenced in the *orpeko* outbreaks) and the occupation by German military forces, by the early 1900s many Maasai had restocked their homesteads, reunited with their families, and reestablished a semblance of their former life. If anything, one might argue that the survivors of the disasters who returned to pastoralism as a livelihood more fiercely embraced their identity as pastoralists. Yet life had changed: many Maasai remained scattered across the land, opting to increase their food security by living interspersed with cultivators with whom they could trade. Others continued to move frequently, in search of better grazing and water for their livestock and strategic social and political alliances. According to Johnston (1902: 829), some Maasai women even chose to remain in the Swahili trading camps or with the Indian workers building the Uganda Railway.

*   *   *

Thus on the eve of World War I, when Britain took over control of Tanganyika from the Germans, Maasai had already witnessed significant changes in their social, political, and economic relations. Inevitably, aspects of the normative gender relations described by Merker and other early visitors changed as well, although these shifts in practice were perhaps not reflected by changes in ideal behaviors. Mutual respect, or *enkanyit,* was central to defining and monitoring appropriate behaviors between and among men and women of different ages, and it still serves, with love (*enyorrata*), as the guiding principle for Maasai social protocols and ideals. As part of *enkanyit,* women exercised considerable autonomy in and authority for their own affairs and influenced the daily collective decisions of their households and homesteads. Moreover, they served as the daily spiritual liaisons with Eng'ai, a responsibility and privilege from which they derived and asserted their moral authority.

The complicated and dynamic picture of Maasai gender, generational, and ethnic relations during this period challenges any easy assessment of women's "status" (cf. Steady 1987; Sudarkasa 1987; Driberg 1932). The available evidence for this period makes it difficult to derive a sense of individual variability among people. But the social patterns and cycles of aging, forging new relationships through marriage and birth, constituting and reconstituting households and homesteads, negotiating rights and responsibilities, and ensuring the well-being of one's family and community, all convey a sense of shifting, intricate relationships of power. Moreover, they indicate that there is no homogeneous Maasai "woman" or "man," rather women and men of different ages, social statuses, and so forth whose interactions, both ideal and real, vary considerably. Thus, the myth of the patriarchal pastoralist with which I began the chapter was, like most myths, an ideological assertion rather than an empirical statement. But why, by the 1980s, would Maasai men wish to declare themselves the sole owners of cattle?

MAASAI PORTRAIT 1: KOKO

The *ilmurran* of the past are no longer.

"*Enchoruet ai!* (My girlfriend!)" called the frail old woman, bent forward, leaning precariously on a walking stick. "*Koko! Enchoruet ai! Takwenya!* (Grandmother! My girlfriend! Greetings!)" I replied, as I neared the small hut where she lived with her grandson, his wife, and their three children. Koko was my closest neighbor when I lived in Emairete, and we spent many hours in my room or in her compound sharing stories, gossiping, and teasing one another. After several months together, she had one day changed the way in which she greeted me from the appropriate "*Siangiki, Sopai!* (Young woman, hello!)" to the more familiar and endearing "*enchoruet ai!*" I was thrilled by this sign of intimacy, as I treasured our relationship and our times together.

Koko[1] is an extremely old woman who was already married by 1916, "when the British fought the Germans." As a widow and a great-great-grandmother, she had tremendous freedom to say and do as she pleased with everyone, men and women, young and old. In fact she delighted in jokes, teasing, and stories that had implicit and even explicit sexual content and flirting with every young man who visited. Two examples still make me chuckle. As I was visiting her one day early in my fieldwork with my assistant Chris, a young Maasai man, we sat around the cooking fire in the hut she shared with her grandson and his family. Chris sat on a small stool, straddling the glowing embers with his legs, one foot on each side of the cooking stones. With impish glee, Koko clasped her hands to her groin, pretending to grimace with pain. "Watch out!" she warned. "If you move too close to the fire you'll burn your penis!" We howled with laughter as Chris sheepishly moved back and closed his legs together. The second example was a running joke between Koko and me that, as a married woman living apart from my husband, I should have sex with her grandson, an *olmurran.* "Warriors are the best, *enchoruet ai!* You should take Steven out into the surrounding bushes and sleep with him!" "But Koko," I would teasingly reply, "I don't like young boys, I like older men. Young boys have no experience." "Shie," she would say, shaking her head in mock disappointment, "old men have no energy. *Olmurran* are the best lovers. And your husband will never know. I mean, surely he has married a second wife by now, since you've been gone so long . . .?!" Almost every time we met, she would raise the issue, even in front of her grandson and his wife.

Koko describes her life as a young girl (*endito*) and married woman in much the same terms as Merker reported for the 1880s.[2] She was born in Olmolog, a Maasai area alienated by the British for settler farms (Chapter 2), so her father moved his family to Sinya and then Longido. (Her husband moved her to Emairete after a brief time in Mfereji.) From the time she was a young girl, she carried wood and water to her home, cared for young children, and helped her mother with household chores. She recalls with special delight the joys of being an *endito* and spending time with *ilmurran* of the Iltareto age-set (who were warriors from 1911–1929 [Mol 1996: 15]):

When we were children, this country was wonderful, not like it is now. The colonial period was better, even though we forget now because things are bad. This life is not good. All that we had when we were adults was great. In that time we had cattle and even goats, children, *ilmurran,* and young women [*isi-angikin*]. When we were young girls [*intoyie*] we flirted with the *ilmurran,* especially those that braided their hair into long pigtails [*iltaikan*]. We would give them milk mixed with blood [*inkipot*] and they would become our lovers [*ilsanjan*]. You would give your lover [*olsanjan*] milk in a large calabash to make him your lover. Our *ilmurran* had braided pigtails [*iltaikan*] and shields [*ilongoi*], and we [young girls] wore metal rings around our legs and arms. We had metal almost everywhere on our bodies! From here to here [pointing from

MP1.1 "Koko" sitting on her bed in the house she shares with her grandson and his family, 1997.

her wrist to her upper arm]. And we had other ornaments as well. I just threw mine out the other day. Even in our ears! And we danced and danced! [She demonstrates, rocking her head and body back and forth, thrusting her shoulders as though she were tilting the broad, beaded circular necklace (*oltirbe*) worn by women.] We would go into the shade of trees to play with the *ilmurran* and sing and dance with them. Those days were really wonderful. But these days in the village? There are no *ilmurran* in the shade these days, they all only wear coats. The *ilmurran* of the past are no longer.

It is striking that her nostalgic memories rest strongly on contrasts between the normative gender practices of the past with those of the present, especially in terms of the behavior and dress of *ilmurran:*

Our *ilmurran* didn't wear these kind of clothes [shirts, pants, and shoes]. And they only wore one cloth, not two . . . and they had swords, spears, and *isursuni*.[3] They danced with us, stole cattle, and killed Ilumbwa[4] to take their cattle. They killed them because they were *ilmurran*, because they were allowed to.

The dress, rituals, and actions of *ilmurran* figure prominently in accounts of cultural change by other Maasai.

Despite her fun times with *ilmurran*, especially her many *ilsanjan*, or lovers, Koko was happy to marry:

D: So Koko, when you eventually married were you happy or sad?
K: I was happy because I could move to this homestead and begin to have children. Our homestead had many cattle and we cared for them. We gave birth to some children who lived and others that died because Eng'ai took them. And those children who lived eventually married and had girls and boys. . . . So I received many good things, since if you give birth and have your children isn't that wonderful?

After bridewealth gifts were exchanged and she gave birth to her first child at her mother's house, her husband brought her to live at his mother's house. She assumed new tasks such as milking and caring for cattle and helping her mother-in-law. Koko claimed that she and her mother-in-law became very close, so close that her mother-in-law gave her four milch cows and a donkey when she was dying rather than leave them to her children. As a junior wife, she loved her husband a lot, even though he sometimes beat her "like a donkey." As she explained later: "He beat me because I did something wrong. Maasai men hit because they are jealous; if you speak to another man you are beaten. But Maasai wives have the habit of loving *ilmurran*, so your husband hits you because you have done wrong." Sometimes, when the beatings became too frequent or unjustified, she would return to her natal homestead with her children and livestock, complain to her parents about the beatings, and wait for her father and brothers to negotiate a reconciliation. For Koko, as for other women, the reconciliation usually involved her husband promising not to beat her any more and giving her some cattle from his personal herd (*inkishu e boo*). Some unhappy women, however, chose *kirtala*, or permanent separation from their husbands.

In time she had six boys and two girls, and her livestock herd increased. Throughout, she had a complicated relationship with her co-wives. Although she depended on them for companionship and assistance in household chores and child care, she also competed with them for the affections of their husband:

You need to have other wives so that you can show them how much better you are loved by your husband: going to lie in the shade with him, eating with him while the other wives are jealous because you are the one he loves. You do this on purpose to make sure that your husband's love for you is visible. Being an only wife is a problem because your husband's love is not evident since there is no one else to compete with, just you.

When she was not busy vying for her husband's attention or otherwise occupied in her household responsibilities, Koko joined other women in walking to markets surrounding Kilimanjaro, especially Machame, to trade for foodstuffs. One item they sought was bananas (*ilmokosho*) which they would cut and place on the roof to dry to make a food called *orkitao;* another was a type of bean she called *orkuroo.* The women carried goods in leather bags (*emokooke*) on their backs or on their donkeys.

Her recollections of the German and British colonists are scattered and fragmentary. Her most vivid memory is of German officers riding by on horseback, carrying guns. Some would stop in and drink milk, others would just come to the homestead to take cattle. She remembers the Germans as being friendly and the British as mean and intrusive. In one interview she described how the British would force them to sell their cattle:

We would see them coming and people would say that they were coming to take our cattle. They would pick a homestead and take the bulls, then tell us to follow them to another place. When you would arrive, they would ask you to show them your animals, then give you money for them, the white money that was around then called *iropiyani* (from "European").

The men would use the money to buy cloth and would often "return to buy the very animals they had been forced to sell!" Such sales occurred infrequently.

Koko gave and received livestock throughout her life. When she was married, she received cattle, smallstock, and even a donkey as gifts from her husband's extended family and her own relatives. She had complete control over these animals; her husband could not take them or sell them. "They were mine. They were animals that I was given." In addition, her husband gave her cattle to care for on behalf of her household (what Gluckman [1950] and others call "house-property"). He retained the right to give these away, but

they were mine. If he wanted to take one, first he had to talk to me. I could tell him not to take that one, take this one, then give it to him and let him go about his business. I could even tell him no, he could not take an animal this time. He would have to ask another wife. When I had children, I gave each child his or her own cattle. I told each of my sons, this one is for you, that one is for him.

D: So your daughters didn't receive any?

K: They each received one animal, but they were going to move away. When they married they would go to their husbands.

She received additional gifts of livestock from her husband, mother-in-law, and other relatives throughout her life, including some of the bridewealth animals received for her daughters (usually a calf). She also gave animals away, not only to her children but also to relatives and friends.

In addition to opinions about the dress and activities of *ilmurran*, Koko had lots of opinions about other changes she had witnessed during her long life (we estimated that in 1992 she was over ninety years old). Swahili was one issue: "Maasai didn't speak Swahili before, even now I still don't understand it. . . . But if I was still young I would learn it, I would love to say 'I speak Swahili.' Look at how you talk to each other and I don't understand. I just sit staring at you until you tell me something." When asked to comment on her grandson, an *olmurrani* who wore "Swahili" clothes and worked in town, as well as the facts that these days *ilmurran* farmed rather than stole cattle and most boys and girls went to school, Koko just shook her head and muttered, "It is as I told you already; we have become Swahilis, life has changed."

In the same interview in which she nostalgically praised the old days when *ilmurran* were "real" warriors, she later discussed the benefits she saw in the present:

The present period is good because Maasai have grabbed the hoe [started farming]. Now, if you have cattle, your hoe can help keep them in your home. Is this not good? We used to wear leather, now we wear cloth. We didn't know the leather was dirty. We young girls loved the *ilmurran*, and just wore our leather in whatever way, it was just our clothing. But if you tell that child (her great-grandson) that we never bathed in the past, just a scrub here and a scrub on the hands and I was done!!?! Be quiet my child, we never knew we were dirty. These days people are clean. Look at these clothes that get washed every day, and people are clean, and even the inside of the house and the containers are clean. When we began to farm, we used those containers from Machame, have you seen them? They were made from a tree that looked like a goat's bell. We didn't have cups to drink tea then.

She then described how they ate without containers and utensils, as well as the details of milk processing. Flour, tea, even sugar were commodities introduced during her lifetime. With animated gestures, she told us how a woman had first showed her flour and how to cook flour with milk to make a thin porridge. "She told us it was called flour, we didn't know it at all. We tried to eat some then threw it outside. . . . We didn't know flour."

She also stressed the value of education:

Aren't those children in school trying to get smart? If you are smart and there are things that you don't know, won't your smartness help you figure them out? . . . When the schools were started, an old man would be told to send a child to school. People complained that their children were being stolen to be given to the *ilmangati* ["enemy," also a derogatory term for Swahilis]. The *ilmangati* were given our children, and the elder Maasai men didn't want to let them go, for fear that they would become different. The children went because they were forced to. But these days everyone wants to go, even if they are not chosen they volunteer themselves. Girls and boys attend school these days, and everyone is happy. But no one liked it in the past.

With education, children could learn Swahili, which everyone needed to cope in the world today.

Koko lived in meager circumstances with her grandson, often complaining that she did not have enough food to eat or showing me the rips in her one cloth. Like most Maasai that I spoke with, she told me about the glory days when every Maasai family had hundreds of cattle. Only a very few homesteads in this area had such large herds anymore; most households had less than ten animals. Even so, her grandson's household was considered poor by community standards—a few chickens, an occasional goat, and a small farm provided their sustenance. Yet she spoke of being *enkarsis,* or wealthy: "I am surrounded by my grandchildren and great-grandchildren. My children have given birth to *ilmurran* and *intoyie,* I am wealthy in this way." Unable to walk very far, she spent most days playing with the children, soaking up the sun on a warm day or huddling over the cooking fire inside the hut in colder weather. But what she was most proud of was being Maasai. "I am completely a Maasai (*Maasai tukul*), a Maasai *"piwa"* [from the English "pure"]. And I would never want to be a white person [*olaisungun,* from the Swahili *mzungu*]."

Koko was still alive during my last visit to Emairete in 1997. In his infrequent letters, Morani, my research assistant, had not mentioned her in some time, so I feared that she had passed away. But as I climbed the hill to her hut, I heard the words that always warmed my heart, *"Enchoruet ai!* (my girl-friend!)" *"Koko! Enchoruet ai!"* I replied, tears of joy in my eyes. She was even frailer and skinnier than before, but the mischievous sparkle in her eyes remained. She proudly told me that the torn black cloth she was wearing was the same one I had given her as a parting gift during my last visit in 1995.

I had brought my second husband to meet her, and after introductions she carefully looked him up and down, up and down, chuckling to herself. Then she went into her hut and returned dressed in her finery—her many beaded necklaces, a clean dark cloth, and full beaded earrings. Slowly she began to rock her head and body back and forth in her chair, thrusting her shoulders and singing a lilting rhyme, as if she were an *endito* (young girl) dancing for a warrior. She gazed lovingly into my husband's eyes, flirting outrageously. "You had better watch out," she warned me, "I will steal your husband!"

MODERNIST ORDERS: COLONIALISM AND THE PRODUCTION OF MARGINALITY

2

In terms of development, the British colonizers didn't do anything for Maasai.
— *Interview with Maasai male elder, 1992*

A nomadic pastoralist without any bounds governing his wanderings and the wanderings of his herds will be a menace to native progress and can only induce chaos and lack of administrative control.[1]
— *1925 Arusha District Annual Report*

Despite over thirty years of experience in British East Africa (Kenya), when the British took over Tanganyika in 1916, they were still baffled by the fluidity and flux of African social relations. Colonial officials were confronted by multiple language groups, overlapping cultural traditions, intermingled populations, diverse modes of subsistence, and fragmented political allegiances. Oblivious to the underlying historical patterns of marriage, kinship, exchange, and power which structured these complicated relationships, colonial officials merely saw chaos, a chaos repugnant to their intertwined notions of order and civilization.

Not surprisingly, the dominant project of the early colonial regime became the imposition of the order so necessary to their framework for political control. Their organizing principle for establishing the requisite "categories of control" was a particular definition of ethnicity based on their preconceived notions of "tribes" as neat, congruent alignments of place, people, and polities. Hesitantly at first, then with increased intensity once the Mandate legitimated their presence in Tanganyika in

1922, the British strove to consolidate and bound people into distinct categories—"tribes"—then place these tribes within demarcated, controllable spaces. Once ethnic identity became spatially enclosed and bounded, colonial administrators could establish and expand their territorially based system of political control through recognition and collaboration with the "chiefs" of these "tribes."

But the colonial project of imposing control through such bounding and ordering was unevenly and contradictorily applied. Certain "tribes" appeared as more threatening and therefore in need of more urgent and forceful "ordering." "The Maasai" had long been described by early traders, missionaries, and travelers in vivid terms as "fierce" nomads who roamed the plains with their cattle, stealing livestock, attacking agricultural settlements, and leading a life free of the domesticating concerns of "modern" man. Johnston, writing in 1886, offers a typical description of this "nomad warrior race" (Hinde and Hinde 1901: x), with its focus on the Maasai warrior and its bizarre mix of fear and fascination:

> The physical appearance of the unregenerate robber Masai is splendid. It is a treat to the anthropological student to gaze on such magnificent examples of the fighting man. It is an example of one side of our multiform nature pushed to an exclusive and supreme development. The Masai warrior is the result of the development of Man into a beautiful Animal. . . . The physical perfection of these East African beef-eating, bloodthirsty warriors is of the prize-fighter's or the rowing man's ideal, rather than the aesthete's. (Johnston 1886: 408–409)

Such stories and accounts, as well as the accompanying picture plates, sparked the imagination and shaped the practices and policies of British colonial administrators, who perceived "the Maasai" as direct challenges to the immediate colonial objectives of establishing political order and, through order, political authority. As nomads, the movement of people and livestock disrupted the neat alignments of ethnic identity with territorial identity so desired by administrators. The presence of the *ilmurran,* or "warriors," renowned for their ferocity and military abilities, and feared for their raids and stock-"thieving" heightened the sense of urgency in controlling Maasai presence and movement.

Development projects in the early colonial period were therefore implemented against a backdrop of related political, economic, and social changes, including land alienation, indirect rule, taxation, monetization, and commoditization. Together, these efforts had contradictory effects: they simultaneously consolidated and expanded male Maasai economic and political power while isolating and marginalizing Maasai as an ethnic group from access to political and economic power with the protectorate. Understanding this broader political, economic, and social context is crucial to assessing how particular development projects were designed, implemented, and received and why some rather than others became sites of struggle between colonial officials and Maasai and between Maasai men and women.

This chapter analyzes how and why the concept of "development" emerged during the colonial period as part of the imperial project of imposing a modernist order on the perceived "chaos" of the natives. Within this framework, I analyze how the formation of ethnic identities as "categories of control" was crucial to the colonial quest for spatial and temporal order and therefore intimately intertwined with and affected by shifting agendas of development. Furthermore, these processes were fundamentally gendered, with profound, although unexpected and uneven, effects on local gendered relations of power. Second, the chapter explores the two key arenas of interventions in this period—water and livestock—to show how they were inherently political (designed to strengthen colonial administrative and land tenure policies) and fundamentally gendered and ethnic. The final section examines the immediate consequences of these early economic and political interventions for Maasai livelihoods, especially in terms of their increased vulnerability to drought and disaster.

Most of the chapter is based on a close reading of archival documents, since few Maasai recall the details of the colonial encounter during this early period. Their memories, as seen in the Portraits and later chapters, are comprised of anecdotes, ideas about the cumulative effects of colonialism, feelings, embodied moments such as spirit possession, and generalized recollections of the attitude and tenor of administrative personnel, whether of admiration or hostility, respect or disrespect. Some Maasai perspectives and actions can also be read indirectly and even directly (in the form of letters and petitions) from the archives. Yet much of this chapter and the next inevitably presents the perspective of colonial officials; the views of Maasai and effects on their lives is more visible in the ethnographic discussion of the contemporary period in later chapters.

Constituting Categories of Control: "The Maasai" and "Maasailand"

Landscapes of Identity: Making "Maasailand" and "the Maasai"

Perhaps the most enduring achievement of the British during the pre–World War II period was the constitution of "Maasailand" as a place and the reconstitution of "the Maasai" as a "tribe." Although both of these related efforts were lengthy, incomplete, and contested, they provided the foundation for other political, economic, and social interventions and thus had long-term consequences for ethnic, gender, and generational relationships. Isolating Maasai spatially, politically, and ethnically disrupted the networks of interaction and exchange upon which their livelihoods and identities were premised. Initially, they struggled to resist colonial restructuring of their space, prompting some accommodation on the part of the administration. Later, however, they were forced to accept their situation and fight to protect what they had in the face of ongoing attacks on their lands and livelihoods.

One of the first British initiatives was to create a Masai Reserve and cajole and coerce Maa-speaking livestock herders to move into the Reserve. The chief proponent of the Reserve was E. D. Browne, a colonial administrator[2] whose "cherished ideal" was "the formation of a Reserve with a self-contained administration," that is, to align people, place, and political rule.[3] Browne's zeal to create a Reserve had several sources. One rationale was posed in moral terms, as a response to what many British perceived as the sad dissolution of Maasai as a "tribe." Although Maasai were still officially relegated to a German-legislated "reserve" prohibiting them from living north of the Arusha-Moshi road, the British encountered groups of Maa-speaking peoples living throughout northern and central Tanganyika.[4] Once the war started, Maasai had moved in search of better lands, steady water supplies, and more advantageous living arrangements, such as proximity to cultivators for ease of exchange of foodstuffs.[5] In some areas such as Arusha Chini and the Pare plains, settlements of Maa-speakers were interspersed with settlements of Chagga or Pare speakers; other areas such as the floor of the Rift Valley were inhabited primarily by Maa-speaking pastoralists, with agricultural settlements in areas of permanent water sources such as Engaruka. Some Maa-speakers herded, others cultivated, many did both. Most administrators attributed the scattering to their continued suffering after the ravages of the epidemics and civil wars of the late nineteenth century and the administrative negligence of the Germans, rather than to a conscious effort by Maasai to diversify economically, reestablish involvement with neighboring peoples, and reassert their own modes of spatial interaction.[6] Upset that such fragmentation and dispersal had occurred among "the Maasai" of travelers' tales and colonial lore, they vowed to restore "the Maasai" to their reputed former glory and vitality as a "tribe" by reuniting the scattered fragments and concentrating them in a single, bounded area.

But the rhetoric of reconstituting the Maasai to their former tribal "vitality" masked more instrumental concerns for consolidating them into a bounded reserve. As the chapter's introductory quotation suggests, the nomadic aspect of pastoralism, with its constant, seemingly incoherent movements of people and livestock, challenged metropolitan ideas of civilization and order, bewildered and frustrated colonial administrators, and thwarted their attempts at control: "Just so long as the Masai owns sufficient stock to permit of his being purely a pastoralist, just then so long will he be of necessity a nomad. Until his nomadic movements are restricted to a definite area, he will roam and encroach at his own sweet will."[7] Such a "menace" was best controlled by restricting such chaotic movement to a designated area. These images defined the appropriate space: one that was virtually unoccupied, that was removed from European settlements and other African "ethnic spaces," and that could contain the vast herds and shifting movements intrinsic to Maasai transhumant pastoralism. Thus, when the Masai Reserve was finally approved in 1922,[8] it encompassed the driest, most desolate lands in north-central Tanganyika. As "pure pastoralists," they were relegated to land where (supposedly) only pastoralism and not cultivation was possible: "I think it should not be forgotten that Masailand under present conditions, is infinitely better employed by the Masai than it could possibly be by any other form of human settlement," wrote Browne.[9]

From the beginning, a constant matter of dispute between Maasai and administrators was the boundaries of the Reserve. Despite claiming to represent Maasai interests, administrators set the boundaries to accommodate the interests of settlers and neighboring administrators and for ease of demarcation.[10] Maasai were seldom, if ever, consulted. The Reserve did encompass vast areas of wet-season grazing land formerly occupied by Maa-speakers before the German occupation, but it contained few permanent waters. More drastically, critical drought preserves and dry-season grazing areas were gradually excised from within the Reserve and alienated to European settlers, who cultivated only small portions of their land but profited greatly from selling water and grazing rights to Maasai.[11] For example, a Dutch settler, Joubert, owned land on the fertile southern slopes of Mondul mountain (also called Komolonik mountain), which included Lemisigie, a mountain stream which was the main permanent water source for the area. In 1930, the stream's output in the dry season was measured to be at least 45,000 gallons per hour, enough to "maintain all the Kissongo herds, and more, free from the fear of lack of water supplies."[12] By 1930, Maasai were paying Joubert £1,000 a year to purchase access to this critical dry-season water source.[13] As Margery Perham scornfully remarked: "Its existence alone made possible 30,000 square

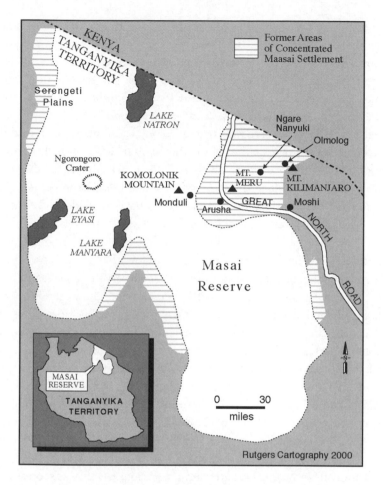

Map 2.1 Approximate boundaries of Masai Reserve, ca. 1923.

miles of dry grazing for the Masai. So he had no need to farm, only sit there and levy toll on them for the use of the water" (Perham 1976: 129). Other controversial settler farms were located in Olmolog, Engaruka, and West Kilimanjaro—all fertile areas with permanent water sources.

In addition, Maasai were forbidden to graze their livestock on the larger mountaintops such as Mondul, Olmolog, and Ngorongoro, which were demarcated as forest reserves to "protect water sources" (Page-Jones 1948: 53).[14] The forest reserve policy was not without its critics among administrators, however, especially those who worked in the field and complained that "the endeavors" were "depriving the Masai of their legitimate dry season grazing and leaving large stretches of land lying dormant."[15] Finally, certain important ceremonial sites were also excluded from the Reserve boundaries, including Ngulat, a section of Mondul mountain which was the long-term site of the Eunoto ceremony, and Olmolog, site of the Olongesherr ceremony (which was divided into farms and sold to European farmers).[16]

Once the Masai Reserve was created, colonial administrators forced those who conformed to their definition of "the Maasai" as (male) Maa-speaking livestock herders to move into the Reserve.[17] Paradoxically, ethnic identity was at once fixed and flexible in the eyes of the British in such moments: in order to retain their ethnic affiliation, Maasai would have to reside in the Reserve; Maasai who refused were told they would have to give up their "Maasai" identity and "become a subject of the local chief, Mchagga, Mweru or Mwarusha as the case might be."[18] Besides having to follow the leadership of another "tribal" group, anyone refusing to reside in the Reserve was perceived as "deliberately severing his connection with his own tribe," and therefore "would automatically be liable to the civic duties as well as the civic privileges of his adopted tribe, including of course the liability for service as a Government labourer or porter."[19] The "Kwavi," perceived as agricultural Maasai, posed a challenge to colonial definitions of Maasai ethnicity, prompting Governor Byatt to urge that the Kwavi either enter the Reserve or "accept the citizenship of the tribes they were living among." Ambiguous ethnic identities would not be tolerated: "They must be definitely Masai or not Masai" (Arusha District [AD] Annual Report [AR] 1925: 8). Not surprisingly, given these threats, "most of the Masai in question expressed themselves as having no wish to break away from their tribe, and many are anxious to move as soon as conditions as to water and grazing permit" (AD AR 1925: 8). Of course, the desire of Maasai to move to the Reserve was interpreted as proof of their inherent tribalism rather than as a desire to retain their social networks and political allegiances. By 1926 some British were boasting about their success at reconstituting "the Masai" as a "tribe": "The Masai tribe is once more a corporate entity recovered from many fragments which were scattering themselves far and wide in the Territory between the years of our occupation in 1916, the collection of which could not commence until 1920 and ensuing years" (AD AR 1926).

Despite the self-congratulatory tone of this excerpt, Maasai refused to acknowledge the authority of colonial administrators to demarcate their space, restrict their mobility, and criminalize their movements across colonially imposed boundaries as "trespass." There were constant reports in the 1920s of

Maasai living outside the bounds of the Reserve as they moved to seek water and grazing and maintain important social networks. In 1928, for example, the district officer from Maswa District reported the presence of 54 Maasai with about 10,000 cattle and 20,000 sheep in the Serengeti Plains. According to the district officer:

> The Masai declined to come in here and explain themselves, they decline to come under Sub-Chief Seni's jurisdiction. They allege that the Masai have no boundaries and as they are short of grazing and water in ther [sic] own country they will use our grazing and water until it rains in their own country. Their attitude is peaceful.[20]

Some Maasai crossed boundaries to continue their grazing and water-leasing arrangements with settlers such as Joubert, despite vocal administrative disapproval.[21] Others used the boundaries to their advantage, moving temporarily into neighboring districts at tax time to avoid paying the higher "Maasai" tax.[22] Special files were kept in Arusha, Tanga, and other neighboring districts on "Movement of Masai and Livestock," and repeated complaints were made about Maasai who trespassed outside the bounds of the Reserve.[23] Administrators in neighboring districts perceived Maasai movement as threats to their control and pressured Masai Reserve administrators to consolidate and contain the livestock and people. While Maasai homesteads in some areas were constantly being removed, only to return again, other settlements were condoned.[24] Large numbers of stock that were found "trespassing" on settler lands were confiscated in 1929 to teach Maasai a lesson, but the experience left them more angry than chastened.[25] Despite their efforts to contain Maasai within the bounds of the Reserve, however, administrators often had to admit defeat: "I trust that capital will *not* be made of the fact that a large percentage of the Masai do not and have not for many years lived within the limits of their Reserve."[26] In the end, they tried to regulate and control such movements by reluctantly issuing "cattle-movement permits" to sanction movement of native cattle onto European areas and grazing arrangements between Europeans and "natives."[27]

While colonial administrators worked to control the movement of Maasai out of the Reserve, they also tried to restrict the entry of certain non-Maasai *into* the Reserve. To discourage "itinerant" traders from entering the Reserve, Browne instituted a pass system in 1924 in order "to have full and legal control over all entrants to the Reserve."[28] But the trading continued, as did the complaints about "surreptitious trade" between Maasai and other groups.[29]

In light of Maasai refusal to obey the boundaries, and despite complaints from district officers in neighboring districts, colonial administrators finally had to concede by expanding the Reserve's boundaries (now officially the Masai District) in 1927 and 1928 to embrace several outlying settlements.[30] As a result, Browne, the senior commissioner who instigated the requests for extension, was accused by fellow administrators such as Hallier, the district commissioner for Moshi, of being biased in favor of Maasai. In contrast, Hallier proudly proclaimed his lack of patience or sympathy for Maasai:

> The Masai have I believe some 20,000 square miles of country reserved for their use, is it sound and right, that they should be given the land . . . which can be put to far greater economic use by Europeans, for no better reasons, than the preservation of barbaric customs; which should in my humble opinion be persistently[,] steadily, and gradually discouraged. The majority of the tribes of this country are advancing rapidly and discarding many of their repulsive customs for a better state of existence in Administration, Education, Scientific agriculture, better houses etc. etc. The Masai will if they do not give up the moran system, wake up one day to find they are the heathen amongst the black men of this Territory.[31]

Hallier's letter foreshadowed themes which would reappear in the 1950s with the drive for higher productivity: that cultivators and settlers could make "greater economic use" of Maasai land than Maasai, that Maasai compared negatively to other more "progressive" "tribes," and that a key obstacle to Maasai development was the *ilmurran* system.

Ironically, at the same time (1926) that Browne was lobbying to expand Masai District to embrace more dry-season grazing grounds and permanent water sources, the district officer for Arusha had convinced the governor to offer fertile land on the southern slopes of Mondul Mountain for sale to settlers. Some 865 acres were immediately alienated, then the land was surveyed and mapped to ease further alienation. Proposals were also made to designate other land in the area as an expansion area for the "surplus" Arusha populations whose own land had become congested and overpopulated,[32] and to sell an additional 3,350 acres, including Joubert's farm, to settlers "without detriment to native interests."[33] Webster, the provincial commissioner, strongly supported these recommendations but noted that there was "also the question of Masai interests."[34] He warned that these proposed alienations, which included a sacred area for the regular performance of the Eunoto ceremony, would anger Maasai and heighten their "attitude of passive resistance to European Administration."[35]

Despite Webster's warning, the government continued to alienate fertile lands in the Masai Reserve, even after it became Masai District in 1926.[36]

Continued bickering between Masai District officials and those in neighboring districts over the presence of Maasai outside of their borders and the positioning of border boundaries led to an investigation and report by F. J. Bagshawe, the land development commissioner. He recommended permitting Mbulu, Arusha, and others to settle in Masai District; removing Maasai from most of their settlements outside their District as well as areas within the District such as the Ngorongoro and Embagai craters, where their interests were believed to compete with those of game; and encouraging alienation of the highland forest areas to European settlers. Murrells, the district officer for Masai, refuted each recommendation "from the Masai point of view," provoked by the report's stress on

> the needs of the Wambulu, the necessities of kindred tribes, the game of the country, the forest reserves, and the iniquities of the Masai. The principal reference to the Masai needs appears to be based on the following principles:—if nobody wants the land the Masai may have it for the time being until they do. That a pastoral tribe must of necessity be banished to the deserts, because apparently the deserts are the most suitable places for them and their stock.[37]

The provincial government's lack of concern for Maasai needs became quite evident in 1930, when Joubert offered to sell his estate to Maasai, who were willing to purchase the entire property to ensure permanent access to the Lemisigie waters. But the provincial commissioner modified the terms of the sale, proposing that the administration buy half of the property for the new Masai District Headquarters and proposed Masai school, splitting ownership of the land and water rights with Maasai.[38] The 1930 Olkiama agreed to pay the purchase price for their share of the farm (2,800 head of slaughter stock by Murrells's estimate), which included financing water pipes and a trough, by assessing levies on each area.[39] Although administrators knew that Lemisigie was "the customary permanent water of the Kisongo Masai,"[40] they perceived no irony or injustice in the fact that Maasai would be purchasing rights to land and water that had historically belonged to them (which the government, not the Maasai, had sold and profited from) and financially subsidizing the colonial administration: "The Masai will have been generously treated and we shall have an ideal site for a permanent station."[41]

Not surprisingly, Maasai were becoming increasingly nervous about their rights—or lack thereof—in land: "The impression seems to exist among the people that much land has been alienated that was not alienated before, and that many new farms have been cut out over and above those alienated by the late German Government."[42] As Murrells acknowledged, "They judge by and from the past, when all these areas were in definite Masai occupation. European district boundaries convey little, to the Masai, who only recognise 'their country.'"[43] Murrells and other district-level administrators who worked with Maasai on a daily basis recognized that the continuing alienation of Maasai lands, including their ceremonial sites, was heightening Maasai distrust of the administration's promises and intentions:

> Hitherto, in contrast to the position in Kenya, all sections of the Tanganyika Masai have regarded the Government with reverence and trust, when however they learn that these areas are to be taken from them, we can be certain that there will be such consternation at what they will consider "rank treachery," that I fear there will be serious unrest among a hitherto peaceful and law abiding people.[44]

Murrells sympathized "a great deal" with their concerns. Not only had "former Masai areas such as Ol Molog, trans-Pangani and the plateau above the west Rift Wall" been alienated, but "they have seen much of their former land and land that is reserved to their uses, destroyed by the alienation of head waters of streams. I refer to Engare Nairobi and Engare Nanyuki."[45] Evidence suggests that Maasai understandings of land were beginning to shift as they absorbed and reworked the colonial ideas that land was a commodity to be bought, sold, and owned and that ownership meant the right to determine who had control, access to, and use of the "property." Murrells reported that fifteen homesteads which had settled with permission in the Kondoa Irangi District in 1929 had "raised a subscription of about 150 head of cattle which they paid over to Kondoa Irangi in order to 'purchase the country.'"[46]

Furthermore, other groups, especially Arusha, were moving in increasing numbers into Masai District.[47] Although the Masai Native Authority, under pressure from administrators, passed several ordinances prohibiting "natives" from other "tribes" from settling in the District without the permission of the "Masai Sub-Chief" of the area, the measures were generally ignored by Maasai elders or used to extract bribes in cattle or marriageable daughters from land-hungry Arusha.[48] Arusha, who shared a language, certain ceremonies, and other features with Maasai, blurred the neat colonial spatial divisions of territory by ethnicity, which enabled them to permeate boundaries which obstructed other African cultivators from entering Masai District. Some administrators believed the solution was to eradicate rather than reinforce the Masai District boundary: "I have always held the opinion that it was a mistake to divide the former Arusha District into two districts (i.e., Arusha District and Masai District) because the tribal affairs of the Arusha, Meru and Masai are closely allied and intermingled owing to intermarriage and cattle distribution.

Tribal customs are very much the same also, and from the point of easy access to Masailand, Arusha has everything in its favor."[49]

These land decisions in the early colonial period—the creation of the Reserve, the negotiation and contestation of boundaries, the alienation of the most fertile land—structured the colonial encounter with Maasai in significant ways. First, by 1927, these early colonial interventions in the formation of "Maasailand" and consolidation of "the Maasai" had produced, to some degree, the social and spatial isolation of Maasai: "The Masai District has been constituted as an ethnological and economic sanctuary; rigidly closed to outside influence and to trade, it has remained for 11 years a stagnant island set in the midst of the most progressive areas of the Territory," wrote Provincial Commissioner Mitchell.[50] The acceleration of land alienation had significant effects on the willingness of Maasai to invest in development and their confidence in the government. Second, the logic that only pastoralists could survive on these lands produced its corollary—that these dry lands were all that pastoralists needed—which was used to displace them from fertile lands inside and outside the boundaries of Masai District. By excising the areas such as dry-season grazing lands, permanent waters, and drought reserves which were critical to sustaining the Maasai form of transhumant pastoralism, administrators gradually undermined the ability of Maasai to support themselves through either pastoralism or cultivation. The consequences of these administrative interventions were exemplified in 1929, when severe drought caused many cattle deaths. Unwilling to admit culpability, administrators blamed the deaths on "overstocking" rather than the structural issues of inequity of land tenure, alienation of dry-season grazing grounds, and restriction of Maasai movement from areas outside of the District.

Making Native "Authorities"

Once the Reserve was formed, the next initiative became the implementation of indirect rule among Maasai. As elsewhere, it was a frustrating and difficult process subject to constant reevaluation and restructuring as administrators expended their limited resources and personnel to produce order and exercise control in the face of evasion, resistance, and challenge on the part of some Maasai men and women. Administrators were overwhelmed by the physical and financial logistics of administering such a vast, sprawling area:

> The Administrative Officer, Loliondo at present, for instance, has half a dozen messengers (half of them not Masai) one office clerk, two Native Treasury clerks-cum-tribal-dressers, one hut-counter, seven policemen, and no motor transport

with which to prevent, detect, and punish stock-theft, collect tax, treat sickness and injury, improve trading conditions, preserve forest and waters, police an inter-colonial border and generally administer about 9000 Masai in a tract of country at a rough guess some 5000 square miles in area. The nature of this country, with its lack of water, human habitation, food-supplies and roads, is in itself sufficient to make this an [word illegible] business. Add to that almost complete lack of assistance or cooperation from the native authority and the task assumes mountainous proportions.[51]

The unwillingness of many Maasai to acknowledge the legitimacy of colonial administration, as evidenced by their refusal to respect the reserve boundaries, and later in persistent noncompliance with veterinary controls and regulations, exacerbated the frustration and distress of administrators who grumbled constantly about Maasai "passive resistance."

The paucity of colonial personnel working in Maasailand in this period had two important but contradictory consequences: as the lone "experts" of daily Maasai life, these men had significant influence in shaping administrative policies and practices in Masailand, yet they lacked adequate personnel and resources to implement their ideas or enforce compliance with orders and regulations. In his caustic review of the "existing state of affairs" of Maasai administration in 1927, when he briefly served as acting provincial commissioner, P. E. Mitchell criticized this individualistic administrative style and vowed "to withdraw the Administration from the 'persona' atmosphere, to the one of administration by custom, procedure and authority alone, supported by 'personality.'"[52] Perceived as advocates for Maasai, especially because of their vocal defense of Maasai land rights, men such as Browne and Murrells had their detractors. F. J. Bagshawe (head of the Land Development Commission), for example, responded to Murrells's comments on a land development survey with a personal attack:

I venture to congratulate Mr. Murrells upon the earnestness with which he champions the cause of the Masai under his care. His remarks are fair comment, from his point of view, which is that of an officer who is concerned solely with one tribe, but knows little and cares less about any other. I have to approach the problems which I am sent to investigate from a different angle.[53]

In a disagreement over whether Olmolog should be reclaimed by Maasai, Hallier tried to challenge Browne's objectivity through similar accusations: "There is not the slightest doubt, that if it had been considered at all feasible to grant this land to the Masai, Major Browne would have endeavoured to get it for them, for it is an axiom that he would have given them Africa if he had been able to do so."[54]

Such disputes highlight the structural tensions among colonial administrators working at different levels: policymakers in the metropole and central government, provincial officials trying to reconcile the sometimes contradictory interests of the different districts and groups under their supervision, and district officers, whose work "on the ground" made them most familiar with (and often protective of) the daily lives and interests of "their people." As the front line, district officers were usually the personal face of colonialism. Moreover, for all of these officers, their prior experiences (such as Browne had had with Maasai in Kenya) and personal beliefs produced divergent ideas about the "proper" administration and development of local peoples. For example, for all their similarities as advocates of Maasai interests in the eyes of their critics, Murrells and Browne seem to have had a tense, difficult relationship, in part as a result of such structural differences. As provincial commissioner, Browne was a bureaucrat: accountable to Dar es Salaam, he decided how to allocate his meager funds among the districts and made strong demands for immediate and convincing results. As a district officer, Murrells had the unpleasant if not impossible task of trying to use the minimal funds to achieve the overly ambitious, if not ludicrous, demands of Browne.[55]

Given the lack of colonial personnel and resources, administrators were forced to create a political hierarchy of Africans through whom to channel and receive information and orders. From the beginning, administrators assumed that the "traditional" "native" authorities were elder men and therefore targeted elder men as useful intermediaries in channeling information and exerting control over other Maasai. In 1916, E. D. Browne, the district political officer at the time, appointed three sympathetic Maasai men as "agents" to replace the German-appointed *jumbes*. He made it a policy, however, to consult with the elders and *ilaigwenak* [traditional leaders] on "tribal matters" and bragged that "these elders were taught that they, as men of influence, must lead their people and co-operate with Government."[56] This system was revised in 1922 to incorporate the *oloiboni* (a spiritual leader, prophet, and healer; referred to as "Laibon" by administrators) as the "Chief of the Masai" to provide a focal point of authority to the pyramid of agents and elders. A key impetus for this change came from Maasai themselves: a deputation of Maasai men requested that Parit, the son of Laibon Lenana who lived in the East African Protectorate (Kenya) be allowed to move from Kenya to Tanganyika to "act as Laibon and Chief of all the Masai in the Territory."[57]

Once indirect rule was formalized as the administrative policy for Tanganyika Territory in 1926, the acting provincial commissioner requested that the district officer for Masai District report on "traditional" Maasai tribal organization in order to search for the "ultimate authority in the tribe."[58] In his report, the district officer characterized Maasai as "an essentially democratic organisation" with no office that could be regarded as a "hereditary chiefship," including that of the Laibon. Three groups, according to the report, had legitimate authority to exercise executive and judicial powers among Maasai: the "Aigwenak" (*ilaigwenak*) who served as the designated representatives, arbitrators, and advisors for each male age-grade; the "Aunoni" (*olaunoni*) who served as the chosen "chief of his 'age,' in whom executive authority is really centred, for his own 'age' only"; and, finally, elder men.[59] As a result of the report, a new system of indirect rule was implemented: the Masai Native Authority (or Masai Council, or Olkiama) was comprised of a council of elder men representing different geographic areas, headed by the Laibon.[60] In 1938, in response to some disagreements which had arisen between the elders and the Laibon, the government took advantage of the death of Laibon Mbeiya to restructure the Masai Native Administration by shifting the Laibon into an advisory role. The result was to further strengthen the authority of these select male elders.[61] Until the 1950s, this system, with several minor readjustments, remained much the same.

Appointments to positions within the Native Administration offered otherwise peripheral men access to power and resources they were unable to achieve within their own society, although they did not gain access to prestige. Many used their positions as intermediaries to extract payments for their services or patronage. Reasonable exploitation of their positions was accepted, even expected, but excessive abuses were not tolerated. For example, Sub-Chief Barnoti was unanimously dismissed by a 1929 meeting of male elders and the Laibon "on the grounds that he used his position for ulterior motives." The list of charges brought against Barnoti by the elders offer a glimpse of the opportunities for misuse of the petty powers granted such native "authorities." The accusations included extracting a one-shilling fee for every head of cattle sold at a local market for himself, permitting cattle to be moved from and to certain areas after he had been paid cattle in the form of a bribe, forcing two Maasai from Kenya to pay him two cows before he would allow them to return to Kenya with stock which they had inherited (even though they had a stock permit), and accepting a bribe "from a certain native who desired to obtain possession of cattle said to have been due him from a native estate. Barnoti is reported to have consented to this seizure and to have given advice regarding the branding of them."[62] After investigating the charges and finding no reason to question the elders' decision, the district officer requested and received approval of the dismissal from the provincial commissioner.[63]

2.1 Provincial commissioner with group of Maasai elder men, 1938. Photo
by Clement Gillman, reproduced courtesy of The Bodleian Library,
University of Oxford (MSS. Afr.s.1175, photo 34/15).

The case of Kapurwa, long a favorite headman among colonial officials,
illustrates the impossibility of satisfying both systems. According to a report
by the district officer for Masai, Kapurwa "has tried to insist on tax collection
when others have not," but his tax-collection figures declined markedly over a
span of three years. The numbers showed "a general exodus from his control,"
primarily, according to the district officer, because he was now considered "'Ol
Meg' [*ormeek*]" by Maasai, that is, "ostracized as being an outsider and no
longer a Masai." "Other Headmen," the district officer concluded, "will risk
the exodus, it means nothing to them; but they will not risk ostracism and all
the penalties and hardships that entails."[64] "It is," he explained, "precisely as
salaried servants of the Government that the Masai regard the Aigwenak or
headmen who make up the Native Authority, although they are chosen by the
people themselves. They are, in point of fact, chosen by the Masai because
they are men who are likely to do nothing, in which case they are tolerated."[65]
But when such peripheral men, such as Kapurwa, tried too hard to ingratiate

themselves with the Government, their Maasai masculinity was called into question, and they were derided as *ormeek.*

Briefly, *ormeek* was a term initially applied to all non-Maasai Africans, especially those who went to school, spoke Swahili, worked in the government, or were baptized. They were often symbolized, for Maasai, by their outfits of trousers, shirts, and occasionally jackets. In time, however, the term was invoked to mark, mock, and ostracize any Maasai man (and very rarely woman) such as Kapurwa who imitated Swahilis, in his case by working for the colonial government as a headman. Later, the term was used to stigmatize Maasai men who went to school or were baptized. The use of *ormeek* as a pejorative term thus signaled new tensions over gender and ethnic identity among Maasai men as they engaged with colonial policies and practices.

The composition of the Maasai Council was not left to Maasai alone to decide. At one Maasai Council meeting, Murrells tried to persuade Maasai elders to dismiss "two ineffectual elders" and replace them with two of Murrells's choosing: "Both are forceful men, pro-Government, will not tolerate concealment of offences, will accept authority as they treat unpopularity with contempt, and generally I should be happy in respect of these two areas with these two men in local charge of the Authority."[66] The Olkiama elders reluctantly accepted Murrells's proposal and nominations, but their comments exposed their awareness of the direct rule lurking behind the flimsy facade of indirect rule. Elder Kuiya, for example, "stated that the Masai of the Central area . . . would accept Elder Engitau as it was the order of Government that they should do so; but Engitau was a stranger to them, and they would have preferred one of their own people."[67] Murrells's response was to slander Elder Kuiya, claiming he was a known drunk and liquor trafficker. Murrells stressed the importance of "the need for a strong rule" to bolster the power of elder men over younger men.[68]

Initially, colonial interests in extending and maintaining administrative controls were intimately bound up with, even dependent on, the authority and control exercised by elder men. In the Maasai case, ongoing colonial anxieties about the threat posed by the dangerous, disorderly warriors strengthened their desire to reinforce the power of elder men and the native authorities: "The present 'age' of warriors . . . has come into power under unique circumstances, and ones which I am of opinion would constitute a menace to the peace of the country, unless steps were taken to ensure that a real strong native administration was existent."[69]

On their part, elder men encouraged administrative fears of *ilmurran* in order to bolster their own authority over younger men and "naturally," women.[70]

They supported administrative efforts to curb cattle-raiding by *ilmurran* in order to protect their own herds from theft (see, e.g. Northern Province [NP] AR 1936: 41) and provided self-interested versions of customary laws to be relied upon in native court hearings. Here their concerns included minimizing cattle theft, discouraging liaisons between their wives and *ilmurran,* protecting their rights in and custody over their children in the case of separation or divorce, and rebuking any disrespect of their authority.[71] Should an *olmurrani* curse an elder, for example, he was supposed to give the elder a cow, a calf, and a bottle of honey or face the threat of death (Maguire 1928: 17).

Despite these "laws" and threats, elders sometimes had to appeal to administrators to intercede when their authority was questioned. In 1930, a dispute arose between Laibon Mbeiya and certain factions of Maasai elders over the Laibon's preference for the company of warriors and his contemptuous treatment of a delegation of elders bringing him tribute (*olamal*). Although this grievance, combined with the Laibon's "general disregard of the elders," was a worry, the "truly dangerous state of affairs" was "the predominant position to which the young warriors were being raised in the Councils of the Laibon."[72] District Officer Murrells intervened immediately. He counseled an influential elder to apologize for a threat he had made that was "most insulting and entirely subversive of the Laibon's authority," and he met privately with Laibon Mbeiya:

> I instructed him that these practices of his were to cease at once, and that he was once again to establish friendly contact with the elders, and that his present practice of surrounding himself with a bunch of irresponsible young men, and excluding respected and wise elders was regarded by me with no favorable eye.[73]

What is remarkable is not only that the elders requested the administration's assistance in resolving this dispute but also that administrators complied so quickly and forcefully in what some might have considered "private" matters.

The implementation of indirect rule, however ineffectual and frustrating it may have seemed to the British at times, was a key factor in reshaping both the relationships between Maasai and other ethnic groups and the relationships of autonomy, mutual respect, and interdependency between Maasai men and women. By extending the authority of men, especially elder men, over the newly emerging domain of "the political," indirect rule broadened and deepened their control over junior men and women. It gave certain men new layers of rights and responsibilities as "representatives" of their communities, including the authority to collect taxes, to enforce livestock decisions, and, in time, to codify customary law. Now elder men met to not only arbitrate inter- and intra-community disputes but also to debate and decide on colonial state interventions. As mediators with the larger emerging state formation, these men were able to exploit their new duties and opportunities to assert their political will.

The absence of women from the "political" spheres of public meetings and delegations was read by administrators as a lack of involvement in politics because of their "greater" concern with the female domains of domestic life. But this gendered separation did not happen just because the British imposed their own model of gender relationships on that held by Maasai; Maasai gender domains overlapped significantly with those of the colonizers, but for different reasons. Since all of the colonizers were men, Maasai protocols of respectful behavior prescribed that Maasai of the same gender and roughly the same age interact with them in formal spheres such as public meetings. As with the British, Maasai men and women occupied separate realms on most public occasions. But these realms were not necessarily unequal or conceived of as distinctly "political" or "domestic." The association between elder Maasai men and British administrators was thus partly a consequence of the gendered nature of colonial administration itself—British men were the officials, and they were only rarely accompanied by their wives. Although Maasai women and British men were curious about one another, in general, young married women kept their distance, while older women, especially grandmothers and post-menopausal women, could interact in a freer and less constrained manner.

The converse of Maasai gendered protocols—that is, that Maasai women considered European women to be their allies and associates, especially in public settings—is evident in the few accounts of their meetings.[74] For example, in her letters home, Jane Fosbrooke[75] wrote of her numerous encounters with Maasai women when she lived and traveled with her husband Henry, an assistant district officer in Masai District from 1934–1935. On one trip to a village in southern Maasailand, Jane described how a group of women approached her as soon as Henry went into a store to hear a dispute:

> Meanwhile I stayed by the lorry and the Masai women came and chattered. . . .
> When they saw me they said "Mzungu" (European) and were very intrigued and
> begged me to show them my hair, at which they exclaimed Ah! Ah! The shop-
> keeper sent down some tea and a generous amount of sugar. They indicated that
> a little would be appreciated, so I let them help themselves. They lapped it up,
> and smacked their lips. I tried them on bananas—some liked them and asked
> for more, others made awful faces and the rest laughed. Then they inspect the
> lorry, especially the headlights, horn and mirror in which they admired them-
> selves with more expression of Ah! Ah! Then Henry emerged . . . [and the
> women quickly left].[76]

The curiosity and fearless interaction of the Maasai women with Jane could hardly be mistaken for docility or shyness. A month later a delegation of twenty Maasai women visited her in Loliondo demanding money to purchase sugar for a newborn baby. When Jane, at the advice of her Maasai carpenter, offered three shillings (after asking her husband's permission) the women were overtly disgruntled:

> They talk an awful lot and won't take it. Jane [she refers to herself in the third person] gets interpreter. "It's not enough they want ten shillings!" Jane departs to house *with* the three shillings. Deputations from the Masai women saying that after all they would like the three shillings. Nothing doing. At last they send the Masai headman who intimated it was all a mistake and they would be so very grateful for the three shillings. So Jane relents and gives him the three shillings.[77]

Like Jane, however, these Maasai women were peripheral to the expansion of male power enabled by the formation of the colonial state. In fact, the paternal paradigm in which colonial administrators tried to cast themselves relative to Maasai—as a father to a son or an older brother to a younger brother—excluded relations with women.[78] In effect, administrators mapped their Victorian gender ideologies onto their understandings of, and interventions in, Maasai life: the male domains of public and political in opposition and superior to the female domains of private and domestic.[79] Their perspective was premised on several assumptions: First, that such distinct domains as "domestic" and "political" even existed; second, that they were spatially segregated; third, that the spatial distinctions between the boundaries of homesteads as "private" domains and more communal spaces as "public" reflected and expressed qualitative differences between the types of power exercised in each domain; and fourth, a presumption that "political" authority was primarily exercised in the public sphere, and conversely that the domestic sphere entailed primarily "private" affairs. In sum, administrators assumed that whatever men were doing must be "important" (and conversely, what women were doing was "unimportant"), thus men were aligned with the public/political sphere and women with the domestic/private sphere.

Money Matters: Of Taxpayers, Livestock Owners, and Household Heads

The third set of interventions were economic. In response to increased pressures from the metropole to incorporate colonial subjects more thoroughly into the global monetary and commodity economy in the aftermath of the Great Depression, administrators in Masai District intensified sporadic earlier efforts to promote monetization among Maasai and commoditization of their livestock and land. Three practices were central to their objectives to extract more Maasai livestock and coerce Maasai men into becoming "buyers" and "sellers" of commodities: taxation, the formalization of monetization and trading, and the expansion of the formal livestock marketing infrastructure. Together, these measures combined to replace the female-dominated barter trade with a male-dominated cash economy and thereby enable Maasai men to thwart women's shared and overlapping rights in livestock in order to consolidate their rights as livestock "owners." Both outcomes disenfranchised women from economic control and autonomy.

Taxation was the government's primary means of implementing a variety of overlapping policy objectives: coercing Maasai to sell livestock, encouraging monetization, and justifying various "development" interventions. First, administrators hoped that taxation would encourage livestock sales and therefore teach Maasai men to treat livestock as commodities. Taxation as an incentive for increased livestock offtake was also praised, since "stock disposal" meant "automatic selection of the herds" and "lessening risks of soil erosion."[80] Second, taxation was supposed to encourage monetization. Thus, a 1933 proposal to collect tax in kind because of scarcity of cash in the Territory was strongly opposed by Baxter, the Masai district officer at the time:

> It is a retrogressive step and would militate against the chances of success of my present policy of education in the uses of money. The Masai must learn to use money and learn soon. His need of money to pay tax is a main incentive at the moment to induce him to bring his cattle in person to an auction where he sells for cash and is introduced to the mysteries of competition in prices, etc.[81]

This principle, as Baxter's comment suggests, was gendered: Maasai *men*, as taxpayers, were to be taught about the mysteries of money and the marketplace. By implication, as will be discussed below, each man was to learn about being the owner of *his* cattle and the head of *his* household. But most often, the "carrot" of development (primarily water "conservation" projects during this period) was used to justify and at times increase the extraction of resources from native populations to finance the colonial administration. For example, of the 10 shillings tax paid in 1926, 1 shilling went to the Masai Native Authority, and the remaining 9 shillings went to the government.[82] Similarly, the increase of Maasai taxes from 10 shillings in 1926 to 15 shillings in 1927 was specifically approved to finance the Masai Water Loan (which will be discussed later). Coincidentally, with the proposed increase, "Government will get 10 shillings instead of 9 shillings and will therefore make £476 pa [per annum] more out of the Masai than it does now."[83]

Tax rates were set throughout the Territory by district, but within Masai District rates were set according to ethnic group: Maasai, Sonjo, and "Aliens" each paid different rates. From 1927 until the late 1940s, Maasai paid the highest rates in the Territory (Tanganyika Blue Books 1927–1948).[84] Administrators justified the disparity by characterizing the large herds of these "cattle-keeping people" as great wealth.[85] "Lest it be thought that this scale of taxation is hard on the Masai," Mitchell computed their "estimated wealth" by listing their total livestock holdings, assigning a flat-rate value per animal, and calculating that an average taxpayer held about £136 in livestock wealth, "so that a 15 shillings tax can hardly be called excessive." Of course, such aggregate figures and stereotypes conveniently masked inequalities in livestock holdings among Maasai. In 1932, Maasai elders refused a "voluntary" tax increase to fund additional water development on the grounds that "although many elders have numerous stock and are wealthy, some are not so, therefore an increase would be oppressive to some." The elders argued further that the "cattle markets have fallen and that now in order to pay one tax they have to sell one beast."[86]

In addition to being explicitly based on ethnicity, colonial taxation policy was also explicitly gendered—a "taxpayer" was an adult man. Circumcised Maasai men were liable to pay the poll tax for themselves and a hut tax, or "plural wives tax," for women they were perceived as responsible for: wives, widowed mothers, married sisters living at home. Permanent exemptions were given to Maasai men who were not "able-bodied" and proved to have no property, as well as senior elders, "who have paid tax for many years and whose property has largely passed to their sons."[87] Acutely aware that the plural wives tax "places wives in the same category as taxable property," colonial administrators in Dar occasionally urged provincial and district administrators to design alternative systems of graduated taxation. Until some viable alternative was available, however, they were unwilling to discard the plural wives tax, as it was a significant source of revenue.[88]

Like all administrative policies in Masai District, taxation was quite difficult to implement in practice. In frustration, the provincial commissioner finally conceded to a proposal by his veterinary officer that four stock inspectors working in Masai District be appointed as tax collectors.[89] The implication of Reid's proposal, in terms of the ongoing rivalry between the veterinary department and administration over who had more expertise and therefore more authority to decide Maasai affairs, was clear: "It is simply that the [veterinary] departmental officers, stationed in Masailand, are in a position to know the area and people probably better than any one else, and can accordingly render valuable assistance."[90] The appointment of stock inspectors as tax collectors was "most satisfactory," resulting in a "considerable increase in the number of taxes paid."[91]

Besides taxation, administrators also promoted monetization and commoditization through expanding the structures, opportunities, and incentives for formal trade in livestock, as well as trade in domestic and personal wares. Although a few Somalis and others had small shops scattered throughout Maasailand, most trading occurred through "itinerant" traders, who traveled from homestead to homestead bartering their wares for smallstock, cattle, and hides. Maasai needed no incentives to trade; administrators acknowledged that informal traders were pervasive and welcomed by Maasai: "Some even set up shop in Masai kraals and are visited by all and sundry."[92] And Maasai women, as discussed earlier, were central to this bartering economy, trading milk, hides, and smallstock for food, tobacco, beads, cloth, and other goods.

But administrators disapproved of this vigorous barter economy. First, the unorganized and unsystematic nature of the trading offended their quest for control and order; they were infuriated that these "hawkers" "[passed] unobserved," "[did] not observe the letter of the law" and "were impossible to control."[93] Second, the invisibility of such trade to colonial eyes meant that it was not only difficult to control but also impossible to tax and license. Shopkeepers paid land rent, house tax, and an annual 100 shillings for a shop license. Traders who attended the cattle auctions paid an annual license fee of 50 shillings for each auction site. But itinerant traders provided no such revenue to the government. A third rationale was to "protect" Maasai, whose "ignorance of money would soon make them the dupes of unscrupulous traders" (Griffiths 1938: 99). Baxter, the Masai District Officer, elaborated:

> The Masai is adverse to the use of money, he does not know the money value of the thing he buys or of the thing he sells. He is therefore at the mercy of the unscrupulous trader. Whether we would be justified in limiting trade to the point where it can be overlooked and controlled is a matter for grave discussion. The Masai must be educated in money values and the only education therefor is trade. The lone hawker has no competitor and can name his price. And it is therefor suggested that he is not a useful agent in education. If, however, the Masai is called upon to buy and sell only in recognized trade centres where competition is rife and where control of the trader is more easily affected, then certainly he is being educated in money values. This appears to be the policy most favorable for adoption.[94]

Fourth, an increasing concern with "overstocking," combined with growing recognition of the economic value of Maasai livestock to the Territory, encouraged the promotion of livestock marketing. The logic was simple: replacing barter with cash and encouraging Maasai interest in trade goods would motivate Maasai to sell more livestock to obtain the necessary cash. Finally, barter was perceived as a far more "primitive" form of economy than cash transactions. The reluctance of Maasai men and women to conduct their transactions in cash was yet another marker, for administrators, of their backwardness and lack of progress. One aim of "developing" them was to instill a sense of things as commodities, the value of competition, and the "natural laws" of supply and demand.

These concerns posed a dilemma to administrators: How could they encourage Maasai to continue their lively exchange of goods with traders but conduct these transactions indirectly through the medium of cash? Baxter, who served as Masai district officer in the early 1930s and was a strong proponent of monetization, instituted several measures to formalize trading and encourage monetization. First, in order to discourage itinerant trading, all traders were required to be licensed, and soon they were forbidden to sell their wares except on legally held trade plots as part of established "trading centres" or at the government-sponsored cattle auctions.[95] Second, a "money campaign" was instituted throughout Masailand in 1933 to educate Maasai men in "money values" and replace bartering with "money exchange":

> The Masai was told that he was now living in the days of new customs; he would admit that in war his old custom of spear & shield was useless in the face of the modern gun & aeroplane: he was to learn that in peace too his old custom of trade by cattle was to be entirely superseded by the new custom of money exchange. He was told that his cattle were subject to numerous diseases, suffered from lack of grass and water, were victim to the lion—while the shilling knew none of these drawbacks. He might contend that the shilling could not produce its kind, but the reply is that neither does the ox or queen cow, moreover money did multiply; the name of its product was "faida," the profit of the trader. . . . The Masai were eventually to learn—the sooner the better for them—that the wiser plan was to retain only a moderate herd of productive stock and to convert all their unproductive beasts into ready money.[96]

Finally, administrators tried to develop schemes to control the sale of sheep and hides, the most prevalent "currency" in the barter economy: "Such sales would only take place at regular auctions and would be subject to much the same regulations as those applied to the cattle trade to-day," wrote Baxter.[97]

In time, these efforts to replace informal barter trade with cash transactions were somewhat successful. The use of cash increased, especially with formalization of livestock marketing, although Maasai men and especially women continued to barter, even in the formally established trading centres: "The Maasai bring in sheep and hides and take away beads, blankets, Americani [cloth], tobacco, sugar, posho, red ochre, etc."[98] Helen Griffiths described how after paying their taxes, Maasai would peruse the wares of traders who had surrounded the auction site with their shops and stands:

> Meantime as the beasts are sold, a long queue of pigtailed warriors has formed, waiting to pay tax and clerks are kept busy early and late making out tax tickets. Then, with what remains of the price of his beast, the owner finds his way to the lines of Indian stalls, where in tents piles of blankets are for sale, and rings of beads are temptingly displayed on large bamboo frames. On the ground are mugs and pots of iron and brass, and steel swords and spearheads for the men. A busy scene indeed. The women stand inspecting the beads, while men squat on the ground fingering the spearheads. But woe betide a trader who is thought at some time to have given bad weight in his store in some distant part of the country. Word is passed to boycott his stall, and he has nothing to do but close it down.
>
> At one end of the line of stalls are two rival restaurants. A motley array of about half-a-dozen cups is spread out on the ground, and tea is served at ten cents a cup, or a meal of meat and fritters for fifty cents. . . . Among the throng of buyers blankets of all sorts are replacing the skins in which the men arrived. Some of the old men might be Highland shepherds in their warm blankets, closely imitating various Highland tartans—and all made in Italy. . . . Strangest of all, are the venerable and dignified old men, and the ferocious looking warriors who now appear in pretty pink and white blankets, marked in large letters "Baby"! (Griffiths 1938: 100)

But Maasai also used money to buy more cattle, often, according to Koko, "the very same animals we had just sold!" (in the case of forced cattle sales).

The "Progress" of "Pastoralists"

By the late 1920s, the categories of "Maasai" and "Maasailand" were taken as givens by colonial administrators, despite continued contestation in practice. Most Maasai were living within the bounds of what was now Masai District, and the distinction between Maa-speaking peoples who herded and those who farmed was linguistically marked between "Maasai" (herders) and "Arusha" (farmers). But when the British spoke or wrote of "the Maasai," or when they considered what policies and practices to implement, they meant Maasai men. And such men were, in British eyes, divided into two categories: elder men, who were "naturally" wise and authoritative, and junior men, or "warriors," who were considered wild and potentially dangerous. Women of all ages were generally missing from the category "the Maasai" and thus from the related categories created and consolidated by British practices, including "taxpayer," "household head," livestock "owner," "buyer," "seller," and "native authority." As these categories suggest, the separate domains of the "political" and "economic" promoted by British practices were primarily male domains.

In addition to providing guidelines on how to administer Tanganyika as a protectorate, Britain's mandate from the League of Nations required her, among other things, to promote "the material and moral well-being and the social progress of [the] inhabitants" (quoted in Iliffe 1979: 247). But the colonial view of appropriate "social progress," with its underlying evolutionary teleology, was not the same for all inhabitants. For Maa-speakers, the British perpetuated the linkage of ethnic identity with mode of production, so that the "pure" Maasai were those Maa-speakers who were livestock holders and did not cultivate, while Maa-speaking cultivators were defined as "Arusha" or "Kwavi." Many British thought of Maasai as a separate and higher "race" than the "Bantu" Africans because they more closely resembled the ideal European physical type (tall, slender, fine facial features; see, e.g., Johnston 1902). But this racist hierarchy based on physical characteristics was contradicted and eventually eclipsed by an equally racist hierarchy ranking peoples by their evolutionary stage according to their primary economic pursuits. As "pastoralists," Maasai were classified as more "primitive" than their more "civilized" neighbors, agriculturalists: "It is a commonly accepted dictum that the pastoralist is a stage behind the Agriculturalist in the process of evolution and development" (AD AR 1925: 6). Progress, for pastoralists, thus meant moving up the evolutionary scale to become settled cultivators,[99] but the process had to be gradual, since "it is felt that the desirability of ensuring that they are really competent to walk before they essay to run cannot be too constantly borne in mind" (AD AR 1925: 25).

The slow economic recovery in the metropole in the aftermath of the Great Depression of 1929 exposed and intensified the precarious economic and political structures of the colonial project. The economic stagnation and high unemployment at home made many British politicians reassess the value of the colonies and the colonial subjects themselves.[100] The passage in Britain of the Colonial Development Act of 1929 marked the ascendancy of British interest in the economic "development" of the colonies over prior concerns with protecting native interests and preserving their "traditional" forms of economic production, social organization, and political self-governance.[101] In the rhetoric of this new economic perspective, natives were no longer "primitive" and "backward" and therefore in need of protection and enlightened guidance;

they were now potential producers of cheap primary goods and consumers of exported manufactured goods from Britain. Proponents argued that integrating colonial subjects into this particular slot in the global economy would revitalize the depressed British economy by increasing demand for British exports, thus stimulating the manufacturing industries and reducing unemployment (for metropolitan perspectives, see Morgan 1980; Constantine 1984).

Within this framework, this section examines the two central domains of early colonial development—water and livestock. It then charts two important shifts in colonial development interventions: the collapse of any significant interventions except for the disastrous Masai Water Loan after the global depression and the attempted reassertion of administrative control and "development" in 1935 following the devastation of Maasai herds. During this period, the rationale for development interventions shifted from predominantly ecological concerns to more economic ones and improved administrative control became explicitly linked with improved economic development.

Water "Conservation"

Water "conservation" projects were some of the earliest interventions, most enthusiastically supported by Maasai; they were also some of the least successful interventions by colonial administrators in Masailand. They were clearly linked to colonial land tenure policies: instead of redistributing land equitably to ensure the successful maintenance of Maasai livestock production and cultivation, the British remedy was to try to convert the temporary wet-season grazing grounds encompassed by the Reserve into permanent year-round grazing grounds through water "conservation."[102] Water "conservation" programs thus emerged as an "ecological" solution to address the symptoms of larger structural inequities in land distribution, deflecting attention from the causes of the structural inequities themselves.

With few alternatives, Maasai eagerly embraced the chance to improve their water situation through these "self-help" (Browne's terms) projects. They paid almost all of the costs, while the government ensured that their funds were "judiciously expended."[103] From 1916–1919, a few water sources were improved, all at the request of individual Maasai who deposited money at the district headquarters in Arusha to pay for laborers to be sent out to do the work.[104] Two dams and a long furrow were constructed in early 1921, financed completely by Maasai. The dams survived the test of the 1921 rainy season, providing "new sources of water for the cattle during the dry season" as well as watering places within easy reach of a main road, thereby encouraging the district political officer "to carry on the good work." Despite very low prices for cattle and sheep in 1922, Maasai continued to pay "willing [*sic*] and generously" for all of the water works, with minor financial contributions by the government.

Colonial administrators strongly identified themselves with the water conservation program. On tour in Masailand they carried tools to work on any ponds and water wells they visited and "kept an eye open for possible dam sites." Aware that water conservation was a means of ingratiating themselves with Maasai, they worked hard to cast government as the paternal, friendly helper:

> As regards the attitude of the Masai towards the work of water conservation it is remarkable how fully and quickly they came to appreciate the effort of Government to help them. After their experience under the Germans the idea of a Government who cared whether they had sufficient water or not was a new one to them, and they were quick to take advantage of it.[105]

Certainly Maasai were eager to improve their water situation, recognizing that water was a major problem on the expanded Reserve: "It is remarkably encouraging with what alacrity the native cattle owners subscribe to the suspense fund for water conservation works in their area" (AD AR 1924). With the encouragement of Murrells, "an enthusiastic amateur engineer" (Page-Jones 1948: 55), Maasai voluntarily contributed almost £3,000 to the water fund from 1922–1925 for the construction of seven dams and three furrows. Although money was also used to repair these same dams, often within two years of their construction, the small-scale water projects were viewed as a success by Maasai and administrators:[106]

> All over the country, wells were widened and deepened, small dams improved, and troughs constructed or improved. In some places, where water was obtained from rocky wells, blasting operations on a small scale were carried out, and in several places buckets and chains replaced the primitive, slow, and wasteful method of hand buckets employed by Masai themselves.[107]

Yet by identifying themselves so closely with the water conservation "successes," colonial administrators set themselves up to be identified with the "failures" as well, as will be seen in the discussion of the Masai Water Loan.

Masai Water Loan, 1928–1935

Despite their success, administrators were frustrated by the limited impact of these earlier sporadic efforts. When Mitchell took over as acting provincial commissioner in 1927, he attributed the "very inadequate results" of water conservation measures to date to "the absence of a properly worked out scheme to tackle this enormous problem." "It is not possible," he continued, "to approach a task of such magnitude piecemeal and without organisation, plant, permanent staff, or a definite programme of works."[108] To address these inadequacies, Mitchell requested a loan of £5,000 from the government to create a "Masai Water Fund," the government's first major development initiative in Masai District. By purchasing an inventory of materials (such as pumps, pipes, windmills, and cement), the fund would enable a "carefully worked out programme" of water improvement by preventing "expensive delays." Once each work was completed, "its cost should be ascertained, and the persons who use it will then be asked to pay for it, the money being credited to the fund, which will thus be constantly replenished, so that further loans will not be required." Recurrent expenditures central to the administration and implementation of the project, such as the (European) foreman's salary and project maintenance costs, would be paid from annual recurrent revenue rather than from the loan.[109]

Although Maasai would pay for these costs by an additional 5 shillings annual tax, Mitchell believed that "the administration of such a fund will be quite beyond the powers of the Masai Native Authority." He recommended that the water fund be kept entirely separate, administered by the district officer and supervised by the provincial commissioner. The Masai Treasury would merely deposit its budgeted contributions "from time to time" in the fund:[110] "The money belongs to the Masai and it must be spent as far as possible in conformity with their wishes, our part being mainly to ensure technical soundness of construction, for which we want a good foreman of works more than a board of experts."[111] The loan and 15 shillings tax rate were approved by the Governor and the secretary of state, who estimated that repayment would take about 28 years.[112]

Some hoped that the provision of permanent water sources would encourage Maasai to settle permanently: "Elders who have paid hundreds of pounds for their wells, pumps and engines, or other water arrangements, do almost become as settled as agricultural people."[113] Others saw them as an incentive for Maasai to sell more stock to finance the projects. Murrells urged Maasai to increase their taxes to finance additional "water development" in order to protect their lands from alienation: "The Masai were informed that it was absolutely essential that they should carry on the development of their lands, or they might lose them by reason of lack of development."[114]

As with the earlier water projects, Maasai were initially very supportive of the Water Loan. They eagerly contributed money (through their increased taxes and loan payments) as well as labor: "Within three days of being asked to produce labour, 30 or 40 young Masai volunteered for the heavy manual work (digging, rock carrying, etc.) at Naberera and Lengijabe."[115] Their enthusiasm was partly due to their realization that the development of water sources was essential to their ability to survive on their allocated "tribal" land. But the Water Loan also offered unique opportunities to assert or strengthen rights over water sources. Despite romantic colonial notions about the "communal" nature of land and water in Maasailand, control and access to both resources were structured by a complex set of rules based on kin, clan, and territorial section affiliations. The improvement of existing water sources as well as the development of new ones was therefore a very political act, as only a few administrators realized, too often after the fact:

> It is important to find out the original owners of the water. One will often be told that the water belongs to some person but close questioning will reveal the fact that the water belongs to some clan that does not just then happen to be occupying it. The need for finding out ownership is all the more important where the Masai themselves subscribe to have a work done and it is most inadvisable to allow a tribe or a clan to pay for work on water that does not belong to them. Waters known as Engare enkishu can be used by the first comer and can be improved without danger but all other waters have an owner or owners. Care should be taken not to allow an individual to pay for a water improvement: if he does it must be on the strict understanding that he has absolutely no right to more than sufficient water for his own cattle, other Masai may use the surplus. In the case of a clan water, that clan should have precedence, but again the surplus should be available to any who want it.[116]

"To illustrate the above dangers," the author described a recent case that came before the local elders:

> A Masai of the Ol Molelian clan made a small dam and trough on a water that belonged to the Ol Mokasen clan. A member of the latter came along and claimed the rights of his clan. The Ol Molelian objected in view of the improvements he had put in. He received no sympathy and was forced to leave the water.[117]

In the case of another borehole: "As an *ad hoc* measure the rights of allocation were here handed to a local water board of leading elders, who immediately allocated the water to themselves: perhaps as good a solution as any!" (Page-Jones 1948: 57). The Water Loan, as well as the previous interventions on behalf of water conservation, thus played into local politics by providing fodder for disputes and the assertion or strengthening of claims.[118]

The incessant demands by Maasai men for water projects overwhelmed administrators' abilities to respond; by 1929, Murrells, the Masai District Officer, complained that

> I have found myself in many cases badgered by the Masai, individually and collectively, and asked what I propose to do to their particular waters, and when. . . . The Masai appear in many cases to have adopted the attitude that as they are paying extra tax in order to support the Water Loan scheme, that they should all benefit as soon as possible, and if necessary each individual should have his claim attended to first.[119]

The reasonableness of such attitudes, although annoying to Murrells, was understood by the document's reader: a handwritten margin note on the document exclaimed: "The Masai are not alone in this!" To persuade "Government" about Maasai support for the project, Murrells shared the following anecdote:

> Masai support for such an innovation is assured, and I have but to quote the case of one individual elder, who, when his water was first commenced upon at Lolbene, was almost an antagonist of the scheme, and remained so for some considerable time, who, only a few weeks ago came to me and asked me to build him another reservoir for storage of excess water from his springs during the rains. I told him that, after I had seen the site where he wanted the reservoir, that such a work would probably cost him 75 head of cattle to pay for, and he was [word missing] man alone. He was satisfied that he would get value for his money apparently, because without hesitation, he told me that I could commence at once on the work, and I therefore engaged another European supervisor for the work, obtained some labour and the work is now in hand. I mention this instance as being illustrative of the Masai attitude towards the works, and to enable me to assure Government that any proposals that I make on behalf of the Masai Loan will surely be endorsed by the people.[120]

Murrells's anecdote is also illustrative of the haphazard nature of the project's implementation, despite Mitchell's bureaucratic vision: projects were initiated here and there through Maasai requests, rather than through any plan coordinating the timing, budget, and resources of projects. Thus, the elder mentioned above could request and receive an expansion of his original project before a project was ever commenced in another area.

In the end, however, despite a few successful projects, the Water Loan was an embarrassing failure that strained rather than enhanced the relationship between Maasai elders and colonial administrators. For each project financed by the loan, the Maasai involved were given an estimate of their repayment obligation in terms of numbers of head of cattle rather than in cash values. Unfortunately, the timing of the loan occurred just as the Depression created a dramatic drop in cattle prices: when the loan began in 1928, average-size slaughter stock were valued at roughly 100/= a head, but the price dropped to 50/= a head in 1929.[121] In 1935, when the last efforts to collect the loan balance were made, the average price was less than 20/= a head: "Thus a work originally estimated to cost 200 head of cattle (£1000) later required 400 head, and later still, for the balance unpaid, five head for every one originally asked for" (Page-Jones 1944: 1). Furthermore, severe miscalculations and poor judgments were made by Mitchell, the district officers, and others involved. Overhead expenses were far greater than originally budgeted, as much of the loan was disbursed to hire extra "native labour" and three additional European supervisors; stock up on tools, equipment, and supplies; and pay for transport. Since, according to the terms of the loan, costs for each project would not be reimbursed by its beneficiaries until the project was completed, Murrells faced a severe cash flow problem just one year into the project.

Second, the government failed in its promise to ensure the "technical soundness" of the projects: "Technical advice was seldom obtained, much enthusiasm and hard work resulting thus in some successes . . . but also very serious and costly failures" (Page-Jones 1944: 1). Most springs that were excavated and "harnessed" so that water could be piped to reservoirs and catchments were discovered to be too "weak" and "insufficient" to provide adequate water (e.g., Lendekenya and Lolbene in 1929). Numerous Petter engines were installed to pump water from wells into storage tanks, but Maasai disliked the recurrent costs of pumping, so these projects fell quickly into disuse, and Maasai refused to repay the total project costs.[122] Of the six projects financed by the Masai Water Loan in 1928–1929, only one (Landenai/Losogonoi), a very expensive gravity-piping project from a harnessed spring, was judged successful by Page-Jones, "a first class-supply." Even so, Maasai repaid only £500 of its £1,700 cost (Page-Jones 1944). After 1930, no more water projects were implemented under the auspices of the Water Loan.

The Water Loan backfired in terms of increasing the Maasai acceptance of colonial presence:

> We have learnt to our cost that the efforts of the enthusiatic [sic] amateur have not only placed our water accounts in a state of financial embarrassment, but by not having shown the Masai any material advancement in the producing and conserving of waters, have caused the people of the tribe to doubt the fidelity of their Administrators. This state will not easily be overcome.[123]

The expensive project failures heightened Maasai distrust, and as they resisted paying, "the Administrative Officer on tour found that his chief function had involuntarily become that of debt collector with damaging results to all current administrative activities" (Page-Jones 1944: 1). While some administrators such as Baxter blamed Maasai for circumventing the terms of the loan repayments by such devious means as searching the country for the smallest cattle they could find, even he had to admit that "the Masai, if they had produced the correct number of beasts average in size, would still only [have] paid half their debt, owing to the fall in prices."[124] Baxter estimated that if the Maasai ever repaid the loan, "they will have to contribute more than three times as many cattle as they were told; and they will never understand the reason why."[125] In 1935 the Masai Native Treasury took over the whole of the remaining debt and agreed to pay £413 a year to the government until the loan was repaid in 1950 (Page-Jones 1944: 1).[126] All Maasai taxpayers now subsidized the government's errors, not just the supposed beneficiaries of particular projects. Direct demands on certain individuals were now replaced with indirect siphoning of funds.

Livestock Development

In addition to water conservation, livestock programs were another key intervention in Maasailand designed to promote "the material well-being" and "social progress" of Maasai in the pre–World War II period. The colonial fixation on livestock-keeping as determinative of Maasai identity empowered the Veterinary Department to take a strong role in policy decisions affecting Maasai, since all such decisions were (in colonial minds) directly or indirectly related to the livestock-keeping function of Maasai. The essentialist reduction of Maasai identity to the terms (male) nomadic pastoralist defined the "problems"—movement and livestock—and thus the "solutions"—control and livestock care. Veterinary policies during this period were closely articulated with land tenure policies: they shared a common goal of consolidating and isolating Maasai and their herds in a distinct bounded area and restricting their movement and interactions outside of that area.[127] The veterinary objectives of disease control and prevention provided administrators with a powerful rationale for constraining Maasai movement.[128] But veterinary officers, like administrative officers, were less concerned with "helping" Maasai than with protecting the land, livestock, and livelihoods of European settlers, and, to some extent, other Africans, from the "dangers" of Maasai interference and entanglements: "The risk of spreading rinderpest or other cattle disease by parties of nomads who are moving about large herds of stock without permission or control requires to be borne in mind."[129]

Although colonial administrators and veterinary staff at times shared common goals and objectives, the ambiguity over whether the focus of their interventions was the Maasai as pastoralist or the Maasai as citizen produced constant wrangling between them over who had more authority and experience to decide the shape and content of interventions in Maasailand. Such disputes are well illustrated by a heated exchange in 1927 between Mitchell, acting provincial commissioner in the Northern Province, and F. J. McCall, chief veterinary officer for the Territory, over who had the requisite experience of Maasai and technical knowledge of livestock matters to determine the structure and policy of the veterinary department.[130] McCall was infuriated by a letter from Mitchell to central administration criticizing the "unsatis-factory . . . division of responsibility" within veterinary administration. For McCall, "the overshadowing paramount factor in Masai life is the livestock," yet "the whole trend of the Acting Provincial Commissioner's report seems to me to show that he either fails to realise this truth or knowingly belittles it." Since "the care of cattle" is "an essential of present existence," "it is evident that primary consideration (I say primary meaning first in the full sense of the word) underlying any change in Masai organisation should be accorded the Veterinary aspect of the problem and who is better qualified than the responsible department." McCall accused Mitchell of lacking experience with Maasai and the necessary "technical" expertise, both of which McCall, of course, claimed to possess.[131] Furthermore, veterinary policies and practices in Maasailand had, in McCall's estimation, been very successful:

> To come to the point tersely, Veterinary administration in Masailand in the past is above criticism, its success is an outstanding tribute to those who evolved it and I feel sure that no person who realised the contrast between present prosperity and immunity from disease and past chaos and threatened starvation would venture to do so in such a manner: those who fail to apprehend such a truth are of themselves ruled out of court.[132]

Despite his attempt to subsume all Maasai affairs as veterinary affairs, McCall conveniently asserted the independence of veterinary concerns from administrative or other concerns:

> It will be observed that I avoid in any way criticising Native Affairs Administration, law, taxation, sociology or ethnology. We are facing a stock problem and my remarks are purely confined to stock matters. Every man to his own trade, the engineer and geologist to water problems, the stockman to stock problems,

> the Administrative Officer to administration. If an operation has to be performed
> in the hospital the Surgeon is responsible, so should it be in all walks of life.

His comments reflected an increasing separation in colonial administration between technocrats (such as veterinary workers or water engineers) and bureaucrats, a cleavage that would only deepen and strengthen as technical departments were institutionalized and expanded. But veterinary matters, for the Maasai, were preeminent: "As in South Africa so in Tanganyika Territory[,] particularly in Masailand[,] the development of Veterinary Science in its widest interpretation is the life and death of the country."[133]

Initially, the Veterinary Department tried to control livestock movement and disease outbreak through two principal programs. The first was a permit system, whereby any significant movement of livestock within the Reserve and all movement outside of the Reserve required permits issued by veterinary officials. The second was the institution of quarantines, whereby all infected livestock were moved to designated quarantine areas, inoculated, and kept in the area until the disease had abated. Both programs were directed at Maasai men, the assumed "owners" of livestock. Men were expected to apply for permits, and men were directed to herd and keep livestock in quarantines. Some additional veterinary interventions, such as the use of Burdizzo Bloodless Castrators and certain veterinary vaccines and medicines, were adopted by some Maasai, but others, such as the proposed branding rules, were adamantly refused.[134]

But the power of the veterinary department in debating and setting policies in Maasailand did not translate into significant interventions or practices, as a lack of personnel and resources restricted the Veterinary Department's ability to implement its objectives.[135] Their efforts were hampered by the vastness of Maasailand, the lack of roads (and vehicles, initially), and the mobility of Maasai and their herds even within the expanded Reserve. Maasai were at an advantage in such terrain—they had no need for roads and were accustomed to long journeys by foot with little food or water during the day. What was difficult and "inaccessible" to district officers and veterinary personnel was familiar, accessible terrain for Maasai. Thus a "very severe epizootic" of rinderpest in 1923 in Maasailand "overwhelmed the resources of the department and had to be allowed to run its course," with estimated cattle deaths of at least 20,000.[136]

The few European veterinary staff had minimal interaction with Maasai. Instead, it was the "veterinary guards" of the African Native Veterinary Service who served as the link with Maasai:

Their duties consist of maintaining a constant patrol of Masailand examining stock for disease, looking out for illicit stock movement, assisting in water conservation, collecting information about tsetse, and forwarding useful information of any nature for the Administration of their own department.[137]

The veterinary guards were widely (and rightly) perceived by Maasai as spies in the service of the colonial administration, gathering information on the location, numbers, and movement of Maasai herds so necessary to the implementation and enforcement of veterinary control measures.[138] At a 1931 meeting with the governor, Maasai elders formally requested "the absolute withdrawal of all Veterinary Quarantine Guards and [illegible] regulations, in fact wanted cessation of veterinary control and interference in their d[omestic?] affairs."[139] Murrells told Maasai later that they themselves were responsible for the continuing necessity for quarantines: "So long as they concealed disease of cattle, or wilfully spread it, then so long would quarantines be necessary."[140]

As far as complaints about the "licentious and extortionate practices of Veterinary Quarantine Guards on duty," it was up to Maasai to report their grievances so that the specific cases could be dealt with by the Native Courts.[141] But complaints about the guards continued: "The attitude of the Guards is stated to be overbearing, insolent and provocative. They demand sheep, girls and service as a right."[142] Complaints about veterinary permit and quarantine policies also continued, despite repeated government claims "that quarantine and Veterinary regulations were enforced for their own good":[143]

Concerning policy, they suggested that with the exception of Rinderpest they were quite capable of controlling their own disease and that these numerous quarantines were causing far more hardship than the risk warranted and asked for re-consideration of policy within Masailand. The control of movement of sheep and goats within the District, and for no apparent reason, was particularly annoying and they saw no cause for this interference with the free movement of small stock. They appreciated the necessity for stock control where quarantine was imperative but protest most strongly against the unnecessary restriction of movement between clean Bomas and clean areas and so on. Why, they ask, should we have to get a permit to move from Monduli to Lolkissale from Kibaya to Naberera from Longido to Gelai and so on?[144]

Maasai communicated their displeasure by avoiding inoculations, circumventing quarantine restrictions, and disregarding the legal restrictions on their movements. Their reluctance to accept interference by veterinary staff with their livestock was perceived as an attitude problem that would soon change once they recognized the "benefits" of veterinary advice.[145]

Despite the department's lack of resources and personnel and Maasai resistance, veterinary polices nevertheless succeeded in disrupting Masai herding practices and social relations. Although Maasai men were adept at avoiding veterinary officers, livestock found outside the reserve without permits were often seized and their owners fined. More drastically, several quarantines were instituted, whereby the owners of infected cattle were forced to move their homesteads to a designated area. Some quarantines lasted years, including a forced quarantine of 42,000 cattle in 1919–1920 during an outbreak of bovine pleuropneumonia (BPP) which was expanded in 1922 to accommodate 80,013 cattle; it still held 61,192 cattle in 1926.[146] Similar quarantines were also created in 1923 in southern Maasailand and in June 1924 on the Sanya Plains because of BPP outbreaks. Despite the extent of the outbreak, quarantine control rather than inoculation was the preferred method of treatment. BPP inoculations in the Masai Reserve from 1922–1925 were minimal and sporadic.[147] Since livestock was a key currency of Maasai social relationships, the system of permits, controls, and quarantines disturbed Maasai transhumance patterns and routines and threatened to disrupt even the most intimate domains of Maasai life.

By 1926, veterinary objectives had expanded beyond disease control and containment to include an interest in "improving" Maasai animal husbandry practices by educating Maasai *men:*

> What we should try to do (and, indeed, are trying to do even now) is to make the Masai a better stock farmer (*he* is by no means bad one now) and add to the knowledge that he has acquired himself that knowledge which the advance of science has brought to European stock farmers. What we need to do is to teach the Masai to (a) dispose of their surplus male stock in cattle and in sheep; (b) castrate poor quality bulls and import some suitable grade bulls; (c) place on the Market the by products of their stock such as hides, ghee and to place a well produced product at that; (d) understand that the young adult males must work . . . and not to expect even if they pay exceptional wages, the natives of other tribes to do their essential services.[148]

Whereas earlier administrators had perceived the large Maasai herds positively as a sign of "wealth" and successful animal husbandry practices, some administrators now inverted that reading, depicting the herds negatively as a "problem of overstocking" and a product of the uneconomic, irrational, and ignorant attitudes and practices of Maasai:

> At present the Masai is a miser of cattle. He allows his herds to increase indefinitely and will only sell sufficient slaughter stock to pay his tax and satisfy his very moderate requirements in cloth and wire. He has no idea of breeding stock for the market and very little idea of selection in breeding at all.[149]

They hoped that the institution of formal markets would encourage Maasai to sell their cattle; "progress" in changing Maasai attitudes was carefully measured through tallies of livestock sales.[150]

The initiative to change Maasai attitudes was prompted by several forces, including the perceived failure of the veterinary department in successfully achieving its objectives[151] and the increasing urgency with which colonial officials now concerned themselves with the "problems" of soil erosion and water conservation (cf. Beinart 1984; Anderson 1984). Rather than admit that the inadequate water and grazing resources of Masai District were due to inequities in land distribution, administrators shifted the blame to Maasai: the problem was not scarce resources but the wasteful surplus livestock populations kept by Maasai. As before, the solution was not the politically sensitive one of restructuring land rights but a politically "neutral" project of changing "attitudes" and thereby practices. Indirectly enticing Maasai to sell their livestock was more politically palatable than more direct methods such as compulsory destocking. Furthermore, increasing financial difficulties in the Territory were shifting the perception that livestock was the source of Maasai wealth to recognition that their stock was potentially an asset to be extricated and exploited in the interests of the colony and metropole as a source of meat for feeding urban populations, a source of export (hides), and a source of revenue (market fees, resale) for the Territory (Veterinary Department [VD] AR 1926).

Frustrated with their inability to increase the sources of permanent water available in the district, some administrators began to blame certain "uneconomic" Maasai animal husbandry practices rather than administrative policies and practices for the "poor" state of the land. The district officer for Masai District, for example, lectured the 1930 Masai Olkiama about "various aspects" of the "question of overstocking" "in relation to soil erosion, loss of stock by starvation, destruction of fodders and grasses, influence of forest destruction upon climatic humidity and permanent water supplies, and economic loss of valuable foodstuffs to the population of the Territory as a whole."[152] He encouraged them to sell their "surplus" stock and deposit the proceeds in bank accounts or face the possibility of forced culling "in order to save the country and land."[153]

Overstocking was not a problem peculiar to Maasai but a general problem attributed to all pastoralist groups. The 1932 East African Governors Conference (comprised of the governors of Uganda, Kenya, and Tanganyika) devoted special sessions and memos to the question of "Administration of Pastoral Tribes with special reference to the problem of overstocking." Although Governor Symes of Tanganyika claimed that there was no problem of overstocking among Maasai, Governor Byrne of Kenya depicted overstocking as a problem produced by the inherently uneconomic practices and attitudes of all pastoralists: their concerns with the quantity rather than the quality of their livestock; the religious and social uses of cattle, especially bridewealth; and, most important, their uneconomic communal use of land, now known as the "tragedy of the commons" (cf. Hardin 1968).[154] The governors agreed that "the 'sentimental' objection by natives to dispose of surplus animals would disappear if opportunities for sale could be afforded," and therefore proposed several "economic measures" to solve the problem: encouraging the establishment of markets and meat factories and increased consumption of meat by natives.[155]

With increasing vigor through the 1930s, both veterinary and administrative officers exhorted Maasai to sell more cattle. Not only would increased sales reduce the "overstocking" problem, but they would increase the money in circulation in Masai District, furnish Maasai with monetary "savings" to survive the dry season and unexpected droughts, and provide needed meat for urban populations and the meat-processing industry. Such pleadings became a relentless chorus at any gathering of Maasai, and often Maasai elders promised to change their "uneconomic habits," if only to silence the badgering and move on to another topic.[156]

The emphasis on making Maasai men better stock farmers was as powerful as the silence about Maasai women, who controlled most of the byproducts administrators wished to "place on the market." Administrators had long recognized the lucrative possibilities of developing local milk and hide industries.[157] Demand for milk in towns such as Arusha far exceeded local supply, and processed milk products such as butter, ghee, and cheese were in demand nationally and internationally. But the production and distribution of milk was controlled by Maasai women, not Maasai men, so administrators never followed through on their ideas. Although it is unclear whether they wanted to "protect" Maasai women from cultural change or deter them from gaining access to a profitable source of income, administrators certainly saw money and "the market" as male domains.

The early veterinary and livestock "development" projects of the 1920s and 1930s thus established an important and enduring precedent: Maasai men, not women, were the targets of these interventions because they were assumed to control not only cattle and smallstock but also the resources such as water and pasture on which they subsisted. Administrators and experts ignored women's roles in pastoral production, as well as their overlapping rights in most livestock and livestock products, and directed all of the training and access to veterinary medicines toward Maasai men. Men were now able to assert themselves as both the "owners" of cattle because of colonial economic policies and as the "experts" on cattle. Women, in turn, were discouraged from exploiting the potentially valuable commodities over which they had control and through which they could have maintained their economic autonomy.

"The Elders . . . Are Crying": Reasserting Colonial Control

By 1935, colonial interest in "developing" Maasailand as an explicit means for increasing administrative control was reinvigorated, at least rhetorically. Hallier, the new provincial commissioner, pressed for the "formation of a general policy for the control and development of Masailand. I certainly feel that Masailand has been left to stagnate long enough."[158] The conjuncture of two events sparked Hallier's renewed interest. First, widespread rinderpest outbreaks combined with drought in 1934 through early 1935 to cause considerable livestock deaths in Masai District: between 1933 and 1935, the estimated cattle population declined from 548,557 to 244,056, while the smallstock population decreased from 500,000 to 97,886 (Tanganyika *Blue Books* [BB], 1933–1935).[159] Second, this devastation of Maasai herds occurred just as colonial administrators were devising strategies to stabilize their shaky financial status through increased extractions from "native" populations in the form of taxes, marketing fees, and other changes. Since Maasai livestock had become increasingly perceived as an asset of the Territory, administrators were shocked by their devastation and determined to protect such national "treasures" in the future.

Preoccupied by their financial concerns, administrators badly misread early signs of the impending disaster. When the rinderpest outbreaks began in early 1934, officials were primarily concerned that the subsequent quarantines and prohibitions on cattle markets and auctions implemented throughout Masai District would prevent Maasai from selling enough cattle to pay their taxes. They were resigned to collecting no more than half of Maasai taxes for the year, despite the "urgent necessity for efficient tax collection in view of the Financial state of the Territory."[160] Livestock sales, however, increased dramatically, despite the abysmally low prices—at an auction in the Kisongo area in July 1934, for example, 1,200 cattle were produced for sale, of which 1,111 were sold; "a normal auction is 200–400."[161] The district veterinary officer proclaimed that the combination of lower prices and increased livestock disposal was a "good thing in many ways—in that it relieves the overstocking problem."[162]

No one recognized the dramatic upswing in sales as a distress signal: lacking grazing land, water, and therefore milk, Maasai were starving, but enforcement of district boundaries prevented many of them from seeking subsistence or exchanging cattle and smallstock for grains and food in areas untouched by the lingering drought. The boundaries designed to contain Maasai intensified their disaster. A poignant letter to the acting district officer for Masai District from the Masai Council of elders clearly attributed Maasai inability to cope with the drought to the government's policies of quarantines and boundaries:

> Greetings. And after greetings, let me explain the following letter. The elders of Longido, Ngarenaibor, Ngare Nanyuki and every place are crying. I ask you as the government to help us with this big problem of drought throughout the country.
> All of the cattle have died from hunger, and soon almost all of the people will follow their path. And we can do nothing because of the government's quarantine. We are dying, but in Arusha-Meru and Moshi areas the white people's fields are full of grass. We Maasai could make arrangements with the white farmers until we recover. Just like God brought his/her compassion. Therefore we ask you men, our shepherds, who have been entrusted by the government to look after us, to make a plan to help us with our problem. Because if you can't help us in any way, then fine, just as we explained at the beginning of this letter, you will bring death to the Maasai by hunger. . . .
> P.S. In Meru and Chaggaland we can buy food with our goats, if the government will help us. If it can't, then fine, let us die.[163]

Scrawled at the top of the letter in pen: "Everything possible is being done by DO Monduli + vo [veterinary officer]. No action."

By late 1934, administrators began to see the devastating effects of the drought, noting in early 1935 that "considerable numbers of stock died in Masailand from lack of water and grazing" (NP AR 1935: 55). The immediate response of administrators was to define the problem as a "technical" one of insufficient water supplies (despite years of water "conservation" efforts and the Masai Water Loan) while, as usual, ignoring the underlying structural inequalities in access to land which had produced the problem. But the only funds available for the maintenance of completed works and for new works was an annual £1,000 "Water Works Contribution" from the Native Treasury.[164] The urgent need for water precipitated a spate of reviews by the Water Board to assess and correct infringements of Maasai water rights by non-Maasai and alien settlers.[165] Hallier, the provincial commissioner of Northern Province, stated the current colonial beliefs about Maasai development most succinctly: "The finding of permanent waters is the basis of any future development."[166]

Their longer-term solution was to try to consolidate and expand their control and "development" interventions to address these enduring "major difficulties." As part of their planning discussions, a frank debate ensued among administrators about the question of supporting Maasai agricultural initiatives: "Is it advisable to encourage Masai towards agriculture or to be pastoralists pure and simply?"[167] The decision was clear and seemed to be undisputed: "It was decided that in considering the district and characteristics of the tribe, all efforts should be made towards furthering of pastoralism. Under no circumstances should cultivation be allowed on permanent waters and [sic] in such cases where families could not maintain a livelihood, without cultivation, owing to insufficient property in cattle."[168] Not surprisingly, Hornby, the director of veterinary services, emphatically agreed: "I do most certainly believe that the best interests of the people and the land will be served by encouraging the majority to remain pure pastoralists."[169]

As a result of these meetings, Hallier proposed a master plan for Maasai development outlined in a chart entitled "Masai District: Improvement in Administration & Economic Development." The chart is fascinating for several reasons. Not only did it reveal how colonial interests in development and administrative control were explicitly intertwined, but it was one of the earliest descriptions of development as specifically *economic* development. The document marked a key shift in colonial development ideology during this period from predominantly ecological concerns (i.e., water conservation) to economic concerns (increased or higher quality production, i.e., "economic/rational" attitudes and practices) (cf. Anderson n.d.; Cooper 1997). But the chart is most interesting because it proposed one of the most comprehensive concepts of development proffered so far; that is, an integrated vision of development as encompassing not only economic concerns but social concerns as well. The list of components included:

1. Closer and better Administrative Control—Means Masai Leaders can be better trained and encouraged to act and take a greater interest in administration of the Tribe

2. Closer and better Veterinary Control—General improvement of stock e.g. breeding from selection. Better beef and mutton production. Ghee production. Improvement in hide production.

3. Schools. Simple education to include Animal Husbandry and Agriculture &c.

4. Trading Settlements—Brings simple wants—clothing, shoes, blankets &c., &c.,

5. Mission Stations—Medical—Hygiene—Care of Children—Protection of young girls—Healthier people.[170]

Of course, this was still a paradigm of "development" within ethnic boundaries, encouraging "improvement" but still keeping things "simple."

Despite Hallier's enthusiastic plans, the continuing colonial financial crisis and fears about the possible return of Tanganyika to Germany resulted in only limited efforts by administrators to develop Maasailand in the late 1930s, although the structures for administrative control and extraction were strengthened. Tax collection was improved with the collaboration of stock inspectors, trade centers were opened and controls of itinerant trading legislated and enforced, and movement of Maasai and their livestock was controlled. Colonial interventions to date had focused on containing and maintaining both "Masailand" and "the Masai." While infrastructure, medical services, education, and other forms of development had been promoted in other areas, Masai District had, as some administrators admitted, received little attention in comparison with these other areas: "The record of progress made during the last 19 or 20 years is almost *nil,* if one faces facts honestly."[171] The situation was "not due to laxity or disinterestedness, for officers in Masailand have, in the past, worked as hard as anywhere in Tanganyika and have, at times, endured perhaps more arduous conditions than anywhere in the Territory."[172] Instead, it was an issue of administrative control: Maguire blamed administrators for having failed to adequately identify the proper "Masai Native Authority." Laibon Mbeiya's sudden death in November 1938 conveniently provided administrators and Maasai elders the opportunity they needed to restructure the "Native Administration" so as to shift power from the Laibon as "Chief" to a Masai Council comprised of elders.[173]

Maasai were becoming increasingly disgruntled with the colonial government's involvement in their affairs: "To them the only forms that Government action appears to take consists of forms to which they, quite understandably strongly object: activities such as tax-collection, the suppression of raiding, and veterinary interference with the free movement of their cattle."[174] Part of the blame, according to Rowe, could be attributed to their disbelief that the government's assistance was "disinterested," and part to the dismal failure of

most government interventions. Whatever the reasons, most Maasai now regarded "the government" as a "hostile element," a "conception" which produced "a total lack of cooperation with—almost passive resistance to—any
Government activity," and a "wall of apathy" so "impermeable" "that it has to
be encountered to be appreciated."[175]

*　　*　　*

The increasing domination of economic interests of the metropole in its
colonies such as Tanganyika had several significant effects in terms of administrative policies, development interventions, and Maasai ethnic and gender
relations. First, the shift from more "ecological" concerns to "economic" ones
in terms of land use and livestock production was accompanied by a shift in
perceptions of Maasai from "rugged pastoralists" to "uneconomic loafers" and
perceptions of their large cattle herds from sources of "wealth" to examples
of "overstocking." Moreover, the emphasis on developing Maasai as pastoralists, and only as pastoralists, combined with their consolidation in the Reserve and the curtailment of their movements and interaction with neighbors,
reinforced the linkage between ethnic identity and economic livelihood and
heightened distinctions between Maasai and other groups.

Furthermore, in their new roles as taxpayers, property owners, buyers, and
sellers, Maasai men took advantage of colonial policies designed to encourage
monetization and commoditization of livestock to consolidate their exclusive
control of livestock and reinforce their own sense that being Maasai meant
being a pastoralist. Gender-specific taxation forced men to seek a source of
cash, and monetization and commoditization made them aware of a lucrative
commodity in their own midst—livestock. Furthermore, as the barter trade
was replaced by commodity purchase, men usurped women's roles as traders:
instead of women bartering livestock products, men began selling livestock to
meet their growing cash needs. Capitalist values, which required the alienabil-
ity of a product, privileged individual male control of cattle, collapsing the
multiple overlapping rights of men and women to use livestock into an idea of
male "ownership" of property. Veterinary services and livestock "development"
projects, directed at only men, facilitated men's appropriation of women's
rights by providing new means for men to legitimate their control of livestock.
The marginalization of women from these "economic" categories, as well as
from the "political" roles of the native authority, converged to disenfranchise
them from their rights over livestock and access to political power.

The monetization and commodization of the Maasai economy had significant consequences for Maasai gender relations. As Maasai men slowly integrated themselves, however peripherally, into the cash economy, they used their position to consolidate their exclusive rights over the disposition of cattle, gradually disenfranchising women from their formerly shared rights of control over these animals. Livestock, especially cattle, became a form of male currency, which men could buy and sell to pay their taxes, hire non-Maasai labor, and occasionally to purchase cloth and other goods from traders.[176] Women generally could access cash only indirectly, through gifts from men or the sale of cattle through their sons or husbands. Precluded from direct involvement in the cash economy, Maasai women continued to barter where possible with the female currency of milk and hides (J. Fosbrooke 1944: 314), but the female-dominated barter trade was eventually displaced from its central position in the pastoral economy by male-dominated cash transactions.

These new forms of property relations introduced new meanings of property that had consequences for gender relations. Taxation classified women as property to be paid for by men, with all the attendant associations of ownership, possession, and control. In order to ensure their access to cash to pay taxes, men asserted their disposal rights over cattle to the detriment of women. In time, the meaning of livestock changed from a store of wealth, source of food, and symbol of prestige to a commodity to be bought and sold like sugar or kerosene.

Furthermore, incorporation into the colonial state extended the formal political power of men in general, and elder men in particular. Women's access to and participation in political decision-making processes was curtailed, and they were relegated to the domestic concerns of home and homestead. As a result, the spatial and conceptual differences between the formerly interconnected spheres of "domestic" and "political/public" were exacerbated, so that they were reconfigured as gendered hierarchies.

Through these processes, the autonomy and interdependence enjoyed by men and women in the late 1800s were replaced by unequal relationships of economic dependence and political control in which men could begin to think about women as property and possessions.

MAASAI PORTRAIT 2: WANGA

The hoe is the same as cattle. . . .
They both have value.

I drove my old Land Rover slowly across the broad, bumpy plain of the caldera around which most of the Maasai homesteads in Emairete, as a result of forced settlement during Ujamaa, are situated. I was distressed by my task that day, carrying the corpse of Wanga's son from the morgue in Monduli to Wanga's homestead. The boy had been the victim of a tragic accident in which he fell off one of the occasional overloaded pickup trucks that carry passengers, animals, and baggage up the steep, precarious mountain road to Emairete. The truck driver, a novice, had misjudged the capacity of the truck's gears, and the pickup had slid backward and overturned, harming several passengers and killing Wanga's son. The men in my car, sons and relatives of Wanga, were silent, brooding and mourning quietly as they had done all morning, first at the police station then at the morgue.

Silence greeted our arrival. A large hole had been dug in the bushes a few yards from Wanga's homestead, and about fifty *ilmurran* and junior elders were gathered at the site. As the men discussed the next step in the procedure, an *olmurrani* came over and told me that Wanga wanted to see me. He was seated in the grass outside his favorite wife's house with four other male elders. He stood up to greet me and gushed his thanks for having helped him. I was embarrassed and kept telling him how sorry I was for what had happened, but he kept thanking me. We sat down together, and he told me that he had known something bad was going to happen. The night before his stomach didn't feel right and even his "spirit" (*roho*) was shaking. Then he heard the news and became very sad. He had seen the boy earlier in the day when he had passed by to tell his father that he was going to Monduli town to buy bean seeds for his farm. Wanga told me that the boy used the profits from the farm to support himself in school, purchasing his uniform, books, and supplies. "But it was God's plan, only God knew. We all die someday, but God is there."

Wanga (his real name) himself died a few years after this incident, while I was in the States. "He asked and asked for you," Morani told me on my next visit. "He pleaded with me to inform you immediately that he was dying so that you would come see him one last time." As Koko was my "grandmother," Wanga had become my "grandfather." He was a widely respected territorial leader, or *laigwenan*, who had worked as a clerk/messenger for the British and as a district councilor for the Tanzanian government; he lived with his five wives and twenty-four children in Emairete. We met during the first days of my fieldwork in 1991, when I visited his homestead to pay my respects. Following Maasai protocols for the proper greetings between a young woman and a much older man or woman, I approached him quietly, head bowed for the touch of his hand. "*Yieyo, takwenya!* (Respected woman, hello!)" "*Iko*," I replied. He grinned at the idea that a white woman had treated him with such respect, and we soon became fast friends. I often turned to him for advice about issues or problems I encountered in my work, and he plied me with questions about life in the United States: "How many cows did your parents receive in bridewealth for you?" "Why do Americans, who live in such luxury with electricity, running water, and good houses, choose to come to Tanzania and sleep in cloth huts [tents] in the bush (*pori*)?" "If the United States is so wealthy, why do some people live on the streets?" "What clans do you have in the States?"

Wanga belonged to the Ilterito age-set, men who were *ilmurran* between 1926 and 1948 (Mol 1996: 15). He was born in Emairete, as was his mother, and his father came from nearby Enguiki. He claimed that he was six years old during the outbreak of World War I and remembered seeing German and then British soldiers pass through on horseback. Men of the Iltareto age-set (warriors from 1911–1929) were forcibly conscripted into the war as fighters and porters: "They were forced to go, it was a very difficult thing." Most returned, and their children and grandchildren live in Emairete today. Wanga recalled other incidents from the colonial period, including his own work as a courier for the government:

W: But I remember when Maasai first saw the whites. We were frightened by their clothes, their coats and pants. I was forced by a Maasai headman to work for the government as a courier when they were building the town of Monduli. I worked for a white man named Bwana Morris who was head of all of the country. I was his guard, and wore a black cloth and a red sign. My job was to search for people to pay their taxes, catch those who broke the law, and to take letters everywhere.

D: And how did you feel doing this work, this difficult work of forcing people to pay taxes?

W: It wasn't difficult work, although we didn't know this at first. In retrospect, we have learned that it was a big help to pay taxes, as this tax paid for the road, water and cattle, and brought medicines, cattle dips and everything. The tax was very small, only something like six shillings a head for each adult man.

D: How did they get the money?

W: They sold their cattle at the market in Monduli.

D: And how much did they receive for their animals?

W: Ahh!! Acha mama!! Those days you would receive two or three hundred shillings for a cow! Really, that British money did some work. A blanket like this one [pointing to the thick blanket draped around his shoulders] only cost ten shillings! Children's clothes cost only a shilling or two, everything was cheap. The hospital didn't sell its medicine, and even cattle medicine was free.

D: Did people see a problem in selling their cattle?

W: They just sold them. There was no problem.

At the time, Maasai had plenty of livestock; they relied on their cattle for milk and their smallstock for meat. "Maasai did not know flour well back then." Wanga worked as a government courier for seven years, when he finally quit. As one of sixteen "pure Maasai" couriers, he earned 15 shillings a month. "Mama, if you heard my salary you would laugh, it was like a joke, really."

Wanga, who was one of the first residents in Emairete, described how more and more people, both Maasai and Arusha, moved into the area. At first there were about twenty to thirty homesteads scattered in the area, all Maasai. Arusha came in 1942, a few at a time:

MP2.1 Wanga seated with author in his homestead, 1992. Note the thatched houses in background. Photo by author.

They farmed small plots then, not like now when they destroy the land. Maasai also began farming a bit, mainly maize as we didn't eat beans then. Men and women worked together to farm. They sold a little then, not like the commerce of today. They would take the food to the weekly market at Matapes (known today as Kampi ya Maziwa). Maasai would take milk and Arusha would take maize.

When Wanga returned from his job as a courier, his father had moved to Mfereji in search of salt licks for the cattle. According to Wanga, many households moved back and forth, spending the dry season on the mountaintop of Emairete and the wet season on the Mfereji plains in the Rift Valley. The British established a camp of four African veterinary guards, Meru and Arusha, at a nearby spring to guard the cattle and monitor their illnesses. Wanga remembers them as being very helpful, especially in dispensing livestock medicines.

But not all his memories of the colonial period are pleasant:

The colonists did not educate Maasai children. It was only when the American missionaries came that our children got a school. It was built in 1964; I built the office myself. But really, we Maasai were very stupid. When the missionaries first approached us, we disliked them. We thought they would take our children and lose them in the bush. Most of the missionaries returned to Kilimanjaro and Arusha to educate those people. After a while, we realized that we had lost a big opportunity. Finally, mama, a *mzungu* (white person) came and built a school here. . . . Hillman.

At first, Father Hillman, an American Spiritan priest (Hodgson 2000a), had to pressure Maasai parents to send their children to school, but "by 1970 Maasai had agreed for their children to be educated." Then, one day, the Tanzanian government nationalized the schools, and "the quality of education was destroyed. It was crazy—children would reach standard seven and not even know 'A'! Really mama, I would stand in front of a public meeting today and say that two, even seven hundred thousand children in Maasai areas are all stupid [because of the poor schools]." At first only boys were educated, "but these days it is clear that it is worthwhile to educate girls."

Wanga was later elected as a *diwani,* or district councilor, from 1962 until 1983. He supported expanding the infrastructure and increasing the availability of social services in Maasai areas. He believed that the postcolonial government has helped Maasai: "It brought water to places that didn't have it, schools, hospitals, everything." He accepted that most Maasai were now farming, rather than just herding. "The truth is that the hoe is the same as cattle. We didn't know this, but they both have value." Maasai began to farm, he argued, "because they realized that their wealth, especially their cattle were diminishing, because of hunger, and they saw and learned from other ethnic groups who were farming." Moreover, he supported the presence of the Catholic church, having been one of a few men baptized in 1972:

We Maasai have been petitioners of Eng'ai for a long time, since we left Kerrio. But we have lacked one thing, which is a church in which to gather together. When the cattle enter and a Maasai woman milks them, she gives some [milk] to Eng'ai before even giving any to her children. She knows that the milk was a gift from Eng'ai. She cannot give milk to her husband or children before this. And she calls Eng'ai by name when she does this.

He described how elder men prayed and even *ilmurran* worshipped Eng'ai at *orpul,* their meat-eating feasts in the bush. "Baptism has helped us increase

our wisdom by teaching us to gather together in one place to worship Eng'ai."
In fact, according to his understanding of the stories he had heard about Jesus,
Jesus and Maa (the first human in his version of the Maasai origin myth
[Chapter 1]) were very similar people: "God sent both of them to help build
the world."

One of Wanga's favorite stories, which he repeated to me many times,
was his account of his involvement in the burial of Edward Sokoine, a Maasai
who had become prime minister then was killed in a suspicious car accident
(Maasai Portrait 4). Sokoine's family lived near Emairete, and the body was
returned to them for interment. "When Sokoine died, my name was communicated around the world. They said that mzee Wanga slaughtered a bull,
brought the special grass, decided that the body should be buried on its right
side, and Sokoine's male children would rub him with fat. Mama, the day
Sokoine died, my homestead was full of army vehicles. . . . They had come to
ask me the history of Sokoine, when he was born, when he went to school,
etc." Wanga prided himself on being the spokesperson for Maasai history:
"The work of telling Maasai history is my work; everyone comes to me. . . .
Even *wazungu* [white people] come to ask me questions. You'll see, one day
you will find my homestead filled with cars. I will go sit on my stool in the
shade of the cattle pen and talk to visitors from America, from other places.
Even members of the National Service have come here, bringing me sacks of
sugar, salt, fat, and even cloth. Many things! The women were shocked!" He
told me about a scrapbook on Maasai history and events that he had kept over
many years, but someone had borrowed it and never returned it.

And he was a historian, telling me stories of events in his life and the
community and describing Maasai social practices and institutions such as
polygyny, engagement, bridewealth, brideservice, clan exogamy, marriage ceremonies, and divorce. What I found most interesting was the centrality of
women's decisions and actions to most of these institutions: an *olmurrani*'s
mother brought her prospective daughter-in-law the first bridewealth gift, a
bracelet; the wife or wives of an already married man were the ones who
"marry" additional wives, according to whether the new wife was to be part of
the right or left side of the homestead[1] (wives often select the new wife then
advise their husband to review their choice); women controlled their household livestock herds, deciding how to distribute milk among their family and
visitors and allocate animals among their children (men's remaining herds,
inkishu e boo, served as a "security bank" against hunger and other drastic problems); unhappy women could decide to leave their husbands permanently (*kirtala*), but had to leave their children behind; and the "seeds" of both the patri-

line and matriline were considered when selecting spouses for one's children ("I don't know about *wazungu* ethnic groups, but we black people have many ethnic groups, some of which don't care how or with whom their daughters give birth!"). He worried about the increasing prevalence of elopement among young men and women, because "bridewealth gave a woman power in her marriage. Her family and clan could just take her away, saying 'where are the bridewealth cattle for this marriage?'" On the other hand, he accused Maasai in Simanjiro and Kiteto of "selling their daughters as if they were at a market! It is a very bad practice and I don't like it. I won't take any of their cattle. What if I accepted fifty cattle for my daughter and they persecute her? How could I pay those animals back? I would have strangled my child like a goat and I want no part of it." Good relationships—between husbands and wives, parents and children—were built on respect (*enkanyit*) and love (*enyorrata*).

In general, Wanga was pleased with his life: "My life has been good. When I first began to work, I had nothing, no children, because I was a young man. Now that I am an elder I am happy. I have children, wives, wealth; I live comfortably. Eng'ai blessed me with children, I have enough wealth, and no problems with my body." But he lamented the lack of respect he saw in young people: "These modern children forget that they need to respect their parents. Every person just goes like the wind. Respect has been lost, faith has been lost." He said of the latest group of *ilmurran* (Landiss in 1992), "Once they were circumcised, their respect went to the bush. They don't know cattle, they don't care about farming; they only care about their stomachs in their mothers' kitchens. It is money they care about, radios." He went on to describe, in detail, how people of different categories should ideally show respect for one another, a standard set of ideal protocols echoed by every Maasai I talked to (involving greetings and spatial positioning, as described in Chapter 1).

When he passed away in 1995, Wanga was buried in the manner of great respect that he had described to me in one of our conversations. "When I die, I will be buried in the center of the cattle pen, my grave will be right there. I am known and respected everywhere, even the government of Tanzania knows me well! I have a black stick that I was given by all Maasai, a calf, a *debe* (container) of honey, and cloth like this one. They come to be blessed in the cattle pen by me. I was the leader not only of my age group, but of all the age groups, of Maasai everywhere."

WHY ARE YOU IN SUCH A HURRY? DEVELOPMENT AND DECOLONIZATION

3

In a world of food shortages, the pastoralist who sells only such stock as will meet his current cash requirements inevitably takes second place behind the agriculturalist; he loses land and he neither likes this nor does he understand the necessity.

(*Masai District [MaD] AR 1951: 2*)

In 1951, British colonial administrators in Tanganyika initiated the Masai Development Plan (MDP), a five-year plan whose seemingly innocuous objectives were to build more water supplies, clear tsetse-infested bush, and experiment with grazing controls and fodder production in a small pilot scheme. But the project was the product of broader British modernization agendas to reassert the legitimacy of empire and rebuild the post-war economy at home and abroad. These agendas reflected a shift in the racialized ethnic premises undergirding the colonial project. Whereas early colonial rule and development had depended on the creation, maintenance, and exploitation of ethnic distinctions to institute indirect rule, ethnic differences were now perceived as barriers to modernization. Ethnic groups such as Maasai, who had been the target of protectionist sentiments in prior years, were now the focus of heightened attempts by the state to coerce them to adopt modern economic ways. Ironically, however, ethnic differences were both disavowed and reinforced by the plan, for although it was designed to overcome cultural barriers by economic means, it was framed, as its title suggests, by ethnic assumptions about what problems "the Maasai" (as opposed to other ethnic groups) faced in terms of their development.[1]

Despite its claims to merely address technical problems, the MDP was therefore deeply intertwined with colonial imperatives to order, control, and compel the progress of their most unruly subjects. At issue were the land, labor, livestock, and livelihoods of Maasai people, as well as contested visions of poverty, prosperity, and progress. As such, the project served to facilitate, justify, and consolidate the expansion of state control into numerous realms of Maasai life, and its implementation became the site of deep contestation between administrators and Maasai. Designed in part to build confidence among Maasai in government and development, the project backfired, failing to meet its own objectives and, more ominously for administrators, fueling anti-colonial mobilization.

The Masai Development Plan: An Overview

Spurred by his familiarity with development initiatives among Maasai in Kenya, the provincial commissioner of the Northern Province of Tanganyika Territory instituted a series of meetings in 1948 between provincial officers, district officers, and representatives from the Veterinary, Water, Medical, Forestry, and Game Departments to present and discuss proposals for a development plan for "Masai & Masailand."[2] According to administrators, the "present situation" of Maasai was full of "most serious difficulties" involving large human and livestock populations subsisting on inadequate land. The 1948 census figures showed 47,000 Maasai, 650,000 head of cattle, and 500,000 smallstock scattered over 23,000 square miles, "of which possibly 70% was useless in the dry season through lack of water or the presence of fly."[3] Previously, the discrepancy between the size of Maasai herds and the available grazing and water had been attributed to problems of overstocking, but now it was blamed on the poor state of Maasai land; specifically, low rainfall areas, the scarcity of permanent water supplies, the spread of tsetse, and the huge numbers of game. Such problems could no longer be solved on a piecemeal basis; instead, "planned development [was] necessary."[4]

The goals were twofold: "the opening up of new areas for occupation at reasonable economic cost" and "the development of the stock-carrying capacity of land under existing utilisation";[5] in short, the "development of Maasailand as ranching country."[6] More precisely,

What Government wants to see is a prosperous Masai tribe breeding good cattle
under better conditions and assisting in the general economy of the Territory by
selling the prime stocks. No tribe has escaped having a money economy, no tribe
stands still; and Government looks forward to the day when the Masai will obtain a name for fine cattle breeding.[7]

After all, "The Masai are fairly good stockmen and the nature of the people
and of their country is such that their future development lies in improved
stock keeping and not in agriculture."[8]

The MDP had three major components: to build more permanent water
supplies, to clear tsetse-infested bush, and to experiment with grazing controls and fodder production. Despite the acknowledged failures of the last
comprehensive water development program in Masai District in 1928, administrators now believed they had the necessary technical expertise, in the
form of a newly created Water Development Department, to build four dams,
one piped supply, and three equipped boreholes during each year of the project. In terms of tsetse clearing, project plans called for clearing most of the
bush breeding grounds for tsetse by machinery, since "local labor" was "insufficient in numbers and quality."[9]

Finally, administrators designated 200 square miles as the Kisongo Pilot
Scheme (KPS), by which they intended to increase the number of permanent
and temporary water supplies, eliminate the breeding habitat for tsetse, and
institute measures to control grazing and conserve fodder by making hay and
ensilage.[10] They hoped that the pilot project would serve as a model to "an-
chor" other groups of Maasai to designated, bounded areas similar to the communal ranches being tested in Kenya: "The Kisongo Pilot Scheme is intended
to be the 'shop window' of the Masai Development Plan and the ability to
extend improved methods of animal husbandry to other parts of the District
is largely dependent upon the success of this scheme."[11] With the aid of "expert" advice and "modern" technologies, Maasai men would become modern
ranchers, adopting labor- and capital-intensive methods of range management and animal husbandry that were spatially bounded.[12]

The MDP represented a significant departure from previous development
efforts, which were judged failures because they were piecemeal, were designed by administrators rather than development experts, and were inade-
quately supervised. These deficiencies were addressed in the complicated bureaucracy of the KPS, which had two tiers of supervisory committees between
the provincial commissioner and the KPS's field officer and a management
committee comprised of representatives of the Veterinary, Agriculture, Water,
and Tsetse Reclamation Departments.[13]

The participation of Maasai, even elder men, in the design and implementation of the MDP was limited. Administrators consulted the Masai Council for approval of already formulated plans and expected little more than "a reasonable measure of cooperation" from Maasai—"they are intelligent critics and must become intelligent cooperators."[14] Confident of the superiority of their scientific knowledge of animal husbandry, range management, and water development, the Masai District team required European expertise and European supervision of every project component.[15] Maasai were, however, expected to make a substantial financial contribution to the MDP, despite their lack of participation in and control over its terms. Of the final project cost of £265,000 for five years, £200,000 was granted by the colonial government from the Agricultural Development Reserve, and the Masai Council was bullied to agree to contribute the remaining £65,000 under threat of losing their lands or having their livestock culled.[16] To soften their demands, administrators claimed that part of the additional money raised by Maasai "will be earmarked for services etc. requested by the Masai themselves."[17] To meet their commitment, the Council opted to levy a local tax of 30 shillings per taxpayer (with 25 shillings contributed to the MDP), to be paid in addition to the 20 shillings government tax already in existence—"the highest taxation paid by any Africans in Tanganyika Territory."[18]

There were other conditions as well. First, Maasai were required to meet "voluntary" annual quotas for cattle sales. Disappointed with the small number of legal cattle sales in Masai District, which tallied 13,779 in 1951, administrators set annual quotas at 20,000 for 1952, 27,000 for 1953, and 34,000 for 1954 and onward.[19] Second, Maasai had to move from certain areas, which the government had decided to alienate to European settlers and non-Maasai cultivators. Finally, they had to allow groups of agricultural Arusha to move into designated expansion areas in their District.[20]

Maasai fulfilled the conditions, albeit reluctantly. They met and even exceeded the annual sale quotas, moved from the Sanya corridor and other lands, accepted Arusha into their District, and paid the £65,000 by the agreed deadline of December 31, 1955.[21] Although Maasai kept their promises and a substantial sum of money was spent, however, little was actually achieved. The MDP was overly ambitious, expensive, poorly planned, and badly implemented, despite the input of technical experts. Year after year, district and provincial annual reports complained that much time and money had been spent on planning, surveying, and purchasing materials but that little work as such had been done. Delays in recruiting staff and receiving and then repairing promised equipment slowed progress in the construction of dams and boreholes during the first three years.[22] The project had high capital and administrative costs, which included hiring permanent European staff, non-Maasai clerks, and laborers; constructing permanent housing and offices; and purchasing a fleet of lorries, vehicles, tractors, and other heavy machinery (much of which was delivered late and was barely used).[23]

By April 1955, less than half the estimated acreage of tsetse-infested bush had been cleared, mostly within the Kisongo Pilot Scheme. The tsetse survey upon which clearing plans and estimates had been based was inaccurate; it vastly underestimated the extent of the tsetse-infested bush and thus the amount of work necessary to clear and isolate fly-free areas.[24] Clearing by machine proved to be prohibitively expensive, and administrators had to search for laborers.[25] A campaign to enlist *ilmurran* failed and non-Maasai laborers were scarce. In terms of water development, the district commissioner listed the following "successful" (quotes in original) water supplies—6 dams, 11 pipelines, 17 boreholes, and 6 haffirs—but acknowledged that the success of these projects was debatable, since many of them lacked necessary equipment or had quickly washed out or silted over.[26] And the KPS, despite large inputs of money and ambitious planning, achieved little in terms of grazing controls or the provision of fodder crops. Maasai searched outside the project boundaries for grazing and water. They refused to feed their cattle baled hay for fear of disease. Little tsetse bush was removed, and the dams soon silted (MaD AR 1952: 4; NP AR 1952: 88; NP AR 1953: 78). Like most colonial projects of the period, the MDP was "top-heavy, involving large outputs of planning and expert personnel, [and] funneling material through a clogged infrastructure" (Cooper 1997: 76).

Nor had anyone planned how the projects would be continued after December 1955. Who would maintain the fleet of vehicles and machines purchased by the project? Who would ensure that the dams did not wash out or the haffirs silt up? Who would prevent the regeneration of bush from cleared areas? Recurrent expenditures for the maintenance of boreholes, dams, and haffirs alone was estimated at £3,000–£4,000 a year.[27] Early documents described the MDP as a "gradually maturing process, tried out for method and cost in the Pilot Scheme, and slowly gaining impetus as the machinery follows the surveys" and noted that "the planning should not attempt to see more than two to three years ahead and should be fluid so as to be adapted to any change in circumstances."[28] Meanwhile, administrators voiced a "confident" hope that the MDP's achievements would "persuade the Masai to finance the continuation of the Development Plan themselves"[29] and "the regeneration of cleared bush country."[30] As the project deadline neared with few visible results, however, administrators grew frantic. The district commissioner admonished the water engineers to finish their projects so as to "secure the complete confidence of the Masai in the scheme."[31] Although administrators tried to cast the project in a positive light, they were embarrassed and frustrated by the project's failure in its own terms. As the district commissioner remarked, "I have always felt that Masailand has not had it's [*sic*] money worth in water development works from the considerable expenditure incurred by the Water Development and Irrigation Department."[32] Negative publicity in the press did not help matters: "Development is Slow in Masailand" read the headlines of one pointed article.[33]

On their part, Maasai were not just disappointed but angry by the end of the project. They welcomed some components, especially the provision of additional water supplies, but complained about delays in drilling and equipping boreholes and the uneven coverage of water development plans.[34] They were also eager to remove tsetse-infested bush from their grazing lands, as long as they were not forced to clear it by hand themselves. They were therefore dismayed by how little their large financial contributions accomplished, given the grand visions of colonial administrators. More significant, however, they resented *how* the project had been implemented, especially in relation to other ongoing colonial interventions; Maasai felt that the colonial government had far exceeded its authority to meddle in their affairs by ignoring their concerns and protestations, betraying its promises, and treating their leaders with disrespect. As a result, the MDP instilled a resentment of government, generating at least one small but growing anti-government faction of influential elders and educated men active in nationalist mobilizing.

To understand the project's failures and its broader consequences, we must examine its objectives in relation to the historical background of changing metropolitan concerns; intensified struggles between colonial administrators and Maasai over land, labor, and livelihoods; and the prior experiences of development of each group. Fortunately, in addition to the rich archival documentation of project plans and implementation, we have access to Maasai perspectives and protestations at the time in the form of the transcripts and correspondence (including Maasai petitions) of the Masai Council, or Olkiama. The Olkiama consisted of senior male representatives (*ilaigwenak*, sing. *olaigwenan*) from each area of Masai District who gathered at least once a year to meet with the provincial and district officers to consider colonial policies, discuss local affairs, make orders and guidelines of their own, and register complaints or requests.[35]

"Development or Death": Origins of the Masai Development Plan

This meeting of the Olkiama is not a regular meeting. You have probably never convened during April before. But this meeting has been called on purpose so that you can discuss one big problem—the development or death of the entire Masai tribe.[36]

Such stark terms—development or death—evoke both the zealousness of colonial ideologies of modernization during this period and the grim alternatives they presented to Maasai. Most broadly, the MDP was a product of two at times conflicting objectives on the part of the British metropole. The first objective was to finance development and welfare programs in the colonies to defuse criticism, reestablish the legitimacy of empire, and justify its perpetuation during a time when imperialism was under attack at home and abroad.[37] The second objective was to rebuild Britain's economy in the post-war era. Despite the rhetorical concerns for social development implicit in the first objective, the demands of the metropolitan economy dominated, and the conjuncture of these two objectives led to the intensification of economic development throughout Tanganyika and other colonies as Britain tried to expand its supplies of raw materials and its markets for manufactured goods.[38] Keynesian economics was in its heyday: development was about higher production, shifting from a "traditional" to a "modern" economy, and promoting "progressive" individuals. Within this dual-economy framework, the obstacles to development were clear: the suffocating, irrational demands of "community" in terms of communal resources and the social obligations of individuals. A new discourse of poverty framed the "problems": Africans in general were "poor" and their "low standard of living had to be raised" by the proposed economic development programs of the metropole.

Based on these metropolitan objectives, administrators throughout Tanganyika Territory saw their mandate as "the urgent economic need to develop the country" (NP AR 1948: 61). Although still colonial subjects lacking the rights and authority of citizens, Maasai and other Africans were now expected to overcome the rigid political and territorial systems based on ethnicity produced by the British and restructure their production systems in the interest of broader civic duties. As pastoralists, the national duty of Maasai was to increase the supply and quality of cattle on the market, through compulsory cattle culling if necessary: "The Masai and indeed all African cattle owners must be taught to regard their stock as an economic asset in a time of world shortage of meat and animal" (NP AR 1947: 78; MaD AR 1951: 8). In an early memo, the director of veterinary services proposed: "The Masai cattle population, with proper water and development, could reach into the neighborhood of a million head in a few good years, . . . [which] should suffice in time to supply . . . approximately a hundred thousand annually."[39] Such fantastical calculations ignited the enthusiasm of administrators eager to demonstrate the economic potential of Masai District.

A key objective of the MDP was therefore to coerce Maasai to increase their taxes to pay for development and sell more cattle to acquire the extra cash:

> It was clear that more cattle must be got out and ways and means were being considered. Again the provision of consumer goods was of paramount important [*sic*]. If the development plan was really successful in the provision of new waters and elimination of tsetse fly, there was little doubt that the Masai would pay still more for these services to continue, *one more way of taking their surplus money usefully from them.*[40]

To encourage livestock sales, administrators instituted provisions in addition to those included in the MDP, such as building new cattle markets, formalizing and increasing the number of stock trade routes, and promoting the establishment of trading centers.[41]

Despite efforts since the 1930s to monetize their economy, colonial administrators still believed that Maasai had little engagement with the cash economy. Yet Maasai men in the 1950s sold cattle when they needed money for taxes or to purchase food and other sundries. Stimulated by their own needs for food rather than fluctuations in market prices, they sold more livestock in bad years when prices were low (since the market was flooded and the cattle were in poor condition). Conversely, a good year for grazing and water meant a large supply of milk and therefore a reduced demand to sell cattle to obtain cash. While this "uneconomic" behavior confused some administrators, others understood its dynamics.[42] Furthermore, Maasai had a keen awareness of differences in price. When they decided to sell, they knew where to get the best price for their animals. In 1946, for example, Maasai strongly opposed a system of "closed sales" whereby they could only sell cattle to the Kenya Livestock Control.[43] They resisted in several ways: selling as many cattle as possible outside the formal markets to Arusha and Chagga friends, livestock traders, and butchers at prices much in excess of the controlled price or bringing large numbers of cattle in such miserable condition that they were rejected. The result was that Maasai "officially" sold only 17,748 head, despite a target of 25,000 (NP AR 1946: 44–45). Administrators were well aware of the extent of illegal cattle sales, but they had difficulty curtailing it (NP AR 1948: 69).[44]

Second, neither culture nor tradition would be allowed to slow down the drive for economic development: "The Native Authorities and Africans have been exhorted on occasions throughout the year to eschew such indigenous laws and customs as are likely to put a brake on political and social development and to adopt others" (NP AR 1948: 60). Pastoralists in general and Maasai in particular became icons of the traditionalism and communalism that colonial officials were now so eager to combat in the name of "progress": "Pastoral tribes are very retentive of their ways. . . . While his cultivator neighbor is being increasingly drawn to economic needs and influenced by urban and industrial development, the pastoral tribesman has tended to remain an anachronism outside modern society, which thus suffers a human loss, for his virtues of pride and simplicity command affection and respect" (East Africa Royal Commission [EARC] 1955: 282).

Because of romanticized stereotypes of them as the "warrior tribe," "noble savages" caught in the web of their own cultural conservatism, pride, and arrogance, Maasai posed a unique challenge to colonial agendas. The MDP was part of a "concerted attack on the minds of the Masai" to convince them of the merits of colonial ideas of progress and prosperity. For colonial officials, prosperity would be the result of increased production for exchange value, not use value, and would be expressed through increased consumption of commodities. Colonial officials readily acknowledged that Maasai were quite wealthy, but they resented how Maasai failed to use their wealth to improve their "standard of living" or that of the nation: "They are rich and well able to afford to pay for the development of their own land but, like most pastoral peoples, they are stultifyingly conservative and slow to accept new ideas."[45] One aim of the MDP was to remove such "cultural" obstacles to economic development through "the encouragement of money-consciousness amongst the Masai and the provision of articles to attract their immense potential spending power."[46] Throughout the project period there were repeated calls by the district commissioner and provincial commissioner to intensify "the attacks" with "closer administration and contact," education, propaganda, and visual aids.[47]

Since the early 1920s, however, Maasai had eagerly promoted certain development projects, financed individually or by Native Treasury funds, including water projects, medical services, schools, and certain veterinary services and medicines. In 1949, the Native Treasury spent over £10,000 on development-related expenditures, including almost £4,000 for water development, over £2,000 to expand the medical program, and more than £1,000 to build five new primary schools. Similar expenditures of over £6,000 were proposed for 1950.[48] Even the district commissioner noted in 1949 the "extraordinary difference" between what the government and Maasai contributed to medical services in the District.[49] Maasai welcomed the proposition for bus services in their District, they accepted the expansion of the primary school system, and both men and women eagerly sought treatment for venereal disease.[50] If anything, Maasai were impatient with the pace of projects they desired, had paid for, and now depended on the colonial government to implement. As one Maasai elder complained, "We see that water projects are going very slowly. That is to say that as soon as work has started, before it has finished, the work is moved to another place. Our water problem will never go away if the work isn't finished any place. Let the water project in one place be finished before moving the work to another site."[51]

Furthermore, British administrators conveniently overlooked their own culpability in reinforcing the very stereotypes they were now intent on dismantling. As a result of the forced relocation of Maa-speaking herders into the Masai Reserve to control their movements and to protect them from outside influences, Maasai were both spatially isolated from other ethnic groups with whom they had a long history of interspersed residence, intermarriage, trade, and friendship and intentionally excluded by colonial administrators from other processes of economic and cultural change for fear of disturbing their "traditional" culture. Ironically, despite colonial claims to modernize Maasai and others by elevating national identity above ethnicity, the MDP was accompanied by some calls for renewed efforts at "repatriating" Maasai who had moved outside the Reserve (now District) boundaries.[52]

Finally, an explicit and overarching objective of the MDP was the need for "closer administration" of Maasai:

> The problem is entirely one of control of the Masai: lack of control in the past
> has permitted exodus into other Districts and promoted the present problem.
> No rehabilitation schemes should be undertaken in Masailand until a system of
> administration is evolved whereby discipline among the Masai is ensured. . . .
> Control such as is necessary means staff, communications, houses, machinery;
> but first and foremost it means drive and no "Masaiitis."[53]

Provincial Commissioner Revington insisted that Maasai be "made to obey
orders—administrative and veterinary—which postulates more staff" and
"forced to make a fair contribution to the economy of the Territory by providing slaughter animals."[54] "The Masai have, in my view, two outstanding
needs—water and discipline; the first is being provided as rapidly as possible
with available means and the second cannot be instilled without adequate administrative and veterinary staff working in close co-operation as discipline
can only be achieved by insistence on sound animal husbandry practice."[55]
Revington wanted to reopen two Masai District substations; hire a new district officer, veterinary and support staff, and police officers for each post; and
build new lockups.[56] In addition, the original proposal for the MDP requested
the hiring of Europeans as development officers, mechanical superintendents,
engineers, and foremen.[57] The provincial commissioner also pleaded with central government that the members of the Masai Development Team continue
as staff for at least five years to ensure the successful and consistent implementation of the project and overcome Maasai distrust. As he wrote to the district
commissioner: "I think the Masai are suspicious and non-cooperative as they
are not aware of our intentions toward them; this suspicion will not be overcome until they get to know individual officers and our aims."[58] They also
requested detailed aerial and environmental surveys of the land, a population
and livestock census, and close studies of the Maasai political system.[59] Although the substations were not reopened, additional staff (including more
police) were hired, and travel and communications were eased by a substantial
expenditure on repairing, upgrading, and building new roads and the construction of a radio relay at Loliondo and two telephone lines to Monduli
(NP AR 1950: 102).[60] In effect, Maasai subsidized increased administrative
surveillance and coverage through their financial contributions to the MDP,
which paid for the salaries of personnel, construction of offices and homes,
transport, and the expansion of infrastructure. Moreover, this closer administration was not just about increasing discipline and coverage but also about
imposing a spatial, social, and symbolic order on Maasai to regulate their land,
labor, and livelihoods.

"Why Are You in Such a Hurry?": Confrontations and Contestations

Land

A central issue of the MDP, and an escalating source of tension between Maasai and administrators and among administrators themselves, was land. Based on their prior experience with colonial development and land tenure practice, Maasai rightly feared either the permanent loss or destruction of their lands. Under pressure to prove their patriotism, Maasai had granted the government permission to farm wheat on several large blocks of land in Ardai and Olmolog during World War II, as well as temporary leases to European settlers for wartime cultivation. Although suspicious about the "temporariness" of the leases,[61] Maasai perceived these loans and the 27,308 cattle they "donated" to the war effort to be part of their obligations as friends of the government.[62] But the consequences of their generosity were disastrous. The Ardai Wheat Scheme destroyed over 20,000 acres of prime grazing land, and the government disregarded its duty not only to return but also to rehabilitate the land.[63] Instead, regrassing of these lands was quietly put into the budget of the MDP, compelling Maasai to partially subsidize the government's obligation. The memory of the "dismal failure" of the wheat scheme haunted both Maasai and administrators.[64]

In addition, the central government reneged on its promise to return the temporarily alienated land after the war. Over the vehement protests of Maasai, the land was leased to settlers: "It is considered that the lands are of more value to the territory agriculturally than they are to the Masai as pasture," explained Page-Jones, the senior provincial commissioner.[65] "It is fine if the Government wants to farm," responded Laigwenan Kotokai, "but we will be very angry if the Government sells the land to a European!"[66] At Olkiama after Olkiama, the government requested permission to alienate Maasai land. Maasai elders consistently denied permission, but the government alienated the land anyway, making a mockery of the consultation process.

The rapid rate of land alienation in this period further heightened Maasai suspicions about the government's intentions. Maasai worried that once additional land was cleared and furnished with permanent water, it would be alienated to white settlers or African cultivators. In 1946, the Colonial Office declared that the government retained ultimate control of the land and sanctioned limited alienation to European settlers in the interest of the "economic development of the Territory."[67] In his 1946 investigation of land disputes in the Northern Province, Justice Mark Wilson found that Maasai had land "plenty and to spare," and recommended ceding much of the most fertile Maasai land to more "productive" European settlers and African farmers as well as repatriating Maasai people and livestock living outside of the District. On the basis of his recommendations, it was resolved to move some 20,000 head of Maasai stock from the Sanya Corridor back into Masai District, to absorb the Tanganyika Maasai who were in the Lake Jipe area, to attract Maasai away from the Serengeti National Park, and to seek in Masai District an outlet for Arusha from the "agricultural slum" of Arusha District.[68]

Three of the most controversial sites of land alienation involved areas of long-term contestation between administrators and Maasai. One, the Sanya Corridor, involved the eviction of both Meru and Maasai, "many of whom, although termed trespassers, have in fact lived in the Corridor for the past thirty years or more" (NP AR 1950: 96).[69] The land was divided into ranching units and farms for Europeans. But by the end of 1952, at least two of the units remained unoccupied, straining the already tense relations between Maasai and administrators: "It is difficult for the Masai to understand why their cattle should not use the unwanted grass on unoccupied farms when there is no grazing in their own areas" (MaD AR 1952: 2; NP AR 1952: 105).[70]

The land issue revealed the tensions and differences between the levels of colonial government. While the metropole and central government could issue bold policy directives, it was the personnel working at the provincial and especially the district level who had to implement them. Since district personnel were more familiar with the daily circumstances of "their people," they often sympathized with their concerns and complaints. District-level administrators forced to implement the Wilson findings were placed in an unpleasant position; most disagreed with the recommendations and knew all too well that they would increase hostility and resentment: "The people are worried and would like to know where it ends," wrote District Commissioner Clarke.[71] The district commissioner complained that 1951 was his most difficult year in Masai District "owing to the unpleasant duties imposed on him in connection with the implementation of the recommendations of the Wilson Report" (MaD AR 1951: 2). He was especially troubled by the lack of compensation to the Native Treasury.[72] Similarly, Fraser-Smith, his replacement, protested the proposed alienation of Lolkisale in 1953, fearing "that a period of from ten to twenty years will be required to regain their confidence and co-operation."[73] Such perspectives only led to accusations of "Masaiitis" by their colleagues.

The MDP was therefore designed, in part, as a response to the rapid increase of government-sanctioned alienation of the remaining fertile areas of

Masai District and the resettlement plans recommended by the Wilson Report, which together intensified pressure on the remaining resources. Since the land was admittedly insufficient to sustain populations, its productivity had to be increased and "expansion areas" had to be developed to accommodate the new immigrants. The extremely low rainfall and tsetse fly which made these areas uninhabitable were to be combated by water development and fly-clearing.[74] From the beginning, district and provincial administrators and the governor discussed the MDP among themselves in terms of a "quid pro quo" for the land alienation.[75] They hoped to both appease Maasai for the loss of their lands and regain their confidence and trust in government and development.

Despite its awareness of increasing Maasai hostility on the land issue, the colonial government continued to alienate land in the name of "increased productivity."[76] Most notably, three 100,000-acre blocks of Essimingor were offered as ranching and farming blocks to settlers after plans for a Native Authority ranch fell apart.[77] While the district commissioners criticized the idea in discussions with the provincial government,[78] they also blamed Maasai for the loss, claiming that the "laziness" of the Maasai leaders in not forcing *il-murran* to clear tsetse bush had caused the alienation by demonstrating that Maasai did not care about improving, and therefore retaining, their land. As one district commissioner admonished a meeting of the Olkiama elders; "If you don't wake up and open your eyes, your land will be taken by Europeans!"[79] When Maasai tried to set the terms, by agreeing, for example, to allocate 1,000 acres to a settler with the proviso that the land would revert to Maasai use once he quit occupying it, the government refused to sanction the transfer, claiming the condition was unacceptable (NP AR 1956: 114). Maasai were also concerned over their dwindling rights to water as the increasing numbers of settlers dammed up or siphoned off Maasai water in both Monduli town and rural areas[80] and water works financed by the Masai Native Treasury in areas such as Olmolog were lost as part of land alienation.[81] Additionally, the government began an aggressive campaign in 1948 to survey the remaining forested mountaintops in Masai District, then demarcate them as either government or native authority forest reserves in order to restrict the grazing and watering of livestock and the felling of trees.[82] Finally, the battle over continued Maasai presence and livelihood in the Ngorongoro Crater and Serengeti National Park angered and politicized many Maasai.[83] In the interests of wildlife conservation, Maasai were expelled from the crater in 1954 and then the park in 1958.[84] They found it difficult to understand why large areas of fertile land were being set aside for the use of game, not people:

"Since we have lived in that area," declared Laigwenan Lekisaka, "we have lived among game animals without killing them. In the past these animals didn't live alone in the forest [without humans], but now they have their own land. . . .We are human beings and we are worth more than those animals!"[85]

Although the MDP was designed to appease Maasai for the loss of their land, the threat of further land alienation was repeatedly used as a measure to ensure compliance with project provisions. As the provincial commissioner sternly warned the 1952 Olkiama, "Those living in Districts in Tanganyika in which there is a shortage of land would be only too willing to occupy and open up those areas of Masailand which you do not at present use if they were allowed to do so, and, if you allow those areas to be idle much longer, Government will have no other choice than to give them to other tribes." After badgering them to force *ilmurran* and junior elders to clear tsetse by hand and to meet the cattle sale quotas, he concluded, "Do not forget that if you do not develop [your country] then there are others and many others who will be willing to do so at your expense."[86]

But Maasai elders were tired of such threats, and their response was quick, direct, and angry. The next day they presented the district commissioner with a handwritten letter in garbled Swahili which outlined their concerns:

> 1) We Maasai elders all together refuse to work clearing the bush or digging a road.
> 2) Since you have been here, you Europeans have met us herding our . . . cattle and sheep. And since long ago we have refused to work with our hands. . . .
> 3) And we do not want to hear news that strangers [*wageni*, referring to African laborers] will be clearing our land so that he can live there or he is looking for a quarrel [*ugomvi*, i.e., a land claims dispute].
> 4) Since long ago when we were merely creatures we knew this name of tsetse. I mean, has any Maasai implied to you that this name was somehow a new/foreign thing to us?
> 5) And also, if you see an Mbulu clearing the bush it is because he was shaken by me [i.e. hired]. If I have shaken him, I will awaken him myself, he will not be woken by another person.
> 6) And also, I ask you why are you in such a hurry? Before I have prepared things for the country of Maasai.

The document was signed by ten Maasai elders, with a side note insisting that "And these things are said by all Maasai, so if you ask who it is, it is the entire country of Maasai who are saying them."[87] It needed little decoding, as the demands and complaints were straightforward: Maasai refused to labor; they feared further land alienation as laborers claimed land by clearing the bush; they chafed at the presumption that they were ignorant of range management, including tsetse control; and they resented and distrusted the accelerated pace of government demands and interventions.

Maasai fears about the consequences of the MDP for their land were, unfortunately, justified. At the conclusion of the project, a member of the Northern Province Land Utilization Board recommended that "various parts of Masailand should be thrown open to alienation as the only means of securing their rapid and permanent development."[88] District Commissioner Fraser-Smith protested vehemently, incensed that "Government should break faith with the Masai and thus shatter any prospect of success the Development Plan might have by alienating those very large areas of land for the Development of which the Plan was formed."[89] Although the land was not immediately alienated, parcels on which Maasai had built permanent water supplies and cleared bush were lost here and there through continuing immigration of Arusha and the expansion of settler holdings.

Labor

As the letter from the elders above implies, the MDP also made labor—an issue administrators had generally avoided—a site of struggle between Maasai elders and colonial officials, as well as between the elders and *ilmurran*. Throughout the colonial period, most Maasai men were sheltered by their livestock holdings from having to seek wage labor to pay their taxes or meet other cash requirements. In fact, wealthy Maasai men were renowned for hiring laborers themselves to farm and to clean out and dig wells for them (MaD AR 1952: 1). Despite endless complaints about the lack of labor in Masai District, administrators had previously left the "warrior" system alone, convinced it would inevitably fade away with modernization (e.g., NP AR 1947: 83). From the beginning of the project, however, administrators began an aggressive campaign to reduce the period of warriorhood and admonished Maasai elders to force the "lazy" *ilmurran* to work as laborers, clearing tsetse bush, digging water holes, and leveling roads (NP AR 1948: 61; NP AR 1953: 81).[90] Administrators saw *ilmurran* as a vast, untapped labor force and believed that hard labor would give them something "useful" to do.

Although some elders initially agreed to make *ilmurran* clear tsetse-infested bush, most *ilmurran* resisted, with the exception of *ilmurran* from the Loliondo area.[91] In protest, besides refusing to work, *ilmurran* launched cattle raids on Maasai elders and neighboring groups, including white settlers.[92] In 1953, the district commissioner estimated that over 3,000 cattle had been stolen since the last Olkiama. He angrily chided the elders for not controlling the *ilmurran* and demanded that they discipline them and force them to work:

"I find it completely disgraceful, here I am working as hard as I can to bring good development to the area, but the thanks I get is to work night and day to capture these thieves."[93] "We do not agree and the *ilmurran* do not agree [to clear tsetse bush]," replied Laigwenak Oltimbau. "At first we agreed, but in the end the *ilmurran* refused, saying that if they went to clear they would die, and even we agree with this advice." Furious, the district commissioner reminded them of the ongoing land alienation, naming each place in a litany of painful memories, and threatened to call in the police to force the *ilmurran* to work.[94] But in 1954, a "serious lack of labour" was still reported: "Since the *moran* refuse to undertake clearing work resort has been had to paid labour, the supply of which during the year has been poor" (NP AR 1954: 97). The *ilmurran* won: the tsetse project was a failure.[95] *Ilmurran* also struck at the heart of the development projects themselves, thrusting their spears into the carefully laid water pipes in more than one site.[96] Frustrated, some administrators blamed Maasai attitudes, accusing them of lacking a "spirit of community self help": "However willing the Masai may be to tax themselves in order to employ paid labour for this work, the results can never be the same and their numbers in any case are too few" (NP AR 1955: 94).

Livelihoods

The MDP and related interventions in Maasailand jeopardized Maasai livelihoods in several ways. The semi-nomadic pastoralism practiced by Maasai was premised on their ability to exploit multiple and shifting localities to counter inherently unstable micro-ecological differences in rainfall, disease, and pasture. And contrary to colonial claims, Maasai implemented and enforced strict controls over access to pasture and water based on section, clan, and residence (see, e.g., Homewood and Rodgers 1991). Several colonial officers recognized the merits of this system, especially those who actually studied the system on the ground, such as the veterinary officer for Masai District: "Providing the land has not become overstocked the Masai himself has evolved an economical method of alternate seasonal grazing on which it is difficult to improve."[97] Rather than strengthen the Maasai system, however, administrators undermined it. They alienated crucial dry-season and reserve grazing lands (which included equally important permanent water sources), increasing pressure on the fragile and unpredictable rangelands, which were themselves unsuitable for the intensified "modern" ranching methods envisioned by colonial administrators and veterinary experts. Additionally, tsetse-clearing caused tremendous environmental destruction, since the process entailed clear-felling all trees and bush in a given acre.[98]

Second, the MDP obstructed Maasai efforts to diversify their economic base and strengthen their food security by cultivation. Throughout the project period some Maasai repeatedly asserted and demanded the right to cultivate their own land. To cite but two examples: in 1950, the *laigwenak* from Olmolog complained about a shortage of flour. "Since you know our land at Olmolog was taken by Europeans," Laigwenak Moluo pleaded, "please don't give the remaining areas to Europeans to farm." "Do you want to invite Kikuyu to come in and farm those areas?" replied the district commissioner. "No, we want to farm ourselves," replied Moluo.[99] Similarly, a year later when told that cultivation would be prohibited in the Ngorongoro Conservation Area, Maasai male elders requested that poor Maasai without stock should be allowed to continue to cultivate their irrigated *shambas*, or farms, and that other Maasai should be permitted to hire cultivators within the Ngorongoro Crater. The government refused their requests, reiterating that "no further cultivation" should take place.[100]

Ironically, despite all of the derogatory stereotypes about pastoralists and their presumed "conservatism," the goal of the MDP, as with both earlier and later development interventions, was to reinforce Maasai livelihoods as pastoralists. Administrators from all levels of government, including the governor, were insistent that Maasai be "encouraged" to remain pastoralists.[101] Even though Maasai demand for grain and other non-livestock food products was rapidly increasing and more and more Maasai were farming, administrators never considered directing resources or training to improving their skills as farmers.[102] Administrators noted increased cultivation by Maasai but generally dismissed it as unimportant, except to rant about Maasai as employers of African laborers:

> There is no doubt that the Masai are turning their minds to the production of maize for their own requirements. . . . The alien cultivator, however, is the Kingpin of Masai agriculture and he is not encouraged by the administration. The solution may lie in contract tractor ploughing in suitable areas contiguous with European farms, the tending of the crops being done by the Masai themselves.[103]

Most tellingly, the regional assistant director of agriculture noted: "It is most unfortunate that there is no member of the Agricultural Department who knows anything at all about Masailand. None of us ever visit it, there is no pure agriculture carried out in it and there is nothing generally to take us there."[104] By 1956, some Maasai were not just farming old homestead sites, but "quite large shambas." "One Masai," the provincial commissioner noted with some surprise, "the court interpreter at Monduli, owns a tractor" (NP AR 1956: 99).

As a result, Maasai were left in a double bind: the fact that they were merely pastoralists was used, as in the formation of the original Masai Reserve, to keep them from better lands where "more productive" agriculture was perceived as possible. Conversely, they were discouraged from farming, perpetuating their dependence on pastoralism as a productive strategy. The alienation of much of their remaining fertile land undermined the viability of pastoralism, rapidly increased the pace of their impoverishment, and intensified Maasai resentment and hostility at what they perceived as the government's betrayal.

Gender

That Maasai men as pastoralists and patriarchs were the target of development interventions becomes very clear when we approach the issue from a slightly different angle. As is obvious from the discussion of the MDP, Maasai women were completely absent as project participants or beneficiaries. Their absence was due less to their invisibility and more to intentional exclusion by administrators. For example, increased production of higher quality hides, a very profitable export good in high demand, was an explicit goal of the Territory and of the Northern Province (NP AR 1954: 69). Administrators knew that Maasai women were responsible for the production, processing, and distribution of hides, although they complained that the final product was a "low-grade article." And they recognized that "the possibilities of the industry are great given adequate skilled instructional staff" (NP AR 1954: 69). But, despite hearty promises to demonstrate the "correct preparation of hides" to improve "what should be a most important export from Masailand" as part of the KPS,[105] nothing was done. Instead, provincial resources were directed at improving and expanding the hide industry among Chagga, where men controlled the process and product (NP AR 1955: 91).

Modernization, at least in the Northern Province of Tanganyika, was not about supporting the progress of some gender-neutral "individual." The "individual" who was to be unleashed from the constraints of communal obligations and protectionist policies was gendered male; it was *his* initiative which was being stifled: "Even today examples are found where attempts on the part of the individual to lift himself above his neighbors and to make himself more economically secure are resisted by his community as a whole" (EARC 1955: 14). The report of the East Africa Royal Commission (1955) is in fact a rich guide to the images guiding administrative interventions during this period. Based on the findings of the two-year investigations of a royally appointed committee, the report is rife with the (gendered) dualities of modernization thought: traditional/modern; communal/individual; subsistence sector/ monetary sector; conservatism/progressivism; stasis/change. Within these binarisms, pastoralists in general and Maasai in particular appear as icons of the traditional conservative "primitive" African. While communal land tenure and tribalism are the twin evils suppressing the (male) "African individual" from economic advancement, pastoralists are equally burdened by their conservatism. "Pastoral tribes are very retentive of their ways," the authors state matter-of-factly (EARC 1955: 282). The old evolutionary duality of conservative pastoralist/progressive cultivator is resurrected: "While his cultivator neighbor is being increasingly drawn to economic needs and influenced by urban and industrial development, the pastoral tribesman has tended to remain an anachronism outside modern society, which thus suffers a human loss, for his virtues of pride and simplicity command affection and respect" (EARC 1955: 283).

Development, Disillusionment, and Decolonization

Ironically, although the MDP was explicitly designed to gain the confidence of Maasai in government and development, it drastically undermined their confidence in both. Maasai frustration over their double bind and their anxieties over government betrayal and increased land alienation were exacerbated by what many perceived to be a shocking lack of respect in their treatment by the government. Elders in the Masai Council complained about their increasingly violent handling by government representatives. In 1949, for instance, elders listed incidents where some of them had been hit by guards, European settlers, and even the district commissioner himself. "We ask our Government to lead us fairly and to respect us as you do other tribes, and as we respect you. If a leader makes a mistake, he must be taken to the district commissioner or DO who will sentence him and fine him, or fine him and dismiss him from his job."[106]

As a consequence, some Maasai elders increasingly supported anti-colonial political groups such as the Kilimanjaro Union, a proto-nationalist movement among Chagga in the Moshi area. In 1949, it opened its membership to "the tribes of the whole country of Tanganyika" and established contact with other groups upset over government land use and soil rehabilitation programs, including Maasai in the Ngorongoro area.[107] In 1951, the district commissioner warned Maasai in Ngorongoro that he had heard that headmen had given support and authorized cash collections for the Kilimanjaro Union: "I wish to make it quite clear to you that the Kilimanjaro Union is not a Government body and has no support from Government." He forbade all salaried headmen from attending any further meetings with the Kilimanjaro Union and warned the elders about contributing money to the union: "Herein lies the danger; if these purposes [for which you have contributed money] are ones of which you cannot inform the Government then you are all treading a dangerous path. I appeal to Laigwenak Oltimbau to use his great influence with the Masai, and to remember his duty to Government, and to put an end to this nonsense."[108]

At the time, Oltimbau was an influential leader of the Masai Council who had been awarded a King's Medal just a few years earlier for his dedicated service in persuading other Maasai to agree to the Gift Stock Scheme during the war (NP AR 1944: 56). His sentiments toward the government had changed, however. In 1952, he wrote a letter to the head of the Olkiama requesting permission to meet publicly with leaders from the Kilimanjaro Union "to discuss the news about the development that was being brought to Ngorongoro"

> because I have misgivings about these Europeans who enter other countries and try to demonstrate development for the betterment of the natives and lo! they really have the objective of seizing the land for their own farms. I have heard much advice from those in Arusha, Meru and other areas. I am not doubtful about the government but I would be happy to reconcile my objectives with the tribes I have mentioned.
>
> Another reason I would like to meet with these three tribes—Maasai, Arusha/Meru and Chagga—is to find out if they want to divide themselves so that each person lives in his own land without working together.
>
> I ask the head of the Monduli Olkiama to give me permission to call this meeting so that we can give the Government "clean words" [*maneno safi*] about our being divided from other tribes. This meeting will cleanse the spirits of all people so that we can live together peacefully, rather than building enmity between us and our neighboring tribes.[109]

This letter was remarkable for several reasons. In addition to his prescient insights into the relationship between imperial calls for development and land alienation, Oltimbau challenged the colonial government's explicit prohibitions on associating with the Kilimanjaro Union and their presumed mandate to determine the residence and political allegiances of each "tribe." Although the colonial government prohibited the meeting, the issue did not fade away. In 1953, when forced by colonial administrators to meet with Sonjo and Kikuyu, Laigwenak Lekisaka reiterated Maasai frustrations: "At this Olkiama we have Sonjo and Kikuyu, both of whom we did not know in the beginning, but who we have joined with now. But those people who we really share things with are the Arusha and Meru, yet we are now told that we are not allowed to work with them."[110]

As a result, the Olkiama elders grew more belligerent. In 1954, the Olkiama refused to discuss plans for the immigration of Arusha into Masai District "until the question of the ownership of the land had been resolved between them and the government." The Council then passed a resolution: "The Masai Council notes that from time to time the government has seized our land and given it to other races and tribes." The ensuing discussion was summarized as follows:

> An answer is required now as to whether the land in this district belongs to government or to the Masai. If it belongs [to] the government, then let the government do what it likes without consulting the Masai Council again. But if the land belongs to the Masai then the Waarusha application will be considered by the Council without consulting the government.[111]

This bold challenge to the hypocrisy of colonial land tenure arrangements was hardly undermined by the district commissioner's official reply: "The ownership of all land in Tanganyika was vested in the Crown, but government held it in trust for the use of indiginous [sic] inhabitants, who must be consulted before any land was alienated."[112] Maasai had already seen what little impact such consultations had in decisions about land alienation.

The MDP in Retrospect

Thus the MDP, like most development projects, was never just about development. Although designed to address technical problems, the MDP was deeply intertwined with colonial imperatives to expand administrative control over recalcitrant subjects. Broad notions of progress and development were used to justify increased interventions into Maasai lives against a backdrop of ongoing disputes between administrators and Maasai over land alienation, labor, and appropriate livelihoods. Furthermore, the MDP was framed in terms of assumptions about the specific obstacles to development confronted by "the Maasai," thereby perpetuating and reinforcing the material and symbolic ethnic boundaries which were so central to colonial political, economic, and social control. Yet Maasai men of all ages resisted such assertions of control over both their resources and their future, contributing in no small part to the failure of the MDP. Although they supported certain types of development, such as additional water supplies, elder Maasai men protested vociferously against project components they felt were unfair, such as forced labor of the *ilmurran*. Most important, they resented the disrespectful attitude and domineering methods by which the project was implemented.

The design and implementation of the MDP thus revealed the fractures and contradictions of imperial rule. Development, as both colonial administrators and Maasai realized, was never merely about addressing some technical problems in the land. The failures of the MDP reflected the failures of the mandate in its last concerted effort to assert its legitimacy and justify imperial rule. Although the government had long been aware of anti-government activity, especially by Maasai in the Monduli area,[113] they were taken aback by the vehemence of Maasai resentment and resistance. For Maasai, the MDP provoked and aggravated anxieties and tensions over colonial rule, prompting some elders to join efforts for decolonization. Many elders simply quit the Masai Council in disgust, ceding power to the educated Maasai men who would form the vanguard of the nationalist movement. These educated Maasai, like elite Africans elsewhere in Tanganyika, were able to invoke the MDP's failures as they outlined their own development visions, visions which became the backbone of decolonization.

Waning Interest

The MDP was the last concerted development effort by the colonial administration in Masai District in part because there was a concerted shift of colonial attention and resources to more politically urgent concerns and areas in response to the emergence of a viable nationalist movement, the Tanganyika African National Union (TANU), under the leadership of Julius Nyerere.[114] The British, who had conceded to Tanganyikan demands to "prepare for self-government" but avoided committing to a time frame, supported the gradual adaptation of the structure of councils, chiefs, and native authorities to a system of national government and advocated a system of multiracial rule with equal representation of the three "races" of Europeans, Asians, and Africans (Iliffe 1979: 475, 483, 485–506). In contrast, TANU wanted a more rapid transition to Independence, the recognition that Tanganyika was "primarily an African country," and the election of African majorities to public bodies (Iliffe 1979: 517). TANU soon mobilized extensive local support through its broad territorial structure with representatives in towns throughout Tanganyika (and, in time, villages), the ability of its leaders to convert a range of dispersed local grievances into collective nationalist agendas for change, the labor of such leaders as Bibi Titi Mohammed and Oscar Kambona in campaigning and recruiting members (see Geiger 1997), and their mobilization of international attention and support through meetings with United Nations delegations and travel and speeches in the United States and Europe.

Insistent on establishing its program for multi-racial rule in Tanganyika, as in Kenya and Uganda, Britain concentrated its resources in a campaign against TANU through the formation of a rival political party, the United Tanganyika Party (UTP), in February 1956, which sought support from middle-class Europeans, Africans, and Asians (Iliffe 1979: 521). In addition, Governor Twining courted the support of the chiefs by forming a Chiefs' Convention in 1957. Although he warned them that "the tribal system and the office of the chief" were threatened by those who "base their appeal on the emotional attractions of extreme nationalism, which in effect is nothing more than racialism," most chiefs, recognizing TANU's power, knew that "their future depended on compromising with it" (Iliffe 1979: 535).

From the mid-1950s, the new colonial objective was to build up an African middle class capable of governing the country with an approach sympathetic to British economic and political interests and "standards."[115] To promote this political agenda, Governor Twining revised the development priorities of the Territory regarding agriculture, land, and education. First, after years of discouraging African capitalist farming in the interest of maintaining social order, "agricultural policy shifted to the 'focal point approach': the concentration of advice on progressive farmers whose example might stimulate their more conservative neighbours." Second, he revised land tenure policy to encourage African freehold land tenure. And finally, the government responded to long-term criticisms from many Africans about the lack of post-primary educational opportunities by proposing to triple secondary school places in the five-year plan for 1957–1961 (Iliffe 1979: 552–553).

Within the context of this struggle for control of the nation-state, both the British and TANU perceived Maasai as an economically and politically marginal people and chose to direct their resources and energies to more politically active groups such as Chagga in Moshi and Sukuma. In 1948, for example, the Tanganyika African Association (TAA), TANU's predecessor, had branches throughout the Province, except in Masai District (NP AR 1948: 65).[116] When the Kilimanjaro Union (KU) expanded its membership from just Chagga to other ethnic groups in 1949, however, it did attract some Maasai supporters, as described above. But for various reasons, the KU soon faded from the political landscape, to be replaced by TANU. Although membership in TANU increased rapidly in the Northern Province, it is difficult to know how many Maasai men joined.[117] Of the 5,952 people who registered to vote in the Northern Province in 1957, however, only 82 were from Masai District.[118]

The lack of political interest in Masai District combined with frustration over the failure of the MDP to produce a marked disinterest on the part of most administrators in any further "development" interventions. Except for the usual lectures at Masai Council meetings urging Maasai elder men to increase offtake, avoid overgrazing, educate their sons, and so on, the Council and Maasai were generally left on their own to cope with "development." Meanwhile, the Masai Council still had substantial sums in its Treasury, and it continued to collect high taxes from its constituents. But most Maasai funds for development were used to try to maintain the water projects built as part of the MDP. The admitted problems with the poor standard of the construction work on the boreholes necessitated constant repairs, and inadequate maintenance service provided by the responsible Government department only exacerbated the problems (NP AR 1955: 93).[119]

Eventually, the government convinced the Council to implement a "second phase" of the MDP, which differed from the first in two significant ways: it was financed solely by Maasai local taxes, and it focused on developing selected areas rather than on district-wide projects. The Kisongo Pilot Scheme was abandoned, replaced by another pilot scheme in the Simanjiro area—the establishment of the first communal Maasai ranch:

> The scheme is designed to provide for closer control over stock numbers and grazing and for the adaptation of the nomadic grazing habits of the Masai to those of rotational grazing and intensive use of the land, by dividing the area into wet season, dry season and reserve grazing areas each with its own water supply. If successful the scheme will be extended to other areas. (NP AR 1955: 78)

In other words, administrators hoped to restrict the seasonal movements of a given number of people and their stock to a delimited area. An area of 250 square miles was demarcated, and three boreholes and two dams were constructed (Stahl 1961: 55). The plan was implemented at the end of 1955 but encountered the one constant in the Maasai environment—the unexpected— this time in the form of fire:

> All went well for the first six months of the year, but just when the Masai were due to move out of the wet season grazing area, a series of fires destroyed the

grazing in the dry season area, and it was necessary to give permission for the majority of bomas to remain for the whole year. (NP AR 1956: 83)

Unanticipated factors, such as fire or disease, as well as the inconsistent rainfall and micro-variations in soil and fodder were precisely the reasons Maasai pastoralism could never be successful "anchored" to one small defined area. But administrators persisted, allocating a fixed number of homesteads to each of the five principal permanent water supplies (although they left it to Maasai to decide which homesteads went where) (NP AR 1957: 75).

Administrative frustration with the heightened refusal of Maasai to see and grasp the benefits of "development" led to propaganda campaigns designed to overcome their "ignorance" and change their "attitudes." In this period, the campaign had two main components: the use of visual aids such as movies and sponsored visits by Maasai elders to "successful" development projects among Maasai in Kenya. A mobile cinema traveled through Masai District in 1952 showing films to Maasai audiences during the cattle markets. According to the district commissioner, "films of local interest and those depicting Masai were very popular" (MaD AR 1951: 10). In 1955, a mobile cinema was purchased, "in order to bring home to the Masai the need for development" (NP AR 1955: 78). It was "immensely popular" despite a lack of films. To support the project, the Masai Native Authority purchased £500 worth of filmmaking equipment in 1956 but had trouble finding someone to use the equipment (NP AR 1956: 84). Local films taken by a visiting anthropologist in 1957 solved the problem (NP AR 1957: 83). While the entertainment value of the cinema was high, its propaganda value in changing attitudes was doubtful.

Besides bringing images of progress and change to Maasai, administrators also tried to bring certain Maasai (elder men, of course) to see for themselves the possibilities and benefits of "development."[120] Mistakenly convinced that somehow Maasai men were ignorant of what was happening among Maasai in other areas, some officers tended to overstate the results of such trips. Thus, in 1956, the provincial commissioner reported that "a visit to Ngong and Nairobi at the time of the Royal Show left a deep impression on the minds of the few elders who made the trip, and they returned full of good resolutions to hasten the development of their people" (NP AR 1956: 84). Such conclusions could be reached only by ignoring the rapid circulation of news about people, projects, and other events through the networks of travel and talk that linked Maasai within and between Tanganyika and Kenya.

Besides the maintenance costs of the MDP water projects, Maasai also continued to finance, through their taxes, the operating costs of their expanding medical infrastructure and subsidize a significant portion of expenses for education.

Education

Until the 1940s, formal education opportunities for Maasai were extremely sparse, especially in comparison with opportunities for other ethnic groups. Initially, only the Lutheran church ran several small primary schools for Maasai boys, the first in Naberera in 1930.[121] During a meeting of Lutheran mission representatives and Olkiama elders in 1930 to discuss opening more schools, the elders stated, according to the district officer, "that the Masai had no children to send to mission schools as all their children were occupied tending cattle." But they acknowledged that "there might be heads of families in the tribe who would be ready and able to send some of their children, and in that case, they should be free to do so. If others did not wish to do so then there was no compulsion, and naturally they could follow their own desires in this particular matter."[122] Their ambivalent response, at once rejecting and accepting mission schools in their midst, reflected the wariness of Maasai about both Christian evangelization and education. Later in the same meeting, they claimed to support the proposed government school in Monduli and even requested that the government build a school for each area of the district.[123] Despite the support of the male elders, the government school did not open until 1937. Much of the delay was due to the sometimes fierce debates among representatives from the Administrative, Veterinary, and Education Departments over who was "responsible" for Maasai and the content of the proposed curriculum.[124]

A key issue in the debate over an "appropriate" educational policy for Maasai was whether they needed the "general" education offered by most government and Native Authority schools or a more "practical" curriculum, including courses in animal husbandry to make them better and more efficient pastoralists. Browne had been a strong proponent of a "special" education policy for the Masai:

> When dealing with a nomadic and purely pastoral tribe like the Masai, we should avoid a system of education which, having inculcated an elementary knowledge of the "three Rs" into the rising generation and then sends them back to their tribe fitted for no other work than, perhaps in a few instances, a low grade native "karani."
>
> What we should try to do (and, indeed, are trying to do even now) is to make the Masai a better stock farmer (he is by no means bad one now) and add

to the knowledge that he has acquired himself that knowledge which the advance of science has brought to European stock farmers.[125]

Not surprisingly, most veterinary officials supported the need for special training for Maasai that was biased toward animal husbandry. Some cited fears that a regular academic curriculum would alienate young boys from their families:

> Book learning, and even the teaching of handicrafts to the cattle tribes, is often synonymous with rural depopulation and sympathy and understanding is accorded the native livestock owner who refuses to send his children to school. The father fears, and rightly so, that his son will acquire tastes unsuited to his walk in life as a stock-breeder, that he will lose interest in animals and in his home surrounding and will finally run away from home, deserting his parents in their old age. His fears in the past have only been too often confirmed and a contented useful unit lost to the tribe. (VD AR 1926: 55)

Proposals for a school curriculum "closely connected with animal husbandry" were put forward, although some acknowledged "that since the Masai hold the view that they know more about cattle than any one else, attendance at such a school might not appeal to them."[126]

Such concerns prompted the acting director of education to ask the obvious question: "Have the Masai expressed, of their own accord, any wish as to the type of school they need? Suggestions have been put to them to which they agreed but they may hold very different views among themselves."[127] Many believed "that the apathy of the Masai towards education will prove to be a great difficulty," and felt that the government "should be in a position, if necessary, to force the school upon the Masai."[128]

The answer—that some Maasai were not only interested in but willing to finance education for their sons—came in 1936 when the Masai Council requested a Native Authority school.[129] The school opened in 1937 with twenty pupils and plans for a four-year "primary course." According to Page-Jones, almost half of the boys were admitted at the request of their parents, three or four were *ilmurran* ("whose insistent demands were hard to refuse"), and the remainder, "at the specific request of the Masai Council, were chosen by the subordinate native authorities from areas, and in numbers, indicated by the District Commissioner" (Page-Jones 1944). By 1940, the school had 80 boarders, and both Maasai and colonial enthusiasm for its success was strong; there were no problems in collecting the annual school fees for each child (NP AR 1940: 38). The Mondul School facilities were expanded over the next few years, more dormitories, classrooms, and housing for teachers were added, and more teachers were hired, including three Maasai teachers from Kenya

(Page-Jones 1944). As further evidence of the support of some Maasai for formal education, in 1938 Purko, Loita, and Laitayok elders asked for a separate school to be built in Loliondo. Colonial administrators convinced them that it was preferable to establish the Mondul School first before new schools were started, so boys from these sections began to come to Mondul in 1939 (Page-Jones 1944).

Not all parents were pleased, however. Some feared "losing their children," or, more precisely, that "the Swahilis" would "take" their children. As one older Maasai man explained, "In the past, during the colonial period, we didn't understand school, it came to this country when we were children. Our fathers prevented us from going. Maasai didn't want their children to be trampled on by the Swahilis, no, they didn't want this at all. They thought that their children would be lost and go off to die." When forced by the government to send at least one child to school, elders reportedly gave the son they liked the least (cf. Saitoti 1986: 53).

The curriculum reflected a compromise solution to the question of general versus special education. Swahili instruction was provided in reading, writing, arithmetic, and practical training in "improved" animal husbandry techniques: "It is generally agreed that education, as far as the Masai are concerned, without animal husbandry, would be unthinkable," wrote the senior veterinary officer to the Northern Province in 1938.[130] Confusion still existed about the objectives of the school, however: was it supposed to train Maasai boys to fill certain "native" positions within the native authority and colonial administration or teach them to be "better" pastoralists? Or was education a means to "modernize" them by broadening their outlooks and changing their attitudes? By 1940, some colonial officials began pushing for expanded educational opportunities for Maasai: "By this time it was realised that if the necessary small number of Masai boys was to be trained as clerk-dressers, teachers, etc. . . . for service in their own country more than a four years' course was necessary" (Page-Jones 1944). The rationale of colonial officials for limiting Maasai educational opportunities was shaped by their own restricted needs for "native" personnel and their "understandings" of Maasai "tradition" and "culture," rather than by the broader interests of the Maasai people: "The number of boys going on to Standards VII and VIII . . . would be small . . . for the number of posts in Masailand is strictly limited and Masai have generally at present no desire to work outside their own country" (Page-Jones 1944). According to Page-Jones, Maasai did not "as a rule" seek employment with the government or the Native Authority; they preferred to employ non-Maasai in "subordinate posts such as messengers and sanitary labourers."

Kenyan Maasai were recruited to fill "native official" positions such as administrative clerks, dressers [medical assistants], and teachers, but their employment was "regarded as transitional only until Mondul schoolboys mature and become available to fill vacancies as these occur."[131] When the first entering class graduated in 1941, some colonial administrators congratulated themselves on helping to form "for the first time in the history of Tanganyika, a nucleus of literate Masai" (NP AR 1941: 37).

By 1943, however, something had happened to dampen Maasai enthusiasm for the school and discourage attendance. For the first time, the provincial commissioner complained in his annual report about a decline in enrollment, attributing it to the "unwillingness of Masai parents to give up the services of their young sons as herdsmen for the as yet unappreciated advantages of education" (NP AR 1944). In 1945, he reported that "the Masai Boarding School continues to be unpopular with parents and only seventy-one children were on the rolls instead of eighty. Five alien children were admitted as an experiment at reduced fees and the small influx of Swahili speaking children has had a stimulating effect on the Masai" (NP AR 1945: 59). A brief note in the 1945 update to the Masailand Comprehensive Report suggested one source of Maasai dissatisfaction: "Elders were forcing children of poor parents to go to Mondul school" ("Education," 1945, MDB/13).

In 1947, a ten-year education plan was approved for Tanganyika that preserved the pre-war emphasis on primary schooling and education adapted to village life (Iliffe 1979: 444–447). But education, as with other development schemes, had been unevenly implemented and received throughout the country, as reflected in attendance figures (only 10 percent of Maasai children attended school in 1951, as compared to 20 percent of Arusha or 64.5 percent of Chagga) and distribution of schools (8 in Maasailand as compared to 22 in Mbulu).[132] Not surprisingly, given the late start and lack of emphasis on education in Masai District, Maasai were still perceived as underdeveloped in comparison to other ethnic groups, and education was fundamental to changing their status. The provincial commissioner voiced his position clearly at the 1947 Olkiama:

> [The] greatest difficulty Administrative Officers now experience is to find sufficient Masai youths who can read and write to assist in administration as Clerks, Veterinary Guards etc., therefore education is needed you may say "we don't want education"—I say that is foolish—it is essential if you are to understand what is going on in the world and you must—you can no longer live apart in the age of cars and aeroplanes—if you still say "we don't want education" you will remain herders of cattle and little better than servants whilst others progress. . . . You

must have literate youths to help you and it is your duty to see that as many boys as possible are educated for the reasons I have given you. You must answer yes—there is no other answer you can give.[133]

Given his bullying tone, the Maasai elders present at the Olkiama had little choice but to agree to the creation of more "bush-boma" schools teaching Standards I and II.[134]

Once the ten-year educational plan was passed by the Legislative Council in 1947, the Northern Province set a "provincial target" providing that 50 percent of all children of school age should be attending school by 1956.[135] Thus, beginning in 1948, there was a rapid expansion of the educational infrastructure in Masai District by the Native Authorities and missionaries, financed partially by grants-in-aid provided by the government. Forced to revise the school system in light of the increased opposition by Maasai elders to the Mondul School, administrators decided to establish smaller primary schools throughout the District, replacing in-school boarding with what came to be known as the "mother and cows system" (Maasai children lived with their mothers and some milking cows in nearby homesteads). Only children attending upper primary schools would board, a situation administrators hoped the elders would find acceptable. The new system seemed to allay the doubts of the elders, and enrollment improved (NP AR 1946: 44; NP AR 1947: 81). In 1948, the government school for Maasai in Loliondo was taken over as a Native Authority school, two bush schools were opened, two mission schools received their first Maasai pupils, and school fees at Mondul School were abolished to encourage increased enrollment. Every local Maasai council now had a school in its own territory. Despite an ongoing problem of a lack of adequately qualified Maasai-speaking teachers, 1949 saw the construction of new school buildings in Kibaya, Mto-wa-Mbu, Loliondo, and Nainokanoka and the opening of Lutheran mission schools in Engasumet, Longido, and Engaruka. Mondul School became a two-year middle school in 1950, with a new classroom and dormitory, and another Lutheran mission school was opened at Arash. A District Education Committee was formed to coordinate the system. By 1951, of the ninety-one children enrolled in the Mondul Middle School, twenty-six were Maasai or of "mixed Masai blood" and the first Standard VIII class began. Three hundred seventy-five children were in "out schools" (day schools, including mission schools) in Monduli Division, and 289 were in out schools in Loliondo Division.[136] Acting Director of Education Sherwood wrote that "education had apparently come to stay."[137] But it was still an education adapted to the "special" needs of pastoralists; the Dis-

Table 3.1 Total 1954 Contributions to Recurrent Costs of District Education, by Institution

District	1954 Total	Government	Native Treasury	Voluntary Agencies
Moshi	£83,837	£69,069	£14,695	£13,873
Arusha	£13,784	£8,524	£2,508	£2,754
Mbulu	£20,870	£10,449	£6,911	£3,510
Masai	£7,709	£4,338	£3,222	£149
TOTAL	£126,200	£92,380	£27,336	£20,286

Source: Northern Province Annual Report 1954: 101 (copy in TNA).

trict Education Committee recommended that the syllabus for primary schools in Masai District "should be recast to give a strong bias to animal husbandry," while boys at the Mondul Middle School attended special lectures on animal husbandry and practical demonstrations on the school farm.[138]

Proposed future developments in 1951 included expanding Mondul Middle School to go up to Standard X and converting the out schools to boarding schools for Standards III–IV, "each with its own dairy herd and grazing reserve." Administrators were increasingly dissatisfied with the "mothers and cows system," claiming that it had failed to adequately feed and house students (NP AR 1952: 108). As Stahl reported, "The system became unsatisfactory, because when the Masai migrated to another area, the mothers left the school, taking the cows with them, and abandoned the children without food. They also tended to use the huts for social rather than educational purposes and during a cattle market they became brothels and hotels" (Stahl 1961: 58). A target of 1,100 Maasai children attending primary school by 1956 was set by the District Education Committee in 1952 (MaD AR 1952). But these plans were delayed while administrators concentrated their efforts on the water and tsetse aspects of the MDP, and the "existing materials and labour shortage" constrained the "building capacity" of the Masai Native Authority.[139] Despite ambitious plans for education, finances were "the great difficulty."[140] Funding was in fact a difficulty, especially since the government spent so little money on education in Masai District as compared with the other three districts in the Northern Province. As Table 3.1 shows, an analysis of recurrent costs in education for 1954 showed that Arusha and Mbulu Districts received roughly two times as much money from the government, while Moshi District received almost sixteen times as much money.

In 1955, another experiment was tested in Masai District—mobile schools which moved with Maasai homesteads as they migrated from area to area. Eight mobile schools were established with an enrollment of 133 boys. Despite some "teething troubles" and some unsatisfactory teachers, administrators hoped "that this type of school may prove the answer to attracting young Masai children to school" (NP AR 1955: 99–100).

And while increasing numbers of parents sent their boys to school voluntarily, many were still forced to send at least one son under community quota systems. Teachers at the Mondul Middle School faced a constant problem with runaway students:

> Some Masai pupils who had run away were sent back to school under escort but ran away again within 24 hours, two at least going on foot to their homes near Loliondo, whence they were sent back again to Monduli only to run away yet again. One Standard VI boy said he would commit suicide if he was sent back to school! (NP AR 1956: 117)

From the perspective of Maasai boys, the experience of being caught and forced to go to school was terrifying. Roving *jumbes* (headmen) tracked and caught runaways and the sons of still-resistant parents. Boys were warned to run away and hide if they saw a stranger with a red hat (the *jumbes* wore a unique hat to advertise their position—a red cap with a black tassel). One elder man recalled how he was chased, caught, and forced to begin primary school by a *jumbe:*

> We were out herding. Jumbe Sirowei, who died recently, was the *jumbe* during that period, which was still the colonial period before independence. He would walk among the herds. If he saw cattle, he would approach them. If he saw two children [herding], he would take one. But if he saw just one child herding, he would leave him. Well, we were three children. So I . . . I mean, if you saw the *jumbe,* that *jumbe,* who had a special hat, well, you knew he was the *jumbe.* We were told that, if you saw a person wearing a hat, run! Because he is the *jumbe.* So when I saw him [DH: Was he Arusha or Maasai? Answer: Maasai.] we ran. I went into the small bushes and hid myself. The others ran. He saw that only two were running, so he knew that one had hid himself. He went around and around, and finally caught me. Then we went to the cattle herd. He didn't only tie your hands so you couldn't run, but also tied you up back here so that he could drive you like cattle. . . . Seven of us were taken to school that day. [DH: Straight?] Straight, without passing our homes. [DH: Oya! Did you cry?] I cried a lot. Anyway, we were taken, we were given food. We met lots of students, since it was a boarding school. . . . The next day, my father came and found me. But that was it. It was the rule. The district commissioner had decided to send the *jumbe,* so there was no asking why this particular child was in school. And so I started school.

Stahl described the problem in terms of stratification and gender:

> Administrative officers are engaged in a constant tussle to get new boys to school and to see that they do not immediately run away. Influential parents keep their children to look after the cattle, with the result that pressure is exerted upon those less able to resist it, the poor fathers or the widows with no husbands to stand up for them and theirs are the children who put in a spasmodic attendance at primary school. (Stahl 1961: 57)

But they still had their moments of success: thirteen students out of nineteen who took the territorial Standard VIII examinations in 1956 passed (NP AR 1956: 117).

Despite the increase in numbers of schools and pupils in attendance, very few Maasai girls were enrolled. Of the 229 pupils registered in the Mondul School in 1947, seventeen were girls—all "alien" girls (NP AR 1947: 81). Of the three middle schools, one secondary school, and two teachers' training schools located in the Province in 1951 which accepted girls, none had any Maasai girl students.[141] Even if they had attended, their curriculum was gender-segregated: While boys were taught "manual work," "the pupils for the girls' middle school were selected from all local areas and the girls were taught domestic science and child welfare and generally encouraged to follow careers eg [*sic*], nursing."[142] Only in 1958 did the Masai Council take the issue seriously, setting quotas for girls primary education, ranging from two to fourteen per school, for a total of seventy-eight. They proposed either that girls live with their mothers in a nearby homestead or in a single-sex dormitory under the supervision of a Maa-speaking matron or teacher.[143]

The masculine bias in the colonial education policy for Maasai was quite marked in its unquestioned acceptance. As many of the above quotations suggest, the discussion was always about how best to educate Maasai boys and for what objectives. Nowhere was there even a discussion about the possibility of educating Maasai girls, even though girls from other ethnic groups were being educated in other government and Native Authority schools. This became quite clear when the government opened a separate school in Mondul for the children of "alien" laborers in 1945 and the provincial commissioner proudly proclaimed that "of the thirty-six children enrolled half were girls" (NP AR 1945: 59).

The stark contrast between the interest of colonial officials in educating non-Maasai girls and their complete lack of interest in educating Maasai girls has several sources, I would argue. First, the absence of Maasai girls from even consideration as possible pupils mirrors the absence of their mothers and other adult women from inclusion in other "development" interventions in Masai District. By midcentury, the coding of pastoralism as masculine by colonial officials was quite fixed: Maasai men were the pastoralists, Maasai women were not. The women were still Maasai but somehow less than Maasai because they were not perceived as pastoralists. Given this image, any "development" initiative aimed at the Maasai, especially if it had any "pastoralist" component, was necessarily targeted at men, since they were the true and only pastoralists. The strength of this imagery and belief among colonial officials, and their complete ignorance about the crucial roles of women in pastoralist production, testifies to the power of the alliance of colonial officials with elder Maasai men. Elder Maasai men, whether through the Masai Council or through more informal interactions with colonial administrators as "friends," dictated the terms of the interaction of the colonial government with Maasai society. The complicity of colonial officials in such an arrangement only further bolstered the power of the elders to control and shape colonial understandings and interventions.

But administrators still yearned for an educated elite:

> The emergence of an educated elite would help to bridge the gap between the extreme conservatism of the elders and modern political and economic trends, and would enable the Masai to be better represented on various bodies, but education remains an anathema as far as the vast majority of elders are concerned and it is believed that there are not half a dozen Tanganyikan Masai who have passed Standard X. (NP AR 1956: 83–84)

In the district commissioner's office in 1956, both clerks were non-Maasai; the only Maasai were two messengers and an interpreter. There were only three Maasai teachers in the Mondul middle school. In the entire district, only a few clerks and a few primary school teachers were Maasai (Stahl 1961: 57). But education was becoming increasingly appealing to some Maasai; the 1957 Olkiama even suggested sending an educated Maasai to England for further study, a proposition that was, according to the provincial commissioner, "unfortunately impracticable" (NP AR 1957: 75). But he did approve of their decision to appoint an educated Kenyan Maasai to act as their adviser and executive officer (NP AR 1957: 75).

Maasai Farmers

Meanwhile, some Maasai were making other changes in their own lives, despite the interventions of administrators. Most notably, more and more were beginning to cultivate. Although some had been farming for years, others began to watch their Arusha neighbors in the Monduli area and other cultivating immigrant communities now living throughout the District.[144] One venerable Maasai male elder told me in 1993 that he had moved to Emairete from Ormuswa in the 1940s *because* he wanted to farm:

I came by myself with one wife, before Wanga and [another elder]. Although I hadn't farmed in Ormuswa, I began after I moved here. I thought farming was a good thing, so I planted maize and beans, food Maasai like. I learned to farm from watching Arusha in Ormuswa and my wives helped me. I had my plot, each wife had her own, and we shared all of the work: planting, weeding, and harvesting. Each person kept the harvest from their own farm.

Other senior elders in Emairete told similar stories of moving to Emairete because of its fertile land in order to farm, learning from Arusha men while their wives learned from Arusha women. In most areas, however, few Maasai men farmed for themselves; rather, the wealthier ones hired non-Maasai laborers (often Mbulu) and the less wealthy (and some wealthy) married non-Maasai wives.

The main stimuli to cultivation were the growing numbers of Arusha families moving into Masai District through both official and unofficial channels and the increasing number of Maasai men marrying Arusha women, their "farming" wives. Provincial-level administrators had long viewed the "empty" sweeps of Masai District as the long-term solution to the overcrowded "land-hungry" Arusha, a position confirmed by the Wilson Report (NP AR 1957: 97). Beginning in the 1950s, large numbers of Arusha were officially resettled by the government in certain designated areas such as Lendikenya, Lashaine, and Kisongo.[145] But many others used their contacts and relationships with fellow Maasai to move themselves. As early as 1950, the district commissioner noted in his annual report that "in the Mondul area it appears that certain members of the Council had—for a consideration—permitted a fair number of Waarusha agriculturalists to settle in the neighborhood."[146] Despite a resolution by a mass meeting of elder Maasai men to withdraw such concessions to Arusha, the gradual infiltration continued. The "consideration," usually a daughter in marriage and some livestock, was as important as the immediate access to maize and beans. And so a similar resolution at the 1956 Olkiama meeting failed: "When it was pointed out that this would mean removing the wives of several of the Masai elders present, the matter was dropped" (NP AR 1956: 86).

Citizens in Need, Citizens in Deed?

On the eve of Independence, the failure of the rains in late 1960 through-out northern and central Tanganyika caused the worst famine since the devastation of the 1890s. The drought decimated cattle herds in areas of Northern Maasailand, especially in the Rift Valley, and caused severe malnutrition and occasional starvation. The government's handling of the drought revealed much about their indifference to Maasai and about their gendered assumptions and practices.

The government responded slowly, denying news reports of extensive starvation with claims that certain groups of Maasai were exaggerating the gravity of their situation to pressure the government to distribute free or subsidized maize in order to avoid selling their cattle.[147] But TANU saw the drought, and the government's sluggish response, as a political opportunity to attract Maasai support. While the district commissioner was still investigating and reporting on the situation, TANU mobilized supporters in other areas of the Northern Province to collect contributions of food from Arusha and Meru to distribute in Maasailand. Unfortunately, the type of food most people donated—bananas—was, as the district commissioner gleefully noted, inappropriate to the situation and "caused some embarrassment." They were bulky, perishable, and not part of the Maasai diet.[148] And TANU members were soon in a dispute with the Masai Council over alleged misuse of Masai Council vehicles to transport the food relief.[149]

But TANU's effort did push the colonial administration to respond. A famine relief committee was organized in Monduli, which included the district commissioner, a Lutheran pastor, and a Catholic priest, to supervise the food distribution and later the free distribution of seeds to cultivators in the area. As with most such crises, the impact was unevenly felt, depending on gender, age, and wealth. Elderly men and women, nursing mothers, and small babies suffered the most because of their weakened state, but the *ilayiok*, young herdsboys, were intentionally neglected, receiving only very small quantities of maize, often on alternate days.[150] The government began distributing about 1,000 pints of milk a day (from UNICEF dried milk) in the district, and eventually set up special camps to ensure that the milk was properly mixed and distributed only to women, children, the very old, and the "feeble"; District Commissioner Clarke reported that "milk is not issued to men unless they are physically infirm from old age or disease."[151] Instead, provincial and district administrators tried to take advantage of the situation to force "able-bodied" Maasai men to labor on food-for-work projects, including maintaining roads, desilting dams, and digging storage tanks. "It must be remembered," the district commissioner noted in a letter to the provincial commissioner, "that hundreds, if not thousands, of Masai are going to be in a desperate position this year and therefore unusually malleable." As if forcing reluctant Maasai men to work was not victory enough, in the same letter he also argued that "conditions in Maasailand are more propitions [*sic*] now for the introduction of rehabilitation and resettlement projects than ever before."[152] But the provincial commissioner, remembering the labor disputes over clearing tsetse flies in the bush, was more cautious. He seemed to lean toward avoiding trouble by just distributing the famine relief food, despite the district commissioner's arguments that the provincial commissioner's position was contradicted by

> the uncontestable principle that all who claim famine assistance, and who have little or no prospect of paying for this assistance within a reasonable period of time, should be required to work for it. Furthermore, if this principle is followed, the chances of claims for famine relief being made by people who do not need it are greatly reduced.[153]

Food-for-work programs were finally implemented but were generally unsuccessful, as most "able-bodied" Maasai men were too busy trying to maintain their herds. Despite a request by the provincial commissioner to the water officer to allow Maasai to graze in the forest reserves and alienated farms surrounding Mt. Kilimanjaro and Mt. Meru (former Maasai lands), the water officer refused, claiming that those areas were also suffering from a water shortage.[154] But Maasai did not care whether they had permission or not; they took their cattle beyond district boundaries in search of water and grass in Arusha and Moshi Districts, producing a flood of "trespass" cases.[155]

The drought lasted through the establishment of Independence on December 9th, 1961, until mid-1962 when the rains, and then the grass and water, returned. Not only did large numbers of Maasai livestock die, but the Masai Native Authority Treasury went bankrupt. In 1961, the Masai Treasury spent £25,203 to finance the staff, food, transport, and food-for-work programs that constituted the famine relief measures. The colonial government only provided £5,603 toward the costs, although they did lend the Masai Treasury £20,000 in an interest-free loan to help them pay their costs.[156] As in the "disasters" of the late nineteenth century, Maasai dispersed to neighboring districts to seek food and economic security, prompting demands a few years later for their return.[157]

*   *   *

So, on the eve of Independence, after almost fifty years of "development," much of it targeted at "improving" water conditions, Maasai were in worse shape than before: the impact of the drought was magnified by the loss of most of their dry-season and drought grazing grounds and water points to land alienation by the government and settlers. Projects designed to build new water sources in order to increase the productivity of the land had only served to decrease its productivity: cattle clustered at the water points, trampling and eating all of the grass in the vicinity, ruining the land. Many elderly Maasai felt betrayed. Having donated cattle to help the colonial government during their time of crisis during the war, they expected the government, as their partners in *osotua* (a special friendship of mutual obligation established through a gift of cattle), to return the gesture and help them in their time of need. Instead, the government shifted the burden onto Maasai and blamed them for their desperate situation: "The growing attitude of laziness connected with famine relief is destressing [*sic*]; were the concept of building a better country in which to live through hard work more prevalent, these troubles which have taken up so much of our time would never have arisen."[158]

MAASAI PORTRAIT 3: THOMAS

I would be very happy if my children all found work—either as employees or for themselves—and used their education well.

I first met Thomas Porokwa[1] in 1984, when he worked at Simanjiro Hospital (which is run by the Catholic Diocese) and I was the coordinator of development for the diocese. A tall, wiry, reserved man, he was always interested in the latest news from Arusha. In his white lab coat, pressed trousers, shirt, and glasses, he was constantly on the move—checking patients, inventorying supplies, hustling around the hospital compound. I kept up with news of him over the years, especially through some of his children whom I knew. During a return trip to Tanzania in 1997, I asked his permission to interview him about his life and his perspectives on the world. He graciously agreed, and we spent two days talking in his sitting room in Simanjiro. As one of the first Maasai boys to receive a post-primary education, he illustrates some of the costs as well as some of the opportunities of the social, cultural, and economic changes that have occurred among Maasai.

Born in 1932 as the third child of his father's second wife, Thomas led the life of a typical *olayioni* as his family moved around the Monduli area in search of pasture and water. In 1942, however, his life was changed forever when his father was forced by colonial administrators to send one of his sons to the Native Authority school in Monduli (the district headquarters), and he chose Thomas. Everyone in his homestead cried, especially his mother, for they all believed that "if a child went to school, he would be lost, become a Swahili, learn different ways of being and a different culture, and become completely lost." With the guidance and friendship of an older boy from his area, he confronted the jarringly unfamiliar new context: the strange food, dorm rooms, mess hall, uniforms, and language. Like many boys he tried unsuccessfully to run away, but in time he found that he enjoyed school and became the top student in his classes. Although he did not feel different when he returned to his homestead during school vacations, he was taunted by his peers as *ormeek*.

When he passed his Standard IV exams and was chosen for further study, his parents urged him to quit and return home. Thomas disregarded their advice and pursued further studies at an upper primary school in Moshi, a predominantly non-Maasai urban area. Surrounded by non-Maasai, his biggest problem was that his fellow students and teachers "feared us Maasai." He tried to be friendly, to show them that Maasai were not mean or aggressive, and in time made friends. As before, he returned home every leave to the welcome embrace of his parents and the taunts of his peers. Although he claimed he still did not feel different, he was careful to change into Maasai clothes before arriving, and his father required that he attend an *olpul* (an extended meat-eating feast by *ilmurran*) during each visit. During Standard VIII he was circumcised and became an *olmurrani* himself, after which he participated fully in *olpul*.

Another milestone occurred in 1951, when he finished Standard IX and was selected to attend a teachers' training college. At the time, he was staying in Monduli Hospital, where his father was recovering from a severe leg injury. Excited and eager to attend, he asked his father's permission. But his father adamantly refused: "No one knows Swahili like you in order to help me." The district commissioner and the provincial education officer both urged his father to change his mind, but he refused. Although despondent over losing the opportunity, Thomas stayed with his father in the hospital for five months until he was fully recuperated.

During his extended stay in the hospital, however, he befriended Christopher Hall, the district medical officer (see Hall 1956). Intrigued by the bright, trilingual young man and eager to help him further his education, Hall asked Thomas's father for permission to keep Thomas at Monduli Hospital and train him in basic medicine. Thomas's father agreed, and thus began Thomas's lifelong career as a rural medical assistant. After extensive training in various hospitals, Thomas worked as a rural medical assistant in government and Catholic hospitals and dispensaries throughout Maasailand until his retirement in 1987. Baptized as a Catholic in 1947 (thus his Christian name), he also volunteered as a catechist and religion teacher and became a leading member of the local Catholic church and diocese. When I asked why he was baptized, Thomas replied that he was "big" at the time and understood exactly what he was doing. Although other Maasai claimed that baptism was just an *ormeek* affair, "I knew that I was joining the good life of God."

These days, Thomas and his family openly live the lives of *ormeek* in a small Maasai village on the Simanjiro plains south of Monduli town. Wearing a crisply ironed shirt, creased pants, and a large silver watch, Thomas spoke to me in the large sitting room of his cement-block house, with its ceiling board and corrugated iron roof. Both days his wife, Mama Joseph, hovered just outside the room, ready to serve us *chai* (milk tea) while preparing our meals (rice with meat sauce). An uneducated Maasai woman, she taught herself some rudimentary reading and math skills and now manages the grinding machine which Maasai women in the area built with the help of the local Catholic church as an income-generating and labor-saving project. Although respected for their financial success and contributions to their family and community, both Thomas and Mama Joseph have been and always will be seen as *ormeek,* as not really Maasai. "Even now," sighed Thomas, "when my wife and I visit our families we are stilled called *ormeek* and *emeeki.*" "Even we call ourselves Swahili now," he admitted later.

The consequences of Thomas and Mama Joseph's difficult decisions to brave the scorn of their community are most dramatically revealed in the lives of their ten surviving children. Of the seven sons and three daughters, all have been baptized Catholic, all but the youngest daughter (who is still in primary school) have been educated through secondary school, and most (including the two older daughters) have pursued post-secondary education. Most telling, in a country where less than 1 percent of the population has the opportunity for a college education (and of these only a handful have ever been Maasai), three of the sons have attended the University of Dar es Salaam. Given the tremendous financial sacrifices that Thomas and Mama Joseph have had to make to educate their children, it is not surprising to learn that Thomas considers education the top priority for Maasai: "As I see it, if a person has been to school, has received a sufficient education, then it is much easier for her/him to make life decisions. It is also easier for them to help bring other people development in forms other than education. I mean, if we had many educated Maasai, we wouldn't lack political leaders and technical experts [to help us]."

Thomas had many opinions about the past and present of Maasai. He recalled the colonial period with mixed feelings: "All together, the colonial administrators had a good relationship with Maasai. They respected Maasai and liked them. But . . . they didn't do any development whatsoever for Maasai. . . . Until Independence in 1961, there were only two or three schools in Maasailand." "But didn't they initiate some projects, such as for water and livestock?" I asked. "Yes," he replied, and listed the few places where the colonial government had built boreholes. He described the veterinary guards: "They were posted almost everywhere to prevent cattle theft and encourage cattle sales. But they were not liked. . . . The police were able to arrest anyone, they could be very mean, they could even beat people and nothing would happen to them. People were therefore afraid and hated them. The veterinary guards and the police." As for the Masai Development Project of the 1950s, "it had no results whatsoever." Just before Independence, he recalled, the British "advised Maasai to unite together, not to mix with other people. They should find their own place, and live by themselves with their cattle, trying not to follow outside customs and traditions."

Thomas had high hopes at Independence but was quickly disappointed. "There were changes, but they weren't good changes for Maasai. We thought that after Uhuru [independence] we would get development like education, water, medicines in our hospitals, everything would be built. But the results, well. . . . Every government project, well . . . take a dispensary. The building would be erected, a doctor and nurses employed, but there would be no medicine. Or if there was medicine, it was only there for a short time. Even if you brought medicine for one month, it would only last one week. So yes, there was development, but little of it reached the people. . . . Even the schools. Many schools were built, but there were no teachers and the few that were there didn't do their work well. When the [Catholic] mission ran the Simanjiro school, about twenty students a year would go on to secondary school. But once the mission left [the school was nationalized by the government in 1970], ten years would pass without even one secondary school student. . . . For Maasai it was as if life went backwards, things stayed the same as they were in the colonial period." He accused the government at the time of preferring to help its own people, such as the Chagga in Moshi, building them more schools and better roads. As for TANU and Chama Cha Mapinduzi (Revolutionary Party, CCM), "they didn't help [Maasai] at all." "One of the main things Maasai wanted was to keep other people from taking their land, but these days most of the land is being farmed by non-Maasai. There are no Maasai. If you look, those people with farms of 2,000 acres, however many thousands, they are not Maasai. They belong to other tribes—whites, Indians, Chagga, and other people."

He mentioned some specific events since Independence, such as the Masai Livestock Development and Range Management Project of the 1970s. At first things went well, "but then, and I'm not sure why, if the government ruined it or the project contract just ended, but suddenly the few things that we had received like veterinary medicines and the veterinary centers were stopped all at once . . . until now." As for Operation Imparnati, the forced villagization program at Independence, Maasai in Simanjiro were not as harassed as in other places, where "people built their homesteads, lived in them for a long time, and suddenly they were destroyed and burnt down. Many lost their property, even their sleeping skins were burnt. And they were forced to move." These days, he is disillusioned by government promises of development: "The government talks a lot about many ways to help people but doesn't come through." The government has helped to provide some services such as hospitals and schools in Maasailand, but these are funded in great part "by the contributions we provide as citizens (*wananchi*)." Even so, he remarked, "we pay a development tax but we don't see any benefits from the tax." "The problem these days," he added later, "is that if you say anything, the government says, 'Start it yourself!' If you fail, then the government will jump in and help." "Many times we fail to finish the list of things we need done!" he said, laughing and shaking his head.

At various times we discussed Maasai gender relations, including women's rights in livestock, bridewealth, marriage, and respect. In terms of livestock, according to Thomas, women never had exclusive rights to cattle in the past, but "they could give cattle to slaughter, for friends, whatever, if they talked about it with their husbands." The cattle of her house "were hers completely. Even if her husband died, no one could take them from her. But she couldn't give them away without permission." These cattle were used in part for her son's bridewealth so that he could marry, and most of the bridewealth cattle received for her daughters went into her household's herd. In fact, Thomas said that women played the main roles in the engagement and marriage of their children, choosing prospective spouses, bringing or receiving small gifts, and meeting with the prospective in-laws.

In his opinion, relationships between Maasai men and women are changing very slowly. "There have been very few changes, *especially* among young people these days. They still haven't learned from other people that women must have equal rights. Just a few [women] want to be treated as equals. . . . They are still afraid to attend a meeting with male elders, to come here and eat together, to see a man eating and chewing and whatever. . . . Very slowly things are changing." Part of the problem is development, which he believes has harmed relationships between people, especially between men and women. "Development has, in some ways, ruined people. People participate in development, which is very new for them, strange, and they don't quite know what to do. . . . Let's consider women's rights in cattle. It's true that every married woman received cattle from her husband. And if there were many, she gave their offspring to her children. And to her father. But now, this business of money and commerce makes many men try to take over all of the cattle or property. He claims it is his because of this business of money. Many old men have become drunks, so they want to take control of all the cattle." "The problem," he said a bit later, "is that people have embraced modern development [*maendeleo ya kisasa*] so quickly, without thinking about 'if I choose this way, where will it take me or will it help me or not?'"

As mentioned before, education is his top development priority. During one of our interview days, two government water engineers drove through town, supposedly to inspect and fix a local borehole. When they arrived at Thomas's house, they were drunk, rude, and belligerent, demanding alcohol and food. Everyone was embarrassed, especially since I was there, but Mama Joseph sat them outside on the porch and quietly fed them a meal. They soon left, but no boreholes were fixed. Later that day, Thomas referred to them when explaining why education was so important: "It would be so much easier to bring development to people once more were educated. If we had more educated Maasai, we wouldn't lack politicians and only have one or two Maasai experts. We would have a water engineer who comes to Simanjiro to help with water development rather than coming to get drunk like those two. Maasai encounter many problems just trying to do their business in town or other places where most people are not Maasai." As an example, he told me the story of an old man who had dropped by earlier when we were talking and left with a young, educated man. "The young man is a seminarian, studying at Segerea. And the old man is from Loiborsirret. The old man's child was in a car accident in Arusha, he was hit by a car. But the old man couldn't go to Arusha by himself to see his child because he doesn't speak the language. He had to ask the young man to go with him. To take him to see his child in the hospital in Arusha. But if it was the young man's child, he could go alone." "Or let's say," he continued, "you need to go to the Arusha Regional Office, or the district commissioner in Simanjiro—these days he is an Mgogo and doesn't know the Maasai language. Or the regional officer, he's a Chagga, he doesn't know Maa." "The first thing we need in Maasailand," he concluded, "is education, then we can work on the other things." And both girls and boys should be educated: "We need male and female teachers, nurses."

Other development needs included health services and water. "Without water, Maasai won't stay here one day. They will rove around, here, here and here. But if they have water, enough boreholes, some good rangeland for their livestock, eh?" But there were still major obstacles, especially "our poverty, the government's poverty. Even if we find the money, the donors don't ever consult people in designing the projects. Or the project starts, but there is still a major part left to do, and suddenly—the money is gone! We wait for more money. But, surprise, all of the money was received, but it was stolen on route, so only a bit dribbles down to the people."

Thomas also had thoughts about the relationship between development and culture. "Every group has its customs and traditions. There are good customs and bad customs, good traditions and bad traditions. So if a group like Maasai are taught to use the good parts of their past culture. . . . Like those who are Christians, they gave up a big part of their culture because the church taught them." He described how most had given up polygyny, seeking help from *iloibonok*, beliefs in curses, and "other parts of their culture which have no meaning in the church. They weren't forced to give them up, but were educated, see?" For Thomas, there were many "good" customs that Maasai should continue. Men's age-sets, for example, where men worked together to help each other with their needs and problems, such as food, conversation, lodging, and marriage. Similarly, he thought the celebrations after women gave birth were a good custom, when family and neighbors gathered, animals were slaughtered, and the birth was honored. "It is cooperation and unity, sharing the happiness of one with everyone present." A woman's post-childbirth confinement for several months was also good, because "she rested and was well-fed so that she could regain her strength." Another celebration took place on the day she left confinement, and then others as the child matured into an adult. "There are many good customs that should continue. They don't prevent a person from participating in development of any kind. And even if they are church members, they don't conflict with church practices. There are various rituals which are just things to make people happy."

Farming these days was a necessity for most Maasai to survive. "In the past, everything was fine, we had plenty of cattle." He recalls that Maasai began farming in the late 1940s. But these days, "almost every Maasai is farming." "In the past," he explained, "they had cattle to sell to buy sugar and maize. These days they don't have any cattle. And those that do have only a few. Not enough to sell to feed and clothe their children. Many farm these days, four, five, even ten acres. If it rains they get enough to feed their families. Almost everyone farms these days." He always cultivated at least a small garden wherever he lived and now farms about five acres. "If things went well, enough rain and such, I could get enough maize and beans to feed us for a year." We had an interesting discussion about farming and other economic activities:

D: How did the Maasai learn to farm, since they were herders?

T: They learned by watching other people, by watching other people.

D: So did the government agents help them?

T: [chuckling] With words. We bring government extension agents to the village, but they don't go out and educate and explain how to farm. They do their own business. If they come here, the first thing they usually seek is a place to farm themselves! [laughter]

D: So what do you think about Maasai farming? Does it destroy their culture or merely change things? You know when white people (*wazungu*) come, they say [in tones of surprised disapproval], "Oh no, the Maasai are farming, oh my goodness!"

T: I don't see it as destroying our culture because first, we Maasai are not wealthy in cattle. Second, even if we don't farm, others will farm and finish our land. It is better that we farm, even if we don't farm all of the land, but farm a bit. We can put a homestead here now and farm later. Third, it helps. If you grow food at home, you don't have to buy maize and other food elsewhere. Or in a long drought like this, you have to sell four or five cattle to buy food, clothing, pay taxes, contributions to government (which are many!), etc. It is all very expensive. But if you have food, you can reduce the number of cattle you have to sell for all this. . . . Most people have very few cattle, *very* few. You will meet an old man with three or four wives who has only five cattle, or a woman who has no cattle, they've all died.

D: So many Maasai have taken to farming. Can you think of other economic avenues that could help Maasai survive?

T: There are many economic opportunities, if the ability is there. There are businesses . . . many Maasai work in the cattle business. Say they buy cattle at Terrat [a nearby market town] for, say, 50,000 shillings, and sell them elsewhere for 100,000 or 200,000 shillings, like that. Many are smart. Buy several cattle, keep some, sell the others. And other kinds of business. Some Maasai have started small stores in places like Terrat or even here. Otherwise there are the cooperatives that the government is urging Maasai to join—for grinding machines, cement factories, crafts. These haven't gotten very far in Maasailand. But other businesses like cattle or smallstock trade are good, even people who haven't gone to school can do them.

D: Are these mainly for men, or can women do some of these businesses?

T: Even women can run these stores. In many places, women have come together to run small stores. There is a woman's store in Terrat, run by Maasai women.

After two long days of interviews, Thomas and I were both tired and ready to quit. Just then, the pilot of the Flying Medical Service airplane buzzed Thomas's house to signal that the health clinics were over and that he was ready to land and take me back to Arusha. But I had one last question for Thomas. "So, if you think about your life," I asked, "what would you like for your children to learn from you or to remember about you?" Thomas replied as follows:

I have lived and worked for a long time. And I know God has helped because I haven't had any major problems in work, habits, laziness or negligence when I worked for the government and mission, until I retired. Even though the quality (*hali*) of my life wasn't very good. You know, life can be difficult. But the work I did, I did well. I would like for my children to copy the life I have lived. If they work, they live the life of work, even though some won't work. To try to be self-sufficient. And maybe to reduce wanting to have many wives and many children, like we did. I mean, life in these days, for a person to have ten children like I do, they will find it impossible to live. Life has become very difficult. Thus, I want them just to copy the way I have lived. I would be very happy if my children all found work—either as employees or for themselves— and used their education well. That is all.

POLITICS OF THE
POSTCOLONIAL PERIPHERY:
GENDER, ETHNICITY, AND
CITIZENSHIP

4

At Independence, development became the legitimating project of the post-colonial nation-state in Tanzania; the African elites who took power embraced the modernist narrative and its agenda of progress. For them, "the Maasai" represented all they had tried to leave behind, persistent icons of "the primitive," "the savage," "the past." For years, most thought of Maasai as an embarrassment better obscured from view. When they did appear, such as in the occasional newspaper article, they were one of the very few groups always identified by their ethnicity—this "Maasai" woman, rather than just this woman, or Ndugu. Photographs of "the Maasai" almost always accompanied the article, and it was de rigueur for a visiting politician to have his photo taken with some "traditional Maasai." Elite Africans, who were intent on integrating the people of Tanzania into a socialist nation by forging links of language, infrastructure, and a sense of national identity translated the former racialized distinctiveness of Maasai into a heightened sense of ethnic difference marked by pronounced cultural and visual signifiers.

Except for their photo opportunities, Maasai were generally out of sight and out of mind. Mocked by the elites as "primitive," accused of "cultural conservatism," and excluded from most state-sponsored development initiatives, Maasai have become increasingly impoverished as their land, livestock, and possibilities for viable livelihoods continue to disappear. Most state resources have been directed to other areas and to people perceived as more "progressive," easier to reach and work with, eager for development. During interviews with me, state officials repeatedly said, "The Maasai don't want development" or "Change? What change? They've never changed!" Most were surprised that I could ever have conceived of such a silly research project. And when development initiatives such as the huge multimillion-dollar USAID Masai Livestock Development and Range Management Project (Chapter 5) have been implemented, their objectives have paralleled the ambivalent goals

of many colonial projects: to leave Maasai culture intact while trying to develop their livestock industry for the benefit of the state.

The dislike and embarrassment of some non-Maasai for what they saw as
the "primitive" habits of Maasai peaked in the late 1960s when they used their
access to state power to wage a campaign to enforce a "modern" dress code
among Maasai. Earlier, a ban had been placed on the mining of red ochre,
used by men and women on their bodies and by *ilmurran* in their hair. Maasai
women still wore beaded leather skirts and capes, while elder men wore blankets and *ilmurran* wore a short robe-like cloth and little else. According to
Hatfield, Maasai and Arusha were periodically warned "that they must wear
proper attire in town or suffer the consequences" (Hatfield 1977b: 16). However, the dress code was only sporadically and unevenly enforced.

But in 1968, government authorities in Arusha Region began a fierce
campaign to change Maasai appearance. They decreed that old men were not
supposed to wear blankets in the daytime, nobody was to wear cloth treated
with ochre, women were to abandon their leather dresses (since they could
not be washed), and *ilmurran* were to abandon their pigtails and treatment
of their hair with red ochre. To ensure compliance, in 1970 bus drivers were
directed to reject passengers who did not comply with the regulations (Ndagala 1990: 47), and "no man or woman was allowed to use a public facility—
shop, bus, dispensary, government office, etc.—unless he or she were wearing
contemporary attire: shorts, trousers, dresses" (Hatfield 1977b: 16). The government, as Hatfield notes, would "make the Masai modern by making them
appear modern" (Hatfield 1977b: 16).

Many Maasai complied with the state campaign by withdrawing from
cities and towns. Elder men met with the regional authorities to complain
about the measures, arguing, for example, that Maasai used ochre to prevent
the spread of lice. But Maasai women expressed their anger directly, cursing
the elite Maasai they saw as complicit in the campaign:

> At Kijungu where the ban was proclaimed, a large group of women from all over
> the South got together to curse the Masai leader of the community, who was also
> Chairman of the Ranching Association. Then they began collecting money for
> an en masse trip to Dar es Salaam to present their complaints to the president.
> The curse was eventually removed by a judicious slaughtering of a number of
> cattle and the women persuaded not to make the trip to Dar. In the North, the
> national parliamentarian [Sokoine] was also cursed. (Hatfield 1977b: 16)

The dress code campaign was soon officially dropped after national criticism,
but the picture of a Maasai *olmurrani* looking after cattle on the Tshs 100/=
notes (popularly called "Maasai") was replaced by a scene of a wheat field

(Ndagala 1990: 47; Knowles and Collett 1989). But the disrespect shown by the government and the hostility of non-Maasai townspeople were not quickly forgotten by many Maasai. Jacobs, for example, reported that in 1977 "*fewer* numbers of either men or women were seen at rural trading centers or in and around urban centers, such as Arusha or Monduli, as compared to 20 years ago" (Jacobs 1978: 12).

But nowadays, as tourism has become an increasingly important source of revenue for the "development" of the Tanzanian nation-state, state officials have put Maasai back into view: to attract tourists, state officials promote "the Maasai" as icons of "traditional," "primitive" Africa through travel brochures and guides, postcards, postage stamps, and other visual and written media (cf. Bruner and Kirshenblatt-Gimblett 1994). The attentive gaze of the tourists has its repercussions for Maasai development, however—the few state-sponsored development initiatives have almost dried up, for fear of marring the "authentic" persona and landscape which captivate tourists and capture their foreign exchange. Simultaneously, however, with increasing First World concerns about ecological "crises" and environmental "sustainability," increasing NGO attention and resources have been directed at sustaining "pastoralists" and "pastoralism" as viable livelihoods. These attempts are marked by the recent plethora of workshops and conferences devoted to exploring the "special" needs and problems of "pastoralist development" and charting the future of "pastoralist" peoples. Maasai themselves have begun to use these images of cultural authenticity to their own advantage, linking current efforts to protect their lands and livelihoods and access development resources to global campaigns for the rights of "indigenous" peoples.

Two recent photos illustrate how representations of Maasai are still used as icons of tradition: the first shows a man in a baseball cap and jacket holding a set of earphones over the ears of a smiling Maasai boy who is dressed in the black cloth, white face paint, and bird-feather headdress of the newly circumcised. The copy reads: "'Sounds great, Ndugu Minister.' This is what this Masai young man seems to be telling Health Minister Philemon Sarungi after hearing stereo music through earphones from the Minister's cassette recorder in Loliondo District this week."[1] The second photo is titled "Blend of Tradition," and shows a woman holding a young boy's hand, walking away from the camera. "What a beautiful contrast!" the caption exclaims. "A Masai traditional wrap blending with *khanga* against shirt, short, trouser and shoes put on by the Masai boy. This Masai mother was apparently visiting a sick relative at the Muhimbili Medical Centre when photographer Seleman Mpochi caught this rare scene."[2] The contrasts the photos are supposed to evoke, between the "modern" Health Minister sharing his "modern" toy with the naive/primitive/duly impressed Maasai boy; and the differences in dress (does one read futures?) in the "traditional" mother and her "modern" son smugly remind all Tanzanian readers of this daily English newspaper—necessarily an educated elite—of their modernity.

In this chapter, I explore the contemporary relationship of "the Maasai" and the Tanzanian state, especially its ethnic and gender dimensions, through the experiences of three communities. In addition to conversations, events, and encounters witnessed while living and working in the areas, I draw on two primary sources of information: a socioeconomic census of all individuals and households taken in 1992 and semi-structured interviews with 150 adult men and women of different generations. My purpose is to show how the legacies of colonial interventions continue to shape images of "the Maasai," "development" interventions, and the administrative, land tenure, and political policies and practices of the nation-state. Moreover, the opinions and perspectives of community members suggest that debates among Maasai and between Maasai and the state over the meaning of "progress" and "prosperity" persist, echoing similar debates in the colonial period. The detailed historical, economic, and social information about the three communities also provides important background information for the following chapters.

From Ujamaa to Structural Adjustment: State Developments, 1961–1993

Socialist Development

Soon after Julius Nyerere was elected president of Tanganyika[3] in 1962, he began preaching and teaching about his radical vision for a socialist policy of "development" designed to meet the unique needs and desires of Africans, particularly Tanzanians. He synthesized his ideas and formally presented them as state policy in the famous Arusha Declaration on February 5, 1967. His policy of Ujamaa, or African socialist development, with many elaborations and revisions, remained the guiding vision of his administration until his resignation in 1985, when Ali Hassan Mwinyi, then president of Zanzibar, replaced him as president of Tanzania.

Briefly, Ujamaa, a Swahili word meaning unity, cooperation, "familyhood," was premised on Nyerere's idealized representation of "traditional African society," especially the African extended family, as it functioned (supposedly) in pre-colonial Africa. In that golden age before exploitation and domination, the means of production were communally owned and everyone who was able "contributed his fair share to the production of wealth" and distributed part of the fruits of their labor to those less able or fortunate. Wealth was shared, everyone was secure, and hospitality was universal:

> Even the Elder, who appeared to be enjoying himself without doing any work and for whom everybody else appeared to be working, had, in fact, worked hard all his younger days. The wealth he now appeared to possess was not *his*, personally; it was only "his" as the Elder of the group which had produced it. He was its guardian. The wealth itself gave him neither power nor prestige. The respect paid to him by the young was his because he was older than they, and had served his community longer; and the "poor" Elder enjoyed as much respect in our society as the "rich" Elder. (Nyerere 1968: 4–5)

Neither "the capitalist," "the landed exploiter," or "the loiter or idler" was known to "traditional African society": "In our traditional African society we were individuals within a community. We took care of the community, and the community took care of us. We neither needed nor wished to exploit our fellow men."[4]

Ujamaa was formulated as a direct rejection of the elements of "feudalism" and "capitalism" which colonial rule had introduced and nurtured, including class stratification, exploitation, individual ownership of land and other resources, and private or corporate ownership of the major means of production and exchange. As such, the Arusha Declaration called for the restructuring of Tanzania as a socialist state based on a list of socialist principles. These included the rights of individuals to equality, dignity, and respect; the rights of citizens to freedom of expression, movement, religious belief, and association; ownership of all the natural resources of the country by its citizens; state control over the principal means of production; and the

> responsibility of the state to intervene actively in the economic life of the nation so as to ensure the well-being of all citizens, and so as to prevent the exploitation of one person by another or one group by another, and so as to prevent the accumulation of wealth to an extent which is inconsistent with the existence of a classless society.[5]

The declaration included a strong critique of external aid, whatever its form, and called for Tanzanians to reject such offerings and be "self-reliant" in working toward their development goals. Money, particularly the belief that more money would bring more development and solve people's problems, was in fact the problem itself:

It is stupid to rely on money as the major instrument of development when we know only too well that our country is poor. It is equally stupid, indeed it is even more stupid, for us to imagine that we shall rid ourselves of our poverty through foreign financial assistance rather than our own financial resources.[6]

According to the philosophy of Ujamaa, people, not money, were the basis of development.

Given the lofty ideals of this seemingly alternative vision of development, it is ironic that the main objective of Ujamaa was the same objective which guided capitalist development policies in the later colonial period: increased productivity in agriculture and animal husbandry. "This is in fact the only road through which we can develop our country—in other words, only by increasing our production of these things can we get more food and more money for every Tanzanian."[7] Tanzania's prosperity lay in increasing its agricultural productivity rather than industrialization. And the conditions for increased productivity, and therefore development, were hard work, the best use of the land in the interest of the nation rather than in the interest of an individual or group, and provision of tools and training in "modern methods" of agriculture.

With its broad vision and sweeping statements, Ujamaa was open to many interpretations as policy was translated into practice. The government consolidated its power by nationalizing many businesses and industries. It formed parastatals (government-owned corporations) to purchase and distribute agricultural produce while forcing farmers to create cooperatives through which to organize their labor and sell their produce. Eventually, in the early 1970s, many rural Tanzanians were resettled from their often scattered homesteads into Ujamaa villages (called Operation Imparnati, Operation Embarnat, or Operation Maasai in Masai District). This "villagization" program was designed to facilitate the provision of government services (such as education, health, and extension work) as well as government control by grouping people in neat, bounded clusters. Villages became the key "unit of development" (see, e.g., Mwapachu 1979; von Freyhold 1979; Scott 1998). Efforts to forge a sense of national identity that superseded ethnic affiliations included the promotion of Swahili as the national language, the nationalization of schools, and the promotion of a standard "Tanzanian" curriculum; the imposition of standardized political and judicial structures; and constant pronouncements in the media (radio and newspapers) about Ujamaa's rationale, goals, and successes (cf. Anderson 1991).

Although Ujamaa claimed to be in part about decentralizing decision-making, control, and funding for economic development to villages, it actually concentrated development interventions in the hands of the state.[8] As a result, the government bureaucracy expanded exponentially to fill the numerous parastatal, administrative, and "management" and "planning" positions created. Layers upon layers of committees were created to plan, approve, implement, and supervise village development projects, so each project had to wend its way through these assorted local, district, regional, and sometimes national committees. Village leaders had to learn the necessary rhetoric and skills to write project proposals and reports, including such concepts as goals, project rationales, impact, evaluation measures, and budgets (as well as how to use typewriters and carbon copies!). Quantification was central to the design, acceptance, and evaluation of many of the village projects: how many people, animals, acres per person, and so forth were needed or would be affected?

Despite these extensive planning and reporting procedures, village development, especially in terms of economic productivity, failed. Agricultural and industrial production declined, while Tanzania's dependence on foreign aid in the form of grants and loans increased. A two-tiered society developed as many urban educated elites used their mid- to upper-level government positions to access government resources; while farmers worked even harder just to maintain their previous production levels under the stifling and inefficient constraints of the parastatals. During this period, Tanzania actually became more dependent on external financing by international donor agencies rather than less so; it relied more heavily on producing for the export market and sank deeper and deeper in debt. In the late 1970s and early 1980s, Tanzania's entry into the war against Idi Amin in Uganda (at a cost of over $500 million [Meena 1991: 169]), the fall of the price of coffee and other export commodities, prolonged drought, rising oil prices, and the breakup of the East African Community only further aggravated the nation's precarious economic position (Meena 1991; TGNP 1994). As the members of the Tanzania Gender Networking Programme (TGNP) reported, "The resulting crisis in foreign exchange led to an acute shortage of goods and services during the early 1980s, and the escalation of corruption and nepotism in government and private circles. There was a drastic reduction in real incomes in all sectors, and a shocking drop in the standard of living of most Tanzanians" (TGNP 1994: 45).[9]

When I first arrived in Tanzania in March 1985, I remember walking through the streets of Arusha gazing at the empty shelves in the closed stores. Most manufactured "necessities" such as cooking oil, sugar, flour, and even diesel were rationed, and "black market" sales of "illegally" imported commodities were thriving. Restrictions on the possession of foreign currency by citizens and expatriate residents as well as government-imposed caps on the exchange rate produced a vigorous parallel market in foreign exchange, with rates often ten times the official rate offered by the government-owned bank. In fact, I thought that "change" instead of "*jambo*" was the proper greeting since that was what almost every young man said to me as I passed him on the street.[10] In contrast to the dearth of manufactured products, primary goods such as fresh vegetables, dried maize, beans, and other staples were available at the large, bustling central produce market. In the rural areas of Arusha Region the stores were also empty, except for high-priced dry goods and the government breweries' beer and gin in the local bars. People spoke in envious tones about the economic progress and array of goods available in neighboring Kenya.

By November 1993, when I left Tanzania after a two-year stint of field-work, Arusha was a bustling urban center, its stores filled with a broad range of commodities from peanut butter and Coca-Cola to apples and white wine imported from South Africa. Several delis, numerous restaurants (including a pizzeria), and more than one ice cream parlor prospered, while the construction of new buildings and hotels and the repainting and remodeling of the exteriors and interiors of older businesses continued apace. The local produce market was overflowing with goods, including special *mzungu* (SW: a white person, a European) vegetables such as watermelon, broccoli, and zucchini. In rural areas, however, the rapidly escalating producer and consumer prices for basic foodstuffs such as maize and beans benefited large-scale wealthy farmers with surplus to sell and capital to survive on during bad seasons but undermined the ability of many rural households to purchase food to supplement their consumption when their harvests failed to meet their needs. In the 1990s, rural stores displayed an assortment of goods—batteries, tinned margarine, plastic combs, cigarettes, candy, flashlights, cookies—beyond the usual beans, flour, rice, sugar, cooking oil, and kerosene. Men spoke disapprovingly about Kenya's oppressive political situation, including government-sponsored violence and widespread fear.

So what happened in the interim? In the early 1980s, international donors took advantage of Tanzania's precarious financial position to reduce their aid in order to pressure the Tanzanian government to accept the Structural Adjustment Program (SAP) of the World Bank/International Monetary Fund. Despite prolonged negotiations, President Nyerere balked at the harsh conditions, but Ali Hassan Mwinyi, who was elected president in 1985, signed a SAP agreement in 1986. The SAP has restructured the Tanzanian economy, but it has also intensified inequalities of gender, class, and ethnicity.

Capitalist Development

The Structural Adjustment Program, or SAP, refers to a set of stabilization and adjustment measures promoted by the World Bank and the IMF since the mid-1980s as the ideal development strategy for developing countries in the Third World. TGNP ably summarizes the broad objectives of structural adjustment:

> The aim is to create a conducive environment for investment and economic growth, by increasing efficiency in allocation of resources, an increase in productivity and output—especially for export, improved balance of payments and a reduction of inflation. . . . The emphasis is on "getting the price right" in order to send the right signals to producers, traders, government officials, workers, parents about what their priorities should be. The prices they refer to include money/currency values, prices of food, of crops, of imported goods in comparison to exports. (TGNP 1994: 46)

Stabilization measures, involving the International Monetary Fund (IMF), refer to financial reforms, including

> devaluation, privatization of banks and/or a mixed approach, liberalization of trade in currency exchange and commodities, budget reform and cuts, withdrawal of subsidies for producers and consumers, abolition of exchange price and wage controls, a credit squeeze, including increased interest rates. (TGNP 1994: 47)

Adjustment measures, involving the World Bank, refer to institutional reforms, including

> promoting export production, reform of industrial and agricultural policies so as to increase efficiency and output, and increase in the role of the private sector, including TNCs [transnational corporations] in production and in social services (reproduction); appropriate tax and tariff structures; appropriate programmes in social services combined with a reduction in the role of the central government, and a shift in responsibility to local governments, families and individuals. (TGNP 1994: 47)

The implicit objective of the SAP, in other words, was to restructure the economies and institutions of developing countries according to free-market principles of competition and privatization, making possible increased investments, resource extraction, and exploitation by multinational corporations. Within the state, the demand to shift resources and investment from "nonproductive" to "productive" sectors of the economy and regions of the country has exacerbated inequalities of class, gender, and ethnicity.

The consequences of the implementation of SAP measures in Tanzania have been generally negative for all but the wealthiest sectors of the population, but they have been especially detrimental to the economic status and social welfare of poor rural women. As Meena (1991) documents, devaluation led to the erosion of real wages of both urban and rural workers, forcing women, as the "'shock absorbers' of socioeconomic crises," to engage in some form of informal activity to subsidize household income.[11] Supposedly gender-neutral policies such as the abolition of price controls to increase farmers' incentives to produce have undermined women's access to land, increased their workload (since, unlike men, they rarely have access to labor-saving technologies such as ox plows, tractors, or even chemical weeders and pesticides), decreased their income (since men tend to retain income from cash crops), and destabilized household food security as farmers shift their land and labor from producing food crops to producing export crops (Meena 1991: 171–175). For the wealthy, however, the flood of imported goods and services, even at exorbitant prices, made possible a much more comfortable, even ostentatious, life. A few citizens and non-citizens have become extremely wealthy from the liberalization of trade, the privatization of businesses and foreign exchange transactions, the encouragement of foreign investment, and other new transnational business opportunities.

In conclusion, first Ujamaa, then structural adjustment, as political and economic visions of the Tanzanian nation, have broadly shaped the "development" agendas and administrative interventions of the nation-state. As in the colonial period, the policies and practices of "development," land tenure, and administrative control have been tightly intertwined but unevenly applied. The remainder of this chapter examines the relationship between Maasai and the state within the shifting paradigms of Ujamaa and structural adjustment through the experiences of the three communities in which I did fieldwork. Here I focus on the ethnic, spatial, socioeconomic, and political aspects of the relationship, while Chapter 5 explores the key "development" interventions during this period and their gendered implementation and effects.

Developing "Villages," Studying "Villages"

Law of the Land

For many anthropologists working in rural areas, the "village" remains an ideal category of study. Its neat, congruent territorial and political boundaries are presumed to enclose a self-contained group of people whose means of subsistence and production are also contained within village borders. Those who regularly cross the village boundaries to labor outside its bounds are labeled "migrants" and may or may not be included within the anthropological gaze. In Tanzania, as in many other nation-states, the "village" is one of the smallest-scale components of a historically created hierarchical grid of political institutions, each with its appropriate leaders who mediate between the levels of the administrative apparatus.

At Independence, Masai District was still administered from Monduli, although it was divided into Loliondo and Monduli Divisions, each with its own administrative and local councils. These divisions remained for over a decade, but in 1974, as part of the big push for "villagization" the government gradually divided Masai District into smaller, more controllable units and sub-units: Masai District was split into Monduli and Kiteto Districts in 1974, then Ngorongoro District was formed from part of Monduli District in 1979.[12]

Within these "Maasai" districts, the question of the kind of political sub-unit which was appropriate for the development and land use needs of pastoralists was hotly contested for over a decade. By 1975, three laws regulated the use of land in these areas: the 1964 Range Management and Development Act, the 1974 National Wildlife Conservation Act, and the 1975 National Villages and Ujamaa Villages Act.[13] The diverse rationales behind these acts reflected contradictory discourses about "the Maasai" as "pastoralists," especially with regard to their relationship to land and their future development. Not surprisingly, therefore, they produced confusion and conflicting outcomes, as illustrated by the changing boundaries and categories that eventually produced the three "villages" in which I did ethnographic research.

Although residential areas of the three villages were distinguished by different place names—Monduli Juu for the mountaintop, Mfereji for the Rift Valley area, Ardai for the southern plains—these names did not refer to distinct political units. The residents of the area considered themselves to be part of a broader territory called "Kisongo" that was governed by explicit networks of residential and clan rights to grazing, water, salt, and other resources within their territory (cf. Homewood and Rodgers 1991; Potanski 1994). Each clan had primary use of certain dry- and wet-season grazing lands as well as water sources, and elders decided when and where herds would graze and water. But a clan's control was not exclusive; livestock from another clan could be watered and fed once permission was requested and granted (almost always) by the clan elders. Failure by a clan member or non-member to abide by their decisions, however, resulted in heavy fines. Much of the Monduli Juu mountaintop was reserved, by general agreement of the area elders, as dry-season grazing grounds, to be used only when other grazing areas were depleted (and even then only with the permission of the elders). Access to Maasai-developed water sources (such as the improved springs in Emairete Crater) was regulated by clan membership, while the dams, pipelines and other water projects built by the government were available to everyone.

But the 1964 Range Management and Development Act (the Range Act) restructured these territorial relationships and disrupted the regulation of access to resources by clans and male elders. Based on the recommendations of a USAID-financed research study, the Range Act was designed to facilitate and encourage the formation of "ranching associations" among pastoralists. The assumptions and objectives of the Range Act evinced a clear scenario of Maasai development according to the precepts of Ujamaa: ranching associations were designed to organize Maasai and other pastoralists into communal, cooperative ranches whose members worked together to design land use plans, finance water projects and other infrastructural improvements and thereby increase their "productivity" of beef cattle. The newly created Masai Commission demarcated several areas in Masai District as suitable for group ranching, then solicited (male) residents to register as association members, promising 99-year leasehold rights, water supplies, and dips as incentives. Ranching associations became the preferred unit of development for "pastoralists" and the cornerstone of the ten-year USAID Maasai Range Project (the project is discussed in detail in Chapter 5). The ranching associations undermined the customary measures of land and resource regulation in two ways: by failing to demarcate land according to Maasai territorial boundaries and by undercutting the authority of the elders in regulating land use by replacing them with an alternative power structure of elected ranch authorities.

The ensuing debates between government officials and Maasai residents over the terms of the Range Act, especially restrictions on cultivation, illustrate the tensions between their contradictory visions of Maasai futures. After the 1961–1962 drought, Maasai who had not farmed before began farming small plots of maize to supplement their household food needs and diversify their productive base, while others who had been farming requested new plots. But these practices clearly contravened government policy: "The policy of developing Masailand as a cattle grazing area through the implementation of the Range Development Plan is the official Government policy at all levels. *The expansion of arable cultivation in Masailand is contrary to this policy.*"[14] Government officials at various levels tried to convince the Masai Council to accept this policy and quit farming, but the Council refused:

> While accepting the fundamentals of the project [the Range Act], the Councillors expressed some fears and doubts. They expressed the desire that Masailand should primarily be a cattle-raising district, but insisted openly that some cultivation should be practiced in suitable areas to avoid the dangers of a one-sided economy. The practice of such cultivation would safeguard the inhabitants from such catastrophes as the 1961/62 famine. If mixed farming could be put into practice in suitable areas then this would probably take care of this problem.[15]

The Council also objected that "people should not be completely 'pinned down' as some areas which get very little rainfall will be almost impossible to live in without having to move away from them at certain times of the year."[16] In Simanjiro, elders also insisted that "it would not do for one part of Masailand to be under one set of laws while a neighboring area was not."[17] Despite pressure from the regional government to accept the proposals and prohibitions immediately, councilors insisted on discussing matters with their constituencies. The range management officer, among others, was outraged at the Council's position: "The foolish contention that the Masai must cultivate in order to avoid a repetition of the ravages of 1961–62 has not the remotest contention with reality, and seems to have been propagated by those ill-informed persons who equate progress with the use of the *jembe* [hoe]."[18] After much debate, a compromise was reached whereby Maasai who wished to cultivate had to request and receive permission from the government. Long lists of names from Loliondo, Monduli Juu, and elsewhere were submitted of those Maasai (men) who were cultivating or who wished to cultivate.[19] Stunned by the numbers, the Masai Council subsequently formally disapproved the implementation of the Range Act schemes for "fear that Masai will be prohibited from cultivating under the scheme."[20] The regional commissioner tersely replied that the Range Act was enacted by Parliament "for the interest of the nation and more particularly for the good of the local inhabitants." It was being implemented as planned, a Range Development Commission was being formed, and it was up to the executive officer of the Masai Council to ensure compliance with the plan. "Do your part," was his closing remark.[21]

One of the first associations demarcated in the mid-1960s was the Komolonik Ranching Association, comprised of the three research localities (Monduli Juu, Ardai, and Mfereji). To convince Maasai of its good intentions, the government financed the construction of several water projects in Komolonik, including a sixteen-mile gravity pipeline for Mfereji, another two-mile pipeline, and several dams and shallow wells. The ten-year USAID project made ranching associations central to its development plans, and Komolonik became one of its two priority ranches. The project built dips, distributed improved bulls, began an artificial insemination program, started a demonstration ranch in Ardai, and eventually began a milk-collecting project in Emai-rete. Most Maasai members made use of the structures and facilities provided by the project, but few complied with the regulations about offtake or felt responsible for the maintenance or repair of what they perceived as government property.

Ongoing debate between the USAID and the Tanzanian government over whether Maasai and other "pastoralists" should live in ranching associations or villages was silenced in 1974 with the passage of the National Villages and Ujamaa Villages Act. Despite pressure from the USAID and administrators of the Maasai Range Project, all Tanzanian citizens, including Maasai, were to live in Ujamaa villages, *not* ranching associations (Jacobs 1980: 8). Under the law, Maasai were forced to resettle into registered villages as part of "Operation Imparnati" (*imparnati* is Maa for "permanent settlement"), radically disrupting territorial and authority relationships once again.

According to Ndagala (1982), rumors about the government's "real" intentions in implementing Operation Imparnati spread throughout Maasai areas:

> At several meetings, for example, the pastoralists claimed that they had heard that the resettlement programme [was] aimed at taking over their personal land and handing it to cultivators. . . . In some areas people believed that "the government wanted all the people to be *wajamaa* by force since persuasion had given little results." And to some, ujamaa meant the sharing of everything including wives and children. (Ndagala 1982: 29)

Seminars were held with regional and district leaders to explain the campaign, stress the need for adequate preparations, and prepare them to hold seminars "to educate the people on the significance of living together in permanent settlements." But ultimately, implementation of the villagization campaign depended on the styles and temperaments of the district and sub-district leaders. For Maasai, Ndagala reports that

> the *boma* [homestead] . . . was adopted as the basic settlement unit, and each could have as many as ten families. Individuals were free to choose the people with whom they wanted to share bomas. Members of each boma-grouping were allocated a plot on which to construct the boma, and were required to complete the construction of its houses as soon as was considered appropriate by the implementation teams. The interval between bomas was to be 1/2 a kilometre with the exception of a few localities in which the bomas could be situated closer to each other. (Ndagala 1982: 30)

The Komolonik Ranching Association was abolished, and members were divided and moved into the new Ujamaa villages of Monduli Juu, Mfereji, Lendikenya, and Arkatan.

Simultaneously, the Conservation Act of 1974 continued the alienation of Maasai lands in the interest of "preserving" wildlife (and promoting tourism) by removing large areas of grazing land in the Serengeti, Ngorongoro, and Tarangire National Parks from use by Maasai herders. The act not only removed land and power from Maasai; it also shifted authority for the future "development planning" of these areas from the Masai District Council to the National Parks (Jacobs 1980: 8).

Finally, the government took advantage of the breaches and dislocations caused by these political restructurings to continue to alienate the remaining fertile lands. In the 1970s, some of the best grazing lands in Ardai were taken by the government to build the training camp that was to eventually become the officer's college for the national army (cf. Jacobs 1978: 6; 1980: 2). A 1971 report documented large-scale cultivation in the Kisongo area by several European and Asian farmers, including 400 acres of wheat in Lendikenya (1 plot), 470 acres of beans in Essimingor (4 plots), and almost 5,000 acres in Monduli Juu (5 plots, "officially" listed as farming 2,400 acres) (Van Voorthuizen ca. 1971). One thousand acres of "unused" land in Emairete was allocated to the Tanzania Beer Company (now Tanzania Breweries) to grow barley and another 1,400 acres to Tanzania Cartons, with the argument that since Emairete was a "grazing" village and few people farmed, the land could be put to more productive uses. In reply to an angry letter by Edward Sokoine, then a Maasai Member of Parliament, about such alienations, one official even contended that "the experts said that if the land wasn't farmed this year it would be ruined."[22]

These laws and practices clearly revealed the development priorities of the government vis-à-vis Maasai livelihoods and Maasai lands. The government felt that certain areas would be better used to "preserve" wildlife and promote tourism (in the process attracting lucrative investments by international conservation organizations such as the Frankfurt Zoological Society and the World Wildlife Fund to "preserve" the land and animals and sponsor numerous expensive research projects [cf. Bonner 1993]). The remaining lands which were not alienated to cultivators could be used by Maasai, but they had to be used in "more productive" ways: Maasai had to reorganize themselves and "improve" their animal husbandry practices in order to increase their productivity and contribute more cattle for the good of the nation.

And so "villages" are products of the Tanzanian government's pursuit of greater administrative control in the name of "development" and have been the cornerstone of the government's administrative and development policies and practices under both Ujamaa and, later, structural adjustment (cf. Pigg

1992). Up to the early 1990s, every ten families had their own leader, or *balozi*, who served on the village council and communicated government orders and directives to his (usually the *balozi* was male) constituents. Representatives of village councils served on the district councils, reporting to regional administrators who interacted with the central government's ministries and departments in Dar es Salaam. The following are brief descriptions of my research "villages" as of the 1990s.

Emairete

Emairete is a village which used to be part of the entire Monduli Juu Village (comprised of Emairete, Enguiki, and Eluwai localities). In early 1992 Emairete/Eluwai established themselves as a separate village, although the boundaries of the villages were still in dispute until mid-1993. Eluwai was regarded by most area residents as a distinct community, with its own school and dispensary and a Lutheran church, but the government still considered it to be part of Emairete village. Residents of Eluwai were not included in my study; instead, my fieldwork covered almost every *enkang'* (except for two remote homesteads) considered by area residents to be part of the Emairete locality.[23] By "Emairete," therefore, I am referring to the Emairete section of Emairete village.

Until 1975, residents of Emairete were settled on the tops of the ridges and hills surrounding a large caldera, or crater. Several older residents still recall the day in 1975 when, without prior notice, government lorries and administrators appeared to implement "Operation Imparnati." The administrators demanded that people take their belongings out of their houses, then used the lorries to run over and demolish the buildings. People and their belongings were loaded onto the lorries, which dumped them in their allocated spots along the crater wall. As women scrambled to construct temporary shelters of hides and poles for the evening, the administrators told the men that they had to build their new homesteads in the designated areas.[24] "The government," one elder man told me bitterly, "just came and tore down our houses. We had no notice and received no compensation."

Emairete is located between 1,800 and 1,860 meters on the upper slopes of Komolonik Mountain, receives good but erratic rainfall, and has adequate land for both grazing and cultivation. Most residents live on the walls of the large crater, grazing their cattle and smallstock on the crater floor and farming on top of the crater and on the floor and slopes of the crater valleys. Fuelwood is available nearby, but water for domestic use is an ongoing problem. During

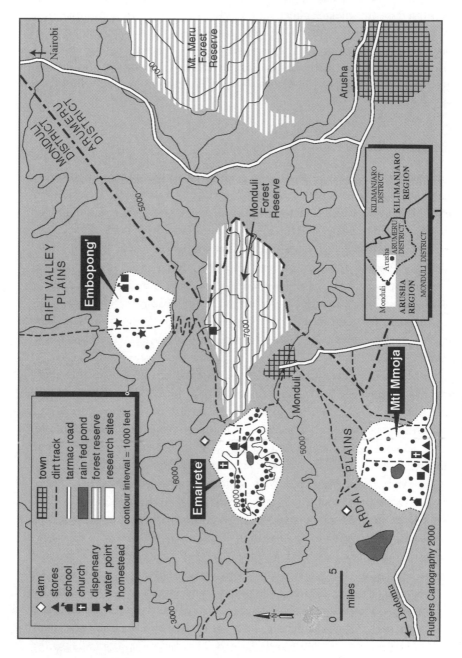

Map 4.1 Research communities (Emairete, Mti Mmoja, Embopong'), ca. 1993

the rainy season, a large seasonal rain pond in the crater and the clan-controlled water holes fill up, but they quickly dry up during the dry season. Women skim the sludge for water or walk with donkeys to the Monduli town spring ten kilometers away. Livestock are watered in the small rain pond or at the large Monduli Juu Dam in Enguiki.

Emairete's convenient location only ten kilometers away from Monduli town, the district headquarters, and its relatively fertile environment have made it the focus of intensive "development" efforts since the late 1950s: a Catholic primary school for Maasai boys was built there during the late 1950s; veterinary extension agents, first provided by the colonial government, later the USAID Maasai Range Project, and now the district government have almost always been present and active in the village, promoting dairy farming, artificial insemination, improved breeding, dipping, vaccination campaigns, and more; Catholic missionaries have maintained ongoing evangelization efforts since 1956 (Hodgson 2000a) and have recently constructed a large Catholic church in the village; a well-stocked, functioning dispensary is located in nearby Enguiki; water projects have come and gone; electricity is provided to one household and promised at the school and other homes; and numerous income-generating projects have been tried and failed, including a dairy collection center, a women-managed grinding machine, and a beadwork-selling project. In the early 1990s, several small stores and two small restaurants, as well as a large weekly market, operated near the school. For Tshs 100/= each way, transport was irregularly provided a few times a day by two entrepreneurs with pickup trucks to or from Monduli town at the foot of the mountain.

Mti Mmoja

Mti Mmoja is actually sections of two different government-created villages (Lendikenya and Arkatan) whose residents consider themselves to be one community. Set between 1,320 and 1,380 meters on the rolling highland plains known as Ardai, which lie southwest of Komolonik mountain, it receives good to average rainfall and has good land for both grazing and cultivation. The name, Mti Mmoja, is Swahili for "one tree," referring to the one large tree which stands near the village stores and dispensary at the border of the rebuilt tarmac highway which connects Arusha town (the regional headquarters and growing tourist center) with the now world-famous game parks. At the height of the tourist season, villagers buying supplies in the stores or waiting for the bus to Arusha can watch endless streams of white minivans shuttling wealthy *wazungu* to and from the parks. A small Catholic outstation church sits behind the stores; it served as the local primary school until the nearby villager-financed school was completed.

Homesteads are fairly evenly spread across the plains and along the road, and farm plots are generally clustered together. Several smaller homesteads farm plots that are adjacent to their residence. If the rains are good, a large rainwater pond fills up to provide water for domestic and livestock use. As the former site of the Northern Province Wheat Scheme, however, the area is completely deforested. Every few days women walk in small groups to the slopes of the mountain to cut and haul firewood—a day-long task. They supplement their fuel supply with corncobs and dried cattle dung.

Embopong'

Embopong' refers to one locality of a larger government Ujamaa village called Mfereji (comprised of Embopong', Endebess, Orbibil, and Puslukunya localities). The name is Maa for a species of candelabra tree that grows on the small hillocks in the area. Set on the floor of the Rift Valley at roughly 1,200 meters (4,000 feet) above sea level, the dry dusty plains receive minimal rainfall. Fifteen kilometers of very bad road, constructed during the 1970s as part of the Maasai Range Project's drought relief program, connects Mfereji to Emairete, but its "difficult" location has meant minimal interaction with development agents.[25] Fortunately, Mfereji's location protected it from the brunt of the Operation Imparnati resettlements, beyond several meetings to "educate" community members about the benefits of working together in an Ujamaa village. As one government official reported in 1969, "It's clear to me that people in Mfereji want an Ujamaa village only because they want a hospital, not because they like the idea of an Ujamaa village."[26] By 1978, district officers were still trying to "educate" Mfereji residents and no resettlements had occurred.[27] Only in 1979 were several homesteads moved, but officials still complained about Maasai insubordination: "Most of the residents just built new houses without moving, and others show not the slightest sign of moving. This state of affairs has sabotaged implementation of the Operation."[28] The sixteen-mile gravity-piped water line constructed in the late 1960s by the Masai Range Commission still intermittently provides water for domestic and livestock uses, though it often took months for the government to repair a breakdown in the system. The district agriculture and livestock development officer had no memory of when the last extension agent worked in the village, claiming it was just too difficult and desolate a place to send anyone.[29] The government dispensary, which had an inadequate stock of medicines and was run by an alcoholic doctor, was often closed. Transport was very infrequent and became virtually non-existent in the early 1990s once the Catholic priest and the anthropologist moved from Emairete (except for a hunting company for tourists). Two weeks and eighteen deaths after a cholera outbreak began in the village in 1992, the District Medical Office, after first denying that cholera existed in the village, finally responded with doctors, medicines, and a partial quarantine of sick patients.

Cultivation is virtually impossible, but the land is good for smallstock browsers and some cattle. Two kinds of families live in the area: poor Maasai who subsist by caring for and herding cattle and smallstock of others; and those who resent state intrusions and choose to live in remote places far from the everyday reaches of state power. The community is reputedly an outpost for cattle thieves, so the police make regular forays to investigate reported thefts and search for stolen cattle. In 1993, the government built a police post in Enguiki to facilitate monitoring of Mfereji. And what was once perceived as remote wasteland is now appreciated for its appeal to tourists and hunters. With the expansion of hunting safaris as lucrative sources of foreign exchange, one hunting company bought exclusive "rights" to hunt on Mfereji land through payment of a large annual fee to village administration for "village development." To add to the "authentic" experience of hunting in the "wilds" of Africa, local *ilmurran* are hired as "trackers," paid so many shillings per day per animal.

Comparative Developments: Village Profiles

The contradictory effects of almost eighty years of "development" and the corresponding shifts in administrative policies and state control are best illustrated through an overview and comparison of the contemporary (1992) economic and social situation of residents in the three neighboring but ecologically distinct communities. Here I will address ethnicity, economic activities, education, and participation in village and national politics. Additional data on household production and consumption is provided in Chapter 5.

Ethnicity: "Pastoral" Maasai and "Farming" Maasai

The two main ethnic groups in the three villages are Maasai and Arusha. But, as earlier chapters have shown, "Maasai" and "Arusha" are not clearly distinct ethnic identities. Both groups speak Maa and share common rituals, age-sets, and clan structures. Arusha Maasai and Kisongo Maasai often have more in common than Kisongo Maasai and other "pastoral" Maasai sections such as Purko Maasai (cf. Spear and Nurse 1992; Spear 1993, 1997).[30] Despite the fluidity and intermingling of ethnic labels and economic activities described by early travelers, the British believed that all "real Maasai" were pastoralists, which led to their separation from the "farming" Arusha Maasai, both ethnically (into separate "tribes" of "Maasai" and "Arusha") and spatially (in the Masai Reserve). Despite these divisions, Maasai and Arusha share complex, shifting historical relationships, including intermarriage, exchange of food for cattle and smallstock, stock partnerships, and participation in the same circumcision calendars and age-set organization. Arusha and Maasai did create separate Native Authorities for their distinct territories in accordance with colonial directives, but these imposed political structures did not stop their common allegiance to the ritual leadership of the *iloibonok* and the political authority of the clan and local elder men. When asked to explain why some people were called Maasai and others Arusha, survey informants generally attributed the distinction to the work of Eng'ai, or God. "Although we are one people," explained an older woman, "Eng'ai gave us different names, according to the places we were from."

While some Arusha began moving back into Maasai areas under the official colonial and post-colonial government "expansion" and "resettlement" programs, most Arusha in the three communities entered informally, through marriage or gifts of stock and other enticements to local elders for permission. By the early 1960s, Arusha settlers were interspersed along the Ardai Plains, with numerous settlements in Monduli Juu. Although many were forcefully removed in the 1960s and 1970s by the government when it was intent on "protecting" pastoralists by preventing "agricultural encroachment," most eventually returned (Jacobs 1980: 11). A 1974 census of the ranching associations found that an average of 13.5 percent of homesteads surveyed were Arusha, although the ethnic composition of Komolonik was not assessed (Hatfield 1975: 20). Migration histories that I took from the elder man of each *enkang'* confirm that some Arusha have lived in the communities for over thirty years, while a second wave entered during the disruptions created by villagization in the 1970s.

The complicated and contradictory relations between Maasai and Arusha were quite evident in the responses to my 1992 census. When I asked adult respondents which ethnic group they belonged to, most replied unhesitatingly "Maasai" or "Arusha" (or "Chagga," "Meru," or other group, in a few cases). For the few people who seemed confused by the question, we read a list of choices (Maasai, Arusha, Meru, Chagga, and other) from which they selected

Table 4.1 Self-Identified Ethnicity by Village and Sex of Adults, 1992

Ethnicity	Emairete		Mti Mmoja		Embopong'		Total	
	Men	Women	Men	Women	Men	Women	Men	Women
Maasai	135	149	65	93	72	93	272	335
Arusha	65	132	21	37	5	19	91	188
Meru	0	7	3	1	0	0	3	8
Chagga	1	0	0	0	0	0	1	0
Other	3	3	1	1	0	0	4	4
Total	204	291	90	132	77	112	367	535

a response. Table 4.1 shows the self-identified ethnicity by village and sex of adult respondents. These figures show that a significant number of residents in Emairete (39.8 percent) and Mti Mmoja (26.1 percent) identify themselves as Arusha. The smaller number of Arusha in Embopong' (12.7 percent) is partly due to the lack of land suitable for cultivation in the area, although that is not necessarily a limiting factor.

Again, it is important to remember that these numbers reflect how people identified themselves for the purposes of this census, which provided no category for "Both." For example, several men perceived by villagers to be Arusha asserted that they were Maasai and were classified as such. One elderly man in Emairete insisted that he was both Maasai and Arusha, despite common agreement by villagers and his sons that he was Arusha. From his perspective, he was one of the first Arusha to move to Emairete, he had been very wealthy in livestock for many years, and he had married several Maasai women. In Mti Mmoja, several Maasai residents told me stories (with great glee) about an Arusha man who lived nearby and had tried for years to "become Maasai." He married only Maasai wives, accumulated large herds of cattle, and refused to farm. Although these accomplishments gained him respect among area Maasai, they still thought of him as Arusha and laughed at his pretensions. Similarly, although ethnicity is ideally patrilineal, some Arusha fathers claimed that the children of their Maasai wives were Maasai, as did many Maasai wives with Arusha husbands.

While distinctions between "Maasai" and "Arusha" were blurred by some respondents, numerous Maasai were very clear about distinguishing themselves as truly "Maasai." Rather than just "Maasai" (masc: *olmaasaindat;* fem: *enkamaasindat*), they would add *tukul* (Maa: completely) or *piwa* (Maa: pure) to their response to emphasize that they were completely and purely Maasai.

When Koko helped me construct her genealogy, she consistently "forgot" the names of the few Arusha women who had married her sons or grandsons (in contrast to her ability to remember the names and genealogies of the "Maasai" wives). Another elder man spoke resentfully about what he perceived as the sneaky ways of the Arusha: "They come at night. You wake up in the morning and there they are. Or they give you gifts—a cow, a daughter—and then they come and ask for land or a place to live. Now that they are your friends, what are you supposed to do?" More disturbingly, some Maasai accused Arusha of witchcraft, refusing to let their children marry into Arusha families for fear of being subjected to Arusha curses. In contrast, some Arusha voiced concerns about letting their daughters marry Maasai men for fear of mistreatment. As one Arusha mother told me, "I want my daughter to marry an Arusha man; he will give her land and won't tie her up in a tree and beat her." Not every perspective was negative, however. One elder Maasai woman admired the initiative and cleverness of Arusha: "They have always been smart. They started to go to school long ago; they are excellent farmers; they dig in the dirt and produce cattle [money and food]; and they are filling up every place. They laugh at us Maasai since we are so stupid we don't know that profit can be made from the land. For these reasons Arusha are smarter than Maasai."

As the census responses demonstrated, claims to ethnicity were situational. To outsiders, especially expatriate development workers intent on helping "the Maasai," many Arusha would claim to be Maasai. In contrast, a few Arusha men in the villages and many in Arusha town proudly told me they were "*not* Maasai" but Arusha, and carefully detailed the differences between their modern outlook and the "conservative" attitudes of Maasai. As one Arusha man I encountered in Arusha town explained, Arusha and Maasai are very different: unlike Maasai, Arusha were mixed farmers, and they were adaptable and keen on development. Arusha were willing to farm, to go to school, and to become "modern" people. No Maasai man or woman, however, ever claimed to be Arusha in my presence. Among themselves, villagers followed the rules of patrilineal descent to ascribe ethnicity, although Maasai men of Arusha mothers were perceived, generally, to be less than Maasai.

Questions on the survey explored people's ideas about the similarities and differences between Maasai and Arusha. Most Maasai and Arusha said they were "one body" (*osesen obo*) or "one blood" (*osarge obo*). Others listed common ceremonies, female and male circumcision, the pulling of the front bottom teeth, dress, and even language (although many noted differences in pronunciation). Many Maasai, however, gleefully mentioned one difference: "Arusha" they said, glancing at my Arusha research assistant, "have red teeth," unlike the Maasai, who have white teeth.[31] Others explained that Arusha and Maasai differed only by their production strategy: Arusha cultivated, while Maasai herded. But they all admitted that this distinction was now a thing of the past since most Maasai were cultivating. "We are Arusha now," one Maasai man lamented; "there is no difference between us." Arusha and Maasai elder men participate in the same clan and council meetings, Arusha and Maasai *ilmurran* are circumcised together and dance together at ceremonies as representatives of the same locality, and Arusha and Maasai women work together in their homesteads as co-wives and in-laws.

Settlement Patterns, Housing Styles: Home on the Range

A historical comparison of settlement patterns, housing styles, and residence relationships in the three villages attests to the contradictory influences of the Arusha, the villagization program, and changing economic strategies. A 1974 census found that the Komolonik Ranching Association was composed of 212 homesteads housing 4,109 adults and children, for an average of almost 20 people per homestead.[32] By 1980, Monduli Juu village itself had 2,910 people living in 537 houses grouped in 56 homesteads. Of these, the Emairete locality consisted of 186 houses in 26 homesteads (Ndagala 1982: 30–31). My 1992 census data, displayed in Table 4.2, shows even greater population density. According to these figures, Emairete now has 251 households that constitute 66 homesteads. Furthermore, while population is increasing, homestead size is decreasing on the average. For Emairete, Ndagala's 1980 census showed an average of 7.2 houses per homestead, while my 1992 census shows an average of 3.8 houses per homestead.

In addition to changes in the size of homesteads, the spatial configuration of homesteads has changed. A thorn fence used to enclose all the houses in the homestead, but in Emairete and Mti Mmoja only the livestock pen in the center of the houses is enclosed, now by thick poles (as Ndagala found in Emairete in 1980). Only the homesteads in Embopong' are still surrounded by thick thorn fences to keep the cattle in at night and the predators out, and they conform somewhat to the ideal type of separate "gates" for each married man; his wives alternate their houses between the right-hand side (1st, 3rd, 5th wife, etc.) and the left-hand side (2d, 4th, 6th wife . . .) of the gate. In Emairete, there are a few distinct homesteads, but the dense concentration of houses on most of the crater wall prevents much spatial separation. In larger housing clusters, houses from different homesteads are interspersed, often with at least one rectangular "man's house" (women's houses were always cir-

171

Table 4.2 Population by Village, 1992

Villages	# Homesteads	# Households	Total Population	Men	Women	Boys	Girls
Emairete	66	251	1079	204	291	291	296
Mti Mmoja	29	114	503	90	132	149	132
Embopong'	21	89	390	77	112	111	90
Total	116	454	1972	371	535	551	518

Source: Hodgson Census, 1992.

cular). In Mti Mmoja, there are a few homesteads comprised of numerous houses and several scattered homesteads either of young men with their wife/wives at the beginning of the domestic cycle or elderly men who often have just one wife and are at the end of the domestic cycle.

Corresponding changes in housing styles, reflecting the influence of Arusha and state interventions, are also evident. One of the first "village" development projects in the 1970s in Emairete was a government campaign to build "modern houses" (*nyumba bora*). The campaign included "education" seminars, government loans for building supplies, training for young men in "modern" house-building techniques, and detailed lists of the names of the men building new houses, with or without loans.[33] Most men used the loans to build rectangular houses for themselves (as opposed to the circular houses built by women), which they used as private spaces for meeting with visitors, storing their property, and even sleeping. In 1980, Ndagala found that in Emairete the "traditional" Maasai houses which looked like small igloos, constructed by women of poles and sturdy limbs then plastered with mud and cattle dung (see Photo 4.1; cf. Jacobs 1971), had almost completely been replaced by the larger "Arusha" type of houses, which are circular, constructed out of thicker poles, and, most noticeably, have thatched roofs. One hundred sixty-one of the 186 houses (86.6 percent) in Emairete were "Arusha"-style homes, and another 14 (7.5 percent) had corrugated iron roofs (Ndagala 1982: 30–31). By 1992, all the houses in Emairete were either "Arusha-style" or rectangular "men's houses" with iron roofs, as were all but one in Mti Mmoja. Many houses also had separate, smaller storehouses for dried maize and beans. Almost every woman in Embopong' was also living in an Arusha-style house, using their recently abandoned "Maasai-style" house as a kitchen, store, and dormitory for *ilmurran* and their girlfriends. One consequence of the change in housing styles prompted in part by the government campaign was that

4.1 A Maasai woman replastering part of her home, 1985. Such "igloo-style" houses are rapidly being replaced by thatched huts. Photo by author.

young men and laborers generally replaced women as the builders of houses, thereby challenging women's long-standing claims to "own" their houses and their ability to control admittance as well as the use of the space and property within (cf. Talle 1987, 1988).

Livestock Holdings: "I Don't Keep Chickens!"

As discussed above, a central component of historical and contemporary ideas about Maasai identity is their commitment to livestock-keeping. From early travelers to colonial administrators to Tanzanian government officials, all have focused on and even tried to reinforce Maasai identity as cattle-keepers. Yet reality is, as always, more complicated. Through the years, many Maasai, especially men, have come to embrace the pastoralist ideal as fiercely, if not more so, than state officials, yet fewer and fewer can afford to subsist solely as herders. "Pure" pastoralism, to use Jacobs's (1965) controversial category, however prevalent it might have been in the past (a debatable point, as my historical evidence has indicated), is now solely the provenance of the very rich and the destitute. Furthermore, customary means of redistribution, such as clientship, stock partners, bride service, and so forth, are disappearing, so that wealthy Maasai and poor Maasai are rigidifying into what one might call class categories. To put it bluntly, the cattle and smallstock have died in large numbers as a consequence of disease (itself a result of lost resistance because of dipping campaigns and the proximity of sick animals to healthy ones) and the long history of alienation of key dry-season grazing grounds and permanent water sources. Despite colonial and post-colonial attempts to buttress the ability of pastoralists to continue to raise livestock through various development interventions, herding is no longer a viable economic enterprise without other means of economic support. Maasai themselves have realized this for several decades and have attempted to diversify economically (with little or no support from the state and development organizations) through farming, trading, small businesses, wage labor, and other forms of enterprise. A comparison of several livestock surveys of Monduli Juu village in 1971,[34] 1978,[35] and 1980 (Ndagala 1982) and my census of Emairete in 1992 provides a sense of the changes and continuities in livestock activities, and the following section explores Maasai involvement in farming.

Given the preponderance of Maasai, Monduli Juu village was designated as a "livestock-keeping" village when it was formed in the 1970s, although residents were allowed to farm food crops. A census in 1971 counted 214 adults and 157 children in the village, and 14,813 cattle, 899 goats, and 969 sheep. By 1978, cattle holdings in Monduli Juu had decreased to 4,590, with an increase in goats to 2,295 and decrease in sheep to 600 (and 220 donkeys). Ndagala's tables, reproduced below as Table 4.3, show that the total livestock holdings of the three Monduli Juu localities were still sizable in 1980. Ndagala's data showed that all of his male respondents "owned" an average of 21.2 head of cattle and 41.8 smallstock; those living in Emairete owned a slightly higher average of 28.7 cattle and 55.2 smallstock (compared to 140 cattle and 17.6 smallstock per adult man in 1971). My data for 1992, shown in Table 4.4, demonstrates a marked decline in livestock holdings. Based on household holdings rather than respondent holdings, my data shows an average of 8.8 cattle per household in the three communities and just 7.5 per household in Emairete. Dividing the total cattle by the number of adult men gives a statistic more comparable to Ndagala's (by male respondent): 9.2 cattle per man in Emairete and 9.8 smallstock, or a third of 1980 cattle holdings (a twentieth of 1971 cattle holdings) and a fifth of 1980 smallstock holdings. Although such statistics are notoriously unreliable, the gross numbers do indicate a striking loss of livestock holdings.

Table 4.3 Total Livestock Owned By (Male) Respondents, Monduli Juu, 1980

Locality	# Respondents	Cattle	Goats	Sheep	Donkeys
Elwai	19	388	323	454	54
Emairete	21	602	691	468	42
Enguiki	20	281	206	381	60
Totals	60	1,272	1,220	1,303	156

Source: Daniel Ndagala, "Operation Imparnati: The Sedentarization of the Pastoral Maasai in Tanzania," *Nomadic Peoples* 10 (1982): 34.

Table 4.4 Total Animals Owned, by Village, 1992

Village	# Households	# Men	Cattle	Goats	Sheep	Donkeys	Chickens
Emairete	251	204	1,879	1,363	632	168	377
Mti Mmoja	114	90	1,588	471	315	76	80
Embopong'	89	77	565	448	311	134	1
Totals	454	371	4,032	2,282	1,258	378	458

Source: Hodgson Census, 1992.

The addition of chickens as a category of domestic animals kept by Maasai women marks the shifting consumption patterns and income-generating strategies discussed below. Maasai residents of Embopong' mock those Maasai women in Emairete and Mti Mmoja who now, like Arusha, keep chickens: "I don't keep chickens!" one Embopong' woman exclaimed during the census; "I am Maasai!"

And as Table 4.5 (also reproduced from Ndagala) and Table 4.6 (from my 1992 census data) demonstrate, such aggregate figures mask large inequalities in the distribution of livestock. As Ndagala remarks, the disparities in livestock ownership became even clearer when the actual figures were examined: "Out of the 21 respondents in Emairete three owned no livestock while 18 owned 899 LSUs [Livestock Units]. While 9 of the livestock owning respondents had under 30 LSUs, and therefore, below the village average, 3 respondents owned 545 out of the 899 LSUs" (1982: 35).

The distribution of livestock by household in 1992, as shown in Table 4.6, shows how stratification in cattle ownership has increased—many households have no cattle, and most have just a few. Instead, the few wealthy cattle owners possess most of the animals: two men own over 300 head each of the 1,879 cattle in Emairete, or about one-third of the entire village holdings.

Table 4.5 Distribution of Livestock Units in Monduli Juu, 1980

Localities (# of Respondents)	Distribution of Respondents according to Livestock Units Owned								
	0	1–5	6–10	11–15	16–20	21–25	26–30	30–40	over 40
Elwai (19)	1	2	5	3	3	—	—	—	5
Emairete (21)	3	4	2	1	—	2	—	3	6
Enguiki (20)	—	2	6	1	4	1	2	—	4
Totals (60)	4	8	13	5	7	3	2	3	15

Source: Daniel Ndagala, "Operation Imparnati: The Sedentarization of the Pastoral Maasai in Tanzania," *Nomadic Peoples* 10 (1982): 35.

Table 4.6 Distribution of Livestock by Household, 1992

Villages (# of Households)	Distribution of Households[1] according to Cattle Holdings[2]									
	0	1–5	6–10	11–15	16–20	21–25	26–30	31–40	41–100	over 100
Emairete (251)	89	105	29	8	4	3	1	3	7	2
Mti Mmoja (114)	10	41	16	18	8	8	3	4	4	2
Embopong' (89)	12	45	15	11	2	1	0	2	1	0
Totals (454)	111	191	60	37	14	12	4	9	12	4

Source: Hodgson Census, 1992.

　　1. "Households" here refers to the separate, usually matrifocal, houses (*enkaji/inkajijik*) which comprise an *enkang'*, or homestead.

　　2. My table and Ndagala's are not directly comparable, as he reports distribution by "livestock units" (a measurement which includes immature stock, sheep, and goats at a pro-rated amount), while my table reports on cattle holdings only. Furthermore, his report seems to be based on a broader definition of household (as a husband and all of his wives) than mine.

Of course, stratification, as measured by unequal distribution of cattle among households, has always existed among Maasai. Despite colonial and post-colonial attempts to represent Maasai as a homogeneous wealthy group, evidence offered by both Maasai elders and some colonial officials revealed large disparities in livestock holdings. Stratification should come as no surprise, therefore, unless we insist on retaining romantic images of homogeneity and communal wealth. The trend toward increased stratification, however, is troubling, for, as we shall see, the mechanisms for assisting friends and family to rebuild or expand their herds are collapsing. Where households in the past could fluctuate between positions of relative wealth or poverty in terms of cattle, these positions are rigidifying into more permanent class divisions.

Cultivating Hunger: Transgressing Boundaries

The increase in stratification, however, is more than a matter of cattle. It is both a cause and consequence of increased cultivation activities in the three communities. Despite continued assertions by a few elder men and some elder women of the pastoralist ideal of only herding cattle, most Maasai in the communities farm, as they have been doing for at least twenty years. A 1974 census of the Komolonik Ranching Association found that almost half of the homesteads surveyed (100 out of 205) were pursuing a mixed subsistence pattern, both farming and herding. The remaining 105 homesteads were identified as "pastoral," with none categorized as solely "agricultural" (Hatfield 1975: 20).[36] By 1982, almost all households in Emairete were farming, and Ndagala reported that "all able bodied persons in individual households participated in agriculture regardless of sex" (1982: 33).

The primary crops are maize and beans, which are often intercropped, and some barley. In the survey, when asked why they were farming, Maasai men and women generally gave one of two (related) answers: the cattle had died or they were hungry. When asked how they learned to farm, Maasai men and women described watching or being taught by Arusha. Arusha men taught Maasai men, and Arusha women taught Maasai women. One older Arusha man in Emairete was named by several Maasai men of his age-set (Ilnyangusi) as their teacher, a fact that he proudly confirmed. His wives, he reminded me, had also taught Maasai women.

In accordance with national legislation, plots of land for farming were allocated within "village" boundaries by the village council. Land is a male asset: when the villages were formed, the village committee allocated up to three acres of farmland to the male "head" of each household. Once men requested and received demarcated plots from the village government, they usually kept a plot for themselves and allocated sub-plots to their wives and adult unmarried sons and sometimes to married female relatives separated or widowed from their spouses and living at home. Men have almost exclusive rights to land. Of the three villages, only two women living in Emairete—a wealthy educated widow and a divorced schoolteacher—had rights to land in their own names. Most women could only gain access to farmland through their relationships with men. They were "given" sub-plots from fathers, husbands, brothers, or sons but lost their rights of access when they married, moved, or separated—in other words, when they severed their relationship with and dependence on a certain man. When a man married, however, he usually retained the sub-plot allocated by his father and requested and received another plot from the village government in his own name. When a man died, certain of his sons inherited his land, and his widows depended on their relationships to their sons to maintain access to their farmland. A widow with no sons, or with sons who did not inherit land, usually moved with her children to her father's or brother's homestead and requested land there.

Ndagala's 21 male respondents in Emairete claimed that their households cultivated an average of 2.4 acres and that they owned 10 ox plows and 51 hoes among them (Ndagala 1982: 34). In Table 4.7, I show the distribution of farming implements in an inventory of all the households. By 1992, the 251 households in Emairete farmed approximately 936.13 acres, an average cultivation of 3.7 acres per household (a substantial increase over Ndagala's figures).[37] The 114 households in Mti Mmoja farmed a total of 505.75 acres (an average of 4.4 acres per household), while the 89 households in Embopong' farmed a total of 22.51 acres, or 0.3 acres on average.

Again, such averages masked substantial inequalities in acreage farmed, as Table 4.8 demonstrates. In other words, while 26 households (10.4 percent) in Emairete did not farm at all, and 141 households (56.2 percent) farmed approximately 235 acres, or 25.1 percent of the total acreage farmed, two households farmed 60 and 36 acres respectively, or 10.3 percent of the total acreage farmed. Similarly, while 15 households in Mti Mmoja did not farm, 56 households (49.1 percent) farmed approximately 98 acres, or an average of 1.8 acres each, while two households farmed 60 and 30 acres respectively. The small size and number of the Embopong' holdings (63 households did not farm, 26 farmed an average of 0.9 acres each) was due to the fact that they farmed on "borrowed" land in Monduli Juu. In Emairete and Mti Mmoja, most of the non-farming households consisted of elderly or infirm adults, although a few households in Emairete consisted of completely impoverished immigrants who had been denied land by the village council. Most "economically active"[38] adult men and women living in Emairete (98.5 percent of the women, 93.1 percent of the men) and Mti Mmoja (97.6 percent of the women, 79.5 percent of the men) farmed, as did almost a quarter of the women living in Embopong' (24.5 percent of the women, 20.3 percent of the men).

Relations of production in farming and herding varied significantly by gender, class, and age. Three predominant configurations were found in Emairete and Mti Mmoja. First, the few wealthy men who owned large areas of land farmed using a combination of capital-intensive and labor-intensive methods. They often rented tractors to prepare and plow the land and hired Mbulu laborers and sometimes wives to plant, weed, and harvest the maize

Table 4.7 Inventory of Farming Implements by Household, 1992

Implements	Emairete (251 households)	Mti Mmoja (114 households)	Embopong' (89 households)
Handhoes	198	95	7
Ox plows	41	16	0
Oxcarts	3	4	0
Wheelbarrows	3	4	0
Tractors	0	0	0

Source: Hodgson Census, 1992.

Table 4.8 Distribution of Households by Acreage Farmed, 1992

Villages (# of Households)	Distribution of Households by Acreage Farmed[1]									
	0	1	2	3	4	5	6–10	11–20	21–30	over 30
Emairete (251)	26	71	46	24	20	11	35	15	1	2
Mti Mmoja (114)	15	23	24	9	11	9	14	6	1	2
Embopong' (89)	63	21	5	0	0	0	0	0	0	0
Total (454)	104	115	75	33	31	20	49	21	2	4

Source: Hodgson Census, 1992.
    1. Partial acreages are rounded up to nearest whole.

and bean crops. While these men would visit the fields to supervise the workers and wives, they rarely worked themselves. Much of the resulting harvest was sold for cash, which the men controlled. They paid the workers, bought gifts for their wives, purchased livestock, and otherwise invested their money as they chose.

Second, the majority of households engaged in small-scale cultivation to meet their subsistence needs, with separate plots for the husband and each of his wives and other adult women living in his homestead. Usually the man prepared the land on all of the plots with an ox plow (owned or borrowed), while women planted, weeded, and harvested their plots and their husband's. Generally, each farmer controlled the harvest from his or her plot, but their obligations differed by gender. While a man could sell part or all of his harvest (although most retained some portion for "emergencies"), women were responsible for feeding their children and households from their harvest. Thus, while maize and beans were primarily cash crops for men, they were mainly food crops for women. A few Maasai homesteads combined their harvests in one store, under the supervision of the senior *enkang'* male, who doled out dried maize and beans to each woman every few days.

Finally, almost every unmarried *olmurrani* in Emairete and Mti Mmoja farmed small plots, performing most of the labor tasks themselves. They sold most of their harvest, investing the cash in livestock or bridewealth.

As Table 4.8 demonstrates, even residents of Embopong' farmed, despite their arid, dusty location. In addition to crossing "ethnic" "boundaries," residents also breached their "village" boundaries. Despite administrative attempts to confine residents, their herds, and their economic activities to the political and spatial bounds of their "villages," Maasai and Arusha transgressed those boundaries in order to diversify their activities, spread their risks, and exploit several different ecological zones. Among the communities I studied, various strategies were used to obtain access to farmland in fertile areas and multiple grazing sites. Women, as sisters, daughters, and wives, were central to all of these strategies.

Wealthy men used polygyny to achieve economic diversity, establishing multiple homesteads and therefore multiple land rights by placing a wife or wives in two or more communities. For example, one very wealthy man (Seuri age-set) had a "herding" homestead in Embopong' and a "farming" homestead in Emairete. His wives alternated between the two homesteads, milking, herding (with some *ilmurran*), and caring for cattle and smallstock when they were resident in the herding homestead, and working in the fields while living in the farming homestead (as well as caring for a small milk herd). As the chief "supervisor" of his wives, his mother shifted between the two homesteads, her importance and his strategy marked by her two houses, one in each homestead. Another younger wealthy man (Ilmakaa age-set) achieved even greater economic diversity through polygyny. Not only did he have two farming homesteads in different villages and a grazing homestead, but he had set up another wife in a distant community with a small shop. In 1992, he cultivated sixty acres of maize and beans in just one homestead, hiring a tractor to prepare and plow his land and employing seven full-time Mbulu laborers to assist his wives and unmarried brothers in weeding and harvesting. His ideas for making money were not limited to herding, cultivating, and small shops, however. He engaged in large-scale cattle trading, co-invested in rights for a gemstone mine, and was looking for a vehicle to purchase and run as a "taxi" along the popular route between Arusha town and the Tanzania/Kenya border town of Namanga.

Less wealthy households accessed grazing and farming indirectly through the marriages of their children. Intermarriage by families in Embopong' with

4.2 Young Maasai man showing the wares in his store in Emairete, 1993. Such stores provide dry goods as well as places for men to gather socially, talk, and listen to the constantly blaring radio. Photo by author.

families in Emairete and Mti Mmoja enabled them to exchange their grazing labor for farmland in the more fertile areas. Many able-bodied women in Embopong' "borrowed" plots of land to farm (usually from their consanguinal or clan relations) somewhere in Monduli Juu or shared a plot with their co-wives. Groups of women were always walking up the mountain to weed and harvest their plots, staying a few nights or even weeks at a time with relatives. In return, men in Emairete kept smallstock and cattle with their affines in Embopong'. For example, one fairly wealthy Maasai man in Emairete had a sister who was married to a man in Embopong'. He "lent" his sister and her co-wife a small plot of land to farm in Emairete. In exchange, her household cared for most of his smallstock. When he wanted to slaughter or sell an animal, he would send one of his sons or grandsons to retrieve it or, on occasion, visit himself.

Finally, very poor households, which were usually monogamous and had no cattle or smallstock, moved to areas such as Emairete where cultivation

181

was possible and begged housing and a small plot of land from wealthier clan members. Both the husband and wife worked in the fields and sometimes contributed labor to their benefactor's fields. Occasionally, a generous family or clan member would lend them a milk cow to care for and provide them with milk. For example, one wealthy Arusha man in Emairete helped two families from Embopong' who had lost all of their animals and moved to Emairete for refuge. One family was an elderly, sickly couple who were childless and unable to care for themselves. He fed them and lent them one of his daughters to bring them wood and water. The second family was comprised of a man, his two wives, and their five children, all of whom crowded into a small house. The family barely subsisted from the small plot they farmed together, the greens and other wild produce the women gathered, and gifts of food they begged from neighbors and fellow clan members.

Although the future of these two families looked bleak, some poor households were able, with the help of family and friends, to recover and improve their situations. After one man "drank" all of his stock (i.e., sold them all to buy alcohol), his wife moved with her three children to live with her brothers. They gave her some land to farm, which she did successfully. When she eventually moved from her brothers' *enkang'* to a house she built nearby, her husband, who had quit drinking, joined her. Their poverty and her accomplishments in farming had produced a shift in their household gender dynamics: she made most of the household decisions, including those about the distribution or sale of their harvest, while he worked meekly by her side on their quite sizeable farm. But as they became more economically secure and invested their surplus in livestock, he gradually withdrew from helping her and began to assert his rights as "head of the household" once again. In their economic activities, therefore, community residents transgressed two key sets of "boundaries": the linkage of ethnic identity with type of subsistence, and the territorial boundaries of "the village" as the self-contained unit of development and economic subsistence.

Education

Soon after Independence, the Tanzanian government nationalized the schools, most of which in the Maasai districts were financed and managed by Christian missions at the time. Part of its socialist development agenda was Universal Primary Education (UPE), the right of every child to a free primary school education. To fulfill this promise, the government built a primary school in every Ujamaa village. But building schools was a different matter than paying for teachers' salaries, schoolbooks, and maintenance costs. As with other development interventions, the government directed its limited resources toward those peoples and areas which were more politically powerful and/or perceived as "progressive." Given the historical scarcity of post-primary educational opportunities for Maasai, most teachers were non-Maasai, and few wanted to teach in the "dangerous," "isolated," "primitive" Maasai areas. Many Maasai were equally reluctant to let *irmeek* or "Swahili" teach their children. Edward Sokoine (a Maasai political leader, see Maasai Portrait 4) tried to ease the situation by encouraging educated Maasai men to train as teachers, which many did, some with financial assistance from Sokoine himself. But they were still too few for the many teaching places, and Maasai schools suffered and still suffer from a shortage of qualified teachers.

Moreover, the government schools, as with schools everywhere, were a primary venue for trying to produce Tanzanian citizens.[39] Swahili, the national language, was the sole language of instruction, and the curriculum taught nationalist ideologies about Ujamaa, appropriate political structures (villages, districts, regions, and the nation-state), economic objectives (cooperation and productivity), and aspects of the dominant majority "culture" of "Swahilis." Children were required to wear uniforms (shirts and shorts for boys; dresses for girls), appear "clean" (i.e., no red ochre smeared on their bodies), and learn Swahili protocols of greeting, politeness, and respect.

As discussed in Chapter 3, when education was first introduced in the colonial period, some parents feared that it would forever change and even alienate their children from them and from Maasai culture. The violent implementation of education in some areas, by which parents were forced to select one child to send to school, runaway children were captured by guards, and fathers were imprisoned for refusing to enroll their children, only exacerbated their fears. But these days, almost every Maasai I interviewed spoke of themselves or their parents as *emodai,* or stupid, for ever having prevented their children from going to school. "Let me just say," remarked a junior elder, "that even I will put my child in school. I mean, I am very *emodai,* but my child will come to prosper." To be *emodai* for them was to be stupid in a particular way; it was to be ignorant of the languages and practices of the nation-state; it was to be unable to operate in a world of courtrooms, hospitals, banks, and politicians.

Thus, despite ongoing concerns about the treatment of their children in schools and the place of "Maasai" in a "Swahili" world, Maasai men and women of all ages desperately wanted to educate all of their children so that they could survive in what they perceived as a rapidly changing land. "The land is now completely wild. There are no cattle, I have only a few left. What shall I do? . . . What happened to the past when people followed cattle?" As one elder Maasai man told us, "I want to educate all of my children, I no longer want one who is blind. I mean, the country has become darkness for everyone." "The wisdom of the past," another elder explained, is worthless; it must be replaced by "the wisdom of the present." Education was perceived as the hope of the future, one of the only means to political power and economic prosperity: "Doesn't this thing called school now run the entire country?" Or, as another junior male elder explained, "If you put your son in school he will study until he gets work as a member of parliament [a reference to Edward Sokoine, Maasai Portrait 4], or he'll get some other important work and he will help you in the future when you are old." Another woman hoped that her educated children would travel to other countries and return home rich. More realistically, many Maasai parents commented about how their educated children would help them if they were sick and had to go to the hospital, if they had to read signs and find places in town, if they needed to understand legal documents and postings, or if they required other such engagements with government workers, most of whom only spoke Swahili. "They [educated children] will help with everything," said an old woman. "I mean if an Or-mangat'i [literally "enemy," also used as a derogatory term for Swahilis] comes to my homestead, my child will know Swahili. I'm a deaf person (*oltung'ani bubu*) [i.e., I don't understand Swahili] who can't understand them. But my child will understand all the affairs of *irmeek* [refers to Swahilis]. If we are told to do a certain thing or be at a certain place, they can do it. Or if there is a legal case they can attend. They can work for both the government and Maasai and become powerful."

A key symbol of the power education was believed to have was the pen. "With the pen and the roads that now pass through the village," one elder man said, "there will be no place that a person can get problems, if these two, the pen and the road, are available." "We people of the past don't know anything," another venerable male elder lamented, "but these new people, these people who know the pen, they have a clear way."

As Table 4.9 shows, the increasing embrace of education is reflected in increased enrollment figures by generation. There were several reasons for the disparities between the expressed eagerness of parents to educate their children and these enrollment figures. Most important, children were a valuable labor force. Boys and girls herded smallstock and calves, while older boys herded cattle. Girls helped their mothers collect wood and water and were primary child care providers, especially when their mothers worked in the

Table 4.9a Percentage Distribution of Last School Grade Attended for Maasai and Arusha, by Age-Set and Gender, for Emairete, 1992

Age-Set[1]	Standards 1–4		Standards 5–8		Forms 1–4		Post-Form 4		Adult Education	
	Males	Females	Males	Females	Males	Females	Males	Females	Males	Females
Iltareto	—	14.3	—	0.0	—	0.0	—	0.0	—	0.0
Ilterito	0.0	0.0	0.0	0.0	0.0	0.0	0.0	0.0	14.3	0.0
Ilnyangusi	0.0	0.0	7.7	0.0	0.0	0.0	0.0	0.0	0.0	0.0
Seuri	7.1	1.2	3.6	3.7	0.0	0.0	0.0	1.2	14.3	8.5
Ilmakaa	7.5	6.3	10.0	47.9	2.5	0.0	5.0	2.1	7.5	10.4
Ilandissy	4.5	4.9	58.0	36.6	6.3	4.9	5.5	0.0	0.0	0.0
Children[2]	56.7	35.7	28.8	24.5	0.0	0.7	0.0	0.7	NA	NA

Source: Hodgson Census, 1992.
  1. As explained in the introduction, age-sets of men and women are not directly comparable: the "age-set" of men is the name of the age-set in which they were circumcised. The "age-set" of women refers to the name of the male age-set who were *ilmurran* at the time the women danced for them as unmarried girls (*esiangiki/isiangikin*). Women of one age-set are therefore roughly the same age as the next junior male age-set, so that, for example, female Makaa are roughly equivalent to male Landiss in age.
  2. Children seven years or older.

Table 4.9b Percentage Distribution of Last School Grade Attended for Maasai and Arusha, by Age-Set and Gender, for Mti Mmoja, 1992

Age-Set	Standards 1–4		Standards 5–8		Forms 1–4		Post-Form 4		Adult Education	
	Males	Females	Males	Females	Males	Females	Males	Females	Males	Females
Iltareto	—	0.0	—	0.0	—	0.0	—	0.0	—	0.0
Ilterito	0.0	0.0	0.0	0.0	0.0	0.0	0.0	0.0	0.0	0.0
Ilnyangusi	0.0	0.0	0.0	0.0	0.0	0.0	0.0	0.0	0.0	0.0
Seuri	0.0	3.3	8.3	0.0	0.0	0.0	8.3	0.0	0.0	0.0
Ilmakaa	5.3	5.3	15.8	15.8	0.0	1.7	10.5	0.0	0.0	0.0
Ilandissy	4.2	8.7	43.8	43.5	6.3	0.0	2.1	0.0	0.0	0.0
Children[1]	46.7	31.6	6.5	7.0	0.0	0.0	0.0	0.0	NA	NA

Source: Hodgson Census, 1992.
  1. Children seven years or older.

Table 4.9c Percentage Distribution of Last School Grade Attended for Maasai and Arusha, by Age-Set and Gender, for Embopong', 1992

Age-Set	Standards 1–4		Standards 5–8		Forms 1–4		Post-Form 4		Adult Education	
	Males	Females	Males	Females	Males	Females	Males	Females	Males	Females
Iltareto	—	0.0	—	0.0	—	0.0	—	0.0	—	0.0
Ilterito	0.0	8.3	0.0	0.0	0.0	0.0	0.0	0.0	0.0	0.0
Ilnyangusi	0.0	0.0	0.0	0.0	0.0	0.0	0.0	0.0	0.0	0.0
Seuri	0.0	0.0	0.0	0.0	0.0	0.0	0.0	0.0	0.0	0.0
Ilmakaa	0.0	2.7	0.0	21.6	0.0	0.0	5.0	0.0	0.0	0.0
Ilandissy	8.3	5.3	27.8	36.8	0.0	0.0	2.8	0.0	0.0	0.0
Children[1]	25.0	17.5	25.0	15.0	0.0	0.0	0.0	0.0	NA	NA

Source: Hodgson Census, 1992.
  1. Children seven years or older.

fields. These demands intensified the emerging class distinctions: wealthy Maasai families hired young boys from poor families to herd their cattle and thereby enabled their sons to go to school. Similarly, young girls were also "lent" to wealthier families to assist in household labor and child care, freeing the wealthier daughters to attend school. As one older woman commented, "Before, we didn't like schools but were forced to send our children. These days no one would prevent their children from attending. But there are differences among us. Some people are very poor and others are wealthy. If you put your child in school, you need to have property to buy uniforms [governments require uniforms every day], shoes, pens, money to contribute to schools funds, etc. . . . Poor people can't afford to put their children in school, but they are forced to." When children from poorer families did attend school, their mothers usually assumed the additional labor burden.

Second, there were structural reasons for school attendance figures involving the development "attention" accorded to the three communities by the state, as is quickly evident from the differences in educational facilities and services. Emairete, the site of one of the first Catholic primary schools for boys, had a large functioning primary school, including several good-quality accommodations for teachers. Initially, only one of the teachers was a Maa-speaker, but in 1993 a local Maasai man who had been teaching in another area was transferred to the school. The close, convenient location fostered a high percentage of enrollment.[40]

Most children from the Mti Mmoja attended the primary school in Lendikenya, which was a long walk. With the encouragement of a Catholic priest, parents in the area contributed money to build another school closer to their homes. In turn, the government promised to provide furnishings, books, and supplies for the school and pay all salaries. A teacher was hired before the building was completed, so she taught classes in the small Catholic church. A wealthy Maasai parent built a concrete-block home with a corrugated iron roof on his property for her to live in until a teacher's house could be built on the school property. She taught Standard I the first year; she added Standard II the next year and there were plans to add additional standards (and teachers) each year. A gifted, committed, energetic teacher, she quickly gained the trust and praise of all the parents. Numerous men and women proudly told me how their sons and daughters had learned to read in less than a year. She moved her classes to the school building once it was completed, but no desks, chairs, tables, or books had been provided by the government by late 1993.

In contrast, only about a fourth of eligible children in Embopong' attended the primary school built with funds solicited by Sokoine in Mfereji.

Few households could spare the valuable labor of all of their children in herd-ing, gathering water and wood, and child care. Those who were students had to walk two to four miles to school, often with only some maize-flour porridge for breakfast to last them the day. Tired and hungry, they often fell asleep in classes and returned to their homes only to help their parents work. Their attendance was as sporadic as that of their teachers. Generally only three to four teachers were posted to Mfereji, most of whom, even though they were Maasai themselves, viewed their posting to Mfereji as a punishment because of the dry dusty heat, the remote location far from their families or even the social life of a town, and the difficult accessibility. Teachers had to find a way (usually by foot) to travel the 15 kilometers over Komolonik Mountain to Monduli town every month to pick up their salary checks. But often their checks were delayed, so they stayed in town to wait. Food was generally un-available for sale in Mfereji (except for exorbitantly priced sugar, Coca-Cola, cigarettes, and a few other commodities brought in by donkey or occasionally by car by an eager entrepreneur) so teachers had to carry in their own food and supplies, either on their backs or by donkey.

Finally, gender was still an issue for parents in educating their children. Most parents claimed in the survey that they wanted to educate both their sons and daughters, but some preferred to educate their boys. The legacies of colonial and mission education, which predominantly enrolled boys in Maasai areas, were evident in such attitudes, but perhaps more important, educated boys were generally perceived as a better investment, for they would (ideally) always help their parents. Girls, however, would only marry and move away to live with their husbands; they could be counted on to help not their parents but their in-laws and husband. Girls were also an important source of wealth, especially for poorer families, through the bridewealth obtained for their mar-riage. Parents also feared that their daughters would be raped or seduced by their teachers, get pregnant by their teachers or male classmates, or elope with lovers of their choosing. These concerns were magnified when they considered sending a girl to one of the secondary schools, most of which only had boarding facilities. None of these fears were groundless, as evidenced by the experiences of several young women, and the cases of these "bad" girls were used to prevent other girls from following in their footsteps. Only a few girls, all but one as-sisted by their educated brothers, attended secondary school, despite the resis-tance of their parents. Paradoxically, although many parents did not want to sponsor the education of their own female children, they did want their edu-cated sons to marry educated women so that the couple "would be alike."

Not everyone shared such gender preferences for boys' education. Several middle-aged women regretted that their parents had not sent them to school. "I was very upset when I wasn't allowed to go to school. But eventually girls were allowed to go to school, so now there are many more. . . . I want all of my children, girls and boys, to go to school since I am still so angry at missing a chance at education. I will put them all in school so they won't be stupid." "These days," another woman confided, "I wish that my father had put me in school, then I would know whether a certain way was dangerous or not. . . . I want my daughters to be smart, even if it won't help me, and my sons as well. These days no one wants to be stupid anymore. I mean stupidity will suffocate us as it has suffocated me since long ago." "My literate daughter-in-law," said one woman, "knows Swahili and has helped me from being like an animal."

Education, therefore, was perceived as a means to achieve wealth and political power, but it was primarily a strategy for males. Such gender bias, especially in the provision of secondary school education, has further contributed to the marginalization of Maasai women from expanded economic opportunities, as well as from the languages and practices of the nation-state. To explore these inequalities, I now turn to a discussion of the ethnic and gender dimensions of Maasai participation in the politics of the nation-state.

Peripheral Politics, Political Periphery: Being a Maasai "Citizen"

"What Is CCM?": Gender, Ethnicity and National Party Politics

For over thirty years, from Independence until 1992, Tanzania had only one legal political party, Chama Cha Mapinduzi (CCM).[41] During this period, the state administrative structure and CCM were closely intertwined: all central, regional, and district officials had to be party members. The state and party had parallel administrative structures, so that, for example, the state-appointed "regional commissioner" had his party counterpart, the "regional development director," and every village was managed by a village-elected village chair, and a government- or party-appointed village secretary.

The relationship between CCM and Maasai was ambivalent at best. As described in Chapter 3, TANU initially made little effort to campaign in Maasai areas during the colonial era. A few elite educated Maasai men such as Edward Sokoine quickly became active party members, but TANU and, later, CCM were unsuccessful (or more likely uninterested) in captivating the involvement of most elder men, uneducated men, or women of all ages. In 1977, Hatfield found in his census that most older Maasai had not joined

TANU, or even if they had they did not consider it "important enough to mention" (Hatfield 1977b: 20). This situation was partly due to CCM's lack of interest in mobilizing such a peripheral people, but most Maasai themselves were not very interested in CCM.

While TANU may not have been interested in the active participation of Maasai, it was still interested in their dues. TANU coerced Maasai men to join the party by requiring that individuals selling or buying cattle (who were almost always men) had to produce TANU membership cards. Anyone receiving famine relief grain (usually a man as "head of the household") also had to show a TANU card (Hatfield 1977b: 20). In 1976, Hess reported that market, veterinary, and other fees plus TANU dues totaled an average of Tshs 50/= ($7) per animal sold. And "if the producer did not have a receipt for previous payment of TANU dues, and invariably the receipts were lost, these were collected repeatedly at the markets as animals were sold" (Hess 1976: 33).

While TANU and, later, CCM had some prominent women leaders and established a women's branch (Umoja wa Wanawake, UWT) early on, the active female members have usually been middle-class educated urban women (cf. Geiger 1997). The very creation of auxiliary women's and youth groups implies that these categories of citizens were never central to CCM's power structure. Very few Maasai women, except for a few who were educated beyond primary school or who married elite educated men, ever became active members of CCM. Like the earlier Native Authorities in the colonial period, TANU and then CCM were perceived as male domains. When Hatfield tried to encourage all Maasai to join TANU in order to influence national decisions such as the dress code, he was told that "neither women nor morani [*ilmurran*] would join." "Of course," he added, "the Umoja wa Wanawake and TANU Youth League could hardly be said to be functioning in most of the rural areas of Masailand" (Hatfield 1977b: 16).

The predominantly male composition of CCM's active membership and the organization's failure to incorporate non-elite women were quite evident in the three communities. As Table 4.10 shows, although 30.8 percent of the women in Emairete, 51.2 percent in Mti Moja, and 25.7 percent in Embopong' said they were members of CCM, a greater percentage of women in Emairete and Embopong' claimed to have no idea what CCM was. When asked during the census if they were members of CCM, at least a third of the women in each village responded "*Kainyoo CCM?* (What is CCM?)." When asked what they thought CCM might be, some thought perhaps it was a religion, others a school, but most said they had no idea; they had never heard of it. In contrast, the percentage of men who did not know CCM was minuscule.

Table 4.10 Percentage Distribution of CCM Membership by Village and Sex

| | Emairete | | Mti Mmoja | | Embopong' | | Total | |
Response	Men	Women	Men	Women	Men	Women	Men	Women
CCM Member	70.0	30.8	82.4	51.2	62.8	25.7	71.5	34.7
Not a CCM Member	20.2	23.5	7.7	14.0	23.1	18.3	17.7	20.1
What is CCM?	3.9	42.6	2.2	33.3	10.3	48.6	4.8	41.6
No Response	5.9	3.1	7.7	1.6	3.8	7.3	5.9	3.6
Total	100.0	100.0	100.0	100.0	100.0	100.0	100.0	100.0

Source: Hodgson Census, 1992.
Figures do not add up exactly due to rounding.

That so many women claimed to be ignorant about CCM was a reflection of the gendered politics of participation in national politics. Women, especially poorer rural women such as Maasai and Arusha, have always been marginal to CCM's exercise of power. Except when trying to mobilize their vote, CCM paid little attention to the needs and concerns of such women, building its rural power base through younger, educated men. However, it is likely that some women who replied "*Kainyoo CCM?*" were in fact quite aware of what CCM was supposed to be. By feigning ignorance, they mocked what they perceived as the wide gap between CCM's endless promises and its meager accomplishments. As one woman replied, "What is CCM? The name for people who don't work?" To question CCM's existence was to scoff at its pretensions, its marginalization of women (except when mobilizing their votes), and its male authoritarian structure.

Masculine Authorities

As in the colonial period, a parallel political structure was created that often exacerbated generational tensions among Maasai men. Elder men continued to exercise their control over marriages, bridewealth transfers, and disputes through their area and clan councils, but some younger educated men, eager for power, participated in the political structure of the nation-state by joining CCM and competing for political offices. But elder Maasai men were not completely oblivious to national politics and the importance of access to power and representation within the administrative structure of the nation-state. Hatfield reported in 1977 that

> there appears to be a small but powerful Masai political machine which tends to determine who campaigns for public office and who does not. While it means

that some potentially able individuals are excluded for one reason or another from the privileges of campaigning, the "machine" is always on the lookout for capable men and will assist them in their strivings. There is also evidence that elections and candidates are observed keenly on the local level. Masai tend to prefer Masai in public office. They respond to past records and promises. (Hatfield 1977b: 20)

Comprised of the *ilaigwenak* and elder men, the male "machine" met together to select a candidate by consensus, then directed everyone under their control to vote accordingly. They encouraged a few young educated Maasai men who were perceived as intelligent and able to run for office with their blessings and the guaranteed support of most people. Edward Sokoine, who eventually became prime minister of Tanzania until his death in a car accident in 1984, was one of the first Maasai politicians backed by the machine, and the most successful. His career (Maasai Portrait 4) illustrates the careful and often difficult negotiations of such men and the power and mutual benefits of such collaborations.

Despite the suspicious deaths of Sokoine and several other Maasai politicians, most elders recognized the necessity for Maasai to compete for political office. Local support for national political campaigns was still mobilized by appealing to voters as "real" Maasai and by using the Maasai male political machine. The hotly contested parliamentary elections for Monduli District in 1990–1991 illustrate the persistent power of this dominant image. The two male candidates were both Maasai by birth. The incumbent, Lepilall ole Molloimet, a former schoolteacher, was elected as a member of Parliament in 1985 with the support of the political machine. The elders from his natal village of Sinya rejoiced, celebrating his victory with a special blessing ceremony and feast, to which I was invited. Molloimet was presented with gifts, including a goat and stick of the *ilaigwenak,* then blessed by all the elders present who circled him, spitting on him and sprinkling him with milk from small calabashes stuffed with green grass, all symbolic practices of blessing. During his first term, Molloimet reciprocated their support, working tirelessly to mobilize NGO support for "development" projects of their (and his) choosing, including water sources, dispensaries, and grinding machines.[42]

But he could not meet the tremendous "development" demands of his constituents, which led many disgruntled elders to complain that Molloimet was just another government/CCM official—full of big promises and small results. Meanwhile, his campaigns for Maasai land rights angered some government officials at the district, regional, and national levels. They encouraged another Maasai man, Dr. Salash Toure, to oppose Molloimet in the 1990

4.3 Lepilall Molloimet, a Maasai member of Parliament, addressing the
male elders in Sinya after a blessing ceremony. Photo by author.

elections. But Toure was an anomaly—he was the adopted son of President
Sekou Toure of Guinea, who had asked for (and received) a Maasai child to
take home with him during a visit to Tanzania in the 1960s. Dr. Toure had
returned to Dar es Salaam as an adult to work as a medical doctor.

The campaign was fierce, with *ilmurran* mobilizing support for Molloimet, who as a member of the Seuri age-set was one of their *ilpiron* (fire-
stick elders), while some elders and educated Maasai men campaigned on
behalf of Toure. Controversy soon began among Maasai as to "how Maasai"
Toure was—as a Muslim, he could not eat the meat offered him during his
campaign tour, forcing his hosts scramble to kill another animal or find appropriate food.[43] But, even worse, he was not circumcised. His opponents repeatedly mocked his supporters by asking how they could elect "a boy" to be a
member of Parliament. Toure lost the election, 11,467 votes to 15,494, but
contested the results for irregularities in voting (people voting more than once
under assumed names) and claimed that Molloimet had "smeared" him by
calling him "a boy."[44] After a long court battle in which Molloimet denied the

Table 4.11 Percentage Distribution of Adult Maasai and Arusha Men and Women
Who Reported Voting in 1990 Election, by Age-Set

Age-set	Emairete		Mti Mmoja		Embopong'		Total	
	Men	Women	Men	Women	Men	Women	Men	Women
Iltareto	—	28.6	—	0.0	—	40.0	—	28.6
Ilterito	85.7	41.7	33.3	57.1	33.3	25.0	61.5	39.5
Ilnyangusi	92.3	51.7	100.0	90.9	75.0	90.9	88.0	68.6
Seuri	85.7	76.8	100.0	96.7	80.0	67.9	88.0	79.3
Ilmakaa	80.0	67.3	94.7	94.7	90.0	59.5	86.1	74.0
Ilandissy	68.8	31.7	89.9	60.7	69.4	57.9	73.8	44.6
Total	75.5	59.8	90.7	85.4	75.3	59.8	79.1	66.2

Source: Hodgson Census, 1992.

accusations, a second election was held, which Molloimet, the "real Maasai man," won.

The success of the elders and *ilmurran* in mobilizing both Maasai men and women to vote in the elections is reflected in Table 4.11. While the percentage of women who voted was very high, with almost 60 percent of the women in Emairete and Embopong' and 85 percent of the women in Mti Mmoja voting, many women openly admitted to me that they voted according to the directions of their husband. Such a high turnout of women to vote for the hotly contested parliamentary election is misleading in other ways, also. Women do not always show up to vote. During the 1993 elections for village CCM chairman in Emairete, ninety-seven men and only three women, educated Arusha sisters, voted.

Women as Children

In the realm of national politics, many women were perceived and perceived themselves to be like children (Hodgson 1999c). They knew little of events beyond their local area and lacked confidence in their own opinions and knowledge of government. While word of mouth provided quick, in-depth news about Maasai events, radios were the main direct source of information about national and international news. Eighteen men in Emairete, six in Mti Moja, and none in Embopong' possessed radios, while only two women in Emairete, the wealthy widow and the schoolteacher, owned them. Many men who did not own radios gathered to listen to them in the stores during the daytime or in the homestead of a lucky owner in the evening. Often several men gathered in a house to listen to the news at night, while women met in another house to talk among themselves. Women seemed to have little interest in the news. The census and the survey confirmed their lack of awareness about basic fundamentals of the Tanzanian state and CCM and their insecurity and uneasiness in answering questions about the government.

The survey included a section of questions probing perceptions about the government's assistance and obligations to the Maasai: What, in your opinion, has the government done to help the Maasai? What, in your opinion, has the government not done to help the Maasai? and What, in your opinion, should the government be doing to help the Maasai which it is not doing? After confident, detailed answers to almost half an hour of previous questioning, many women quieted down, claiming ignorance of ideas or opinions about the government, repeating *mayiello, mayiello, mayiello,* "I don't know" for question after question.

When pressed, they would repeat *"mayiello, mayiello"* or mutter something along the lines of "How should I know that?" Some older women and a few younger women had more thoughtful answers—the government has built schools, provided food when there was hunger, built hospitals, and so on. No man hesitated to answer these questions; all had opinions about what the government had done to help them and what should still be done. Their answers described basic needs—schools, clean water, hospitals, roads, veterinary medicines, and so on—that they felt the government either had supplied or should supply. As to how the government had *not* helped the Maasai, few men or women had anything to say other than *"metii,"* "there is nothing" (literally: "It is not there").

Another question asked if there had been women among the leadership (*enkitoria* or *erikorei*) of the Maasai in the past. Almost everyone responded "no." When asked why, the most common response by both men and women was "they, women, are ignorant" (*emodai*), and the second most common response was that it was not women's work, but that of men. When asked if there were presently women in the Tanzanian government, most men and women said yes—but they were there because the government put them there (*etipik*), and, many implied, not because they deserved it. Not surprisingly, only one Maasai woman—the wealthy widow—served in local village government; she was one of the twenty-three members of Emairete's village council, while no women were on the councils of Mti Mmoja or Embopong'.

In the domain of politics, women were not only accused of being ignorant, and therefore unable to fill leadership positions, but they had internalized this image so that many were unaware of basic institutions of the Tanzanian state such as CCM, and many more professed ignorance of any worthwhile opinions or ideas about the government.

*   *   *

As these village profiles and commentaries indicate, Maasai have been disenfranchised from political power and economic opportunity in the nation-state. The difficult relationship between Maasai and the state has been fueled by persistent images of Maasai as "primitive" and "conservative." These images have been used by state officials either to direct their resources to more "progressive," politically powerful groups or to justify harsh interventions such as villagization and the dress code campaign. Moreover, if Maasai men are second-class citizens, Maasai women are third-class citizens (if they are citizens at all). Yet Maasai men and women persevere, crossing ethnic, political, and cultural boundaries to take advantage of whatever opportunities are available within the constraints of increasing impoverishment and stratification.

MAASAI PORTRAIT 4: EDWARD MORINGE SOKOINE

I would very much like for us all to examine our customs and beliefs in order to set aside our bad customs and nurture our good ones, in light of our self-respect as Africans.

The estate of *marehemu*[1] Edward Moringe Sokoine, the former Maasai prime minister of Tanzania, sits to the left side of the bumpy dirt road that winds over Komolonik Mountain from Emairete down to Embopong' in the Rift Valley. Three large cement-block houses, one for each of his two widows and another for his mother, are behind the high wooden fence that protects the estate from the road. Outside the fence there is a guardhouse, which is manned year round by police to protect the privacy and security of Sokoine's family.

I first entered the compound on April 12th, 1992, to attend the eighth annual memorial of Sokoine's death at the invitation of one of his widows. His raised cement grave lies behind one of the houses, and is surrounded by a chain fence and sheltered by a corrugated iron canopy; it has a large wooden cross and plaques on top of it. Several Maasai elite were in attendance—the member of Parliament and other district and regional government and party officials—and several students, dressed in black, from the teachers' training college in Monduli. The local Catholic priest, an American Holy Ghost Father, arrived and held a brief ceremony at his graveside, with two Bible readings, a Psalm ("The Lord is my shepherd . . ."), prayers, and a short sermon. (He apologized that he could not offer mass, as it was Palm Sunday.) First family members and then the most important government officials took turns putting wreaths on his tomb. The member of Parliament, whom I knew well, asked me to take his picture laying the wreath, but his camera wouldn't work. Afterward, the men went to the senior wife's house and the women to the junior wife's house for food and drink. As we waited, Sokoine's younger wife proudly showed me her photo album, including pictures of her children, studio portraits of her and Sokoine, Sokoine with President Nyerere, and Sokoine in China shaking hands with a group of female dancers who had blackened their skin and wore crop tops with *khangas* (printed squares of African cloth) tied around their waists. With the other women, I ate *pilau* (a spiced rice and meat dish of Indian origin), fried potatoes and bananas, and cabbage salad and drank sodas (beers and alcohol were reserved for the men). We sat in the ornate living room, full of pictures of Queen Elizabeth, Prince Philip, other royalty, and Sokoine and his family; Maasai beaded jewelry; a large porcelain vase; and Christmas lights draped on the mantelpiece. One of Sokoine's teenage daughters, dressed in a shiny dark blue polyester dress with a back slit and black slip peeking out was slouched in front of the brand-new stereo system, listening to tapes, switching them back and forth. After the meal we watched a video of *Hatari*, a John Wayne movie that was filmed, in part, in Tanzania, on their huge new video monitor. As I recorded in my field notes: "Everyone was mesmerized—lots of comments about the rhino attacking the car. Was the man who was zipping up the woman's dress her husband? Why did the one man punch the other? One woman kept imitating the shrill woman's voice to the amusement of the other women. Lots of muttering when Dallas [the female lead] was lying in bed first with John Wayne, then Red Buttons, then a third man walked in. . . ."

References to and stories about Sokoine recurred constantly in my discussions with Maasai. For many, he was a mythic figure. His life was central to their understanding of the changes that had occurred in their past, and his death marked their sense of despair about the future. "When Sokoine was alive," they would say, "he told us to go to school." Or, "he told us to quit moving about and settle on our land to protect it." "The government only cared about us," one man told me, "when Sokoine was alive. He helped us to get water, schools, and a hospital. Now that he is gone—poof! Nothing!" "In the time of Sokoine," said another male elder from Embopong', "dams were built for us, a church was built for us, we were given farm land, and even if the cattle died you wouldn't die from hunger." But these days, without Sokoine to represent their interests in national politics, many Maasai from the area feel vulnerable to continued attacks on their rights, especially their land rights.

Sokoine was born in 1938 in Emairete and raised in Monduli Juu. He began primary school in Monduli in 1949, then passed his exams and entered the Monduli Middle School in 1953.[2] He was not interested in attending school to become a "better pastoralist"; he loved education for its own sake. He was circumcised and became an *olmurran* in 1957 (of the Seuri age-set), the same year he entered Umbwe Secondary School in Moshi. The fire-stick elders (*ilpiron*)—led by Wanga ole Nyati (described in Maasai Portrait 2), a famous and respected leader himself—selected Sokoine to be the *olaigwenani* for his age-group in the area. At a special ceremony in the Emairete Crater, they blessed him and presented him with the short black stick that symbolized his position. At this meeting, he is reported to have lectured the other *ilmurran* on the importance of education given the broad changes taking place in the world. Soon afterward, he was baptized a Catholic and took the Christian name "Edward." (His biographer even claims that earlier he had seriously considered entering the priesthood [Halimoja 1985: 109].) A diabetic, Sokoine had to quit secondary school in 1958 because of health problems. Despite his poor health, he was still able to move to Mfereji to coordinate the distribution of milk and food during the 1960–1961 famine.[3]

In a 1961 letter he wrote to the district commissioner of Masai District from Mfereji, he outlined his early position on the future of the Maasai:

> How often have I heard neighboring tribes saying that they will encroach into this country when the British restraint has been removed and farm it; I have a sickening feeling for time is now in the "near vicinity." For they will do all they can with this land. Personally, I think our best way lies in the intensive development of our country. For we shall be accused of occupying land without developing it properly, while others who know how to develop it need land thirstily. I am not talking about one particular place but the whole district as a whole. It is really dissappointing [*sic*] to see that people are shifting from one place to another and leave behind them "deserted ruins."[4]

The idea that only vigorous promotion of Maasai development would protect their land rights remained a central tenet of Sokoine's political vision.

He consolidated his power base in 1961 when he joined TANU and became the assistant secretary of the Masai Council (he became secretary a year later). As an *olaigwenani* in the Maasai political structure, an officer in the Masai District administrative structure, and one of the few active Maasai members of the national political party, he was now poised to rise rapidly through the ranks. In 1965, after two years studying finance and leadership in West Germany, he ran with the backing of the Maasai political machine for member of Parliament for Masai District. The incumbent, Edward Mbarnoti (who had been appointed "chief" of the Masai Council during the last few years of colonial rule), was now perceived as ineffective by some constituencies in representing Maasai interests. The machine mobilized Maasai men and women to vote for Sokoine, and his victory was overwhelming: 6,977 votes as opposed to only 871 for Mbarnoti. Much of Mbarnoti's support came from non-Maasai living in the towns of Masai District who feared the consequences should Maasai gain political power.

Sokoine quickly established himself as a vocal representative of Maasai rights, asking fifteen pointed questions during one of his first days in Parliament. Many were about Maasai loss of land rights and control in the Ngorongoro area. Others included:

• Why have Maasai in Ngorongoro been forbidden to farm, yet some of them have no livestock to feed themselves?

• Since in this nation there are tribes that have progressed and others that are still backward, what plans does the Government have to educate those backward people so that they will be the same as their comrades?

• Although the Masai District Council requested a law requiring all children in Masai District to go to school until graduation, the Ministry of Education refused to enact such a law. Could you explain why such a law is not possible? (Halimoja 1983: 25–26, 32–33)

As part of the activist modernist agenda reflected in these questions and others like them, he was also committed to cajoling, coercing, and even at times forcing his Maasai constituents to embrace education, improve their animal husbandry practices, settle in permanent communities, and otherwise pursue "development." Several elder men from Emairete told me how Sokoine had urged them to stay in Monduli Juu when they wanted to relocate in order to avoid the increasing numbers of Arusha moving in to the area. "That is how Maasai keep losing their land," Sokoine told them, "and there is no more land to move to. Stay and protect your rights and your land."

Progress for Sokoine also meant a change in certain Maasai cultural practices. As he told Parliament in a speech in 1965: "I would very much like for us all to examine our customs and beliefs in order to set aside our bad customs and nurture our good ones, in light of our respect as Africans" (Halimoja

1983: 38). As his example, he described the food taboos of *ilmurran* (no food other than milk, blood, and meat) as cultural practices that needed to be changed, in order for *ilmurran* to adopt "modern ways" (Swahili: *njia za kisasa*) such as farming and other economic activities and lessen their reliance on livestock. Similarly, as head of the Masai District Council, he was a prominent voice in the government's campaigns to ban Maasai from mining and wearing ochre in the mid-1960s. As he wrote in a letter to the regional commissioner:

> The [Masai] Council has been unhappy with the use of olkaria [red ochre] by Masai, and particularly with the habit of painting it with [*sic*] their bodies or dying their clothes with [it]. Apart from the fact that the ochre makes people appear dirty, a danger to good health, it has been a displeasing sight to foreign visitors. After a long consideration on the subject the Council has passed a resolution to pursuade [*sic*] the Masai to dispense with this tribal custom. It further suggested that if it is the "reddish" colour of the mineral which is appealing to the people shopkeepers will be advised by the Council to sell national dresses made of a colour most pleasing to the people.... The Council decised [*sic*] to request Government to make it illegal under the law to mine red ochre for sale, and also to revoke the right of local people mining the mineral under tribal rights.[5]

In a subsequent letter, he claimed that "many Maasai had criticised this custom and called for its abolishment but the former colonial Government wasn't in favour of this as it thought the custom deserved perpetual preservation."[6] Besides closing the mines, lecturing Maasai to change their practices (including wearing two pieces of cloth to fully cover "the necessary parts of the body"), and encouraging stores to sell red cloth and clothing, Sokoine demanded that all Maasai government officers, however low-ranking, serve as examples by wearing "modern" clothing (i.e., shirts and pants). But he supported some Maasai practices that others opposed, such as polygyny. Although baptized a Catholic, he married two wives (one in 1960, the other in 1969) and had a total of eleven children with them.

Despite these (moderately successful) attempts to force Maasai to conform to national ideals of "modern dress," his demands for more schools in Maasai areas, the required attendance of every Maasai child in primary school, the formalization of Maasai land rights, and provision of increased services confronted the prejudices and limited resources of the nation-state and were routinely rejected. His campaign to strengthen Maasai land rights through the provision of 99-year leaseholds succeeded only, at the time, for his home area of Monduli Juu, the only Maasai area to receive such a certificate (Jacobs 1980a: 11).

Despite these confrontations and his limited successes in funneling state resources to Monduli and Ngorongoro Districts, Sokoine retained strong support among Maasai and gained increasing popularity among other Tanzanians as his reputation for fighting corruption spread. His support among Maasai is best seen from the election results. He ran uncontested in 1970. In 1975, a non-Maasai dared to challenge him and lost by over 12,000 votes (14,911 to 2,644). He ran uncontested again in 1980. As a member of Parliament, he served in various ministries, which culminated in his appointment as prime minister in 1977. He was a close confidante of President Nyerere and ably executed national directives such as coordinating the war with Uganda in 1978–1979 and implementing fierce campaigns against corruption, "black marketeering," and hoarding.[7] These campaigns earned him the respect and appreciation of many Tanzanian citizens and the title "Man of the People."[8] But his 1983 anti-corruption campaign (which focused heavily on corrupt government officials), as well as his battles over illegal alienation of land in Monduli District to some expatriates by other government officials, made Sokoine numerous enemies among his fellow officials and politicians.[9] The circumstances of his death in a car "accident" on April 11th, 1984, prompted both national mourning and intense suspicion that the accident was in fact no accident but a plot arranged by his adversaries. The equally mysterious death of his replacement as member of Parliament, Joseph Lemomo, while training at the national army's officers' college in 1985 (allegedly from a heart attack), only further confirmed Maasai suspicions that the state would not tolerate powerful Maasai. Some elder men now warned their ambitious sons about the dangers of participating as a Maasai in national politics.

Like many famous people, Sokoine was a man of contradictions. Although he was a powerful defender of Maasai political rights, especially land rights, he put constant pressure on Maasai leaders to change certain social beliefs (such as resistance to education) and cultural practices (especially in terms of dress and appearance) to conform with national, "modern" ideals. Yet he himself, a Catholic, married two wives, in keeping with Maasai custom but contrary to Catholic teaching. For some, he was a visionary, showing "his people" the way of the future; for others, he was an arrogant dictator, demanding that all follow his directives. Paradoxically, while his local reputation among Maasai was based on his ardent defense of their land rights and his respected status as a *olaigwenani* of his age-set, his national fame was partly achieved by the erasure of his ethnicity in the media—the educated, intelligent, "modern" Sokoine was a "man of the people," a preeminent Tanzanian citizen who was hardly a "real Maasai."

POVERTY AND PROGRESS: GENDER, ETHNICITY, AND PASTORALIST DEVELOPMENT

5

"The Maasai," as Chapter 4 documented, continued in the post-colonial period to be perceived as "primitive," "conservative," and "backward." These persistent images shaped the relationship of Maasai with the Tanzanian state, as evidenced in the village profiles. This chapter continues the analysis of development during the colonial period by examining contemporary development interventions, particularly their gendered and ethnic assumptions and effects. My purpose is to explore the continuities and changes between the ideas and experiences of development in the colonial period and those of the post-colonial period. What were the post-colonial legacies of the colonial development interventions in terms of the design and implementation of development projects, the relationship between Maasai and the state, the meanings and practices of "being Maasai," and the gendered relations of power between and among Maasai men and women?

After tracing the contemporary masculinist constructions of "the Maasai" as "pastoralists" and their development "problem," I explore how these images shaped the largest Maasai "development" project to date, the Masai Livestock Development and Range Management Project (MLDRMP). Like Ferguson (1990), I analyze the images and assumptions which shaped the objectives and implementation of the project. I also examine the consequences of the project as one more in a long list of development failures in the lives of Maasai. Given the dominance of economic paradigms in shaping development goals and practices for over fifty years, I focus this analysis on the cultural and social dimensions of the gendered consequences of commoditization and monetization. I then turn to a more recent development agenda, that of "indigenous development," and explore how gender, ethnicity, and nation are articulated in the origins, objectives, and practices of two Maasai indigenous development organizations (IDOs).

From Backward Pastoralists to Modern Ranchers

As in the post-war colonial period, the drive by the government to increase productivity, now in the name of Ujamaa, renewed and intensified attempts to "develop" the beef industry as a potentially lucrative source of state revenue. Not only did urban areas of Tanzania have a large unmet demand for beef, but beef was also a profitable export commodity.

In 1959–1960, an economic mission from the International Bank for Reconstruction and Development (IBRD, the World Bank) visited Tanganyika to formulate a program for the economic development of the country.[1] In their dense report (IBRD 1961), the experts claimed that Tanganyika's "recent development" had been "highly satisfactory," and they foresaw "little difficulty in maintaining a reasonably satisfactory rate of growth of production and exports over the next few years" (IBRD 1961: 3). They did, however, worry about "the problem of maintaining the growth of production in the longer run" once the post-war boom in commodity markets subsided, and because of the "existing African methods of agriculture and pastoralism [which] lead increasingly to depletion of soil fertility and, in places, to erosion" (1961: 3–4). The solution to these problems "was made more difficult by the smallness of government financial resources" (IBRD 1961: 5). But there was hope. Within the country, the "main development task . . . is to improve the methods of peasant agriculture and cattle keeping, or to transform present methods and organization into systems making more productive use of the land" (IBRD 1961: 5). Meanwhile, "since Government expenditures play a key role in stimulating and making possible increase in production," the IBRD experts had an unsurprising suggestion: "Development in Tanganyika could benefit greatly from increased grants from the outside world and from external loans bearing low rates of interest, long repayment periods or liberal periods of grace before service becomes due" (IBRD 1961: 4). Their report detailed the areas in which government expenditures could be usefully expanded to stimulate increased production. But much of the report was also concerned with "questions of planning and method," since "the greater Tanganyika's success in making effective use of the limited resources at its disposal, the more it will appear to merit financial and technical assistance from the outside world" (IBRD 1961: 3–5).

And pastoralists, of course, had a distinct role in furthering the development of their country. The problem of production was conceived of as one beyond history: "As with crops, so with livestock, existing African methods differ little in essentials from those practiced from time immemorial, and lead to a combination of low yields and deterioration of the land" (IBRD 1961: 79). More precisely, the degradation of the land was seen as a problem of the "tragedy of the commons" (cf. Hardin 1968):

> The combination of communal ownership and grazing of the land with un-restricted individual, or family, ownership of stock results in both low productivity and deterioration of the land, because it immediately leads to disregard of two essentials of successful ranching, namely, adjustment of stock numbers to carrying capacity, and pasture management. Neither the individual nor the community exhibits any interest in these matters; what is everybody's business is nobody's business. (IBRD 1961: 80)

Instead, "each *man* is anxious to increase his herds and to possess as many beasts as possible" (my emphasis; IBRD 1961: 79). As before, the entire history of the constant resettlements, voracious land alienations of the most fertile areas, and prior attempts to increase production which produced the problem was ignored. And not only have "African methods" changed little since "time immemorial," but they were also "communal," a term which collapsed all the distinctions between the ways different groups control access to grazing and water by clan, territory, and other affiliations. The smug arrogance of the experts and their contempt for everything "African" was displayed in their litany of the sins of African pastoralists: "gross overstocking," their "desire to possess as many animals as possible," their "indiscriminate" and "uncontrolled" breeding of livestock, the "poor quality" of the stock, "low" standards of animal husbandry, and so on. The implicit opposition between the wild, uncontrolled, ignorant (primitive) African and the controlled, rational, wise (modern) American was hard to miss.

The sum of all these problems was that "the pastoral areas are contributing far less than their potential to the income of Tanganyika" (IBRD 1961: 81). As such, "the Mission" (an apt title) had two categories of recommendations: an improvement approach and a transformation approach. The improvement approach meant the usual gradual modifications of the "traditional pattern," for which there were "encouraging signs towards increased productivity": "in some areas stock owners are showing an increased tendency to regard their animals as a cash crop, and to take a more active interest in disease control, pasture management, improved animal husbandry and better quality stock" (IBRD 1961: 143). But since "it is likely to be many years before the traditional African cattle industry can be raised to anything approaching a reasonable level of efficiency and productivity," the Mission also recommended a more radical transformation approach: group ("partnership") cattle ranching. These organized, large-scale ranches, established in selected localities on land cleared from tsetse and provided with water supplies, would be run under the "expert management" of the Tanganyika Agricultural Corporation supervising the "tenant cattle keepers" (IBRD 1961: 160).

With Independence, this particular plan of government-managed ranches with African cattle-keeping tenants was never realized, but the idea of group ranches persisted. In 1962, at the request of the Tanganyikan government, USAID financed a study to prepare a "livestock and range management program" for Masai District which could be used as "a model for extending improved practices and production" throughout the district (Deans et al. 1968: 2).[2] The study's recommendations formed the basis for the Range Management and Development Act of 1964, which provided the legal basis for "increased livestock production and improving land use on 155,000 square miles of grazing land in Tanzania." Under the act, local herders could form ranching associations with 99-year leasehold rights, and district ranching commissions would be formed to supervise, set policies, and manage the activities of such associations within their area (Deans et al. 1968: 2).

A Masai Commission was formed under the auspices of the Ministry of Agriculture to supervise the formation and management of ranching associations for the entire Masai District. One representative from each of the five divisions in the district was appointed, as well as six government officials as ex-officio members.[3] Progress, however, was slow:

> By 1969 registration drives to form only four widely scattered ranching associations had begun. Each of the four was targeted to comprise some 350–550 herding families (that is, 1,800–3,000 persons) in control of some 400–500 square miles. . . . Maasai were urged by their local political leaders to seek such association partly in order to secure collective leasehold rights to pasture lands that would permit them to keep out agricultural and pastoral trespassers, and partly because they were promised special assistance from the Ministry and Range Commission in developing their resources, such as new water supplies, veterinary services, roads, schools, dispensaries, and so forth. Indeed, a small demonstration ranch, involving a cattle dip and small dam, was established by the Ministry on the Ardai Plains southwest of Monduli in 1968 precisely in order to serve as a model of the innovations that ranching association members could expect to receive if they registered. (Jacobs 1980: 3–4)

In 1964, Komolonik, covering 220,000 acres near Monduli (including the three study communities), was the first area chosen for the formation of a pilot demonstration ranching association (Map 5.1). To prove that the government "was really serious this time," the Masai Range Commission financed over 210,000 dollars' worth of improvements on the land, including a sixteen-mile gravity pipeline system with six tanks in Mfereji, a two-mile pipeline supplying one watering point and a dip, other dams and water points, road construction, and cattle dips.[4] A thirty-member steering committee (of Maasai men) selected by Maasai (men) was formed to mediate between the Masai Commission and the Komolonik Association members, but by 1969 the association was still not registered. Maasai refused to accept the budget for the improvements or the stock quotas presented by the commission and saw little reason to form such an association.

Meanwhile, the concentration of water and dips in Mfereji was creating problems:

> In less than a year it had become starkly clear that a new problem had already been created. Not only was the rest of the area without adequate dry season water and dips, but even the other dry areas bordering on the part which now had water, had hardly any reliable sources of water for the dry season. The island of abundant water created in Mfereji became the focus of livestock convergence in the dry season as herds from all directions streamed in to drink water. The result was acute overgrazing. The area was in danger of turning into a dustbowl. (Parkipuny 1979: 141)

But overgrazing was not the only problem. After their five-month study of the association in 1968–1969, Dean and the rest of a five-man USAID team of "experts"[5] concluded that

> the move by the Range Commission to get the backing of the Masai through capital improvements has not succeeded. The Masai feel little responsibility for the improvements made, possibly because they were not involved enough in the planning and construction of improvements. They definitely do not feel it was a partnership arrangement. Their attitude is that the government has done this much, let them finish the job.
>
> The majority of the Masai have not perceived the need for an association nor how an association would work. They have difficulty in seeing how their needs will be solved by the scheme presented by the Range Commission. The Masai feel strongly that the government officials do not fully explain their proposals so that they can understand them. What they do not understand, they distrust and hesitate to commit themselves to support. The Masai have been suspicious of the Government and the Range Commission, primarily because they have not understood what the Commission and its officials are trying to do and why. (Deans et al. 1968: 56)

Despite these indications of Maasai reluctance (if not resistance), the recognized problems of accountability, participation, and communication, and the rapid, acute overgrazing in Mfereji, the ranching association concept became

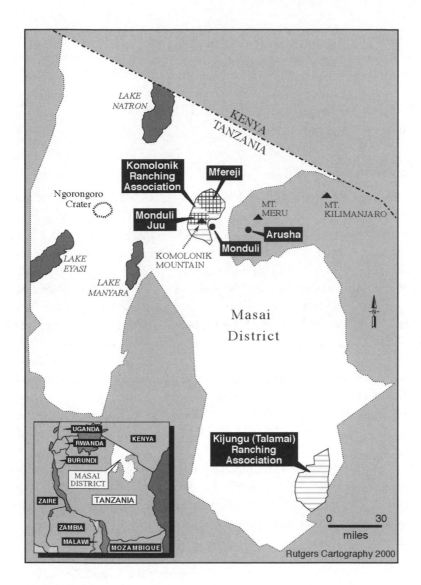

Map 5.1 Masai District ca. 1970, showing approximate location of major
Masai Range Project Ranching Associations. Adapted from USDA map
(Deans et al. 1968: Figure A).

the cornerstone of the largest development project in Maasailand yet, the multimillion-dollar, ten-year-long USAID Masai Livestock Development and Range Management Project.

Masai Livestock Development and Range Management Project

An Overview

Based on the above 1962 and 1968 studies, USAID designed and implemented a series of projects over a ten-year period (1969–1979) in Tanzania, known collectively as the Masai Livestock Development and Range Management Project (MLDRMP; the project), contributing over 10 million dollars to a total project cost of 23 million dollars.[6] The project's goal, explicitly set by the nation-state and not the Maasai, was "to assist the Government of Tanzania to achieve its objective of self-sufficiency and an exportable surplus to earn foreign exchange in the livestock sector" (Utah State University Team 1976: 5).[7] To reach its implicit economic goal of converting Maasai into commercial beef producers, the MLDRMP's purpose was phrased in economic terms: "to achieve a high level of livestock offtake in the Masai District consistent with proper resource management and Tanzanian development goals" (Utah State University Team 1976: 6). Seven specific changes in herd management (e.g., a decrease in calf mortality) were designated to measure the successful realization of this purpose.

From the beginning, therefore, the project was explicitly about developing livestock, not people, for the benefit of the state, rather than for the benefit of the people themselves. Maasai were conveniently characterized as a homogeneous amenable group with "potential" in similar terms as the language used to describe their land:

> The project operates in a clearly defined, relatively insulated, homogenous geographic area having a generally favorable climate and an extensive but protected vegetative natural resource base, not as yet unduly subject to the pressures of human or animal population; there is, therefore, a demonstrable potential for increased production and animal agricultural development.[8]

To meet its goals, the project launched an ambitious array of project components designed to improve range and livestock management, control diseases, assist in the development of security of land tenure, train Tanzanian specialists, develop training for Maasai and Tanzanian livestock and range officers, and assemble baseline data on all facets of Maasai population, economic life, range conditions, climate, and other topics.

Ranching Associations as the Unit of Development

Central to the project's objectives was the formation of ranching associations similar to those formulated in the 1960s, groups of Maasai who would register with the government in return for rights of occupancy and certain water rights. The ranches had three purposes: 1) "to develop an improved herd and raise improved bulls for distribution to upgrade member herds"; 2) "to serve as an educational instrument to introduce modern range and livestock management practices"; 3) "to make the ranch economically profitable and pay for its development as well as improvements in the Association."[9] In order for an association to be officially registered, at least 60 percent of the prospective members had to consent, a range officer was posted to the area, a census was taken of members and their stock, and a ten-man steering committee was elected by members (Parkipuny 1979: 141). Most of the financing came from regional development funds, which constructed a manager's house, a dip, a permanent water supply, and stock pens and paid herders for each ranch and promised to continue its financial assistance until the associations became "profitable."

The average association covered some 300,000 acres and had 500 families and 200,000 livestock units (Hoben 1976). Although by the end of 1975 there were eight ranching associations in various stages of development in Tanzania, only three of these associations had been granted rights of occupancy by the end of 1976, and the legal status of even these rights was being questioned by the end of that year (Holland 1987: 20). By that time, Operation Imparnati had been implemented and the government had opted for settling Maasai in registered Ujamaa villages. When the project team realized that they could not fully implement ranching associations throughout the district, they selected two associations, Komolonik and Kijungu (Talamai), as their priorities. Since several water facilities had already been constructed in the Komolonik Association by the Masai Range Commission prior to the beginning of the MLDRMP, project administrators focused their attention on Talamai.

Maasai responded positively to some of the project components, especially the construction of new facilities for stock watering and the provision of veterinary services, including dips (which killed flies and ticks and thus the diseases they carried), for improving animal health. Maasai men sometimes traveled long distances to use dips, contributed cash to the construction of dips, and paid dipping fees during the first two years of the project. About 60 new dips were constructed (bringing the total number of dips in Maasailand to 94), and over 28 million cattle, 6 million sheep, and 7 million goats were dipped during the project period. Dipping in Talamai was highly successful: calf mortality was reduced from 60 percent to 5 percent by January 1973.

As in the case of Mfereji (above), the concentration of water sources and dips in the two associations attracted large numbers of people with their livestock from other areas. Most of these people became association members, but even non-members were allowed to graze within the bounds of the association:

> For example, a new dam was constructed at Monduli Juu during the past year. The area was previously grazed properly because of a lack of water. When the dam was constructed, many people moved into the area. The people that were there began to keep cattle for other people. The results were overgrazing around the dam and the use of all the water in the dam. The water was completely used and most of the people had to leave the area.[10]

"The results of this development," according to the range management specialist, "are that the most developed associations are the worst overgrazed."[11] As early as 1976, experts were forecasting disaster if the project continued to supply water and dips without a concurrent program to limit livestock numbers: "I feel that the continued existence of the Range project in its present form significantly increases the probability that Masailand will become a desert due to overgrazing."[12] To address the problem, a grazing plan was written for Komolonik by a range officer, specifying wet, dry, and reserve grazing areas. At the time a production-utilization range survey showed that Mfereji appeared to be overstocked, while Emairete and Ardai were both understocked. The plan recommended, among other things, resettling some people from Mfereji in Ardai and Emairete. Once written, the plan circulated through the district bureaucracy for approval, but none of the residents participated in designing or approving this attempt to divide and bound people, their herds, and their land.[13] A similar decision to "scatter development" throughout Monduli and Kiteto Districts to prevent the concentration of people and livestock never transpired either.

In 1975, Komolonik Ranching Association submitted a loan application of Tshs 1,296,250/= for the establishment of the Taresaro Ujamaa Ranch. The objectives of the 40,000-acre ranch, located on the highland plains west of Ardai, were to 1) be a commercial supplier of improved bulls to farmers; 2) purchase immature stock for fattening and resale; and 3) train association members in modern techniques of livestock management.[14] "Improved" bulls

were provided to ranching associations, but preference was given to "progressive" stockmen, "most of whom were members of the associations' steering
committees, had large herds, and were involved in political and business activities at the extra-association level" (Parkipuny 1979: 149). Even these Maasai
soon realized that the "improved" bulls program had several problems. First,
in contrast to local Zebu cattle, the bulls had difficulties surviving in the harsh
conditions (especially the long treks for grass and water), needed more food
and water, and were more susceptible to East Coast fever (ECF) and other
diseases. About 110 bulls, over 50 percent of those distributed, died during
the first two years (1971–1973) of the program. Second, the "improved" bulls
serviced fewer cows than the local bulls; "one man was quoted as saying that
while his local bulls mounted about five cows a day in the season, the imbecile
exotics barely managed one" (Parkipuny 1979: 150).

Although Maasai were initially reluctant to form ranching associations,
reports of the success of dips and the provision of water points in Talamai and
Komolonik spread, and soon Maasai demands to form associations surpassed
the capacities of project personnel. The problem was no longer how to entice
Maasai to form associations but how to meet the overwhelming demand for
new associations with dips and water: "'Range' became the magic word, overshadowing everything else including the government and party in the minds
of the stockmen. That is how in some parts of Maasailand the newest age
group was given the name Range" (Parkipuny 1979: 145). But delays and even
failure to build the promised dips and water points soon stifled Maasai interest. Problems also developed with embezzlement of membership dues and
other funds by some ranching association officials (Parkipuny 1979: 147).

Paying for Development

Although the United States contributed over 10 million dollars to the
Maasai Range Project, Tanzania paid dearly for the project, including substantial payments to the United States in the form of "local contributions" for
the support of USAID personnel, the purchase of U.S.-manufactured equipment and supplies, and long-term debt obligations to the United States. In
terms of "local contributions," the Tanzanian government agreed to cash contributions of Tshs 21,600/= per man-year of services for each U.S. technician
funded by USAID, housing and appliances and furniture in Arusha, medical
services, local transport, office facilities, and "nights out" allowances.[15] Second, the MLDRMP included a 1.7 million–dollar loan agreement with the
United States with seemingly generous repayment terms.[16] But the loan car-

ried other provisions: the Tanzanian government was required to purchase equipment and operational components as well as services "required" for the project exclusively from the United States, and all loan repayments had to be made in U.S. dollars (Parkipuny 1979: 142–143).

Given its financial difficulties, it was hard for the Tanzanian government to ignore the lucrative lure of large loans and grants in the name of "development," but officials often scrambled to find ways to spend the huge sums of money in ways that met the loan conditions. So when, for example, the Talamai Ranching Association applied for a loan of Tshs 100,000/= to clear bush and construct a dam (under the auspices of the Ujamaa Corporate Ranch Livestock Credit Project, a large loan to the Tanzanian government financed by the World Bank), they were advised to resubmit their application for a loan of Tshs 1.54 million to establish an Ujamaa ranch (Parkipuny 1979: 156). These large sums necessarily encouraged the design of large-scale, capital-intensive projects, with top-down control in order to ensure that the terms of the loan were met.[17]

The Best-Laid Plans

As with the Masai Development Plan in the 1950s, the hugely ambitious, bureaucratically top-heavy project sank under its own administrative weight. The reams of fine-tuned detailed plans could not overcome the logistical problems of transport delays, inadequate equipment, staff shortages, and erratic funding that are part of any project's implementation.[18] A major problem was the maintenance and recurrent cost of the boreholes and dips, many of which quickly ceased functioning.[19] The size of the project only magnified the effects of these problems.

But as Vorhis, the project's hydrogeologist, reported, there was perhaps a positive side to the project's limited success in constructing new water sources:

> The rate of borehole completion has been very slow, but one of the consolations has been knowing that the country could not afford a rapid rate. Each borehole now costs around Tshs 123,000/=, headwork costs another Tshs 138,000/=, and the cost of an operator and fuel about Tshs 5,000/= per year. If boreholes had been completed at the rate of one a week, well within the capability of the equipment, the GOT [government of Tanzania] would have had to budget about Tshs 6,000,000/=. With funds appropriated of only Tshs 250,000/= one appreciates what a financial strain "success" would have caused![20]

But, as with prior development projects, no provisions were made as to how the project should be run and maintained once USAID ended its involvement.

Ultimately, the project failed even to meet its own goals of increasing the sale of Maasai livestock on the Tanzanian market to supply beef for domestic and international markets. The numerous terminal evaluations of the project were overwhelmingly negative in their assessments. While better access to water and dips created an increase in stocking levels, Maasai did not increase their commercial offtake. Instead, some project areas such as Talamai, which attracted large numbers of people and stock, soon experienced high stocking levels, land deterioration, bush encroachment, and inadequate water supplies to meet the inflated demands (Arhem 1985: 38).

Development "experts" attributed the limited offtake to a lack of market incentives in Tanzania. But evidence indicated that Maasai were in fact selling large numbers of cattle "illegally" in Kenya:

> Given six years of poor rainfall during 1970–76, the deterioration in infrastructure services to Maasailand, high livestock auction fees and low market prices offered within Maasailand, the need to bribe policemen as much as 300–600 shillings if caught driving cattle into Arusha District for better prices, and the "two-for-one" blackmarket rate in exchange of Kenyan for Tanzanian shillings, it is not altogether surprising, nor entirely irrational, that many Maasai have taken to marketing their livestock through Kenya. (Jacobs 1978: 18; cf. Jacobs 1980: 12)

Based on "discreet inquiries" among Maasai, Jacobs estimated that from 60,000 to 100,000 head of cattle per year were being sold "illegally" by Maasai in Kenya, as were a similar number of sheep and goats (Jacobs 1978: 18). Disgusted with the outcome, CCM imposed a mandatory 10 percent destocking rate in the Maasai districts, a measure which not only failed, but also increased Maasai resentment and resistance.[21]

As in the case of the Masai Development Plan of the 1950s, Maasai were once again blamed for the failure of a project not of their own design or choosing. Several of the evaluation reports repeatedly cited the unwillingness of Maasai to participate in either the implementation or the maintenance of most project components, noting that once the government subsidized such services, the Maasai attitude was characterized as "they have done this much, let them finish it" (DEVRES 1979: 90). Many of the thirty-eight "Important Assumptions" on which the project objectives were based assumed a willingness on the part of Maasai to voluntarily change fundamental aspects of their lives (including their semi-nomadic movements, their livestock management techniques, and their attitudes toward cattle and land) when shown the "advantages" of alternative modes. Furthermore, given these "obvious" advantages, the project assumed that Maasai would be willing to contribute labor and share the costs of the projects. But as the following example illustrates, Maasai saw the government-designed, government-financed, government-controlled projects as the government's property and responsibility:

> The . . . dip was not operating because the iron water pipe had rusted through in one 10 foot section. When asked why there were so few cattle and so much grazing, the herders, standing at the water trough, reported that there was much ECF [East Coast fever] and that the dip had not been operating for 18 months. When asked why they didn't fix the pipe, an easy task, . . . they expressed surprise that we thought they should do this and explained that they were waiting for the Mifugo [Livestock] Office to do it.[22]

In fact, according to Jacobs, Maasai were explicitly prohibited by the government from financing the construction of water supplies "because the government argued that such installations should be provided free by the government, even though the government did not have the resources to do so themselves" (Jacobs 1980: 12).

While the project evaluators severely critiqued the project's design and implementation, Maasai were not as critical. One evaluation team was told by some Maasai that the new wells, dams, reservoirs, and tank trucks for emergency distribution were the "Project's greatest contribution to them and it was the project activity they would most like continued" (DEVRES 1979: 46). Although the evaluation team found faults in the water project component of the project, including continual delays in project implementation and rapid silting of some boreholes, these problems (based on project, not Maasai, criteria) did not sour the evaluation of the Maasai—they were satisfied with their net gain in access to water.

Questions of Control

Relations between Tanzanian government officials and USAID project personnel seem to have been tense throughout. A conflict developed from the very beginning of the project over the legal and ideological relationship between the "ranching associations," which were the fundamental building block of the MLDRMP, and the "villages" central to the philosophy of Ujamaa. USAID officials and other proponents of the ranching associations argued that they were merely a pastoralist version of a Ujamaa village, modified to suit the "animal husbandry–based" lifestyles of the "pastoralist" Maasai and their environmental conditions. Many Tanzanian government officials, however, thought the associations were merely "special treatment" for Maasai. According to a letter written by regional administrative officials in April 1971,

The use of land as stipulated by the Range Development Act as it stands now is capitalistic in its formation as well as its execution, and it probably aims at preserving the Maasai as pastoralists, an idea which we are now fighting to eliminate. It is imperative that the Maasai should be engaged in other economic activities and not only in herding their cows. (Cited in Jacobs 1980: 5)

They insisted that Maasai be treated like all other Tanzanians and be forced to move into planned communal villages.

USAID even froze its orders for heavy equipment in April 1971 in protest until the issue of "the rights of occupancy for ranching associations and farmers" was resolved (Jacobs 1980: 6; Parkipuny 1979: 144). During a visit to the Masai Range Commission in July 1971, the Minister of Agriculture informed Maasai leaders that although the provisions of the Range Development Act stipulated that ranching associations should be given rights-of-occupancy certificates as soon as they completed registration, "politically this was not desirable as it may create perpetual friction between the ever developing Ujamaa villages embedded within the Associations as well as dividing the Maasai themselves. This appears to conflict with the national political concept of Ujamaa."[23] Instead, government policy regarding Masai District was to develop the area primarily for livestock production rather than crop farming "because the economic return is higher per acre than the crops which suffer from scanty and unreliable rains."[24] Under diplomatic and financial pressure from the United States, government officials eventually relented and claimed to support the formation of ranching associations, promising official rights of occupancy to the associations. Procurement activities resumed in November 1972, but the conflict between ranching associations and Ujamaa villages continued:

The problem we are facing is that the [Maasai] citizens themselves can not understand why they have to move into villages and at the same time contribute cattle to start Ranches. . . . We had to completely drop the Lossimingor Ranch because the entire Lossimingor area was taken over by an Ujamaa village. . . . The political leaders of this district advise you that if citizens are forced to start Ujamaa Ranches and Ujamaa Villages at the same time, they will be completely confused.[25]

By 1978, villages had completely displaced ranching associations as the appropriate units of development for Maasai,[26] and only Komolonik Ranching Association ever received a right of occupancy.

As Parkipuny notes, issues of control and accountability between Tanzania and the United States were problematic from the beginning, since the project began as a "national" project, but was almost completely financed by the United States. As a "national" project, the MLDRMP was accountable to the central government in Dar es Salaam, specifically the Ministry of Agriculture, rather than to the local district and regional authorities in which it was situated (Parkipuny 1979: 143). Meanwhile, the main project office was in Dar, and the local project offices and staff residences were in Arusha (the regional headquarters) rather than Monduli (the district headquarters) (Parkipuny 1979: 143; Jacobs 1980: 4). Besides preventing any real local participation or control, these overlapping bureaucratic hierarchies inevitably created problems in integrating project components with the planning and projects of the various government departments. The problems were not resolved by the passage of the National Decentralization Act in 1972, which decentralized authority for planning and development to the regional and district authorities, thereby shifting management of the project to the district development director, specifically the district livestock officer, in 1973.[27] Nor were they eased in 1978, when this shift in control was reversed through "regionalization," which transferred responsibility for project funds and equipment away from the districts and placed them under regional control, invested in the new Tanzanian project manager.[28]

But USAID also underwent significant changes; the project period covered a major shift in USAID development philosophy. Initially, the project was seen primarily as a technical intervention, applying the modern scientific expertise of American scientists to the technical problems of Maasai animal husbandry. In the mid-1970s, USAID discovered that people were part of development and started demanding that its projects contain components devoted to the "social" development of the people involved to ensure that each project was not only financially sound but socially and environmentally sound as well (Hoben 1976; Jacobs 1980: 9). The project's goals were revised to reflect these new humanitarian concerns; rather than being designed to help the Tanzanian government, the project was now designed "to assist the Masai People in improving water and range resources, control livestock parasites, and decrease diseases and increase animal production through integrated ranges and livestock management systems."[29] Now it was anticipated that these projects would improve the "well-being" and "quality of life" of the Maasai by raising income and helping them to establish village life. The indicators which would be used to measure their improved status included income, job opportunity data, and the number of villages and ranching associations established.

While the actual project components remained much the same, they were now modified in project documents to at least show concern with the "impact the project is having on cultural habits of the Masai." Such culturally sensitive "assistance" would now include "1) accelerating the Range Management Planning using practical approaches applicable to Masai culture; and 2) development of information about Masai culture and the maintenance of communication levels with the Masai and their leaders so an evaluation can be made as to how project activities are received."[30]

A project sociologist was hired in 1975, and a Maasai man was hired to train, both overseas and in Tanzania, as his counterpart. Alan Jacobs, an anthropologist who had done research among Tanzanian Maasai in the late 1950s, was also hired to return in 1978 for a short project evaluation. His mandate, according to his assignment letter, was to provide his insights "on the future of the Masai as a cattle herding people, and how they may cope with this future."[31]

Finally, all of the evaluations described the generally "negative" attitude of Tanzanian government personnel toward Maasai, concluding that the "regrettable paternalistic attitude" shown by these people toward Maasai impeded instructional efforts and project operations in many respects (DEVRES 1979: 89). Not only did the government fail to provide promised support and personnel, but it allowed (if not encouraged) farmers to settle in several key project areas in direct contradiction of its promise to control further settlement by guaranteeing land tenure to Maasai in range and ranch areas. The greater political influence of agricultural groups with the state was clearly revealed in the results of competition for land tenure. As in Kenya, some Maasai perceived the ranching associations as a means to secure land against further encroachment by cultivators. Once the government reneged on its promise to guarantee land rights and allowed further encroachment into Maasai areas, the ranches became less desirable.

The ambivalent position of the government was clear: it was hard to resist the large amounts of money provided by the MLDRMP and the lucrative possibilities of increased livestock production and offtake, but it was disturbed that these resources and attention were being funneled to Maasai. As in the colonial period, however, "development" interventions were a useful means of consolidating state control. Ranching associations and the provision of dips and water points became the first steps toward resettling Maasai in villages. The data collected by the project, such as the censuses of Maasai and their livestock and detailed land-use surveys, further facilitated the government's villagization plans. The project's goals were set by the state, not Maasai, and the primary project beneficiaries would be the state's urban populations and foreign exchange accounts, not Maasai. Maasai reluctance to participate in aspects of the project could be read as efforts to evade and resist such control.[32] They voted with their feet by participating in those project components that they perceived as beneficial (the dips, veterinary services, and water facilities), and ignoring components (increased offtake) they found unhelpful. The disparity between the state's agenda and Maasai objectives was revealed by the failure of Maasai to translate their increased herd size into increased offtake, an outcome that the state and project designers had assumed as given.

Gendered Effects

The gendered assumptions of the project are clear from the language used in almost any project document: the "cattlemen," "stockowners," "herdsmen," and "decision-makers" are all male. "Since the Masai cattleman is proud, independent, and conservative he must be convinced not coerced" writes Hess (1976: 15), for example, in a report on the ranching associations. The androcentric assumptions that pastoralists must be men blinded project planners to women's roles in pastoral production (which include caring for sick animals and smallstock, milking, and sometimes even herding and watering) as well as their overlapping rights in most livestock. They directed all of their training, access to veterinary medicines, and membership in ranching associations only to Maasai men, which contributed to the project's failure. As Bennett remarked in his evaluation, "No role for women was envisaged by the project from the beginning. The team considered this to have mitigated against improvements in calf mortality and weaning, since Maasai women are mainly responsible for raising calves" (Bennett 1984: 108).

As with the Masai Development Plan, USAID "experts" assumed that Maasai raised cattle for beef rather than milk. This was partly due, as Kettel (1992) has noted for pastoralist development projects generally, to Western assumptions that since women were involved in milking, milking could not be that important economically to the maintenance of the household. Despite the retinue of livestock "experts," the fact that Maasai breeding and production strategies were designed to increase milk rather than beef production was only seriously noticed in the final year of the project. As the USAID animal production specialist meekly noted in his 1979 end-of-tour report (ten years after the project began):

> It has not been earlier recognized that the Masai are also very much involved in milk production. Besides for reasons of security and wealth, large numbers of cattle are needed to provide for a preferred milk diet. When visiting a boma one is not offered roast meat but a cup of milk. When one asks about the condition

of the boma the reply most often comes in terms of how much milk is available. People who become sick are often considered sick because they are drinking only a little milk. When one discusses improved bulls, female offspring are judged not only on their size but how much milk they produce.[33]

Of course, once the economic potential of dairying was finally acknowledged, project personnel ignored the roles and rights of women in managing and controlling milk and directed their efforts toward men. The Monduli Juu dairy project registered households according to the (male) head of household, facilitating the appropriation by men of the milk and income earned (see below). And when fifty dairy cattle were introduced to local farmers, those farmers were all men.[34]

The gendered assumptions and effects of the MLDRMP were also clearly evident in the training and extension components. From the beginning, a key objective was to train thirty Tanzanians (all men, most Maasai) in U.S. universities in the various technical specialties necessary for "livestock development" (such as range management, animal production, and livestock production). No Maasai women were sent or even considered for training.[35] Similarly, when the shift in USAID development policy to more "social" concerns prompted an increased emphasis on training by extension workers in the field, funds were allocated for the construction of a rural training center in Monduli to provide instruction to men in animal husbandry and to women in nutrition and maternal child care.[36] But when the center was finally opened in 1978, its first two seminars were for 48 Maasai (male) leaders, and 15 (male) elders from Komolonik, including lessons on animal parasites, some disease conditions, care of improved bulls, care of dairy cattle, artificial insemination, castration, and cleaning and using a syringe. Twelve guides on various aspects of range management were also completed and "field-tested," then printed in English and Swahili: "The guides have been designed for use in an outreach program involving Masai [male] community leaders in the planning of their own range management systems."[37] Only when such "female" concerns as health and nutrition were proposed for study through the center in 1977 did Maasai women become the "target" of possible interventions. As the project sociologist wryly commented, "The fact that it focuses on women means that a major segment of Maasai, who have virtually been ignored, would be given special attention."[38]

The project reinforced the economic and political disenfranchisement of Maasai women that had begun early in the colonial period. The discursive practice of "experts" treating Maasai men as the "individual" "owners" of cattle, and therefore directing all animal husbandry training, advice, and inputs to them, made men the de facto livestock "experts," undermining women's roles in pastoral production and their rights in livestock. Furthermore, since rights in land (however tenuous) were vested in the association members, men became the controllers, if not the "owners," of the land as well. Once Maasai were resettled in villages, farm plots were "naturally" allocated to men as the "head of households."

Devastating Development

The MLDRMP had other long-term consequences besides the gendered effects. In its aftermath, the state ceased almost all development interventions among Maasai, including maintenance and repair of the project dips, water supplies, and other constructions. Financially crippled by the economic crisis of the early 1980s, state administrators directed their meager funds and energies toward "development" among less "difficult," more politically powerful peoples. The lack of roadworthy vehicles, equipment, even money for "nights-out allowances" made travel and therefore work in the vast, inaccessible terrain of the Maasai districts impossible. When they were not out trying to make money in various ways to supplement their own meager salaries, district and regional officials sat in their offices and drew up plans—for water projects, cattle dips, and extension training—and waited for money.

The consequences of the almost complete withdrawal, after the ten-year deluge of inputs and investment, were devastating. One result was a violent resurgence of East Coast fever and heartwater in the mid-1980s in many areas of Maasailand, killing thousands of cattle which had lost their resistance from the years of dipping. Several years of fairly regular dipping of cattle during the MLDRMP had reduced the prevalence of these tick-borne diseases and resulting cattle mortalities. But the lack of maintenance and failure to repair dips by both the state and Maasai themselves (who did not feel responsible) led to the eventual cessation of dipping as the dips slid into disrepair. The foreign currency crisis of the 1980s also forced the state to withdraw its subsidies of acaricides (the chemicals used in dips), so that even hand-spraying became prohibitively expensive. The result was a fierce resurgence of ECF and heartwater (*olmilo*) and the death of thousands of cattle.

Emairete, which had a long history of ECF, was one of the first areas where cattle populations were devastated. Once the Monduli Juu Dam was rehabilitated in the early 1980s, it became the primary dry-season water source for livestock in the area after the rainwater ponds and smaller dams dried up. The concentration of cattle facilitated the rapid spread of ECF and heartwater, killing cattle from Emairete as well as those from Mti Mmoja, Mfereji, and other areas. Evidence of the devastation is shown in the sharp decline in the average number of cattle per adult man between Ndagala's 1980 survey in 1978 (21.2) and mine in 1992 (9.2) (see Chapter 4). But one does not need numbers—the signs are immediately visible in Emairete: the large, sturdy cattle pens hold only a few scrawny cattle in the evenings. By 1991, there were so few cattle left that it took them months to graze down the thick grass in the crater. The localized drought and repair of the dam in 1992, however, brought thousands of head of cattle from surrounding areas to Monduli Juu to graze and water, quickly depleting both the grass and the water.

The widespread drought and ensuing famines throughout East Africa in 1983–1984 eventually drew the attention of the international media and NGOs constituting the international development community. The Tanzanian government was neither financially nor materially equipped to meet the food demands created by the food shortages, so the NGOs took over. In the Maasai districts, the Catholic church mobilized food aid through USAID and created an informal committee to coordinate the receipt and distribution of the food. Token payments were collected from villagers and held in village accounts to be returned to the villages toward development projects of their choosing. With the end of the food relief efforts and the need to return the money to the villages in the form of development, this informal committee was institutionalized as the Arusha Diocesan Development Office (ADDO), which became one of the key development institutions working in Maasailand other than the Lutheran church and World Vision International. Although none of these organizations was very active in the three research communities, their emergence marked a shift in the financing and control of development interventions from the Tanzanian state to NGOs. One consequence has been the scattering of development attention according to the preferences and priorities of these NGOs, with little attention paid, as usual, to the establishment of mechanisms to ensure the maintenance and continuity of projects. Meanwhile NGOs generally continue to consider only men to be pastoralists, design their projects accordingly, and further reinforce male control. Even women's development projects, as we shall see below, have not ameliorated the precarious economic predicament of Maasai women.

Commodity Control: Eluding the Money Men

So what have been the gendered effects of all these "developments"? We have seen in chapter after chapter how commoditization, the intensification

221

of the market economy, and increased needs and uses for money have been changing the meaning and use of key economic resources in Maasailand—livestock, agricultural crops, and land—in ways similar to those seen throughout many parts of the world at different historical moments. Livestock has shifted from a resource with multiple intertwined layers of control and rights to an individually (male-) owned commodity, agricultural crops have been redefined as primarily food or cash crops, and land has changed from a shared, abundant resource to a bounded, scarce, individually controlled asset. These processes, promoted since the early colonial period by development interventions, have created separate male-controlled political and economic domains. Men control not only land and livestock but money as well. While women do have a few sources of income—selling milk, alcohol, or tobacco, or, for a very few, providing midwifery or circumcision services—none of these activities provide a substantial income. These gendered effects, and their influence in shaping contemporary development projects, are explored in this section in terms of livestock, milk, cash crops, and women's development projects.

Men of the Cattle

The commoditization of livestock began in the early colonial period. Throughout the years, first the British government then the Tanzanian government tried to encourage, bribe, coerce, or force Maasai to perceive their cattle as commodities and sell them. While these efforts were only partially successful, they did succeed, as I will demonstrate below, in consolidating male control over cattle.

In his 1980 survey of 60 men, Ndagala asked who controlled livestock and milk in their households. Of the 59 men who responded, they all claimed that only men (whether as fathers, elder brothers, or husbands) and not women controlled the livestock; 43 said that women (mothers or wives) controlled subsistence milk. But the 52 who sold some milk said that only men controlled the cash from the sale of milk (1982: 37).

Similarly, in our survey, we asked several questions first about cattle, then about smallstock, exploring what rights a person had over the animals, who they identified as the owner (*olopeny* [masc.] or *enopeny* [fem.]) of the animals, and who controlled (*aitore*) their milk. There was a significant difference between the responses of different generations. In all three villages, most older men and women spoke about joint ownership of both categories of livestock, of almost equal rights in animals (to give as a gift or to slaughter for a ceremony, for example), and shared decision-making in selling. "In the past, we didn't sell animals, we just slaughtered them or gave them away," was one response. Several older women advised me that control and decision-making over the buying and selling of livestock depended on the quality of the relationship between a husband and wife. "Only women who get along with their husbands can buy livestock," said one older woman. "Or a widow ... like Mary" (Maasai Portrait 5), she added. One woman claimed individual ownership, especially over smallstock. "I am truly a pastoralist," she said. "I myself had many goats. When I started my alcohol-selling business, I bought goats and cattle—two calves and four goats." "Cattle bring me respect," she added. "With my cattle I can solve my problems—I can marry with them, I just get respect from having them in my homestead. I'm seen as respected and a well-liked person." "Of course I buy livestock," replied another older woman. "Especially when I am selling milk, I most certainly buy them."

But younger men and their wives presented a different picture—while women could contribute an animal to *osotua* (exchange friendship usually based on close consanguinal or affinal relations), rarely did they claim the right to give an animal to a friend or to slaughter or sell one. *Maidim, maidim, maidim* was the recurring answer of women to these questions: "I am unable." When probed further, women explained that the animals belonged to their husbands—men were the cattle "owners" and made the livestock decisions. "Even if there were one hundred women here, they wouldn't control the cattle!" proclaimed one Maasai woman. "I don't control cattle, I control chickens!" responded another. A few young women disagreed. Some claimed they were allowed to purchase smallstock and even, occasionally, cattle, usually through their adult sons or husbands as intermediaries. But few were allowed to sell. "I'm a woman, only men can sell cattle," replied one young wife. "Men constrain women," remarked another young woman, "but when I tell them to sell my goats or sheep, they sell them." "I sell cattle to buy my children clothes and hire laborers for my farm," responded another. The responses of most of the younger married men confirmed such a scenario—without hesitation they claimed exclusive rights and sole ownership over the animals, sometimes even over their milk, a resource historically recognized as controlled by women. "Goodness, don't I control them? Don't I control the children [women] and the cattle?" remarked one young husband.

There is, of course, often a discrepancy between the public ideologies and private realities of control and rights over livestock (cf. Oboler 1996), but the differences between generations in their attitudes toward and rights in livestock mark a progressive deterioration in women's rights in livestock. Some of the generational differences could be attributed to women's increased power with age (cf. Udvardy and Cattell 1992), but most women perceived the changes as a loss of rights. Many women complained about it openly and bitterly. As one older woman explained, "In the past, women were not ruled by men. I mean, wasn't every old man born of a woman? But these days, men are like judges!" "Men treat us like donkeys," complained one group of young women, a remark I heard repeated in many places. But while they expressed dissatisfaction and frustration (and the issue is an acknowledged source of friction between certain men and women) most of the women felt powerless to regain their lost rights. Women's increasing loss of rights in livestock has been partly produced by the changing perception of livestock shaped by the intensification of the market economy and the increased need for money to pay for medical care costs, school costs, food supplies, and development taxes, among other things. Rather than just a shared store of wealth, a source of food, and a symbol of prestige, livestock is now also a commodity, to be bought and sold like sugar or kerosene.

Milk Money

Women in Emairete have not felt so powerless in other, similar situations, however. Ndagala (1990) recounts how in 1977 a small milk-collecting plant was built in Emairete to purchase milk from local villagers. Under the sponsorship of the Food and Agriculture Organization (FAO), the Northern Dairies targeted men for the project, registering each family in the name of the "head of the household" and therefore giving the money to the men. Although a few women, exercising their traditional control over milk, initially brought and sold it, many men soon took over from the women, selling the milk themselves and keeping the money. During the first two months of the project about 12,750 liters a month were collected, increasing to more than 30,000 liters of milk per month during the rainy season of 1978 or 1979, at a price of Tshs 1/80 a liter.[39] But this time, according to Ndagala's account, the women fought back when men encroached upon their rights—the women watered down the milk so much that it was unacceptable to the plant, and soon the project closed down (Ndagala 1990: 160; cf. Ndagala 1982). Today, the small concrete building stands roofless and empty, symbolizing yet another failed project. But the effect of the commoditization of milk, in addition to increasing the conflict between men and women, was to limit circulation of surplus milk to poorer kin and neighbors. The surplus is now usually sold, and those who lack milk purchase it from neighbors (cf. Ndagala 1982: 36). When "important" unexpected guests such as a respected elder man or the local anthropologist visit a house where there is no milk, the woman of the house will often send a child scurrying (shillings in one hand, a bottle in the other) to a wealthier female neighbor to purchase milk for tea.

Cash Crops

Like the example of the milk-collecting plant, the case of cash crops supports the argument that where sums of money are involved, men are ready to invoke women's "childlike" qualities as excuses for denying them access to or control over such goods. In 1990, Tanzania Breweries began offering contracts to farmers in Emairete and Mti Mmoja to cultivate barley. The procedure since the beginning has been as follows: once a farmer signs a contract, Breweries provides seeds, a pesticide, a weed killer, and the use of a combine to harvest the barley when it is ready. The farmer is paid, by check, a set price per kilo for the harvested barley, less the cost of the inputs provided by Breweries. In 1991, for example, Breweries paid Tshs 71/= a kilo for harvested barley, but it deducted Tshs 113/= for a kilo of seeds, Tshs 3,890/= for a liter of weed killer, Tshs 9,000/= for a liter of pesticide, and Tshs 4,000/= an acre to harvest the barley with its combine. An average farmer collected between Tshs 75,000–85,000/= an acre in profit, after paying all the Breweries' charges. While there are several problems and risks in cultivating barley—poor rains, bad seed, delays in harvesting, delays in payment, alternative use of the land for food crops—barley cultivation is recognized as a potentially lucrative enterprise.

Except for two educated Maasai women in Emairete (one a widow, the other divorced), all the contract farmers in Emairete and Mti Mmoja were men, cultivating between one and forty acres of barley, with most cultivating two or three acres each. One obvious reason for this gender difference was the responsibility of women for feeding their children and their limited access to land. While women had to cultivate enough beans and maize to feed their children, leaving little land, if any, available for alternative crops, men, free from such responsibility, could easily convert some or all of their land to barley production. Furthermore, men, but not women, could always request more land from the village. But men could also request more land to give to women, so, noting the gender difference in barley cultivation, we asked in the open-ended survey, "Are women able to farm barley?" If a person answered "No," we then asked, "Why can't they grow it?" or if they answered "Yes," we asked "Why then do so few grow it?"

In response to our questions, most men and women stated that women

225

were unable to grow barley; the most common reason given was that it was just too difficult (*egol*) for them. The "difficulties" referred to here were not the physical difficulties of the actual farming tasks, since the chemicals and combine, by precluding the need for the back-breaking labor of weeding and harvesting, actually made barley a physically easier crop to cultivate than beans or maize. Instead, one explanation of the "difficulties" focused on the technological differences between cultivating barley and cultivating maize and beans. As one man explained: "[Women] are not able [to cultivate barley] . . . because barley cannot be farmed by hand (*to nkaik*)." Another man elaborated: "[Few women cultivate barley] because the work is difficult because a machine comes to harvest." So one "difficulty" is a gendered view of who can control agricultural technology, whereby women can farm by hand but only men can control machines, just as they control ox plows.

But later discussions revealed that the more important "difficulties" involved women's supposed inability to function in the public realm necessitated by the Breweries contract: to interact with Breweries agents, to sign a contract, to supervise the combine, and to receive and cash a check. For these reasons and others, "[Barley cultivation] is not their domain, their command (*enkitoria*), it is the domain of men"; "[Women don't farm barley because] they don't have much command, much rule (*enkitoria*)"; "Only a husband has the ability to do all [that is required to cultivate barley]." Men did not, however, identify language or literacy as "difficulties"; most of the male barley farmers do not speak fluent Swahili and are illiterate.

Finally, men thought that women just could not handle such large sums of money—women were too irresponsible, they would just run away, they would get drunk and neglect their children, and so on. As one man summed it up: "[Women] just can't hold on to money." (Of course, these are the same complaints made by women about men's use of the barley money.)

While the responses of many women echoed those of men—barley is just too difficult for women to grow—a few women rejected this reasoning, offering an alternative explanation that recognized the underlying gendered structures of power being created and maintained by such statements: they believed women were able to grow barley but did not do so because men did not allow it. In the words of one older woman:

> If I cultivated barley now, I would be sick. Only women who are not controlled by men can cultivate it. If I did cultivate it now, I would be robbed (*nikioruni*) of any money I got, since a wife is unable to control all of her money. My husband would rob me, saying *basi*, I am going out drinking.

Or as another woman bluntly put it: "[Women don't farm barley because] they have no power."

Thus, women's supposed childlike qualities—their innate irresponsibility, their inexperience, their selfishness, their inability to wisely manage money— are here used by men to justify their exclusion from a potentially profitable venture, thus increasing their economic inequality and furthering their economic dependence on men. But, as we have also seen, while many women seem to have absorbed and internalized this cultural image of themselves, believing that barley is in fact too difficult for them to grow, some women reject such explanations as illusory, as falsifications of reality. These women realize that references to the supposed "childlike" qualities of women which make cultivating barley so "difficult" for them are less about the inadequacies of women and more about men's strategies of control. Such statements, as these women recognize, are no more than justifications to create and maintain a certain structure of power relations between men and women, especially between husbands and wives. If women cannot grow barley, if they cannot operate in the public world of contracts and banks, if they cannot supervise combines—it is not because of any innate inabilities on their part, but because men have not allowed them to learn or to try these tasks.

Women's Development

With the emergence of Women in Development (WID) as a key paradigm of development in the late 1970s, a few development projects were introduced among Maasai which were specifically targeted to meet the (sponsor-perceived) needs of Maasai women, including income generation. Two such projects were introduced in Emairete, both by an English woman working as a volunteer schoolteacher at the secondary school in Monduli (now called Sokoine Secondary School). A brief overview of the design, implementation, and results of these projects provides further insights into the emerging relationships between gender, development, and money.

The first project was a beadwork project designed to help women purchase beads; sew "traditional" necklaces, earrings, and bracelets; and sell these items to tourists in Arusha, usually through souvenir shops. Small loans were obtained to enable wholesale purchase of the beads from distributors in Kenya (the plastic beads which long ago replaced the glass beads of Arab and Swahili traders are all manufactured in the Czech Republic). The volunteer arranged for several souvenir shops in Arusha to sell their wares. She encouraged the

227

women to choose officers—a chair, secretary, and treasurer—from among themselves to administer the project. Since the jobs required literacy and basic math and bookkeeping skills, the women chose the three most educated women among themselves, selecting the wealthy widow as chair.

The women were elated. Sewing beads was an enjoyable craft, and it gave women pride and allowed them to express their distinct workmanship and styles.[40] Beadwork fit in well with their workdays, as it could be done in the company of other women or picked up and put down through the course of a day's work. Finally, unlike milk, it was one of the few female activities and products that men could not co-opt.

After the first women sold their beadwork and received large (to them) amounts of cash, the project grew quickly. Women within Emairete worked hard to sew as much beadwork as they could, while women from Embopong' and neighboring areas joined the project. Inevitably, supply soon exceeded demand, and the chair began storing the surplus jewelry in a trunk in her house. The backlog in supplies meant that women were not being paid immediately for their work; many did not understand, grew disgruntled, and accused the officers of stealing their payments. The volunteer returned to England, leaving the project in the hands of the officers and their suspicious project members. When the trunk was stolen from the chair's house one day (allegedly by the widow's son), the loss of thousands of shillings of beadwork marked the end of the project.

Although the project had been over for more than two years when I began my fieldwork, the women still spoke about it forlornly. For them, the beadwork had been their *maendeleo* (Maasai use the Swahili word for development), in contrast to the other development projects, which were the *maendeleo* of the men. When I explained to a woman I had just met in Embopong' that I was studying *maendeleo*, she furrowed her brow in confusion, "Beads, you mean?" Others spoke longingly about the large amounts of money they had made, then angrily about their mistrust of the educated officers. Several wondered if I, yet another white woman, might help them revive the project. (I did not.)

The second project was the construction and management of a maize-grinding machine in Emairete village, organized with the help of the English volunteer under the auspices of the local UWT chapter, the women's branch of CCM. The machine would not only reduce women's labor (they either ground maize by hand or carried it to the grinding machines available in Monduli town) but would also provide the cooperative who managed the machine with income. Women interested in joining the cooperative had to pur-

5.1 A Maasai woman in Embopong' sewing beads onto a leather skirt for her daughter's wedding, 1992. Photo by author.

chase shares to help finance the building materials, the labor, and the connection to the one electric cable that passed through the village.[41] They scrambled to beg the money from male relatives or earn the money selling beadwork, alcohol, milk, or other commodities. When the first machine was stolen just two days after it was installed, the women requested and received a loan from SIDO (Small Industries Development Organization) to purchase a new machine.

As with the case of the beadwork project, the bookkeeping, bill paying, and other aspects of the grinding machine project required that literate women manage the project. Two of the three beadwork project officers were selected, including the wealthy widow. The women hired a man to run the machine, then organized a schedule among themselves to take turns working at the building to collect money and supervise the grinding. Although constant electricity blackouts limited the use of the machine, it was well used when it was running. But the money received by the officers, or, better put, the money they deposited in the project account, never sufficed to pay the electricity bills and loan payments, and the project's debts mounted. Meeting after angry meeting was held among the members, who accused the officers of using their "knowledge of the pen" to steal the revenue. In 1992, SIDO removed the machine because of the cooperative's failure to meet their loan payments. In desperation, the officers organized a buy-out whereby two men in the village would repay the loan balance on the women's behalf, then replace and run the machine. The buy-out went through, much to the distress of the coop members who after years of losing their profits now lost their capital. In an angry confrontation, they accused the project officers of pilfering the project funds, which, under threat of curse by an elder, they admitted to. Although the machine was still owned by the two men, everyone put on a happy facade a few days later when the national secretary of CCM visited to honor the grinding machine project as an "exemplary" women's development project. Dressed in a shiny polyester skirt and tunic, draped with beads, the chair read a statement to the assembled dignitaries thanking them for their support and proudly reviewing the "successful" history of women's development in the village.

Ethnicity Reinvigorated: Indigenous Development

The latest phase of development began in the early 1990s with the emergence of Maasai indigenous development organizations (IDOs, cf. Hodgson 1999b; Igoe 2000). A growing priority among Euro-American NGOs in recent years has been to promote and finance IDOs, that is, development organizations created, staffed, and controlled by members of indigenous populations who set and fulfill their own development agendas. Marked by such events as the United Nations "Year" (1993), the International Decade of the World's Indigenous People (1994–2004),[42] and publications such as *Cultural Survival Quarterly,* this policy is politically attractive to Euro-American NGOs for several reasons: it avoids the neo-colonial taint of sponsoring local NGOs staffed and often supervised by expatriates, it fulfills current "progressive" interests in empowering groups perceived as historically marginalized and disenfranchised by their nation-states, and it uses the rubric of development to bolster claims about the non-political nature of such interventions.

But indigenous development has emerged simultaneously from the grassroots as well, as groups of historically marginalized peoples have organized themselves to demand certain cultural, political, and economic rights. As part of their effort to gain international moral and financial support for their initiatives, they have often intentionally manipulated and projected homogenized,

exoticized versions of their cultural identities to accord with "Western" stereotypes of "indigenous" peoples. At once local and global, indigenous development is therefore the product of current First World interests in empowering
marginal groups and the success of certain Third World peoples in strategi-
cally essentializing their own identities to defend rights, mobilize resources,
and advance seemingly progressive agendas (e.g., Conklin and Graham 1995;
Jackson 1995; Turner 1991).[43]

Partly in response to recent global campaigns for the rights of "indigenous" peoples, several "Maasai" development organizations have emerged in
the past decade in Tanzania organized around claims of a common indigenous
identity based on ethnicity, that is "being Maasai." The first, Korongoro Integrated People Oriented to Conservation, or KIPOC, was officially registered
under the Tanzanian Societies Ordinance in late 1990, while the Maa Pastoralists Development Organization, or Inyuat e-Maa, was registered in 1993.
Since then, numerous Maasai IDOs, many based on territory or clan, have
been organized in Tanzania, over twenty at last count, including assorted um-
brella groups. Both KIPOC and Inyuat e-Maa, the main groups I will consider in this chapter, position themselves in similar ways relative to local,
national, and transnational development agendas. These IDOs combine two
functions: they are both the community representatives and the bureaucracy
which facilitates and administers projects vis-à-vis international donors. Posi-
tioned in this manner as "gatekeepers" (Igoe 1999: 19) between communities
and donors, they effectively circumvent, if not replace, the position of the
state. These partnerships between local IDOs and international donors have
been facilitated by several factors, including first, the failure of the so-called
developmentalist state to fulfill the development demands of this marginalized group of citizens (cf. Escobar 1992: 31; Friedman 1994) and the group's
subsequent search for development elsewhere; second, the recent implementation of democratization measures in Tanzania which have expanded the opportunities for grassroots organizing (cf. Neumann 1995); and third, the current preoccupation of international donors with the plight of indigenous
peoples, an agenda intimately related to global concerns with environmental
sustainability.

Although all of these factors are important, here I wish to emphasize the
significance of the new category of "indigenous" for linking global concerns
and institutions to the local efforts of marginalized populations and the consequences for ethnic and gender relations and identities. KIPOC, Inyuat e-Maa,
and the other Maasai IDOs define their agendas and objectives through explicit links to transnational discourses about the rights of indigenous peoples,

the privileged relationship between indigenous peoples and their environment, and the necessity for development projects which are environmentally "sustainable." Like Indians in Columbia (Jackson 1995), Penang in Borneo (Brosius 1999), and peoples elsewhere, Maasai are "learning to see themselves as belonging to new categories" (Jackson 1995: 9).

The category of indigenous has, in fact, facilitated the assertion and rigidifying of more "cultural" identities, often along "ethnic" lines (cf. Friedman 1994). In order to appeal to these new global initiatives to protect and help "indigenous" peoples, Maasai leaders have appropriated and reconfigured the fixed ahistorical image of "the Maasai" produced during the colonial period and now used by state officials to attract tourists. For example, in a project document written to publicize its program and funding needs to international donors, KIPOC argues that the dominant "national culture" conceives of the "modern Tanzanian" as a Kiswahili speaker and either an active farmer or of "peasant origin." In contrast, the few "indigenous minority nationalities" in Tanzania are defined by KIPOC as either pastoralists or hunter-gatherers who have "maintained the fabric of their cultures":

> They are conspicuously distinct from the rest of the population in dress, language, transhumance systems of resource utilization and relationship to the environment. Pastoral and hunter-gatherer peoples persevered, through passive resistance, to hold on to their indigenous lifestyles, traditions and cultures. (KIPOC 1991: 5)

Although stigmatized by the dominant culture as "static, rigid [and] hostile to cultural interaction and exchange," these indigenous cultures have in fact never been "irrationally opposed to economic development nor uncompromising in dealing with external interests and forces." In reality, these people have been "left out of the development process," especially in terms of the allocation of resources to social services and economic infrastructure (KIPOC 1991: 5–6). The Maasai struggle, therefore, is "part of the global struggle of indigenous peoples to restore respect to their rights, cultural identity and to the land of their birth" (KIPOC 1991: 7).

Based on the above analysis of their situation, KIPOC (which also means "we shall recover" in Maa) proposed, among other initiatives, to assist "pastoral and other marginalized indigenous peoples in Tanzania to identify, design and plan projects rooted in the principles of sustainable environmental management and development to meet basic community needs" and to study, as well as raise "community consciousness" about, the need for "integrating community development with nature conservation," that is "sustainable utilization of natural resources to ensure improvement of living conditions without com-promising the welfare of future generations" (KIPOC 1991: 12).[44]

But what lies behind this invocation of "indigenous"? Specifically, what kinds of social divisions are masked and perhaps even reinforced by these ap-peals to international concerns for the rights of indigenous people and the desire for environmental sustainability?

First, and most obviously, it is important to look at the organizational structure of KIPOC, Inyuat e-Maa, and other IDOs. When one does so, one quickly realizes that the leaders and active members of IDOs who assert themselves as the "authentic" "indigenous" representatives are mostly well-educated men who are "junior elders" (ages 35–45) within the Maasai age-set system. No elder men, the customary leaders, are involved, nor are many uneducated men. The marginalization of women in both the organization and practices of KIPOC and Inyuat e-Maa is immediately evident: no women, educated or uneducated, work in the central organizations, although some IDOs have created peripheral structures ("women's wings") to placate the few donors who insist on attention to women's issues. Both KIPOC and Inyuat e-Maa have a "women's wing" (in the case of KIPOC, a "women's and children's wing") and a "youth wing," none of which operate on a continuing or system-atic basis (KIPOC 1990; Inyuat e-Maa 1991c).

The donors and NGOs who support and finance the IDOs are com-plicit in enforcing these gender and class differences. For these organizations, younger educated men are the preferred representatives of "indigenous" groups. NGO representatives, like colonial officials before them, presume that education means enlightenment and modernization so that these "progres-sive" men will unselfishly care for the greater good, but to these representatives education also means literacy and multi-lingualism, so that they can fulfill administrative duties such as maintaining correspondence, writing project proposals, preparing financial reports, and addressing (however superficially) the required women's and environmental components of development proj-ects. For these reasons, NGOs are most comfortable with such men, just as earlier colonial administrators were initially more comfortable with elder men as the "natural" "traditional" "native authorities."

NGO support and resources enable these educated Maasai men to cir-cumvent both the state and elder Maasai men to gain access to substantial material resources and political power. As the acknowledged representatives of "indigenous" people, they obtain numerous opportunities for international travel, further education, and significant financial resources in the form of travel allowances, honoraria, and stipends which most save and use for personal projects at home: building a house, purchasing livestock, or buying a vehicle. The curriculum vitae of one prominent Maasai IDO organizer was replete with trips to international workshops that lasted from several days to several weeks, which he attended as *the* representative of *the* Maasai to discuss "indigenous peoples." Furthermore, for several years, he was also *the* Maasai representative in the country, serving as a consultant to various projects and workshops sponsored in East Africa by international organizations, including the International Institute for Environment and Development (IIED, London) and USAID.

The ability of such "representatives" to accrue these resources not only improves their individual situations but also enables them to select and finance their particular gendered visions of development. Since women do not participate in the planning and administration of the development projects organized by the IDOs, such projects take little account of the needs, desires, or perspectives of Maasai women. Although some projects (such as water projects) help women in terms of their household responsibilities, most replicate and reinforce existing patriarchal relations of power by assigning control for the design, implementation, and management of the project to men (usually educated) in the community. Ironically, at the same time that the leaders of this new transnational form of organization mobilize around promises of "progress" and "modernity," they justify the exclusion of women by appeals to "tradition" and "culture."

A compelling example of these gender politics occurred at the First Maasai Conference on Culture and Development in 1991, where Inyuat e-Maa was founded. Organized by an educated man who claimed to be Maasai (many of his friends and colleagues told me that he was in fact Kikuyu) and sponsored by three Nordic development agencies, the conference attracted over 180 delegates from outside and inside the country, including "traditional leaders" from twenty-five Maasai localities, educated Maasai, government and party officials, religious leaders, development workers, and scholars. The gender hierarchies presented and reinforced at the conference, which I attended as an invited participant, were strikingly clear: while the meeting room was full of Maasai men, two educated Maasai women, and a scattering of Euro-American scholars and development workers, uneducated Maasai women were relegated to the balcony outside the main conference, where they were supposed to display their beadwork for conference participants as part of a "Maasai Women's Cultural Exhibit." In a conversation prior to the conference, when I questioned the organizer about this gendered divide, he replied that including the women in the main conference would be "against tradition," as "women were never included in the meetings men held to decide community affairs." "Since when," I curtly replied, "was a 'First Maasai Conference on Culture and Development,' comprising men of all ages, clans and areas, ever considered a traditional meeting?" In reply, he just shrugged and reiterated his claims of supporting Maasai "tradition." In the final conference report, he justified the exclusion of women from the main conference because of their "traditionally" greater concern with moral and cultural issues, as opposed to the political and economic issues which interest men (Inyuat e-Maa 1991b: 23). This particular appeal to "tradition" is of course very different from that used by several elder men who angrily walked out of the conference on the first day after demanding to know why these elite young men were usurping their authority as community leaders and decision-makers.

Of course, Maasai women are themselves hardly a homogeneous group; they are stratified by wealth, education, marriage, and class position. Despite the organizer's attempts to keep them on the periphery of the conference (both literally and figuratively), Maasai women did not passively accept their marginalization. Two young educated Maasai women attended, one of whom spoke passionately about the desperate need to support female education and castigated the men present for their lack of attention to gender issues and inequalities. On the last day of the conference, a group of uneducated women in customary dress entered the conference hall and loudly protested their exclusion from the conference: "If this is a conference on Maasai development and culture," one woman exclaimed, "then why were we women not invited to contribute? Are we not Maasai?" Stunned, the organizers tried to placate the women with promises that they were trying to represent the women's best interests, but the women soon walked out.

In addition to challenging the claims of the conference organizer about the "traditional" roles of Maasai women in public meetings, this story demonstrates that non-elite Maasai women themselves are all too aware of the gendered strategies and effects of these IDOs. Their collective public criticisms have been repeated in many private conversations with me and others. Some see the IDOs as just one more strategy for certain Maasai men to further solidify their political and economic power over women; others carefully point out the new vehicles, houses, and businesses of some of these leaders and wonder about their (mis)use of resources given in the name of all Maasai for their individual self-advancement. And a few women, such as the wives, mothers, and daughters of these men, benefit materially from their new incomes which enable them to reproduce and elevate their class status.

What is important here is not just the gendered practices of educated men, but the complicity of donors and NGOs in accepting such practices and appeals to "tradition." None of the donors sponsoring the conference seem to have questioned, much less challenged, the exclusion of women from the conference. Similarly, no donors have criticized the exclusion of women from the organizational structures of the IDOs or their failure to include women in the selection, design, and implementation of most projects. The concern of donors and NGOs with promoting the mobilization and agendas of "indigenous" peoples seems to have obscured their sense of the differences which inevitably exist among such peoples. I should note that I am not questioning the ability of elite men or women to represent groups, but I am challenging the unquestioned assumption by donors and others that they are the "natural" and inherently enlightened representatives.

In response to the complaints of Maasai women, pressure from one NGO, and (to a far lesser extent) my interventions, the same IDO which organized the First Maasai Conference on Culture and Development sponsored a "Maasai Women's Conference" in 1996 (after the Second Maasai Conference held in 1994 again restricted women to exhibiting their beadwork on the balcony). Although not the equivalent of integrating women into the administration of the IDOs and their projects, the conference was still a first step toward identifying and incorporating the needs and perspectives of Maasai women.

Unfortunately, but perhaps not surprisingly, attendees of the Maasai Women's Conference were almost exclusively elite Maasai women, many in fact the wives of IDO organizers (Inyuat e-Maa 1996). It seems that non-elite women were not even invited, although the status of the women attending would not necessarily be clear to donors unfamiliar with individual Maasai families. The class status of the attendees does not discredit their effort, but it does reaffirm the necessity to carefully examine the complicated gender, ethnic, and class politics of indigenous development.

Two additional examples offer important insights into how issues of gender, ethnicity, and class which we have already examined in terms of the organizational structure of the IDOs play out in some of their practices and projects.[45] One of the central objectives of IDOs has been to protect Maasai lands from further encroachment and alienation by the state, commercial enterprises, and wildlife conservation efforts (including the expansion of park boundaries and creation of "buffer zones" to protect wildlife migration routes). Against the long history of land alienation in the colonial period described in earlier chapters, and at a time when customary rights of determining land tenure have been threatened by proposed national legislation revoking customary tenure in favor of surveyed village-owned land deeds (Presidential Land Commission of Inquiry 1994), protecting land rights is clearly an urgent matter.

The first example is a village survey and registration campaign initiated in 1985 by Maasai activists with the support of the Catholic church, which sought to establish government-recognized legal boundaries around non-nucleated rural Maasai communities as a means of clarifying and legitimating community-level tenure claims. KIPOC quickly took up and supported this project as a key strategy to prevent further land alienation and as a first step toward community-based land-use planning. In the face of heightened threats to the legal status (and therefore to the tenure) of their lands, formally surveying and registering community lands as government-designated villages was a pragmatic short-term response. But it has had unfortunate unintended consequences in terms of gender and class relations. As Diane Rocheleau, Louise Fortmann, and others have noted, "Women's spaces are frequently nested between and within lands controlled by men," whether as "thin strips of bush separating homesteads or even single trees scattered amidst a husband's cultivated fields" (Rocheleau, Thomas-Slayter, and Edmunds 1995: 62; cf. Rocheleau, Thomas-Slayter, and Wangari 1996). Their invisibility often means that "exclusive ownership rights become vested in male-headed households or male-dominated community organizations as a result of mapping and land reform initiatives uninformed by gender analysis" (Rocheleau, Thomas-Slayter, and Edmunds 1995: 62). Certainly this has been the case with IDO-sponsored village mapping and registration exercises among Maasai. The registration campaign has centralized control over land allocation and access in the hands of a few men, those who constitute village councils. (Very few, if any, women are council officers.) Now that the boundaries of land are legible to the community and state, corrupt leaders among these men can and have "sold" village land to urban elites, dishonest government officials, and even non-Tanzanian expatriate commercial farmers and ranchers. Numerous Maasai women, who are dependent on their fathers, husbands, or brothers for access to land, and therefore have the most marginal and precarious claims, report that the resulting shortage of cultivable land has curtailed their access to separate plots in which they would control the harvest and profits. Of course, women still labor in their husbands' fields for the benefit of their household and the profit of the husband. Although I do not have the necessary data to examine the question from my own field sites, work by Elliot Fratkin and others suggests that the declining resource base of pastoralist women in similar situations in Kenya has adversely affected the health and nutritional status of themselves and their children (Nathan, Fratkin, and Roth 1996; Fratkin and Smith 1995; Fratkin, Roth, and Nathan 1999).

Furthermore, as discussed in Chapter 4, the focus on "villages" has obscured boundaries and land-use agreements already recognized by Maasai groups resident in the area. Existing divisions of land into pasture types (or farms) with complicated rules of access controlled and monitored by territorial sections (*iloshon*) and clans were ignored (and thereby undermined) in favor of the neat boundaries demanded by government surveyors and land registration offices. As a result, informal exchanges of farmland for access to grazing land between communities, such as occurred between two of my three research sites, which are often arranged through and for the benefit of women, have been threatened. Finally, the explicit focus on land and the physical extent of village territory ignored particular resources on the land such as water and salt licks, as well as female-controlled resources such as wild greens, gourds, and firewood. Once surveyed and bounded, access to these formerly communal resources can be circumscribed, disrupting female networks of resource provision.

The second measure I want to examine are proposals by Inyuat e-Maa and some other IDOs to create a pastoralist reserve, which would set aside land for the exclusive use of Maasai pastoralists. Participants in the fifth meeting of the Pastoralist Network in Tanzania (PANET), all of whom were primarily representatives of Maasai IDOs, made the following recommendation in 1994:

> PANET should support the declaration of certain districts/land units as "pastoral areas." Demarcation, allocation and titling of lands for pastoralists in perpetuity should be promoted as a way to protect pastoral lands from landgrabbing. Consideration should be given to new institutional frameworks based on the traditional system, to facilitate negotiation between villages and communities for sharing and co-management of range resources. PANET should commission more studies on what institutional frameworks are appropriate for different pastoral groups. (PANET 1994: 6; cf. PANET 1993: 7)

In 1997, the directors of Inyuat e-Maa were contemplating the creation of a pastoralist reserve along similar lines. Following the model of game reserves and hunting reserves, and simultaneously seeking to ward off encroachments by these same competing land uses, this group argued for state recognition of protected status for a large area encompassing critical pastoral resources, critical dry-season grazing areas, and strategic drought reserves.

This proposal is controversial, and it raises numerous issues such as the historical irony that Maasai themselves are calling for a reserve similar to that imposed on them in the early colonial period and that elite Maasai men with little experience or interest in herding are demanding that an area be restricted solely to livestock production. What I want to address are the gendered consequences of demarcating and linking physical boundaries on the landscape with economic and cultural boundaries, that is, restricting the reserve to pastoralism as the sole mode of production. As a result of their different productive skills and pursuits as milk managers, traders, and gatherers, women have gained a different experience of and knowledge about their environment than men (cf. Rocheleau, Thomas-Slayter, and Edmunds 1995: 63). Yet because of their lack of representation in the IDOs, their experience and knowledge has been ignored, and they have been excluded from debating and designing plans for land use and natural resource management such as the creation of a pastoralist reserve. This inattention to women's economic and environmental rights and responsibilities has produced a proposal that would not only restrict women from pursuing their diverse productive roles, it would also further reinforce male claims to prestige and authority as the "true" pastoralists. Given the particular gendered history of Maasai ideologies and practices of pastoralism, a pastoralist reserve would be a preeminently male domain in which women were economically, politically, and culturally subordinate.

In conclusion, although a particular image of Maasai identity is being used to promote a seemingly more "progressive" agenda than that implemented by colonial officials and state administrators, the effects for most Maasai women are still very much the same: continuing, if not increased, economic, political, and cultural disenfranchisement. As elite men assert their power as "authentic" "indigenous" representatives to attract international resources and attention, they subsequently transform local power relations. The marginalization of women and uneducated men is, as discussed earlier, clearly evident in the organizational structure and administrative practices of the IDOs. As evidenced by their protests and boycotts at the First Maasai Conference, however, these groups are voicing their own critiques of the IDOs. Yet, as the village registration and pastoralist reserve proposals suggest, such gender and class disparities in who is designing, controlling, and implementing environmental and development projects can have significant consequences for those excluded from the planning process.

*   *   *

The masculinist constructions of "Maasainess" and "pastoralists" which emerged during the colonial period continue to shape "development" interventions in the contemporary period. One consequence of the androcentric assumptions and practices was to reinforce the categories of identity produced by economic development projects such as the MLDRMP—livestock owner, household head, and project officer, for example. Maasai men have taken advantage of these new political and economic identities to consolidate their control over not only livestock, land, and crops, but over money itself. Even when traditionally female-controlled products such as milk become commodities, men try to appropriate the product and the profit. Only beadwork seemed immune from male control, but not, it seems, from male deceit. However, men are not the only ones greedy for money. Some of the few elite educated women who are qualified by virtue of their literacy to serve as project officers also take advantage of the opportunities offered by development to exploit others to make money.

MAASAI PORTRAIT 5: MARY

Oh Dorotea! Children these days . . . I just don't know what to do with them!

Mary, as I shall call her, was a wealthy educated widow.[1] She lived with her seven children in a large cement-block house, one of the "modern houses" (*nyumba bora*) built as part of an Ujamaa village development project. Next to her house was a rectangular mud-and-wattle building with two rooms that she used as a kitchen and storeroom and a third small building with a cement floor that was one of the only latrines in the community. She had met her husband when he was a teacher and she was a student at Ngorongoro Girls Primary School, a school (and the only girls' school) briefly run by the Catholic church in the 1960s. As she told me one day:

> I loved school. I wanted to continue and study in secondary school, but my father and Edward [a pseudonym for her future husband] tricked me. They told me that I was pregnant, and that I had to drop out and get married. I did, and married Edward, but it wasn't true. They lied to me to get me to quit school and marry.

As her husband worked his way up the government hierarchy to eventually become a top district official, Mary had children,

241

cared for the house and homestead, and learned how to be a "proper" wife in Swahili terms. Nevertheless, her husband married a second wife many years later, with whom he also had children.

When I met her in 1991, Mary was a robust, energetic woman busy trying to achieve and retain economic security for herself and her children. She had many economic ventures, including raising cattle and smallstock; farming maize, beans, and even barley (she was one of the only women to farm barley in the area); buying salt, tomatoes, oranges, and other food in Arusha or Monduli to resell (or have one of her younger daughters sell) at the weekly market in Emairete; and renting a small house to teachers or other outsiders. For a while she even had one of her sons work with his friends to run a transport business in their old Land Rover, but the boys ran wild with the vehicle and spent all their earnings. She was always on the go—walking up and down the mountain to Monduli town on some errand, often lugging her newborn baby with her (although sometimes she left her at home with one of her older sisters). She served on the village council (and had done so for over ten years), supervised the grinding machine that was one of the village's women's development projects, and kept her eye open for any and all opportunities to make money. When farmland became available in another Maasai area, she quickly used her government connections to "buy" fifty acres and hired Mbulu laborers to farm and tend the land for her. At home, she usually had a man living in a shack on her property, working her fields, managing her livestock, and serving as a handyman in return for room, board, and a small salary. On Sundays, she would usually dress up with some of her children and walk to the new Catholic church to attend services.

We met frequently, and we talked often about her life and the lives of her children. "Oh, Dorotea! Children these days. . . . I just don't know what to do with them!" So far, her older sons had only brought her grief. One died a few years ago, supposedly as a result of being cursed (*emoti*) by women in the village for having stolen their beadwork projects from his mother's house. Steven, another son, had been studying in a technical school in Dar es Salaam, but he had dropped out. Most of the time he hung out with his friends at home, sleeping, eating, and listening to very loud music on his boom-box. Steven often yelled at his mother, demanding money and food, and harassed his younger sisters. Invoking the rules of patrilineal inheritance, he would yell, "I am the boss here! You are living in my house, and your money is my money!" Inevitably she would give him some to quiet him down, and he would run off to Monduli town or Arusha with his friends for some trouble.

She had more success with her daughters. Her oldest girl, Sara, had been semi-adopted by an American couple and lived with them in the United States while studying in secondary school. I only met her once, when she visited in 1992. She looked like any middle-class American teenager—blue jeans, a tight-fitting cotton shirt, permed hair, and make-up. She was spunky, funny, and seemingly more mature than her years. A few days after she returned, a huge fight ensued between the (non-Maasai) schoolteachers and Maasai parents in the community over the planned circumcision of her younger sister, Naserian. (Mary had made sure Sara was circumcised before she left for the United States, as she knew she would never agree later.) The teachers were upset not only about the circumcision, but that Naserian's was planned for the week before she was scheduled to take the national exams for secondary school placement. Since Sara had never participated in the ceremonies that preceded circumcision, Mary wanted Sara and Naserian to go through them at the same time.

In the end, a compromise was reached. First, Sara went through the adult naming ceremony (*orkiteng' lentomon*) that precedes circumcision for girls and boys. (The ceremony had already been performed for Naserian.) One evening, some elder male lineage and clan relatives filtered in to Mary's homestead at sunset. They sat outside the kitchen, drinking and talking among themselves. After Mary had milked her cows, she, the elders, Koko (Maasai Portrait 1), and I went inside the kitchen and sat around the cooking hearth. Sara was called and joined the group reluctantly, a look of annoyance and boredom on her face as she sat down between Koko and me. Grilled meat was passed around for the men to eat; they cut pieces to share and passed some to me. They talked among themselves about a teasing name to give Sara and decided on one (I didn't catch it). They asked her what her name was (Mary had told me earlier that the elders would probably give her the same name she already had, since she lived overseas). Throughout, Sara continued to look bored and above it all, and she asked Koko several times if she could leave. Once the meat was finished, Koko took a small gourd filled with water, milk, and stones and showed Sara how to cup her hands, turned up, right over left. Koko poured some of the mixture in Sara's right, Sara sipped it, Koko poured, Sara sipped. The procedure was repeated twice using Sara's left hand. Then Sara took the gourd and performed the process on Koko's hands. An elder man said, "Mother of Sara," and Koko replied. He called out the teasing name several times, and finally said Sara's Maasai name, to which everyone assented. He prayed for her well-being, for many children and cattle. Another elder repeated the same routine, beginning with the teasing name. Afterward, a bucket of fried fat was passed around, and Sara, Koko, and a few other women in attendance were given pieces. Mary brought *gongo* (distilled liquor) for the men, and everyone sat around and talked. Sara fled to her room as soon as she could. The men left quickly after finishing the *gongo,* and the women stayed back and finished up the meat. They sang boisterous songs about their lovers and boyfriends, interspersed with Christian hymns.

A few days later, another ceremony took place, *orkitupukunit,* at which two sheep were slaughtered in the morning, one for each girl to be circumcised. This ceremony was performed exclusively by women, including the suffocating, slaughtering, roasting, and eating of the sheep (men were given only the neck meat to eat). Each girl had to sit inside the kitchen while the women suffocated her sheep, then they could wander away while the women slaughtered. I was impressed by how adept the women were at slaughtering, since this was the only time I had witnessed women cutting up an entire animal. (The same ceremony is reportedly also performed for boys, by women, two days before their circumcision.) Throughout the day, women from the community wandered in to eat meat, and I was eventually given a meaty thigh piece to share with another woman. During the day, some of the women painted Mary's kitchen with water mixed with ochre and other dyes, others brought firewood and water, and the rest just sat and talked. The storeroom next to the kitchen was cleared, and a small bed was brought in. Men stayed far away from the kitchen and surrounding area most of the day.

The next day, the household bustled with women cleaning the main house, others cleaning 50 kilos of rice. (They—Maasai and Arusha schoolteachers and two educated Maasai women—laughingly told me that Mary had asked for "Swahili" women to clean the rice, since she didn't trust Maasai women to find all the stones.) Relatives filtered in, including Mary's brother and his family. At sunset an old woman, the circumciser, arrived, dressed in two bright black-and-red-printed cloths (*khangas*). Mary teasingly introduced her to me as "the person who liked to take other people's blood," and the women chortled with laughter. Soon the kitchen was filled with women cooking, talking, and laughing together. Men sat in the sitting room of the main house, while women congregated in the kitchen and storeroom-turned-bedroom. Food (meat fried with onions) was served, gossip ran wild, and then a small meeting between Mary, her brother, and two close friends took place in her bedroom to make a schedule for the following day and determine which guests would sit where and who would serve them. (I was asked by Mary's brother to serve food in the sitting room.) I soon went to bed, but the teenagers, including Sara and her sister, danced to loud disco music in the sitting

MP5.1 Maasai women slaughtering a sheep after first suffocating it, as part of the *orkitupukunit* ceremony preceding female circumcision, 1992. This was the only time I saw women slaughter livestock, and I was impressed by their knowledge and skill. Photo by author.

room until the wee hours of the night, and the adult women sang songs in the kitchen.

By dawn, the household was already bustling. I sat with some women, including Koko, in the kitchen, tending the fire and cooking some porridge and tea for breakfast. At one point, Mary walked in with a small clay bowl and gave it to the circumciser, who filled it with water and ash. "The water of the girl (*enkare e ndito*)" she told me, setting it aside. The women were vehemently discussing the confrontation with the schoolteachers over Naserian's circumcision. "I'm so sad that circumcision will probably fade away," said Koko. "It's fine if they don't let us stretch our earlobes or wear Maasai clothes, but to quit circumcising our girls?" "Why is it so bad for girls not to be circumcised?" I asked. "It's just bad. A man will pay all those cattle and be cheated, he'll receive an uncircumcised girl!" Mary soon walked in again, looking disgruntled. "I tried to get Sara out of bed, because we have to prepare for the ceremony, but she refused and went back to sleep!" The women in the kitchen laughed and shook their heads. Sara soon appeared outside the door. The women told her she had to bathe in cold water as Naserian, who stood shivering in a *khanga,* had already done. Sara angrily grabbed the water and walked away. The women laid a dried cowskin in the doorway of the kitchen and asked Sara to sit on it when she returned. She refused, the women cajoled her, and she grew more and more upset. "I'm not so stupid that I'll agree to sit on a cowskin!" she yelled, stomping angrily back to the main house. Perplexed, the women went into the kitchen to consult Mary. "I don't know what to do," she said, wearily shaking her head, glancing at me. They decided to send an emissary to try to coax Sara back, and the woman succeeded in convincing Sara to return to the kitchen. The women now put a small wooden stool on top of the cowskin and told Sara she could sit on that. Sara refused, and her younger sister clucked in disbelief at her sister's cheekiness. Finally she quickly sat on the stool, then got up and left the room (since she had been circumcised a few years before) as the women laughed among themselves. Naserian was then asked to sit on the chair, which she did slowly and reluctantly. She hesitated about opening her legs. ("She's not afraid, just shy" the women muttered among themselves.) As a few women watched, the circumciser took a razor blade and quickly nicked Naserian's inner thigh just enough to draw some blood. She then signaled to the women outside, who started ululating and laughing among themselves. Naserian stood up from the stool and walked outside, hitching up her cloth to look at her nick in bemusement. A few hours later, four *ilmurran* and two *intoyie* (uncircumcised girls) in customary dress walked up, carrying two thin trees (*elaitin*) to be planted, according to tradition, outside the entrance where the girls were circumcised.

Preparation for the feast began in earnest. A group of male elders took Steven, Mary's eldest son, to the center of the cattle pen to bless him as a stand-in for the duties of his deceased father. Obviously annoyed, he sat on a folded skin on a wooden stool with grass on his shoulders and inside his sleeves. The elders threw a mixture of water and milk on him from small gourds, let the cattle out of the pen, then sat next to him to drink. Steven sat glumly with his best friend, speaking in Swahili and mocking the elder men. "Look at that silly hat!" "How about that dirty one blowing snot from his nose?" I asked Steven if he could take the grass off and he told me that it had to fall out of its own accord. I walked back to the house, and soon afterward he and his friend left for the rest of the day.

The festivities continued through the day and much of the night. Mary

MP5.2 "Mary" receiving the gift of a goat from a delegation of guests for the post-circumcision celebration, 1992. Photo by author.

dressed up in a skirt and top she had sewn herself, then draped a wide beaded Maasai necklace on top and tied a wide beaded headband around her hair. Guests arrived throughout the day, singing as they entered the homestead, whereupon a delegation of women would walk down, singing, to meet them and receive their gifts, including goats, maize, money, and honey beer. Delegations of *ilmurran* arrived, singing songs and dancing in the cattle pen with the *intoyie* as some adult women sang and danced outside the pen. I quickly became the official photographer; there were endless requests to take pictures of guests handing over their gifts, dancing, or just sitting in their chairs. Several elders were shocked to see the supposedly circumcised girls walking about, but the women just laughed knowingly among themselves. Pilau (an Indian dish of rice, potatoes, meat, and spices) was served, as was alcohol, bottled beer, and honey beer. At one point I found Mary and a group of women dancing and singing near the *elaitin* trees. Mary and another woman each grabbed a tree and started singing raucously while dancing and jumping wildly. Other women took their turns. Later, a Maasai elder man who was also the village catechist said prayers for the girls in the sitting room, followed by other elders. By nightfall, most of the guests left, and the teenagers started another disco in the sitting room. Mainly *ilmurran* and young boys were dancing, although Sara and a few other girls (who were drinking alcohol with some boys in a back room) danced every now and then. Everyone giggled with embarrassment when one *olmurrani*'s mother started dancing, but she soon left the floor. Naserian's and Sara's fiancés were both there: John, a born-again Christian who was the son of an elite Maasai family, dressed in a crisp white shirt and bow tie; and Chris, in pressed pants and a collared shirt. Once the disco started, John sat by himself on the front porch listening to Christian songs in his Walkman. "It's better than that dance music," he told me.

I spoke to Mary later about what had transpired that day. "I didn't let them fully circumcise Naserian because of the teachers," she explained. "I agreed with them that it was stupid to circumcise her just before her exams, since it usually takes at least a month to recuperate. But as soon as her exams are over and school is out, I will have her fully circumcised. For now, however, it seemed best to go through with the ceremonies and celebration as if she had been circumcised. I don't know what I'll do when we really circumcise her." "I don't know Dorotea," she continued. "I mean, everything is changing. I can't even force them to get married, or else I would be wealthy with cattle!" I talked about circumcision with other educated Maasai women that day, all of whom claimed to be circumcised. "But will you circumcise your daughters?" I inquired. "No," one women answered. "Female circumcision is a thing of the past, it has no meaning anymore." "I'm not sure," said another woman. "It is such an important part of our culture."

Mary's adapted circumcision ceremony for her daughters was just one of many topics that villagers gossiped about. I was told endless stories about her: how she had refused the attentions of her husband's brother, how she had many lovers, how she was selfish and cruel. Many claimed that she had a "mean/bad spirit." There was endless speculation about who was the father of her newborn daughter, since she was born long after Mary's husband had died. Was it one of her workers? A certain Catholic priest? Perhaps Koko's grandson? I was told that at the annual Easter baptism ceremonies, the American missionary priest had refused to baptize her daughter until she named the father. Insulted, Mary had left the services, head held high, and the name of her daughter's father still remained a secret.

As a wealthy educated widow, Mary crossed all kinds of boundaries of appropriate female behavior. She was the sole and successful economic provider for her family, the sole decision-maker for her household and home-stead, and she was sexually independent. In many ways she was one of the main proponents of "development" in her community, with her modern house, latrine, assorted income-generating projects, educated children, and adapted customs and ceremonies. It was not the least bit surprising, therefore, that her life and habits were such a common topic of gossip and disdain. On her part, she nurtured her relationships with the few other educated Maasai women in the area (including Sokoine's widows), trying, like them, to navigate the best path toward the future for herself and her children.

THE GENDERED
CONTRADICTIONS OF
MODERNITY AND
MARGINALITY

6

This book has told a story about the experience of a group who have been constituted as "traditional" yet are struggling to live in world shaped ever more forcefully by "modernity." What is it like when a certain configuration of masculine attributes—being a nomad, a pastoralist, a warrior—persist for more than a hundred years in defining who you are to other people? How do the men whose masculinities have been shaped by such images reconcile the contradictions which are produced? How do the women, at once subsumed and excluded by these representations, make sense of themselves and these processes? Finally, what happens when none of these pursuits are possible anymore, when the development props that sustained you as "traditional" in a "modern" world collapse? What are the experiences of Maasai women and men as they have lived and coped with the contradictions of being at once marginal and modern?

Negotiating the Contradictions of Modernity and Marginality: Maasai Men

One result of colonial and post-colonial efforts to perpetuate and sustain the linkage of Maasai ethnicity and culture to cattle herding, nomadism, and warriorhood, and to mark all of these pursuits as male, was to privilege and fix certain masculinities. Being "Maasai," as I will demonstrate, came to be understood by Maasai themselves as being a pastoralist and a warrior: a "traditional" masculinity forged in opposition to "modernity" and sustained by development interventions. Conversely, Maasai men who in some way embraced aspects of modernity, and therefore did not conform to this dominant configuration of masculinity, were stigmatized and ostracized. But these days, as increased land alienation, declining livestock populations, forced settlement, and continuing marginalization from economic and political resources within the state make such "traditional" pursuits untenable, the dominant Maasai masculinity is being reforged to uneasily embrace both the "traditional" and the "modern."

The shift in dominant Maasai masculinity is most clearly seen in terms of the configuration then reconfiguration of the masculine category of *ormeek* (pl. *irmeek*) (Hodgson 1999c). (The Maasai language is gendered, and "or" is a masculine prefix. *Emeeki*, with the feminine prefix "e," is the rarely used feminine equivalent.) As described in Chapter 2, *ormeek* emerged during the colonial period as a derogatory name for "Swahilis" or non-Maasai, that is, those Africans who were educated, spoke Swahili, worked in the government, or were baptized. They were often symbolized, for Maasai, by their "Western" clothing. In time, however, the term was used to deride any Maasai man who imitated the Swahilis, who adopted the practices or fashions of modernity, who sought to be anything other than a "real" Maasai man.

Ormeek seems to have first been applied by Maasai to other Maasai men in the 1930s, when it was used to deride elder men who worked for the colonial government as "headmen" or *jumbes*. In time, the meaning of *ormeek* was broadened to include those men and boys who attended school. A common reason elders gave for refusing to let their children go to school was the fear that they would become *ormeek*: "Those elders who refused to send their children to school . . . said 'Oh! if my child goes he will become ormeek!'" *Ormeek* was also used to describe Maasai men who were baptized. Both Lutheran and Catholic missionaries and teachers encouraged their Maasai students to seek baptism. Although most parents refused to permit their sons to be baptized, some boys, especially those who pursued post-primary education, decided to be baptized anyway (cf. Saitoti 1986). Maasai elders I interviewed perceived baptism to be even more incompatible with Maasai culture and masculinity than education. One said, "If they only learn things like how to write and read, a regular education, but are not baptized, *basi*, when they come home, they will be normal people like other Maasai. But once he is baptized, he will have a different faith. He will separate from us completely." Conversion to Christianity by Maasai men marked a fundamental change in their male identity for several reasons. Maasai men, especially *ilmurran* and junior elders, were not perceived as particularly religious; male converts had to promise to not marry any more wives, and they had to recognize and submit to another authority as superior to their own ritual and political leaders. Initially, few baptized boys continued to actively participate in the church once they had completed their education. Those who did remain active adherents, however, were stigmatized as *irmeek*, especially if they worked as catechists.

Ormeek was therefore an implicit critique of all that modernity represented to Maasai: education, institutionalized religion, even the political structure and language of the nation-state. The senior and venerable elders I interviewed, who grew up with this strictly enforced dichotomy of the dominant Maasai masculinity and the disparaged *ormeek* masculinity, described the difference between Maasai and *ormeek* in mutually exclusive terms. As opposed to the ideal of Maasai men as pastoralists, for example, *irmeek* were ignorant of herding and cattle (*"meyielo ataramat inkishu,"* lit. "they did not know how to care for/about cattle"). The use of *ataramat*, from the verb *eramatare*, is significant here, as *eramatare* denotes more than just herding (*enkirritare*) but encompasses all aspects of cattle care. To care *for* cattle one must have the pertinent animal husbandry knowledge, but to care *about* cattle implies an emotional bond and commitment. Given the centrality of caring for and about livestock to Maasai pastoral identity, economic production, social organization, and prestige structure, this statement marks *irmeek* as profoundly not-Maasai.

Others described them in spatial terms as rootless, ungrounded, wandering: "Those people have no place where they live. They come and go with work. They come like people from far away, but don't distinguish themselves. And their seed is not known." Although this senior elder's description could be read as depicting *irmeek* as roving nomads, the reference to their unknown seed suggests that it is more of a commentary on *irmeek*'s perceived lack of community and attachments. Seed is a symbol of the patriline; it occurs constantly in discussions of marriage arrangements when parents or elders debate the quality of a future bridegroom's seed or the seed that spawned a future bride: "[I wouldn't want my daughter to marry an *ormeek*] because I don't want a seed I don't know, that I don't know the habits of. How will I know if he is nice? His background might be that he is a troublemaker and I wouldn't know." These descriptions imply profound differences that cannot be easily overcome: one either knows about cattle and herding or one does not. One cannot be grounded and rootless at the same time. And one's seed is either recognized and respected or unfamiliar and suspect.

During this period, the *ormeek*/Maasai opposition masked the complexities and contradictions of cultural change. In many ways, *ormeek* became as much a stereotype as the dominant Maasai masculinities had become by this time, in part because the characteristics of *ormeek* transcended age-grades—any Maasai man, whether *ilmurran* or elder, could become an *ormeek*. But neither the dominant masculinities nor *ormeek* were essential, static categories, and as the meaning of one changed, so did the other. That some Maasai men embraced that which had been defined and stigmatized for years by Maasai and colonial administrators as not-Maasai destabilized the dominant masculinity. And as the scope and pace of interventions into Maasai life increased, the meaning of *ormeek* broadened to encompass each new arena of imposed social and cultural change, further heightening the contrast between them.

Furthermore, *ormeek* refracted the opposition in gendered terms—it was rarely applied to Maasai women. If being a traditional Maasai was about being male, then its opposite, *ormeek*, was also a masculine category. Maasai women were in many ways doubly excluded from this identity dilemma: not only had they become devalued as less than Maasai, but they were also denied many of the opportunities for change available to Maasai men. Only a few Maasai women were called *emeeki* (the feminine form), either because they were one of the few to attend school during the colonial period or, more often, because they married *irmeek* schoolteachers and politicians and adopted Western clothes and Swahili hairstyles. Baptized women, however, unlike baptized men, were rarely called *emeeki,* in part because so many Maasai women converted to Christianity (see below).

Although the commentary of the senior and venerable elders marked the *ormeek*/Maasai distinction as a vast, unbridgeable gap, several Maasai men during this time struggled to reconcile the seemingly stark differences. As the lives of Thomas (Maasai Portrait 3), Sokoine (Maasai Portrait 4), and others attest, the configuration of Maasai masculinities, and thus the meaning of *ormeek,* has shifted. One reason is that the number of *irmeek* has expanded as the first generations of *irmeek* have raised their children as *irmeek.* Like their fathers, these men use their education, knowledge of Swahili, and capacity to operate in the political realm of the nation-state to work for salaries, vie for development resources, and struggle for political power. Because of the changing political economic situation of Maasai, these men (and some women) are far better situated than their uneducated cohort to adapt, survive, and even prosper. Pastoralism has collapsed in many areas, so Maasai throughout Tanzania have turned toward farming as a means to feed their families and toward education as the hope for their future. Most senior and venerable elders now speak of themselves as *emodai,* or stupid, for ever having clung to a masculine mode which embraced pastoralism and rejected education, farming, and involvement with the state. The irony here is striking: while *irmeek* were stigmatized by many of these same men for being ignorant of cattle, and thus not really pastoralists, this ignorance has little resonance now that pastoralism it-

6.1 Alais Morindat, an educated *ormeek,* poses with his first wife during one of the celebrations which marked his transition from *ilmurran* to junior elder, 1987. Photo by author.

self is increasingly less viable. Instead, it is precisely the knowledge of *irmeek* that is now valued and the ignorance of traditional pastoralists that is discredited.

And now that all men, both old and young, struggle to overcome the constraints of a dominant masculinity that rejected modernity, the category of *ormeek* is being reforged in less derogatory terms. As all elderly Maasai men embrace education as necessary to the future of their children, and as more of their children and grandchildren—the younger men—go to school, participate in national government, or even join the church, the dominant masculinity of Maasai-ness is being reconfigured to contain the attributes of modernity historically associated with *ormeek.* As a result, *ormeek* has been recast either to represent minimal differences or, more commonly, has become a category empty of any meaning at all. Younger men spoke of *irmeek* as merely signaling a difference in language—"they speak Swahili"—or a difference in dress—"they wear pants." In contrast to earlier meanings of *ormeek,* such differences were more external and flexible and were not mutually exclusive: one could both speak Swahili and speak Maa, or one could wear a red cloth in the morning, put on pants to go to town, then return in the evening to home and the red cloth again.

The transformation in the meaning of the term was evident in one elder man's comments:

> In the past they said that an *ormeek* did not know how to care for cattle. . . . But what do we mean now by *ormeek*? I don't know this thing called *ormeek*. I mean, I am called *ormeek* and him over here [referring to my assistant], he is *ormeek*, and this child sitting here is *ormeek*. Now what will we do with this term *ormeek*? I know that a smart person is called *ormeek*, so maybe an *ormeek* is a smart person with a white house and a tractor—that is what we are learning and that is what we want.

Other elders, junior elders, and young men shared his sense that as more and more Maasai became like *ormeek* the term was losing any fixity of meaning; it was a sign without a referent:

> I don't know what an *ormeek* is, I just don't know. I mean this name *ormeek*, if I am not wrong, we use it to slander those we meet on the road, or when we see an *ormakaa* [junior elder] resting in his pants. That is what we mean by *ormeek*. It came in as a name, but it is a mistake. I mean look here—this woman [me] who is sitting here is an *elaisungun* [European], but although she is *elaisungun*, we don't know what kind of *elaisungun* she is. They have lots of tribes themselves—there are Americans, English, Indians, Boers. Similarly, if you look within our Maasai, there are Arusha, Sukuma, Chagga, and Meru. So if you try to find the meaning of this word *ormeek* you will fail. I am unable to know the meaning of this name called *ormeek*, I just don't know.

While the senior and venerable elders lamented the past and berated themselves for having clung so desperately to a certain way of being, a masculinity they now derided as *emodai*, the junior elders, and even more so the *ilmurran*, sought to forge new ways of being a Maasai man which could embrace the claims of the past and the demands of the present. Unlike their more senior elders, all of the *ilmurran* and junior elders spoke Swahili, and some could even converse in rudimentary English. Increasing numbers of young men attended school and pursued alternative economic activities, including salaried employment as teachers and government workers. And while the senior and venerable elders relied on their wives and sons to farm for them, the elders, junior elders, and young men eagerly cultivated maize, beans, and occasionally barley to eat and sell.

Other contrasts with the dominant masculinities described for the early

6.2 A Maasai man, trained as a rural medical aid, vaccinates a baby as part of a mobile mother and child health (MCH) clinic, 1986. Photo by author.

twentieth century are even more remarkable. Age-sets are still an organizing principle of masculine subjectivity and social relations, and their fundamental apparatus has remained much the same: male circumcision is still a prerequisite to becoming an adult man, each age-set is still given a unique name, and men advance from age-grade to more senior age-grade together. But the experience, attitudes, and practices of being an age-set member have changed. In these Maasai communities, as in many others, few young men had time to spend in the numerous activities which build solidarity within their age-set: the liminal period after circumcision has been dramatically shortened as most boys must return to school, *emanyatta* (warrior-villages) are a rare occurrence, and *ilmurran* have infrequent opportunities to congregate with each other as they pursue farming, education, waged work, and other opportunities to make money. Many only selectively observed the dietary prohibitions, and obviously none could sustain themselves solely on milk, blood, and meat alone given the demise of the cattle herds. They wore an array of clothes depending on the context. At home, some wore a long cloth knotted over one shoulder and fastened to their waist by a belt, while others wore blue jeans and t-shirts. All had pants, shirts, jackets, and shoes to wear to town, political meetings, and other public venues.

Not all venerable elders liked the interests and pursuits of the younger men. A few complained about their lack of respect, their individualistic ways. One venerable elder was quite terse in his criticism: "If you look closely, all that [the younger man] is interested in is money; what he cares about is his radio, his watch. He doesn't know cattle, and when he farms all he cares about is his radio and watch. . . . He can't know if his father is hungry; he can't know if his mother is hungry; he can't know if his child is hungry." Such scathing diatribes about the selfishness of younger men challenged both the communal ideal of *ilmurran* and the ideal of generosity of the elders. It invoked an early critique of *irmeek* (that they didn't "know" cattle) but extended and complicated it: what these young men knew was money and material goods, but their self-interested obsession with accumulating their individual property blinded them to the basic needs of their families. The radio and watch were also potent symbols of the changes which had occurred among Maasai men: listening to radio broadcasts in Swahili solidified their linkages with the nation-state, and their preoccupation with their watches confirmed the new salience of time in their lives.

Maasai women, especially older women, could also be quite scathing about the differences between the *ilmurran* of long ago and the *ilmurran* of today. As Koko (Maasai Portrait 1) told me scornfully,

The *ilmurran* of the past didn't die for no reason. They didn't get fevers or any sicknesses, but only died during cattle thefts. But these *ilmurran* of today who eat flour inside the house? Would you ever have seen *ilmurran* of the past eating flour in a house? They didn't eat meat that had been seen by married women [and] they drank blood that had been mixed with medicines (*ormukuta*) so that they had the strength/abilities to steal. But those [*ilmurran* of today] who eat flour mixed with shortening, that was forbidden (*enturuj*) for *ilmurran* in the past!

Given the significance of their former roles as promoters and defenders of the male order, it is not surprising that older women were so caustic in their critiques. Some of their anger was also due to their hostility about their progressive loss to men of economic autonomy, rights in livestock, and political authority. Yet many of these same women depended on the success of these young men, as their sons, to find ways to support them in their old age.

Younger women were more tolerant, although bemused. Like the younger men, most described the difference between Maasai men and *irmeek* as superficial, a matter of language and clothing. Some women believed that marrying an *ormeek* would give them greater freedom than if they married a more traditional man. The increasing number of elopements, especially among educated men and women, attested to the willingness of women to challenge the prerogatives of their parents to arrange their marriages and to the shifting meanings of "father" and "husband" which have accompanied the reconfiguration of masculinity (Hodgson 1996). Other women, however, still dreamt of having a "real" *olmurrani* as a lover and mocked the aspirations and attitudes of *irmeek*.

But whatever their current survival strategy, Maasai men of all ages asserted a very modernist dream: for the village, they wanted a hospital, a good school, a grinding machine, more cattle medicine, a better road, and cheap public transport to the nearby district headquarters. When asked what they personally wanted, most replied with some version of "I want everything; there is nothing I don't want," then proceeded to list a house with a corrugated iron roof, a car, a tractor, a bigger farm, more cattle, and more children as the most common elements of their dream. And they hoped that their sons, their warriors-become-scholars, would help make these dreams come true.

But in a curious echo of the earlier British ambivalence about changing Maasai culture, they were also aware of the tensions and contradictions that such aspirations entail: "But really, I don't want our culture to be changed, because if we change our culture we will all be stupid. But I also don't want development to be lost, because if it is lost we will all go to the bush." Or, as another elder complained: "I don't want our Maasai culture to be changed at all; I don't want our children to be changed; I don't want our cattle to be changed so that we don't have them anymore. . . . I don't want this area to be cultivated even though I want a farm, but I don't want it to be farmed so that the cattle have to be fenced in."

Embodying the Contradictions of Modernity and Marginality: Maasai Women

How, then, have women negotiated the gendered interventions and effects of development and modernity? I suggest we examine the domain in which they have asserted and expressed themselves, "the religious." Specifically, I want to explore the symptoms and spread of *orpeko*, or spirit possession, which, I argue, marked the penetration, impact, and reshaping of "modernity" and all its contradictions: Maasai women's increasing disenfranchisement from their historical rights over certain economic resources, their political marginalization, and their exclusion from the expanding opportunities for education and income generation (cf. Hodgson 1997).[1] But *orpeko* was simultaneously a "counter-hegemonic process" (cf. Boddy 1989: 5); it not only critiqued the intrusion of "modernity" and the consolidation and reinforcement of patriarchal authority in the lives of Maasai women, it also strengthened relationships among women and partially enabled them to create an alternative community beyond the gaze and control of Maasai men.[2]

Most studies of spirit possession examine cases of long-established spirit possession cults that have complex rituals and procedures for identifying, appeasing, and negotiating with rich pantheons of spirits but rarely cast them out permanently. Further, many of these spirit possession cults operate in societies with a significant Muslim influence and presence. The distinctions of the Maasai case are therefore intriguing: First, Maasai have no long-term tradition of spirit possession; instead, spirit possession, or *orpeko*, emerged through Maasai interaction with Muslim-influenced spirit possession practitioners and cults and spread in tandem with increased missionary activity by the Lutheran and Catholic churches. Secondly, most Maasai interpret *orpeko* as possession by "the devil" (*esetan*) rather than by a range of individual unique spirits. Finally, rather than seek ways to accommodate and appease the spirit in a long-term relationship or through institutionalized spirit cults, most Maasai seek a permanent "cure" for the "sick" and "inoculation" for the "healthy" through Christian baptism. But there are similarities: as in most cases in Africa, the preponderance of possessed Maasai are women, generally younger married women.[3]

Orpeko is vividly perceived by Maasai men and women as an outside force that has entered and disrupted their lives. The "otherness" of *orpeko* is immediately evident both linguistically and spatially. First, the word *orpeko* is not indigenous to the Maa language but is an adaptation of the Swahili word *upepo* (spirit, wind). Second, *orpeko* spread from the outside in—the first cases occurred in the south, near the borders with non-Maasai peoples, then slowly spread northward, into the heart of Maasailand. Maasai stories about *orpeko*, as well as the case histories, emphasize its foreign origins: *orpeko* emerged from Maasai contacts with non-Maasai peoples, both African and Euro-American. Maasai say that the first cases of *orpeko* were brought by Maasai who had dispersed to "Swahili" lands after the devastation of livestock and people in the late 1800s wrought by rinderpest, bovine pleuropneumonia, and smallpox, as well as the resulting famine and inter-sectional wars. Although *orpeko* seemed to have faded for years after a spate of outbreaks in the 1930s, it reappeared dramatically in the mid-1950s and spread rapidly throughout southern Maasailand (Hurskainen 1985: 9–11). By 1971, when Peterson made his study, hundreds of Maasai women were reportedly possessed by *orpeko*. Most women he interviewed claimed that their first symptoms occurred from two to fifteen years earlier. The renewed outbreaks coincided not only with incursion by non-Maasai healers who specialized in identifying and treating *orpeko* cases, but also with rapidly expanding evangelization activities by the Catholic and Lutheran churches (Hurskainen 1985: 9–11; Hodgson 2000a).[4] Slowly the outbreaks spread north, with occasional cases being recorded in Monduli District in the mid-1970s and significant numbers occurring in my three research communities by the early 1980s (Hurskainen 1985: 11).

The earliest recorded case of spirit possession is that of Nanoto (DP/3),[5] an elderly woman who told Peterson that she was first possessed between 1900 and 1910, when she was in her late twenties. Her story, as summarized by Peterson, is as follows: Although she was born in northern Maasailand, she was living at the coast near Pangani during this period. The elders took her to a non-Maasai healer for treatment when their normal methods for treating her symptoms, a fever and a rapid strong pulse, failed. He diagnosed her problem as spirit possession, concocted a brew of medicinal herbs for her to drink, and charged twenty-one cows for the treatment. For three months following the treatment, she was far worse—she had no appetite, rarely slept, and refused to talk to anyone. Just when her family thought she was going to die, she recovered, was better for a while, then suffered a relapse of the same symptoms. In 1930, a Lutheran evangelist and another man visited her *boma*, telling people to gather around and hear God's word. "She heard this, came, listened and became very, very happy—'like the white cloud on top of a mountain.'" After the evangelist left, she ate and slept well for four days, then began to hear voices directing her to go to church. She convinced her father to let her go, partly by reminding him of all the cattle he had lost trying to heal her. She walked to the mission, attended devotions that evening, then stayed on in the area to attend baptismal instruction classes. "After hearing the First Commandment on her first day of baptismal instruction, she began to shake and wail and then the demon left her for good. She then finished instruction and was baptized."

The details of Nanoto's account provide a template through which to examine the symptoms, diagnosis, and treatment in both early and contemporary cases. As in Nanoto's case, *orpeko* most commonly afflicts women of childbearing age, although a few cases of possessed men have been reported and recorded.[6] A range of symptoms could be diagnosed as *orpeko*, including headaches; pains in the head; fevers; pains and burning sensations in the womb and/or stomach; back aches; swelling in the neck, breasts, and often belly; general listlessness and apathy; lack of appetite; and insomnia. Later symptoms often included wailing, shaking, thrashing fits, choking sensations, and nightmares (cf. Hurskainen 1989: 43). The most prominent symptoms seem to cluster geographically, so that, for example, women in Naberera complained of fever, while most from Kisongo spoke of terrible burning sensations in their stomach/womb. In the communities in Monduli where I studied, the acute symptoms of *orpeko* were fits characterized by body rigidity, vigorous shaking, and a low, growling moan. Ongoing symptoms included a general malaise, negligence of household duties, rudeness, and terrifying nightmares. Many of these symptoms, of course, could be attributed to other diseases and maladies—it was the naming as *orpeko*, usually by other women, that made the difference.[7]

These symptoms, I believe, signify the contradictions that development has produced in the lives of Maasai women. Earlier chapters showed how colonial and post-colonial development interventions contributed to the economic, political, and cultural disenfranchisement of Maasai women. As being "Maasai" came to mean being a male Maasai who was a warrior, pastoralist, and patriarch, Maasai women (and *irmeek* Maasai men) became marginal to this rigid, gendered configuration of ethnic identity. At the same time that Maasai women have gradually lost both prestige and power, their workloads have increased. Many have been compelled to cultivate to subsidize household consumption as livestock resources have dwindled, and most walk farther in search of fuel wood and water now that sedentarization has depleted nearby resources. These processes have converged to displace women from their rights and roles and heighten their sense of despair and isolation.

The one obvious alternative open to women—to embrace modernist notions of progress—is neither an easy nor an attractive option. Not only do most women lack the economic or political means for such a direct challenge to the consolidation of patriarchal authority, they are also unclear about whom or what they would be opposing. Maasai women have a ritual means of organizing (*olkishiroto*) which involves cursing, physical attacks, and the destruction of property to rebuke individual affronts by men or women to certain cultural rules (cf. Spencer 1988: 201, 205). But the gradual overlapping changes which have empowered Maasai men provide no *specific* violation to be condemned or individual to be punished. Women cannot launch a ritual attack of words and beatings on all men. Instead, silenced from either verbal or violent forms of protest, women have initiated a powerful moral critique of development and its gendered effects on their lives in the language of their bodies. Through spirit possession, women voice their complaints about their disenfranchisement, at once internalizing their despair and expressing their predicament.[8]

Considered broadly, *orpeko* is a metaphor for women's outrage at the changes in their lives. In my discussions with men and women, they stressed *orpeko*'s association with devastation and disease. They obliquely referred to it as *emuoyian,* or "sickness," but a sickness that came from outside and afflicted only women. Like modernity, *orpeko* had ambiguous origins, multiple manifestations, and devastating gendered effects. One cluster of *orpeko* symptoms, for example, signified the perceived source of these undesirable changes: "the other," that is, outsiders, non-Maasai—the external, imposed processes, practices, and people over which women exerted little control. For example, possession fits were often triggered by "foreign" sounds, such as radios and drumming, and when possessed, some women spoke in "strange" languages in which they were not fluent, most often Swahili or Arabic (cf. Benson 1980: 55). But the terror of women over the changes in their lives was most evident in the nightmares they described to Peterson, nightmares filled with signs of the invasion of "the other." Many women spoke of a sense that "darkness" or "a black cloud" was descending on them, suffocating and even strangling them:

> She would wake up at night with a start as "darkness" would come and try to strangle her. Being very frightened, she would cover herself quickly before the "darkness" could cover her and then she would scream. After this she was unable to sleep for the rest of the night. She also began to feel something very heavy in her chest. (DP/1)

Sometimes the choking sensation came from within themselves, rising from their stomach to their chest and throat:

> The first occurrence of trouble was in 1969 when this girl became quite sick with a fever. A few days later she saw "darkness," felt that she was being strangled and ran out of the boma. She was caught by her family and they decided that she was crazy. From then on she would shake every day—first on one side, then the other and then her whole body would shake. She always had a burning sensation in her stomach and felt something very hot moving upwards to strangle her. She felt like a dying woman at this time, and she almost did die. (DP/5)

Most women complained that their symptoms were always worse during the night, in the darkness. In a few cases, "the other" was symbolized by whiteness: a few women dreamt that something or someone white was either coming toward them or beckoning them—a white light or moth, a white man, or a half white/half Maasai man. Perhaps the white men represented the white settlers and administrators infiltrating their lives and lands, or the white cassocks of pastors and priests.[9]

If these symptoms identified the source of women's increasing despair, another cluster of symptoms marked the dimension in their lives where they felt most threatened and therefore the most anxious—their roles as mothers. Being a mother, especially the mother of sons, was fundamental not only to attaining respect and prestige as a woman but also to ensuring one's maintenance and subsistence in old age. Although important, their roles as wives, daughters, and sisters were less prestigious and critical. Pregnancy, or anxiety about pregnancy, was therefore central to most occurrences: not only was possession prevalent among infertile women, but pregnancy could trigger possession, and possession was said to cause miscarriages (cf. Boddy 1989, especially Chapter 5). One of the most common symptoms could be read as an embodied expression of women's anxieties about pregnancy, motherhood, and reproduction: many women reported a burning, painful womb or stomach, occasionally with a hard lump in it. In other words, women feared the effects of the changes on their lives with regard to both their biological and social reproduction.

Finally, as Pastor Stanley Benson has argued, another cluster of symptoms expressed the isolation women felt: possessed women would run away from their families and communities or enter into "a coma-like trance where no communication is possible" (Benson 1980: 54). Peterson described how possessed women would often cover their heads, faces, and eyes when talking to him, as if to hide and distance themselves (1971).

Paradoxically, while *orpeko* thus marked the structural crisis of individual women, it also enabled their "healing" in two ways. First, *orpeko* strengthened relationships among Maasai women: when a woman became possessed, it was usually other women who helped her. Once *orpeko* cases became more prevalent, it was mainly other women, often Christian women, who diagnosed or "named" a woman's symptoms as *orpeko*. Sometimes they would beat *debes* (metal containers—also a foreign import) to confirm their diagnosis and invoke, then appease, the spirit, causing the woman to dance and sing until she was exhausted or the spirit had subsided. Non-Maasai traditional healers could also temporarily appease the spirits through *ngomas,* or dances with drumming, but most *ngomas* were performed for the afflicted woman or women by other Maasai women (as they are today).[10] Also, when a possessed woman had acute attacks of fits and thrashing, other women would gather round and physically hold and comfort her until the fit had passed. Finally, Christian women would encourage the afflicted woman to go to church or, if a church was not nearby, instruct her themselves in the teachings of Christianity. Most of Peterson's findings still hold true today.

Orpeko, in other words, has enabled women to establish multi-dimensional, textured relationships among themselves. Through physical touch, emotional bonds of empathy and sympathy, and the sharing of knowledge and experience, women have addressed their increasing isolation, despair, and loneliness. Although women might not be able to describe the source of *orpeko* beyond attribution to some foreign, outside "other," they can name the symptoms of *orpeko,* and through such naming, begin to work together toward healing.

Orpeko has also enabled women's healing by facilitating the creation of an alternative female community within the Christian church: the most popular and prevalent means to heal *orpeko* has been to attend baptismal instruction, become baptized, and participate regularly in the Christian church. The pattern in Peterson's earlier cases was for men to take possessed women to non-Maasai healers, to *oloiboni/iloibonok* (Maasai healers and ritual experts), and/or to doctors in government hospitals and dispensaries, all of whom failed to cure the women. Their impotence in the face of *orpeko* could be understood as women's rebuke of the increasing powers of "traditional" patriarchal authorities and the male medical institutions of development. And so possessed women, such as Nanoto, would eventually be taken, usually by other women, to church, where they would find permanent healing.

Such was the case with another woman interviewed by Peterson, who described her early symptoms, which began after a miscarriage. On the advice of the elders, she took a trip to a traditional doctor, who beat drums for her. She danced and thrashed so hard on the ground, however, that she miscarried again:

> After this second loss of a child, she returned home sick, very weak and with the same symptoms as before. They fed her cow and goat fat in their efforts to give her strength. When they saw that she wasn't getting any better, the elders decided to send her to another traditional doctor. She, however, refused to go because she had heard from Masai Christian women at Ngojoha who had been cured that Christianity was the only true cure. The elders consented so she went to church in about 1966. She was taught by a Masai evangelist . . . and then baptized on the 24th of September, 1967.

As soon as she began baptismal instruction, she started improving as far as the shaking, the burning sensations in the groin and the headaches. All of these symptoms left her before baptism. She still had occasional problems mentally, i.e. confused thinking, amnesia. These mental lapses continued until baptism.

The day before baptism when she first heard she was to be baptized, all the original symptoms returned in full—yelling, dancing, shaking, burning sensations. They continued until the moment when she was baptized (first application of water). Afterwards she became normal and has been so since that time. When she was baptized, she said she felt a heavy feeling pass over her and then afterwards she felt very relaxed. (DP/8)

All of Peterson's, Hurskainen's, and my accounts emphasized this point: that only the Christian churches could permanently heal *orpeko*.

So what is the appeal of Christian churches to Maasai women? As I have discussed elsewhere, despite the persistent efforts of Lutheran and Catholic missionaries to convert Maasai men, the vast majority of converts have been women (Hodgson 2000a). The appeal of the church is partly due to women's greater religiosity: Maasai women perceive themselves and are perceived as far more religious and closer to God (Eng'ai) than Maasai men. As women themselves say, the church enhances their already substantial religious life by providing a place to sing and pray to God. Some women even emphasize their spiritual superiority over men by characterizing their attraction to the Christian church as an inherent, embodied difference between men and women. They claim that their *oltau* (heart, soul, spirit) is more open to Eng'ai, closer to Eng'ai, while "the spirits of men just don't want to go to church." One woman argued that men, like wild animals (*olowuaru*), had no spirits. Moreover, the invocation of men as wild animals suggests a sharp moral critique of the changes in Maasai gender relations, simultaneously casting men's increased political and economic power as evil and an affront to Eng'ai while affirming the moral superiority of women in the face of such betrayals.

But the church also overcomes women's isolation by providing a forum to gather as a group. Unlike ceremonies and celebrations which provide only infrequent opportunities to gather, the church enables women to gather together on a frequent, regular basis. In addition to the class or service, women meet beforehand to chat in small circulating groups and often remain long afterward to talk. Finally, the church is also described by some as a place where one can learn new things and gain wisdom (*eng'eno*). Women go to church so that they can "get that wisdom (*eng'eno*) which is taught to people."

Although *orpeko* is still spoken of as a sickness (*emuoyian*) which has spread through Maasai women, the association between *orpeko* and Christianity is now quite direct: most contemporary Maasai now interpret *orpeko* as

265

possession by "the devil" (*esetan*) and believe that Christian baptism is the only way to exorcise the devil and achieve permanent healing.[11] As one elder man explained:

There is a sickness (*emuoyian*) which has spread into this area recently which was not here before, this thing called *esetan*, this *orpeko*. It hasn't entered men, but women. But when you take a woman to the oloiboni he says "she is cursed." And if you take her to another, "she is cursed." Basi, . . . this wisdom of Christians showed that a thing called the church (*ekanisa*) could heal this sickness. When we put women in there they were healed, really it helped them. Shie, why else would so many have joined? Also, it is said that a healthy person who is baptized cannot be possessed.

Or as another elder man commented:

Another thing which often admits women [into church] is *esetan*, they have entered church because of *esetan*. I mean, many have gotten *orpeko*, and they say that church is the only cure, since they have seen many others who became ill with *orpeko*, went to church and were cured. Others decided to go to church so that they wouldn't get *orpeko*.

One woman, when asked if she attended church services, answered quite bluntly: "I have not gone to church; I don't have Satan (*maata esetan*)."

Despite the appeal of the Christian churches, most women have to receive some man's permission—most often her father or husband—to attend baptismal instruction and church services. Several women interviewed by Peterson, such as Nasirian below, spoke of the difficulty obtaining permission from reluctant men:

Upon returning home [after visiting several traditional doctors whose treatments failed] a Christian woman told her if she would accept her instruction about Christianity, she would be healed. Her husband became very angry and refused. Her grandmother said, "If you play around with Christianity, you will become like an Mswahili." However, when her husband saw that she was getting no better, he consented and she began instruction from this woman. . . . [After eight days of instruction from this woman she was cured]. . . . Now that she was alright again, her husband and others in the boma tried to keep her from having anything to do with the church. She did manage to sneak off to church occasionally but suffered a lot of grief because of this. Finally her husband allowed her to go because she began having the same trouble again and another wife and a daughter also became possessed (they also went to church). (DP/12)

As in the above case, other women told Peterson how their husbands were very reluctant about their continuing involvement in the church:

> Although the rest of the boma inhabitants think her cure quite amazing, she has suffered a lot of grief because of her husband who is a type of local medicine man. He doesn't like at all the fact that she is a Christian. He thinks it is an excuse for moving towards civilization and Swahili ways. (DP/9)

The only baptized man interviewed by Peterson suffered continual harassment: "He is really bothered by other Maasai men. They come and ask him, 'Are you the one who sits among women and children? You aren't worthy to be a Masai!'" (DP/13). Many Maasai men whom I interviewed spoke disparagingly about the church, dismissing it as the mere "nonsense" of women, a waste of time.

Orpeko has helped women overcome men's resistance to their participation in church. Listen to one woman's story, as paraphrased by Peterson in 1971:

> There are eighteen women in her boma who are Christians, and when they heard that she had a demon they gathered and sang for her. Three of these women who had been demon-possessed are in her immediate family. (In this boma demon possession became such a common thing that husbands of women once possessed but now Christians, gave their wives permission to have their children baptized. Up to this time, permission for baptism was given only to those who were possessed.) (DP/2)

Orpeko continues to overcome the reluctance of Maasai men to allow their wives to become involved in the church. As one young married woman told me:

Men just don't want it [baptism]. There are men, for instance, like mine, who insult the church and say, "Shie, child, where are you going? Church? And what do you intend to find there? Have you changed? Have you become an *emeeki*? If you go, you'll leave a bad omen here."

But they all have to put you in that house of God (*ena aji Engai*) on the day when Satan comes inside you. If you are unable to cook his uji and he is stricken by hunger, then he says, "Shie, yesterday I slept without eating, perhaps my wife is crazy with *orpeko*, let me take her to church."

And he doesn't know what else to do to cure her. I mean, he left her for a long time until the day when he missed his food because Satan prevented her from cooking. Then and only then did he take her [to church]. But when he takes her, she will embarrass him there since she might jump about and tear off her clothes. But he left her [at home] without taking her so that she could pray to God when her spirit was still good (*supat oltau*); he left her until she got blemishes on her spirit (*ildoai oltau*), then and only then did he take her.

Several women spoke of how they became sick and their husbands had to "put" them (*etipika*) in church. Even men spoke of "putting" a sick wife in church to cure her of *orpeko:* "I put (*atipika*) one wife in that house [the church], I took her to be baptized. . . . I mean she had *orpeko,* that was the reason I put her in. . . . Everything else I did failed." Disputing notions of individual choice, one man claimed that women did not want to go to church but were forced to go by *orpeko:*

If you examine the women from here who are there, you'll see that what makes so many go is the sickness called *orpeko* which had infected them. If there is a young Maasai woman who does not want to go to church, she is taken anyway by this craziness. It is the place to wipe out this curse, the church is the only place. So, as I see it, it is not that the women badly want [to go to church], but that they are afraid of this sickness. The sickness has not yet spread much among men, or else many of them would also enter the church.

This theme of involuntariness—that *orpeko* is forcing women to do things such as join the church, which they would not otherwise choose—is repeatedly expressed in numerous early and present-day accounts. Other people (usually women) would diagnose or "name" the symptoms as *orpeko*. Moreover, possessed women often refused to go to church, despite insistent pleas by family and friends. Most were forced to go to church, often physically dragged to church for the first time, only to run away or have violent possession fits in the doorway. Finally, just before baptism or the application of water, a woman's symptoms would occasionally return violently, as if making a final statement of her unwillingness and lack of intention (see, e.g., DP/8, above).

The very ambiguousness and ambivalence of *orpeko* in terms of questions of women's agency and intentionality is crucial to its ability to resolve, in some measure, women's dilemma (cf. Boddy 1989: 5). Even men who are reluctant to allow their wives or daughters to join the Christian churches can hardly argue with the demands of the devil. By displacing responsibility for going to church from the women to either the devil (*esetan*) or decisions by men, women get what they want—to go to church—without directly threatening the authority of men. Husbands can either allow their wives a weekly respite from their heavy workloads to attend church or suffer the stark social and economic consequences should a woman become possessed and quit working altogether. Once *orpeko* spreads through an area, it is often enough for women just to invoke its possibility to receive permission to join the church. Many also receive permission to baptize their sons and daughters as a precaution.

Orpeko, in summary, has emerged and spread alongside a particular historical conjuncture between the increasing pressures and alienation produced by the intensifying economic, political, and social disenfranchisement of women and the alternative possibilities for female community and solidarity provided by the Christian missions. But the symptoms of the "sickness" spreading through Maasai women has, I have argued, embodied and expressed Maasai women's anxieties about their increasingly isolated and precarious position (cf. Alpers 1984; Stoller 1994). Paradoxically, however, *orpeko* has also enabled women to resolve their structural crisis by strengthening relationships among women and facilitating the formation of alternative female communities under the auspices of the Christian churches. Bedeviled by the malevolent forces shaping their lives, Maasai women have had the spirit to critique and transcend their isolation and anxieties.

*   *   *

As the story of development continues and the rigid masculine stereotypes of "being Maasai" persist, Maasai men and women are both finding ways to negotiate the disjunctures between images and realities, between "tradition" and "modernity." One consequence has been that men and women have come to interpret what it means to "be Maasai" in different ways. For many Maasai men, as for government officials, scholars, and others, "being Maasai" has come to be understood in primarily economic terms (being a pastoralist), a definition that, over time, has been used to exclude women. In contrast, as Maasai women have been marginalized both materially and symbolically from the pursuit of the pastoralist ideal, they have intensified their sense of identity as Maasai based in the realm of the spiritual, in their privileged relationship with God, Eng'ai.

So while one venerable elder still plaintively asserts that "We Maasai are people of the spear," another elder marks the shift in masculinities and his hope for the future in contrasting terms: "The spear of our grandfathers is finished; the only source of power now is the power of the pen." And women, lacking access to the power of the pen, seek their power in the spirit.

CONCLUSION: MAASAI PASTS,
MAASAI FUTURES

Commerce and cattle disease will do much to open up Masailand, which is the finest country in Africa. The one will soften and the other will tame these fierce people. The increasing love of trade goods impels them to encourage the arrival of coast caravans, and the loss of their cattle, as before explained, will force them to till the soil. Then as my old Masai friend prophesied, they will all become Wa-Kwavi, and if the original nomad Masai be a fierce, intractable, insolent bully, he no sooner becomes a settled agriculturalist than he changes into the nicest, quietest, honest, mildest inhabitant in Africa. Therefore, although they may fail to see it, the greatest boon En-gai can confer upon them is to sweep their cattle off the land. (Johnston 1886: 425–426)

Johnston's prophecy has, it seems, come true; the "once intrepid warriors" have now become farmers, teachers, laborers, and politicians. Yet the stereotypes which inform his prediction—of fierce, uncontrollable, culturally conservative pastoralists—persist. Development has been central to both the transformations in Maasai life and livelihoods and the endurance of the stereotypical images of what it means to "be Maasai." Although the form, content, and context of development interventions have varied, the underlying objective has generally remained the same: to protect Maasai "culture" through preserving and occasionally improving Maasai pastoralism, guided by an image of pastoralism as a purely masculine endeavor. As a result, development has further reinforced and rigidified the distinctions between Maasai as "traditional" and others (whether British colonial administrators or Tanzanian elites) as "modern." The complex intertwining of modern interventions and reified cultural differences has had substantial material consequences; as an ethnic group, Maasai have been marginalized from both political power and economic resources in first the colonial and now the post-colonial state.

At the same time that Maasai as a collectivity have been disenfranchised, however, these same interventions have reinforced and expanded the political and economic power of Maasai men over women. Monetization, commoditization, and "development" have produced separate male-dominated domains of the "economic" and "political," as opposed to the female domain of "the domestic." Meanwhile, the gendered modernist ideologies of "individualism" (individual male control of property), "rationality" (male "thinking" over female "feeling"), and "progress" (increased productivity for profit) have empowered Maasai men to consolidate their control over these realms through such categories as taxpayer, head of household, and livestock owner. These processes have converged to displace Maasai women from their former rights and roles. Furthermore, the oppositional categories of modern and traditional have been mapped onto Maasai gender relations: Maasai men have been valorized as the cultural ideal, promoted as symbols of tradition—an image of "being Maasai" that has been increasingly reified in the images of warrior, pastoralist, patriarch. The result of this rigid gender-coding of Maasai ethnicity has been to further marginalize women, in this case from their sense of "being Maasai."

As a celebration of Western progress, civilization, and rationality, the idea of the modern, as Hall (1992) among others has argued, is consciously built on a difference with another; the modern not only presupposes but requires the existence of the traditional to acquire its meaning (cf. Escobar 1995). The Maasai case demonstrates how such a dichotomy between modern and traditional was inscribed on the categories (such as ethnic identities) that were formed as part of the imperial project of imposing a modernist order on the perceived chaos of the native. Furthermore, it shows that the very development interventions that were critical to implementing the modernist project were crucial to sustaining and intensifying these oppositions. Thus, paternalistic efforts in the early colonial period to design and implement development projects that would protect Maasai culture by enforcing the political-economic isolation of Maasai and sustaining them as pastoralists reified the distinction between Maasai as traditional and other Africans as modernizing. The abrupt shift in policies and practices in the 1950s, and the accompanying pressures for Maasai to change rapidly, further heightened (and stigmatized) such differences. In turn, Tanzanian elites used such images to further marginalize Maasai from political and economic power in the post-colonial period; more recently they have used these images to market them as relics of Africa's primitive past to lure tourists. But recently the simultaneous decline of developmentalist efforts by the state and rise of transnational interest in "indigenous" development have enabled some elite Maasai men to use these stereotypes to circumvent the state and pursue their own development agendas.

The experience of development has therefore been an uneven process about which most Maasai feel deeply ambivalent. As the "power of the pen" replaces the "power of the spear," Maasai face an uncertain and difficult future. Despite the increasing numbers of educated men and women, some of whom participate in regional and national politics, they are still, as a group, peripheral to state power. Even the renewed interest in "pastoralist" and "Maasai" development by international donors is problematic: although it has increased their access to economic resources, it has also engendered increased resentment from Swahilis and others whose cultural profile is not "exotic" or interesting enough to merit such attention.

Many Maasai I interviewed commented on differences in the colonial and post-colonial periods in terms of the government's attitude toward and concern for Maasai affairs. Some recalled the colonial period with fond memories; they remembered it as a time when the government cared about Maasai welfare. "These days nothing is good," remarked one senior male elder. "It was far better in the past when the British were here." Others complained about the current lack of development in Maasai areas in comparison to other areas. "The government these days doesn't help us," explained one venerable male elder. "It doesn't help Maasai get land for farming . . . or repair the water projects. The government helps everybody except Maasai!" The reason for the current problems, according to one elder, was that "black people can't lead." "Colonial officers were better. . . . Black people (*iltunganak oorok*) are nasty . . . they chew us like dogs." These comments and others referred to the lies, corruption, bribery, and discrimination they believed characterized the "Swahili" government. As one older woman explained: "For example, we are told to give money to the [village] chairman so that he can meet with the government about one plan or another. He takes everything and doesn't bring back anything. He 'eats' [steals] it all! Once," she continued, "we held a protest [about corruption] at a large government meeting. . . . When the government saw the protest, they killed two of their bulls, fed everyone, and the meeting went well. These days they are just selling us off." Maasai felt most vulnerable in legal matters. "Before," observed one senior elder, "people with legal cases could speak the truth and be heard, but now matters are decided by corruption and bribery. The person of truth should not be beaten by the person with property." For many, the relationship between Maasai and the government changed drastically once Sokoine died (Maasai Portrait 4). "The government helped us a little when Sokoine was alive," said one old woman. "They built us the water project. But once he died, it was the end of any help from them." And not everyone had positive views on colonialism. "They [whites] colonized black people," remarked one venerable male elder, "so how can black people ever catch up?" "White people have caused all of our problems," said a middle-aged woman to my assistant, Morani. "Except for her [referring to me]; she's different."

Many recall the past in nostalgic tones and fear what the future will bring. They describe the social transformations that have occurred in terms of an increasing lack of respect between spouses, between parents and their children, between state officials and Maasai. "There is no respect these days," observed a venerable female elder. "What is left if there is no respect in the world?" she wondered. "I want the old life where people respected each other," lamented another old woman. Others are disturbed by the social transformations and dislocations. "Before," explained one venerable male elder from Embopong', "an elder was called an elder, an *olmurrani* was called an *olmurrani*, and a woman was called a woman. What are they called these days?" One senior female elder attributed the social problems to alcohol: "Alcohol has destroyed the world. I mean, if a small child drinks and an adult drinks, where will respect be found among drunks?" For another senior female elder, the source of the problem was money. "[If I was given a lot of money] I would throw it away. . . . Just having a few things destroys people, much less many things. What could you do with so much money? I wouldn't want it at all. I would throw it in the bush." One venerable female elder blamed greed and selfishness: "Life in the past was better because there was respect. Now I can faint from hunger and there is food in this house, but the people won't offer me any when I pass by. . . . Before, people used to help one another."

But some are more hopeful. "Life has changed a great deal," said a young educated Maasai man. "We [Maasai] were behind, but now we see the light, our head is filled with some brightness. Just look at how the country has changed. Before, we didn't know how to farm and others did, and now we want to farm. The world has changed. The changes I want are for Maasai to get farms and to quit staying in the bush, and I want children put in school so they won't be stupid." "The customs of the past were stupid," commented another senior female elder. "Everything has changed and we should just accept it." "I don't know what to say about the changes in Maasai life," said a middle-aged woman. "I live in the present, not the past."

C.1 What will the future bring for this young Maasai girl and the younger brother she is holding in her arms? Photo by author, 1986.

For Maasai, development has been a profoundly gendered process in its constitution, representation, and effects. Despite the economic and political disenfranchisement of women, many men and women perceived that women were on the forefront of development. One senior elder spoke of women's embrace of development: "Frankly, I don't know the meaning of development. . . . We are old men. . . . Women lead us now. When you become old you become their [women's] workers. Women have really led development. These days they pay the taxes, when before elders would pay with their cattle." "The government should put Maasai women in office," suggested another senior woman, "since they are far more progressive than men!" "Girls will rule their fathers," warned a senior female elder, "if they become educated." While many men regretted how much life had changed for Maasai, a number of women, especially younger women, were eager for change. "The good life for me," explained one woman, " is to have more and more development." "Development," remarked another woman, in reference to the women's grinding-machine project in Emairete, "has given women a voice and power."

The Past and Future of Development and Modernity

So how does this study contribute to the study and practice of development and its counterpart, modernity? The experiences of Maasai suggest that the legacies of colonial and post-colonial development efforts resonated far beyond the goals and results of specific projects and programs. Development had been central to the assertion and expansion of state power by ordering and rationalizing Maasai lives and livelihoods to conform to colonial, and then national, agendas of "progress." The supposedly technical objectives of, for example, improving the productivity of animal husbandry or increasing the number of permanent water supplies masked other, more political, agendas. Lack of access to adequate grazing land and water supplies were not technical problems but political problems, the result of ongoing, extensive alienation of the most fertile land (dry-season grazing lands) and permanent water supplies in favor of "more productive" cultivators and game parks and reserves, among other uses. Not only did the significant restriction of the resource base available to Maasai diminish the viability of pastoralism, it also undercut their attempts to diversify their economic activities, especially through farming. In other words, the "problems" attributed to Maasai were, at least initially, problems of the colonial government's own making. Furthermore, these problems occurred because of marked differences between Maasai and government views of the future of Maasai land, livestock, and livelihoods. Development, in other words, was never just about technical problems; it could only be understood in terms of the broader historical, political-economic, and cultural contexts in which it operated.

What has happened to Maasai challenges and complicates the idea that development is either good or bad. Rather, the issues are about power, culture, and history (cf. Dirks, Eley, and Ortner 1994; Cooper and Stoler 1997). Who controls and participates in the design and implementation of development projects? What and whose agendas are being advanced by particular projects? What kinds of representations and misrepresentations about people's realities shape development ideas and practices? How do the legacies of prior development efforts influence people's participation in current endeavors? Maasai were never adverse to development on their own terms. They sometimes paid huge amounts to finance or subsidize projects and eagerly participated in those projects or project components they supported, including veterinary medicines, water projects, hospitals, and even, eventually, schools. But they recognized and resented the cultural messages conveyed by government officials and technical experts that privileged "modern" ideas of progress and prosperity and stigmatized Maasai ideas and practices. Furthermore, and perhaps most important, Maasai were offended by the ways in which development projects were repeatedly implemented: the lack of consultation, the overblown promises and disappointing results, the misdirected blame, and the incessant diatribes about changing their ways, all of which they understood as a lack of *enkanyit,* or respect.

In addition, the Maasai case raises larger issues about the relationship between the experience of development and the formation of individual and collective subjectivities. Identity formation is not just a matter of individuals engaging directly with broader structural forces; it is always mediated by collective crosscutting allegiances to social categories such as gender, generation, ethnicity, and class. Not only did the meanings and practices of "being Maasai" change; Maasai men and women also came to interpret what it means to "be Maasai" in different ways. Thus, while contemporary Maasai men base their sense of ethnic identity on their economic pursuits as pastoralists (even if, in reality, most combine livestock production with farming, wage labor, or other economic pursuits and Maasai women are still central to livestock production), Maasai women voice an alternative perspective. The resulting contradictions of being both marginal and modern have been expressed and experienced in different ways: for men through the shifting meanings and referents of the masculine category of *ormeek* and for women through their engagement with *orpeko,* or spirit possession.

The book, I hope, illustrates the value of ethnographic research, of studying not only the texts but the contexts in which development operates. The combination of participant observation, life histories, interviews, and careful readings of archival documents enables us to go beyond mere discursive readings of the practice of development. Instead, we gain a partial understanding of how some Maasai men and women have experienced and coped with the contradictions produced by their encounters with development and, through development, modernity. By providing a sense of the temporal and spatial dynamics of development, ethnohistorical analysis demonstrates that development is never a totalizing process, but is always a site of mediation and negotiation.

EPILOGUE: THE LAST
OF THE MAASAI?

In 1901, Sidney and Hildegarde Hinde published *The Last of the Masai*, in which they predicted the imminent extinction of the "nomad warrior race" (1901: x) of "pure" Maasai. As Hinde explained, "By the 'Last of the Masai,' I do not mean the last individuals of the race, but rather the last of the rapidly decreasing band of pure blood, whose tendencies, traditions, customs and beliefs remain uncontaminated by admixture with Bantu elements and contact with civilisation" (1901: xiii). Almost ninety years later, a co-authored book of the same title, *The Last of the Maasai* (Amin, Willetts, and Eames 1987), was published, with lavish photos and similarly dire predictions. As the jacket copy advised:

> To 19th century Europeans, they were the "noblest savages," an elite corps of painted and feathered warriors, strangely aristocratic in their disdain of other people's civilisation.
> For the Maasai, no advance during the last 100 years has been of any great interest or advantage; not peace for war; money for cattle; nor cities and settlement for the plains and open boundaries of their land across much of southern Kenya and northern Tanzania.
> Their isolation, their land, their traditional codes and values, have all been defended in a long, mostly passive war of resistance carried out by a society structured as a standing army.
> But it's all over, almost. . . . [The Maasai] are on the final retreat to the point of individual choice: either across the line of time and cultural advance or all the way back to the reservations—to whatever dry land is left to them.

Neither the Maasai of the present nor the Maasai of the past bear much resemblance to the stereotypical images of them that pervade, and have always pervaded, Western and African media. Instead, they have embraced a much more dynamic and historical sense of the relationship between economic, social, and cultural change. Throughout the last century, they have changed their practices, ideas, and sense of identity in response to economic and political opportunities and threats, interactions with neighbors and strangers, and their own needs and desires. Thankfully, those who predict "the last of the Maasai" are not only misguided but also wrong.

When I began the major phase of field research for this project, I held meetings in each of the three communities to explain my project and request permission to pursue my research. "Government officials, development workers and other outsiders all seem to have an image from the past of what Maasai life is about," I explained. "I would like to learn about and describe the present realities of your lives, so that people can understand the changes and continuities that have occurred. I would also like to ask questions about your desires for your future and that of your children." After much discussion and debate, the leaders and residents of each community eagerly welcomed me to live with them, talk to them, and tell their stories. I have done so now, and I hope that this account of their past and present will help them work toward a future of their own making.

Glossary

Words which appear only once in the text are not included in the glossary. Also, there are various differences in the pronunciation of Maasai dialects and no standard orthography. I have relied on Mol (1977, 1996) but have altered spelling to reflect Kisongo pronunciation where applicable. For example, *ormeek* appears elsewhere as *olmeek* and *olmeg.*

Maasai nouns are gendered:
e/en/eng/er: feminine singular   *o/ol/or:* masculine singular
i/in/ir: feminine plural   *i/il/ir:* masculine plural

ol–	*aji*	full age-set
en–	*dito/in-toyie*	young uncircumcised girl
	kainyoo?	what is it?
en–	*kaji/inkajijik*	house
en–	*kang'/inkang'itie*	homestead (SW: *boma*)
en–	*kitoria/in-kitoriat*	command, rule
ol–	*kiyama*	meeting, for British; occasional meeting of the full Maasai Council
	koko	grandmother, elderly woman
o–	*laigwenani/i-laigwenak*	age-set leader
o–	*layioni/i-layiok*	young uncircumcised boy
o–	*loiboni/i-loibonik*	ritual expert, "prophet"
	maendeleo	SW and Maa for "development," progress
	maidim	"I am unable," from *a–idim,* to be able
e–	*manyata/i-manyat*	special homestead for *ilmurran*
	mayiello	"I don't know," from *a–yiello,* to know, understand
or–	*meek/ir-meek*	non-Maasai African, a "Swahili"
e–	*modai*	stupid, ignorant
e–	*muoyian/i-muoyiaritin*	sickness
ol–	*murrani/il-murran*	age-grade of young circumcised men, "warrior"
	mzungu/wazungu	SW for European, white person
E–	*ng'ai*	God
e–	*ng'eno*	wisdom, knowledge
or–	*peko*	spirit possession (SW: *upepo*)
ol–	*piron/il-piron*	fire-stick elder
ai–	*ruk*	to believe, to agree, to be converted
e–	*setan*	a devil, Satan

279

e-	*siangiki/i-siangikin*	young circumcised woman
o-	*sotua*	special friendship based on stock exchange
ol-	*tau/il-tauja*	heart, mind, soul, spirit
a-	*tipika*	to put in, place
	Ujamaa	SW for unity, "familyhood"

Notes

Introduction

1. I am grateful to John Stiles for sending me these articles.

2. Where possible, I use the preferred spelling "Maasai," although I have retained "Masai" when it is used by others in writings, letters, and other quotations. There is a huge scholarly literature on Maasai, especially Kenyan Maasai. Some key works include Arhem (1985, 1987), Bernsten (1976, 1979, 1980), Galaty (1979, 1980, 1981, 1982a, 1982b, 1983, 1993a, 1993b), Homewood and Rodgers (1991), Jacobs (1965), Kituyi (1990), Ndagala (1990), Parkipuny (1975), Rigby (1985, 1992), Spear and Waller (1993), Spencer (1988), Talle (1987, 1988), and Waller (1976, 1978, 1984, 1985a, 1985b, 1988, 1993a).

3. Some of these districts have since been subdivided into new districts.

4. "Offtake" refers to the animals sold, traded, or otherwise disposed of from a herd.

5. Gordon and Douglas (2000) explore similar issues in their compelling analysis of the "myth of the Bushmen" in Namibia. See also Schrire (1984) and Wilmsen (1989).

6. Other scholars who have examined images of Maasai include Collett (1987) and Knowles and Collett (1989).

7. In my endeavor to combine anthropology and history, I have been greatly influenced by Feierman (1990), Moore (1986), and, more broadly, by Dirks, Eley, and Ortner (1994) and Cooper and Stoler (1997).

8. Similar efforts for Africa and other parts of the world include Fratkin (1991), Pigg (1992, 1993), Croll (1994), and Gupta (1998).

9. See Cowen and Shenton (1996) for a thoroughly compelling analysis of "development's" much earlier history.

10. For other ethnohistorical analyses of development in the colonial period in Africa, see Van Beusekom and Hodgson (2000).

11. See Cohen and Adhiambo (1989, 1994) for works on ethnicity which evoke the myriad ideas, images, and practices which reproduce and reconfigure multiple meanings of Luo ethnic identity.

12. A similar "history of women" school has developed among historians; much of the contemporary work uses life histories and personal narratives to explore and express women's ideas, practices, consciousness, and agency (cf. Geiger 1986). The life history of a Maasai woman, Telelia, co-authored with Paul Spencer, is included in the *Being Maasai* collection (Chieni and Spencer 1993).

13. These ideas are more thoroughly discussed in Hodgson (1999a, 2000b, 2000c).

14. See, for example, Driberg (1932), Dupire (1963), Klima (1964), Elam (1973), Dahl (1979, 1987), Beaman (1983), Wienpahl (1984), Ensminger (1987), Curry (1996),

Jowkar and Horowitz (1991), Horowitz and Jowkar (1992), Moore (1986), Hutchinson (1996), Oboler (1985), and Hodgson (2000b).

15. The work of Okeyo (1980), Kettel (1986), and Oboler (1985) have influenced my thinking here. Other scholars who have addressed aspects of Maasai gender relations include Llewelyn-Davies (1978, 1981), Kipuri (1978, 1989), and Talle (1988).

16. There is a vast feminist literature which debates the analytic usefulness of the concept of "patriarchy" in describing and understanding gender inequality in Africa and elsewhere. Some important works include Walby (1990), Stichter and Parpart (1988), Schmidt (1991), and Hodgson (1996).

17. For other examples of this in Africanist scholarship, see Hodgson and McCurdy (1996, 2001) and Grosz-Ngate and Kokole (1997).

18. Because chronological age is difficult for a Maasai or a researcher to discern, I have categorized men and women by age-set: men by their age-set of circumcision, women by the male age-set they danced with as *intoyie* (young, uncircumcised girls). As such, men of the Ilmakaa age-set, for example, are roughly the same age as women of the Seuri age-set (i.e., women who danced with Seuri).

19. In August 1992, I was robbed by the son of my landlady, then evicted from the house by her. With little time to find another place and few other options in the communities, I rented a room in the house of a friend in Arusha to use as a home base and stayed with my assistant during trips to Emairete. As I had done previously, I visited Arusha about once a week for water, diesel, and other supplies, but I would often stay two nights in town rather than just one so that I could type my notes and take care of correspondence and other administrative tasks. In Mti Mmoja, I always stayed in one central homestead, where I had long-standing relationships. In Embopong' we shifted our overnight stays between three homesteads.

20. I interviewed one of Morani's clan sisters while he waited outside, as her exaggerated "respect" behavior took the form of silence in his presence. Morani interviewed one elder man in my absence. We had failed numerous times to interview him because he was either sick or absent, so Morani, who lived nearby, took advantage of a moment when he knew the man was present, healthy, and willing to be interviewed.

21. "Respect" behavior was also, ideally, expected between Morani and his clan sisters, but was, with one exception, loosely observed, if at all.

1. Gender, Generation, and Ethnicity

1. The narrative is a summary from the transcription of a longer, disjointed version told to me during an interview with Wanga in 1992.

2. The following section is drawn from Bernsten (1979), Sommer and Vossen (1993), Sutton (1990, 1993), and Galaty (1993a).

3. Similar confusion exists about the place of Torrobo (or Dorrobo, Ndorrobo) among Maa-speakers: are they just "poor" Maasai who have lost their cattle and are forced to hunt and gather, or are they a separate ethnic group with distinct cultural and linguistic genealogies? Since few Torrobo live in the communities studied, I will not explore these issues in depth, but see the important work of Kratz (1980, 1994) and Blackburn (e.g., 1974, 1976) on the Okiek, as they call themselves, and the work of Klumpp and Kratz (1993) on negotiations of identity using beadwork by contemporary Okiek and Maasai women in Kenya.

4. Writing in 1860, for example, Krapf, a Church Missionary Society missionary,

spoke of the "Wakuafi" and "Masai" as two almost identical tribes, sharing the same language, nomadic lifestyle, disdain for agriculture, diet, religious beliefs, and physical characteristics; even more, they called themselves by the same name: "Orloikob" or "Loikob," which Krapf translated as "possessors of the land" from the root *enkop,* or "land." Despite these similarities, Krapf claimed that "the two kindred tribes, the Wakuafi and Masai, hate each other mortally" (1968 [1860]: 359–361). Nearly twenty-five years later, when Thomson traveled through Maasailand in 1882 and 1883, he described the Maasai and "Wa-Kwafi" as merely two divisions of the same tribe: the Maasai being the pastoralists and the "Wa-Kwafi" the agriculturalists. Thomson claimed the Wa-Kwafi were forced to cultivate because of their tremendous losses of livestock and people through unsuccessful raids, famine induced by locust invasions, and, finally, devastating attacks by "the Masai of the plains" (Thomson 1968 [1885]: 239–241). See Galaty (1993b) for a different reading of the use of the terms in these early accounts.

5. Merker (1867–1908) was based at the German military station in Moshi but traveled extensively throughout Maasailand. He had hoped to return to Moshi with his new wife after a vacation in Germany in 1903 but was sent to Dar es Salaam to train new recruits. He and his wife were sent back to Germany in 1906 because of bad health. He returned alone in 1907 to take over the military station in Mwanza, where he died of a lung infection in 1908. First published in 1904, Merker's *Die Masai: Ethnographische Monographie eines ostafrikanischen Semitenvolkes* (Berlin) was partly revised and expanded for a second edition in 1910. My references are all to the 1910 edition; I used an extremely accurate English translation (author unknown) verified and supplemented by the additional translation assistance of Lisa Vanderlinden. Merker's ethnography is particularly valuable because it offers a picture of Maasai life in Tanganyika at the time, not Kenya. While Merker's time in German East Africa obviously coincided with German colonial rule, it also occurred just after a series of disasters (which I discuss later) had struck Maasailand. Although some parts of the manuscript are problematic, such as his argument that Maasai were the lost tribe of Israel, other scholars of Maasai have also acknowledged the rich detail of his ethnography. See, for example, Bernsten (1980) and Waller (1978).

6. These additional accounts include Baumann (1894), Krapf (1968 [1860]), Farler (1882), Wakefield (1870, 1882, 1883), Last (1882, 1883), Thomson (1968 [1885]), Gregory (1896, 1901), and Johnston (1886, 1902). As Bernsten (1980) cautions, these early reports by missionaries and travelers must be used carefully, since many accounts are based on secondhand information reported by Swahili traders, non-Maasai Africans, or coastal missionaries; and second, of those authors who did visit Maasailand, few spoke Maa, and most stayed for only a very short time (e.g., three days in the case of Last).

7. Merker (1910 [1904]) provides detailed descriptions of these sartorial and linguistic markings in Chapters III, VIII, and XVI.

8. Merker (1910 [1904]: 72), however, claims that girls circumcised between the beginning of the circumcision of one age-grade of males and the beginning of the next were considered members of the first age-grade.

9. Some Maasai men traveled even farther afield—they appeared in the Berlin Exhibition in 1886. According to Merker, they used the money they earned to purchase the "freedom" of relatives who had become "slaves" after the cattle plague. More likely they compensated families who had housed and cared for their wives and children in order to retrieve them (Merker 1910 [1904]: 119).

10. Wakefield (1870, 1882) describes several trade routes based on information provided to him by caravan leaders.

11. There is a large feminist literature on the domestic/public dichotomy. Some authors see the distinction as a central explanatory principle for the "universal" subordination of women, who are always confined to the less prestigious domestic sphere (Collier and Rosaldo 1981). Such an explanation assumes that such distinctive spheres are universally present, that they are unchanging through history, and that they have fixed, universal meanings. For one critique of such "universalist" arguments, see Yanagisako (1979).

12. Although Merker marks Eng'ai as male, the term is actually gendered female in the Maasai language. Contemporary research suggests that Eng'ai has both female and male aspects (Voshaar 1979; Hodgson 2000a).

13. Women from each group would exchange an unweaned child with each other, briefly nurse the infant, then return him or her (Merker 1910 [1904]: 102–103).

14. Sacks (1979) provides a useful early study of the contradictory roles and rights of African women as sisters and wives.

15. See H. Moore (1986) for a provocative analysis of the centrality of women- and female-controlled spaces among Marakwet, an agro-pastoralist group in Kenya.

16. See also Johnston (1886: 425), Last (1883: 525–526), and Thomson (1968 [1885]: 95, 160).

17. For a detailed analysis of these crises, see Waller (1988) and Koponen (1996, esp. 24–25).

18. Baumann (1894: 32) describes how Maasai parents would offer him their children in exchange for meat. When Baumann refused, the adults would abandon their children in the camp. "Soon our caravan was swarming with Masai children and it was touching to see how the porters cared for the little urchins. I employed some of the stronger men and women as cowherds and thus saved quite a number from death by starvation."

19. Maasai prostitutes were reported to be working in Nairobi at this time (White 1990: 34).

20. According to Koko, her father belonged to the Iltalala age-set. They were warriors from 1881 to 1905 (Mol 1996: 13).

21. For an exhaustive study of the German colonial period in Tanganyika, see Koponen (1994). See also Iliffe (1969).

Maasai Portrait 1: Koko

1. Koko and all Maasai personal names used in the book are pseudonyms, except for historical figures and where otherwise specified. "Koko" literally means "grandmother."

2. Her father belonged to the Iltalala age set, who were *ilmurran* from 1881–1905 (Mol 1996: 13).

3. Mol (1996: 379) describes *isursuni* as balls of feathers stuck on top of spears as a sign of peace.

4. It is unclear who constituted *ilumbwa,* except that they were not Maasai. Mol (1996: 238) describes them as a group of Nilotes living in the area prior to Maasai migration (cf. Bernsten 1980: 2).

2. Modernist Orders

1. 1925 Arusha District (hereafter AD) Annual Report (hereafter AR), p. 9, Tanzania National Archives, Dar es Salaam (hereafter TNA), Secretariat Files (hereafter Secr) 1733/1.

2. Browne administered Maasai first as district political officer of Arusha District

and later as senior commissioner then provincial commissioner once the Northern Province was formed. As soon as he arrived in the Territory in 1916, he began lobbying the governor for the creation of a Masai Reserve in Tanganyika similar to the one he had helped form in Kenya. Browne, Provincial Commissioner (hereafter PC), Northern Province (hereafter NP), to Chief Secretary (hereafter CS), Dar, 15 March 1926, TNA, 17/37. See Waller (1976) for historical perspectives on the Kenyan Masai Reserve and Sandford (1919) for a colonial version.

3. Browne, PC, NP, "Memorandum on the Formation of the Masai Reserve and the Administration of the Masai 1916–1925" (hereafter "Memorandum on the Formation of the Masai Reserve"), 15 March 1926, TNA, 17/37. The attainment of this "ideal" became a personal project, even obsession, of Browne. See also Browne, PC, NP, to CS, Dar, 15 March 1926, TNA, 17/37.

4. One report estimated that at the outbreak of the war there were 17,000 Masai scattered among five administrative districts: Kondoa-Irangi (3,000), Moshi and Arusha (9,500), Mwanza (1,000), Pangani (3,000), and Usambara (500). Even this figure was recognized as "well below the actual number" and failed to include Maasai living in Dodoma and Morogoro Districts. Browne, PC, NP, "Memorandum on the Formation of the Masai Reserve," 15 March 1926, TNA, 17/37.

5. Chief Veterinary Officer (hereafter CVO), Dar to CS, Dar, File Notes, ca. 1925, TNA, Secr 7077/3.

6. A few administrators, however, believed that the Germans had in fact helped Maasai to reconstitute themselves as a "tribe" by "assisting them to obtain cattle by employing them as ruga-ruga in native wars etc and paying them in stock, and in general, encourag[ing] them to start afresh." Murrells, District Officer (hereafter DO), Masai District (hereafter MaD), to Land Development Commissioner, 18 May 1930, TNA, 17/37.

7. Murrells, DO, MaD, to PC, NP, 13 December 1930, TNA, 17/37.

8. Despite recommendations for specific reserve boundaries as early as 1917, however, no serious efforts to formalize the boundaries were made until 1920, after the war was over and the Treaty of Versailles and then the Permanent Mandate formalized the British presence in Tanganyika. During the extensive negotiations to delineate the reserve boundaries, the proposed reserve was expanded from the area now known as northern Maasailand to include present-day southern Maasailand. By 1922, the reserve was approved, although the "Wakwavi" of Morogoro District were added in 1923. Browne, PC, NP, "Memorandum on the Formation of the Masai Reserve."

9. Browne, Senior Commissioner (hereafter SC), NP, to CS, Dar, 10 February 1926, TNA, Secr 7077/3.

10. For instance, "In 1922 for the sake of having the Ruvu River as a convenient Eastern boundary to the reserve, Masai were removed from excellent and well-watered grazing lands along the East bank up to the neighbourhood of the Pare Hills." Author unknown, notes to CS, Dar, n.d., TNA, Secr 7077/3.

11. By 1929, Masai District included twenty different farms, although some settlers owned more than one farm. Pelham, DO, AD, to PC, NP, 2 November 1929; PC, NP, to DO, AD, 16 December 1929; both in TNA, 17/37.

12. Murrells, DO, MaD, first page missing, March 1930, TNA, 17/43.

13. Webster, PC, NP, to CS, Dar, 7 March 1930, TNA, 17/43.

14. The Germans had demarcated the first forest reserves in 1899, but the British found it impossible to maintain the reserve boundaries and prevent encroachment during their early years. In 1920, however, a Forestry Department was formed, and by 1921 legis-

lation was passed reinstating the former German reserves. "Forestry," among documents submitted to the East Africa Royal Commission (hereafter EARC), Public Records Office (Kew) (hereafter PRO), CO 892/11/2.

15. Lloyd, Acting DO, MaD, to PC, NP, 16 March 1925, TNA, 17/43.

16. Murrells, DO, MaD, to PC, NP re "Land Alienation, Arusha and Moshi Districts," 12 May 1928, TNA, 17/37. In general, see the documents in TNA, 17/37. A 1929 request argued for the return of Olmolog to Maasai not only because it was the site of the Olngesherr ceremony, but also because it was revered as the birthplace of Laibon Mbatian and was "regarded by the Longido and Engare Nanyuki Masai as their natural reserve pasture in times of drought." Furthermore, Maasai had improved the land by digging a series of wells. The request seems to have been denied. Dallas, Assistant DO, Longido, to PC, NP, 16 November 1929, TNA, 17/37.

17. Browne, PC, NP, "Memorandum on the Formation of the Masai Reserve."

18. Assistant DO, Longido, to DO, MaD, 18 April 1928, TNA, 17/37.

19. Ibid.

20. Morgans, DO, Maswa, to PC, Mwanza, 25 June 1928, TNA, 17/37.

21. Maguire, Administrative Officer (hereafter AO), N. Masailand, to Joubert, Rasha Rasha, 2 December 1924, TNA, 17/37.

22. See, for example, McMahon, Acting PC, NP, to Treasurer, Dar, 9 March 1934, TNA, 69/27/MS; McMahon, Acting PC, NP, to CS, Dar, 10 April 1934, TNA, 69/27/MS; Page, Acting CS, Dar, to PC, Tanga Province, 3 May 1934, TNA, 4/723/I.

23. See, for example, SC, Mwanza, to CS, Dar, 19 January 1926, TNA, Secr 7077/3.

24. Browne, SC, NP, to AO, N. Masailand, 26 November 1924, TNA, 17/37.

25. Murrells, DO, MaD, to PC, NP, 7 August 1931, TNA, 69/47/MS.

26. Maguire, AO, N. Masailand, to SC, NP, 28 November 1924, TNA, 17/37.

27. Murrells, DO, MaD, to PC, NP, 31 August 1926, TNA, 17/37.

28. Browne, SC, AD, to CS, Dar, 7 April 1924, TNA, 17/37.

29. In 1925, for example, a complaint was registered about "dozens of Wasukuma selling tobacco, meal, etc. to the Masai" who had "no trading licence or anything of that sort." Russell to unknown, 15 July 1925, TNA, 17/37. See also Hallier, DO, Moshi, to PC, NP, 2 March 1927, TNA, 69/7/2.

30. Mitchell, Acting PC, NP, to DO, MaD, 23 April 1927, TNA, 17/43; Murrells, DO, MaD, to PC, NP, 29 August 1926, TNA, 17/37; Acting DO, Longido, to DO, MaD, 18 April 1928, TNA, 17/37. A further series of extensions was requested in 1929 that included areas to the north (Loliondo and Palalet), south (Essubugu lo'l Datwa), and west (the Serengetti plains) that were outside the extended reserve but occupied by Maasai: "Each of these areas has been continuously occupied by Masai of one or other of the clans since before the first European occupation." It is unclear whether any of these new extensions were approved. Dallas, Assistant DO, Longido, to PC, NP, 16 November 1929, TNA, 17/37. For a detailed description of the "Boundaries of the Masai Reserve" as of October, 1929, see Webster, PC, NP, to DOs and Senior Veterinary Officer (hereafter SVO), NP, 8 October 1929, TNA, 17/37.

31. Hallier, DO, Moshi, to PC, NP, 16 May 1925, TNA, 17/37.

32. Three small Arusha settlements had already been established at Musa, and Kitching predicted that "other settlements will follow as soon as the fear of subsequent alienation is removed. Ultimately, and in the course of a few years there will be a general occupation of the whole of the Mondul slopes." Kitching, DO, AD, to PC, NP, 27 April 1928, TNA, 69/205/AR/B.

33. Ibid.

34. Webster, Acting PC, NP, to CS, Dar, 18 May 1928, TNA, 69/205/AR/B.

35. Ibid.

36. PC, NP, to Assistant DO, Kibaya, TNA, 17/43. By 1930, it was estimated that 53,000 Maasai occupied an area of 25,624 square miles; an additional 10,000 were estimated to live above the Rift Wall. Two thousand seven hundred Sonjo and 657 "aliens" also lived in Masai District. Their estimated livestock population was 700,000 cattle and donkeys and 750,000 smallstock. Murrells, DO, MaD, to Land Development Commissioner, Dar, 18 May 1930, TNA, 17/37.

37. Murrells, DO, MaD, to PC, NP, 13 December 1930, TNA, 17/37.

38. Joubert's price was £4,000 and a grant of 250 hectares in Arusha District. Webster proposed that the government pay £2,000 and grant the 250 hectares, while Maasai pay £2,000. Webster, PC, NP, to CS, Dar, 7 March 1930, TNA, 17/43.

39. Murrells, DO, MaD, to PC, NP, 16 September 1930, TNA, 69/47/MS.

40. Ibid.

41. Webster, PC, NP, to CS, Dar, 7 March 1930, TNA, 17/43. See also Murrells, DO, MaD, first page missing, March 1930, TNA, 17/43.

42. Murrells, DO, MaD, to PC, NP, 7 August 1931, TNA, 69/47/MS.

43. Ibid.

44. Dallas, Assistant DO, MaD, to PC, NP, 16 November 1929, TNA, 17/37. In the letter, Dallas used the logic of development to justify his request for formal recognition of Maasai tenure: "If they are not to be expelled, what security of tenure is to be offered to them, such as may justify the outlay of their money on development and conservation of water supplies etc."

45. Murrells, DO, MaD, to PC, NP, 7 August 1931, TNA, 69/47/MS.

46. Murrells, DO, MaD, to PC, NP, 30 January 1931, TNA, 17/37.

47. Murrells, DO, MaD, to PC, NP, 29 January 1929, TNA, 17/37. See Spear (1993b) for detailed historical accounts of the Arusha expansions and migrations.

48. For example, see orders made by the Masai Native Authority dated 1 September 1934 and 22 August 1935, TNA, 69/54/6/MS/2.

49. Hallier, PC, NP, "Masai District," September 1935, TNA, 17/43.

50. Mitchell, PC, NP, to CS, Dar, 16 March 1927, TNA, 17/43.

51. Rowe, Assistant DO, MaD, to PC, NP, 19 December 1935, TNA, 17/43.

52. Mitchell, Acting PC, NP, to CS, Dar, 16 March 1927, TNA, 17/43.

53. Bagshawe, Land Development Commission, Dar, to CS, Dar, 21 December 1930, TNA, 17/37.

54. Hallier, DO, Moshi, to PC, NP, 16 May 1925, TNA, 17/37.

55. See, for example, Browne, PC, NP, to Murrells, DO, MaD, 1 November 1926, TNA, 17/43 (cf. Spear 1993: 17). Oral data suggests that the different structural position of colonial government officials affected Maasai perceptions of and relationships with them, although not as much as individual differences of attitude, behavior, and reputation among the officials. Some district and provincial officers are remembered fondly by their nicknames, others less so.

56. Browne, PC, NP, "Memorandum on the Formation of the Masai Reserve."

57. Ibid. Who constituted this delegation and why they wanted to bring the Laibon is unclear. Perhaps they wanted yet one more barrier between themselves and the administration or wished to dilute the power of the headmen.

58. Mitchell, Acting PC, NP, to CS, Dar, 16 March 1927, TNA, 17/43. Earlier ad-

ministrators had relied on Hollis (1905) and Merker (1910) as sources of ethnographic information on the Maasai political system. See, for example, Dundas, CS, Dar, to SC, NP, 4 November 1925, TNA, Secr 2860/35, enclosing translated excerpts from Merker; Maguire (1928).

59. Murrells reminded the PC that "the Masai are as a general rule, respecters of age, and that many of their difficulties are settled by them, in council with elders, not necessarily Aigwenak, by discussion and agreement." Murrells, DO, MaD, to PC, NP, 28 February 1927, TNA, 69/55/MS.

60. Browne, PC, NP, to CS, Dar, 15 March 1926, TNA, 17/37; Mitchell, Acting PC, NP, to CS, Dar, 16 March 1927, TNA, 17/43.

61. Page-Jones, DO, MaD, to PC, NP, 5 December 1938, TNA, 69/47/MS/2.

62. Davey, Acting DO, MaD, to PC, NP, 24 August 1929, TNA, 69/47/MS.

63. Ibid.; PC, NP, to Acting DO, MaD, 3 September 1929, TNA, 69/47/MS.

64. Cited in Acting PC, NP, to CS, Dar, 21 July 1934, TNA, 69/27/MS.

65. Rowe, Assistant DO, MaD, to PC, NP, 19 December 1935, TNA, 17/43.

66. Murrells, DO, MaD, to PC, NP, 1 May 1930, TNA, 69/47/MS.

67. Murrells, DO, MaD, to PC, NP, 16 September 1930, TNA, 69/47/MS.

68. Ibid.

69. Ibid.

70. Other examples of the collaborative relationships between elder African men and colonial administrators are detailed in Chanock (1982, 1985) and Mbilinyi (1988). For a study of contemporary attempts by male elders to ally themselves with the state in controlling their "disobedient" daughters, see Hodgson (1996).

71. See, for example, "Sheria la Mahari za Kimaasai, ca. 1930s," TNA, 17/250/14; Maguire (1928).

72. Murrells, DO, MaD, to PC, NP, 1 May 1930, TNA, 69/47/MS.

73. Ibid.

74. See, for example, Mallet (1923), especially 96–99.

75. As Jane Fosbrooke proudly told her family and others, she was only the second European wife to live in Maasailand. Wives were not allowed to accompany husbands assigned to Maasailand until 1934. As it was, in this period colonial officers had to complete one full tour and be hired permanently before they could marry and bring their wives back to Tanganyika Territory. Tawney interview with J. Fosbrooke; J. Fosbrooke letters; both in J. Fosbrooke deposit, Rhodes House Library (hereafter RHL), Mss. Afr. s. 1906. I am grateful to the late Henry Fosbrooke for allowing me to read and selectively quote from Jane's letters.

76. The rest of the letter is missing. "Concerning Loliondo," September 1934, J. Fosbrooke deposit, RHL, Mss. Afr. s. 1906.

77. J. Fosbrooke, "Loliondo," 29 October 1934, J. Fosbrooke deposit, RHL, Mss. Afr. s. 1906. Fosbrooke later reports a similar encounter by a delegation of women demanding money from another wife, Trude Rowe.

78. See, for example, Browne, PC, NP, to CS, Dar, 15 March 1926, TNA, 17/37.

79. For analyses of the middle- and upper-class Victorian gender ideologies which informed British administrators of the time, see Poovey (1988) and Davidoff (1995).

80. Murrells, DO, MaD, to PC, NP, 7 August 1931, TNA, 69/47/MS.

81. Baxter, DO, MaD, to PC, NP, 7 August 1931, TNA, 69/47/MS.

82. Mitchell, Acting PC, NP, to CS, Dar, 16 March 1927, TNA, 17/43.

83. Ibid.

84. See the Tanganyika Territory *Blue Books,* 1926–1929 (Dar es Salaam: The Government Printer). Copies available in the Library of Congress, Washington, D.C.

85. Murrells, DO, MaD, to PC, NP, 7 August 1931, TNA, 69/47/MS. See also Page-Jones, DO, MaD, to PC, NP, 12 February 1939, TNA, 17/H/1/1.

86. Murrells, DO, MaD, to PC, NP, 7 August 1931, TNA, 69/47/MS.

87. "Memo on Liability for Poll Tax, Masai District, 1935"; Page-Jones, DO, MaD, to PC, NP, 12 February 1939; both in TNA, 17/H/1/1.

88. Kennedy, CS, Dar, to all PCs, Confidential Circular No. 10971/149, "Native Taxation," 9 June 1937, TNA, Secr 10971. See also Kennedy, CS, Dar, to all PCs, Confidential Circular No. 10971/91, "Native Taxation," 11 January 1937, TNA, Secr 10971.

89. Reid, Provincial Veterinary Officer (hereafter PVO), NP, to Director of Veterinary Services, Mpwapwa, 8 March 1935, TNA, 69/27/MS.

90. Ibid.

91. Hallier, PC, NP, to CS, Dar, 29 August 1935, TNA, 69/27/MS.

92. Baxter, DO, MaD, "Trade in Masai," 17 August 1933, Masai District Book (hereafter MDB), 242.

93. Ibid.

94. Ibid.

95. Ibid., 242–245; Typed addenda, 20 November 1933 and 25 May 1944, MDB, 244, 247; Baxter, DO, MaD, "Trade in Loliondo," 7 February 1935, Arusha Region Book (hereafter ARB), 259–260. See, generally, documents in the file "Rights of Occupancy over trading plots—Mondul," TNA, 69/207/MS/17; and "Establishment of Trading Centres," TNA, 17/218.

96. Baxter, DO, MaD, "Trade in Masai," MDB, 244–246.

97. Baxter, DO, MaD, "Loliondo Veterinary Matters," ARB, 261–262.

98. Baxter, DO, MaD, "Trade in Loliondo," 7 February 1935, ARB, 259–260.

99. Not everyone shared this objective: "To advise a nomadic Maasai to settle down and lead a farmer's life is not helpful; he simply cannot do it, the nature of the country precludes the possibility. Improved stock management he can understand, the advantages of wells, bores and windmills appeal to him, and a cow that gives twice as much milk as his other cows is an abiding and tangible joy. He does not want to change and it is questionable if for many years to come he or his animals could survive any marked alteration in his environment" (Veterinary Department Annual Report, 1926, p. 55; hereafter VD AR).

100. See, for example, Hansard, House of Commons, vol. 229, col. 1277, 3 July 1929; cited in Constantine (1984: 190).

101. The following draws on Constantine (1984) and Cooper (1997).

102. Browne, PC, NP, "Memorandum on the Formation of the Masai Reserve."

103. Ibid.

104. The following sub-section is drawn from Browne's memo, ibid., and the 1944 Masailand Comprehensive Report. The Masailand Comprehensive Report was compiled by Page-Jones in 1944 as a summary of development initiatives that had taken place in Masai District since British colonial rule. Copies are available on CAMP and in the TNA. All quotations are to Browne's memo, unless otherwise stated.

105. Browne, PC, NP, "Memorandum on the Formation of the Masai Reserve."

106. For example, the Lashaine Dam was built in 1922; repaired in 1923, 1925, and 1928; and finally abandoned in 1930. Ibid. and Masailand Comprehensive Report. See also Page-Jones (1948: 55).

107. Browne, PC, NP, "Memorandum on the Formation of the Masai Reserve."

108. Mitchell, Acting PC, NP, to CS, Dar, 16 March 1927, TNA, 17/43.

109. Ibid.

110. Ibid.

111. Mitchell, Acting PC, NP, to CS, Dar, 3 May 1927, TNA, Secr 7077/4.

112. Mitchell, Acting PC, NP, to DO, MaD, enclosing copy of 29 March 1927 "Minute by the Governor," 23 April 1927, TNA, 17/43; Cameron, Governor, Dar, to Secretary of State, London, 6 April 1927, TNA, Secr 7077/4; Amery, Secretary of State, London, to Cameron, 11 May 1927, TNA, Secr 7077/4.

113. Government of Tanganyika Territory, Memorandum, 6 March 1932, PRO, CO 822/44/4.

114. Murrells, DO, MaD, to PC, NP, 7 August 1931, TNA, 69/47/MS.

115. Mitchell, Acting PC, NP, to CS, Dar, 4 January 1928, TNA, Secr 7077/4.

116. "Water Conservation," 7 February 1935, ARB/366.

117. Ibid.

118. Pauline Peters (1994) has described how borehole development projects in Botswana fostered similar disputes between elder men over ownership and access rights to the new sources of water and surrounding land.

119. "Memorandum in Reference to Item 10, Water Conservation, in Masai Native Treasury Estimates for 1929/30," 1929, TNA, Secr 7077/4.

120. Ibid.

121. Baxter, DO, Ma, to PC, NP, 11 October 1933, TNA, 69/27/MS.

122. For example, Naberera (£1250 of £1800 cost repaid); Engurtoto (£100 of £1,100 cost repaid); Makame (none of £1,000 cost repaid) (Page-Jones 1944). See also Murrells, DO, MaD, to PC, NP, 7 August 1931, TNA, 69/47/MS.

123. Lloyd, Acting DO, MaD, to PC, NP, 16 March 1935, TNA, 17/43. Lloyd reviews the failure as part of calling for "the technical advice of an expert" in setting and implementing future "water policy."

124. Baxter, DO, MaD, to PC, NP, 11 October 1933, TNA, 69/27/MS.

125. Ibid.

126. In 1944 the debt was settled with a final lump payment of £2,300 from money collected mainly through the Masai War and Development Fund (Page-Jones 1944: 1).

127. Lowe, SVO, NP, to PC, NP, 2 November 1927, TNA, 17/37.

128. CS, Dar, to SC, Mwanza, 8 February 1926, TNA, Secr 7077/3.

129. SC, Mwanza to CS, Dar, 19 January 1926, TNA, Secr 7077/3.

130. Mitchell, Acting PC, NP, to CS, Dar, 16 March 1927, TNA, 17/43.

131. McCall, CVO, Dar, to CS, Dar, 6 April 1927, TNA, Secr 7077/4.

132. Ibid.

133. Mitchell responded to the chief veterinary officer's criticisms by claiming that their differences were a "question of direct versus indirect rule"; the chief veterinary officer had already informed Mitchell in a long conversation that he was not a supporter of indirect rule. Mitchell, Acting PC, NP, to CS, Dar, 3 May 1927, TNA, Secr 7077/4.

134. "Notes on the Masai Native 'Olkiama' held at Monduli on 23/7/1937," TNA, 17/252; Masailand Comprehensive Report 1944.

135. In 1919, the veterinary staff responsible for northern Maasailand consisted of one (British) veterinary officer, two (European) stock inspectors, and 8 (African) veterinary guards. By 1926, the staff had increased to one veterinary officer, two or three stock inspectors, and twenty-seven veterinary guards, whose responsibilities included coverage of southern Maasailand.

136. Hayes, Acting SVO, NP, to PC, NP, 4 March 1926, TNA, 17/37.

137. Ibid.

138. Memorandum by the Government of Tanganyika Territory, 6 March 1932, PRO, CO 822/44/4.

139. Murrells, DO, MaD, to PC, NP, 7 August 1931, TNA, 69/47/MS.

140. Ibid.

141. Ibid.

142. DO, MaD, to PC, NP, 29 June 1934, TNA, 69/27/MS.

143. Murrells, DO, MaD, to PC, NP, 7 August 1931, TNA, 69/47/MS.

144. DO, MaD, to PC, NP, 29 June 1934, TNA, 69/27/MS.

145. For example, Browne, PC, NP, to CS, Dar, re: "Masai Administration," 15 March 1926, TNA, 17/37.

146. Hayes, SVO, NP, to PC, NP, 4 March 1926, TNA, 17/37. See also VD AR (1926: 15–30) for a thorough discussion of the history, etiology, and treatment of BPP among Maasai in Tanganyika Territory written by Hayes.

147. One thousand ninety hundred eight BPP inoculations were given by veterinary personnel in 1922, 7,298 in 1923, 271 in 1924, and 10,534 in 1925 for a total of 20,011 during the period. Browne, PC, NP, to CS, Dar, 15 March 1926, TNA, 17/37.

148. My emphasis. Browne, PC, NP, to CS, Dar, re: "Masai Administration," 15 March 1926, TNA, 17/37.

149. Hayes, SVO, NP, to PC, NP, 4 March 1926, TNA, 17/27.

150. The first formal stock market was organized in Arusha in 1923 with sales twice a week; other markets soon started at Kibaya and Mbulu. Total sales for 1926 were minimal, however (AD AR 1925: 10, 22; VD AR 1926).

151. Governor, Minute, 22 August 1926, TNA, Secr 7077/3.

152. Murrells, DO, MaD, to PC, NP, 16 September 1930, TNA, 69/47/MS.

153. Ibid.

154. "Memoranda by the Governments of Tanganyika Territory, Kenya, and Uganda; Recommendations of the East African Governor's Conference," April 1932, PRO, CO 822/44/4.

155. Ibid.

156. See, for example, Murrells, DO, MaD, to PC, NP, 16 September 1930, TNA, 69/47/MS; "Notes on Masai Native 'Olkiyama' held at Monduli on 23/7/1937," TNA, 17/252.

157. See, for example, "Notes on Masai Conference held at Monduli on the 15th April, 1935," TNA, 472/P554.

158. Hallier, PC, NP, to Director of Veterinary Services, Mpwapwa, 6 March 1935, TNA, 17/43.

159. These *Blue Book* statistics, although notoriously unreliable, do reflect significant gross changes in livestock populations. Note that for these years the figures exclude the Loliondo subdivision of Masai District.

160. Webster, PC, NP, to Director of Veterinary Services, Mpwapwa, 27 June 1934, TNA, 69/27/MS.

161. Gurning, Acting DO, MaD, to PC, NP, 16 July 1934, TNA, 69/27/MS.

162. Reid, DVO, NP, to PC, NP, 30 July 1934, TNA, 69/27/MS.

163. Masai elders to Acting DO, MaD, 21 January 1935, TNA, 69/246/MS. My translation from Swahili original.

164. PC, NP, to DO, MaD, 25 October 1933, TNA, 69/27/MS.

165. For example, Gilbert, Acting DO, AD, to PC, NP, 15 February 1935, TNA, 69/246/MS; Lloyd, Acting DO, MaD, to PC, NP, 6 June 1935, TNA, 69/246/MS.

166. Hallier, PC, NP, to CS, Dar, 29 August 1935, TNA, 69/27/MS.

167. "Notes on Masai Conference held at Monduli on the 15th April, 1935," TNA, 472/P554.

168. Ibid.

169. Hornby, DVS, to VO, NP, 14 May 1935, TNA, 472/P554.

170. Chart attached to Hallier, PC, NP, to CS, Dar, 29 August 1935, TNA 69/27/MS.

171. Maguire to DO, MaD, 12 March 1937, TNA, 69/54/MS/II.

172. Ibid.

173. Page-Jones, DO, MaD, to PC, NP, 5 December 1938, TNA, 69/47/MS/2.

174. Rowe, Acting DO, MaD, to PC, NP, 19 December 1935, TNA, 17/43.

175. Ibid.

176. Baxter, DO, MaD, "Trade in Masai," MDB/242.

Maasai Portrait 2: Wanga

1. Customarily, wives of the same man are assigned to alternate sides of the gate, the first wife to the right side, the second to the left, the third to the right, and so forth. Women and their children on each side of the gate form an alliance in matters of marriage, property management, and inheritance. Contemporary evidence suggests that this practice is fading, especially as more and more men are monogamous.

3. Why Are You in Such a Hurry?

1. For a sense of popular images of Maasai during this period, see, for example, the numerous articles in the *East African Annual,* such as E. H. W. (1943–1944), Tate (1949–1950), author unknown (1949–1950), "Bwana Kongoni" (1951–1952), and "Kilusu" (1956–1957). Fosbrooke (1948) provides a detailed, if partial, overview of Maasai social organization at this time.

2. Minutes, 13 August 1948, TNA, 471/949/A/I; Minutes, 15 October 1948, TNA, 471/949/A/I; Minutes, 28 March 1950, TNA, 471/949/A/II. Their discussions were based, in part, on a detailed report by Gower on the conditions in southern Maasailand, which I have been unable to locate. But for comments on the report, see Clarke, DC, MaD, to PC, NP, 15 April 1948, TNA, 471/949/A/I. Gower's report was itself a response to the findings of the Wilson Commission, discussed below.

3. "Minutes of Provincial Advisory Committee held in Arusha 22–23 May 1951," TNA, 17/45/II.

4. Clarke, DC, MaD, "Masai Development Plan," 19 April 1951, TNA, 17/289/III (hereafter Clarke, MDP).

5. Clarke, MDP.

6. "Masai Development Plan" (outline), 6 August 1950, TNA, 17/289/III (hereafter MDP [outline]).

7. MDP (outline), Annexure A.

8. "Masai Development Plan" (text), 6 August 1950, TNA, 17/289/III (hereafter MDP [text]).

9. MDP (outline). According to the initial calculations, the cost per acre of clearing by tractors would be 17/97 shillings compared to an estimated 16/00 per acre if manual

labor was used. Tsetse-infested bushes were unevenly scattered on the land, especially along vegetation edges and drainage lines, and thus occupied only 5 to 10 percent of the total area. If six tractors had been used, approximately 375 square miles of land per year, or 1,875 total square miles, would have been freed of tsetse. The final proposal, however, requested only three tractors, which modified the cost/benefit calculations. Young, Provincial Tsetse Officer, NP, to Director of Tsetse Survey and Reclamation, Arusha, enclosing "Proposals for Masai Mechanical Bush Clearing Unit," 6 July 1950, TNA, 471/949/A/II; MDP (outline).

10. MDP (text).

11. Fraser-Smith, DC, MaD, to PC, NP, "Draft Estimates 1953," TNA, 471/949/ 1/II; NP AR 1950, 90.

12. Hornby, for example, envisioned Maasai adopting the system of "the old Trek Boers in South Africa who every winter moved their flocks and herds from the High Veld to the Low Veld, to the great advantage of animals and pastures." Hornby, "Impressions of a Masailand Trypanosomiasis Problem," 18 September 1949, TNA, 471/949/A/II.

13. Clarke, MDP.

14. Ibid.

15. Although Clarke, the district commissioner during the design and early implementation of the plan, argued that "the indigenous people should have some sort of stake in the various Development Schemes, African and non-African, which now hold the stage," his views were ignored by others. Clarke, DC, MaD, to Senior Provincial Commissioner (hereafter SPC), NP, 17 November 1950, TNA, 471/949/A/II.

16. MDP (outline), Appendix I and Annexure A; Fraser-Smith, DC, MaD, to Chairman, Local Councils Board, 14 March 1955, TNA, 17/103/A.

17. Administrators had numerous suggestions for additional services, which included improving boarding accommodations for students, abolishing market fees, instituting a public bus service, offering loans to purchase cattle, and even creating a consumers' cooperative society. MDP (outline), Annexure A.

18. Clarke, DC, MaD, "Masai Development Plan—Progress Report for Year 1951," 13 December 1951, TNA, 17/289/III. The Masai Council consistently rejected government proposals for a graduated tax based on livestock holdings because of a principled disagreement with wealth-based taxation and the difficulty of sorting through overlapping rights in animals. MDB, 229; NP AR 1949: 71; Fraser-Smith, DC, MaD, to Political, MaD, 30 April 1955, TNA, 17/164. In 1953, this extra tax was incorporated into the general tax for a total tax of 50 shillings per taxpayer (MaD AR 1952: 1). In addition, the Masai Council levied an additional tax of 10 shillings per taxpayer in 1954 and 1955 to supplement their contribution to the MDP (NP AR 1954: 87). This tax supplemented the £11,000 remaining in the Masai War and Development Fund and the balance of £10,000 in the Native Treasury.

19. Fraser-Smith, "Memorandum on Land Utilization in Masailand," 20 November 1953, TNA, 471/D.3/2 (hereafter Fraser-Smith, Memorandum); Fraser-Smith, DC, MaD, to PC, NP, enclosing draft of press handout "Development in Masailand," 20 January 1955, TNA, 471/D.3/2.

20. "Masai Development, Tanganyika," *Commonwealth Survey*, 14 May 1954, p. 62 (RHL).

21. Fraser-Smith, Memorandum; Fraser-Smith, DC, MaD, to PC, NP, enclosing draft of press handout "Development in Masailand," 20 January 1955, TNA, 471/D.3/2; Fraser-Smith, DC, MaD, to PC, NP, 2 July 1955, TNA, 17/103/A.

22. Clarke, DC, MaD, to SPC, NP, enclosing "Masai Development Plan—Progress Report for Year 1951," 13 December 1951, TNA, 17/289/III; Troup, Acting PC, NP, to Member for Local Government, Dar, 12 March 1953, TNA, 471/949/1/II (Estimates); Fraser-Smith, DC, MaD, to PC, NP, 15 April 1955, TNA, 17/103/A.

23. MDP (outline).

24. "Minutes of a Meeting of the Masai District Team Held at Monduli on the 8th of May, 1952," TNA, 471/949/II (Estimates).

25. For example, 7,500 acres of fly bush were cleared by machines and non-Maasai labor was hired at a cost of £19,000, an exorbitant amount rightly termed "uneconomic" (NP AR 1952: 87; NP AR 1953: 78).

26. Fraser-Smith, DC, MaD, "Memorandum, MDP (Part II)," 15 November 1953, TNA, 471/D.3/2; Fraser-Smith, DC, MaD, to Director of Water Development, Dar, 28 April 1953, TNA, 471/949/1/II (Estimates); Fraser-Smith, Memorandum; Fraser-Smith, DC, MaD, to SPC, NP, 17 March 1954, TNA, 17/103/A.

27. "Development Plans," ca. 1956, TNA, 471/D.3/2/II.

28. Clarke, MDP.

29. Fraser-Smith, DC, MaD, to PC, NP, 15 April 1955, TNA, 17/103/A.

30. Clarke, DC, MaD, to SPC, NP, 30 September 1951, TNA, 17/289/III.

31. Fraser-Smith, Memorandum; Fraser-Smith, DC, MaD, to Director of Water Development, Dar, 28 April 1953, TNA, 471/949/1/II (Estimates). See also Troup, Acting PC, NP, to Member for Local Government, 12 March 1953, TNA, 471/949/1/II (Estimates).

32. DC, MaD, to PC, NP, 5 December 1955, TNA, 471/D.3/2/II.

33. "Development Is Slow in Masailand," *Sunday News* (Tanganyika), 9 January 1955, p. 3.

34. Fraser-Smith, DC, MaD, to DWD, Dar, 28 April 1953, TNA, 471/949/1/II (Estimates).

35. These either took the form of written petitions in Swahili signed (with fingerprints) by the *ilaigwenak* or individual speeches to the gathering.

36. Mkutano wa OlKiama [Olkiama Meeting], 16 April 1954, Arusha Branch, TNA (hereafter ATNA), 284/II.

37. Financing for these initiatives came primarily from the Colonial Development and Welfare Act of 1940, whose primary purpose was "to promote the prosperity and happiness of the peoples of the Colonial Empire." To meet its objectives, the act included several innovations over prior development financing: it promoted social services, it financed recurrent expenditures rather than just capital costs, and it encouraged colonial governments to design comprehensive development programs rather than just individual projects (Constantine 1984: 258–259). See also Cooper (1997).

38. For more detailed background on the relationship between metropolitan and local development agendas during this period, see Constantine (1984), Anderson (n.d.), Cooper (1997), and Cooper and Packard (1997).

39. Reid, Director of Veterinary Services, Dar, to SVO, NP, May 1948, TNA, 471/949/A/I.

40. Emphasis added. "Minutes of Meeting of NP Provincial Department Heads and DCs, 26–27 November 1951, Arusha," TNA, 17/45/II.

41. The government built five new cattle markets and four permanent crushes [holding pens] in 1948, and the MFC built four more permanent cattle markets in 1954 (NP AR 1948: 69; NP AR 1954: 105). By 1952, five principal stock routes traversed the North-

ern Province and twenty-eight trading centers were spread through just the Monduli Division of Masai District. Macgregor (for Regional Assistant Director of Veterinary Services) to Assistant Commissioner of Police, Arusha, 6 February 1952, TNA, 17/NR.35/I; "Trading Centres—Masai District," attached to Fraser-Smith, DC, MaD, to PC, NP, 5 October 1955, TNA, 17/218.

42. As the provincial commissioner wrote in his 1950 annual report: "The drop in sales was due largely to excellent grazing conditions and a freer supply of milk, leading to a reduced demand for maize flour and thus a reduced need to sell cattle to obtain money" (NP AR 1950: 89).

43. As part of the war effort, livestock from Tanganyika was sold via the Kenya Livestock Control to the Liebegs processing plant to provide bully beef (canned or corned beef) for the armed forces (NP AR 1944: 64).

44. See also Clarke, DC, MaD, "Notes for Provincial Annual Report, 1950, Masai District," TNA, 69/63/20. One reason Maasai often received better prices when they sold on the informal market than at the government-sponsored markets was that Somali buyers in particular cheated Maasai by "ringing" the market, agreeing in advance to bid for alternative pens in order to lower the price (Griffiths 1938). Maasai constantly protested to government about such "ringing" and only agreed to meet the voluntary Masai Development Plan quotas if district officials would ensure that the buyer from the main meat-processing facility would attend the sales to prevent the practice. "Olkiama, 6–8 February 1952," ATNA 284/II.

45. Fraser-Smith, Memorandum.

46. Clarke, DC, MaD, to PC, NP, 4 January 1950, TNA, 471/949/A/II.

47. A pet project was a mobile cinema unit to make and present films to Maasai in order to persuade them through visual media of the need for (certain) changes. Fraser-Smith, DC, MaD, to PC, NP, 21 June 1955, TNA, 17/103/A.

48. Clarke, DC, MaD, to PC, NP, 4 January 1950, TNA, 471/949/A/II.

49. Meek, DC, MaD, to PC, NP, 24 September 1949, ATNA 284/II.

50. "Olkiama, 6–8 February, 1952," ATNA 284/II; Bassett, Government Hospital, Arusha to McKenzie, 17 May 1948, TNA, 471/949/A/I.

51. "Majibu ya wazee katika Olkiama" [Replies of the Olkiama elders], 19 September 1949, ATNA 284/II.

52. Meek, DC, MaD, to PC, NP, 14 April 1949, TNA, 69/57/1/II.

53. SVO, NP, to PC, NP, 9 February 1949, TNA, 69/57/1/II.

54. Revington, PC, NP, "Memorandum on Masai Development," 16 September 1948, TNA, 471/949/A/I.

55. Revington, PC, NP, to Member for Agriculture and Natural Resources, 18 November 1949, TNA, 471/949/A/II.

56. Ibid.

57. MDP (outline).

58. Revington, PC, NP, to DC, MaD, 13 February 1948, TNA, 471/949/A/I. See also Revington, PC, NP, to CS, Dar, 18 August 1948, TNA, 471/949/A/I.

59. Maasai protested news of another census: "In terms of the issue of counting our cattle by the Europeans of the Veterinary Department in order to get cattle for the markets—we do not want our cattle to be counted; Masai will bring cattle to market like always." Masai Olkiama elders to DC, MaD, 6 February 1952, ATNA 284/II.

60. The declaration of a state of emergency in Kenya in October 1952 was used to justify a further expansion of the police force and "constant vigilance," especially in north-

ern Maasailand near the Kenyan border where many Kikuyu lived with Maasai friends and relatives (NP AR 1952: 85; NP AR 1953: 84; NP AR 1954: 83).

61. The PC reported in 1946 that the decision to grant temporary leases for several thousand acres of land in the Oljoro area mainly in Masai District "without prior consultation with the people has created some doubt in the people's minds as to Government's intentions in spite of our efforts to explain the over-riding necessity of the maximum possible production of food" (NP AR 1946: 41).

62. In August 1940, at the request of colonial administrators, the Masai Council agreed that Maasai would donate 6,000 head of cattle annually for sale at a fixed price for bully beef for the troops. One-third of the sale proceeds would be given to the Tanganyikan government as a "free gift," one-third would be loaned to the government interest-free, and the final third "retained in the Native Treasury for immediate development works" (NP AR 1940: 32–33). Although administrators stressed the "voluntary" nature of the contribution, the cattle were donated in exchange for a promise by colonial officials not to compulsorily recruit Maasai men to serve in the military or work as plantation laborers (Fosbrooke 1980: Annexure II, 3–4).

63. When the Ardai lands, by then "a vast expanse of bare earth," were finally returned to Maasai in 1948, the government contributed £1,000 for their rehabilitation, despite awareness that no answer to the problem "will cost a mere £1,000" (NP AR 1949: 76; NP AR 1948: 62; MDP [outline]).

64. See for example, Game Warden, Moshi, to PC, NP, 21 May 1948, TNA, 471/949/A/I.

65. Maasai Olkiama to DC, MaD, 17 September 1950, ATNA 284/II; Page-Jones, SPC, NP, to CS, Dar, 7 October 1950, TNA, 471/949/A/II.

66. "Masai Local Native Council (Olkiama) 1947" (minutes in Swahili), TNA, 17/252.

67. Hall to Battershill, 21 February 1946, PRO, CO 691/186, cited in Iliffe (1979: 451). The guiding principle, according to Iliffe, became "how land could best be utilised for the territory's benefit." For much of the land, the decision was alienation: a doubling of the European population from 10,648 in 1948 to 20,598 in 1958 was met with an increase of alienated land from 660,961 hectares in 1948 to 1,284,647 hectares in 1959 on first 33-year leases, then 99-year leases (Iliffe 1979: 450–451).

68. *Report of the Arusha-Moshi Land Commission, 1947* (Dar es Salaam: Government Printer, 1947), copy available in ATNA; MDP (text).

69. See Spear (1997) for a more detailed account of the confrontation and Mbise (1974) for a somewhat fictionalized account.

70. The two other areas were Oljoro and Olmolog (NP AR 1950: 94–95).

71. Clarke, DC, MaD, "Notes for Provincial Annual Report, 1950, Masai District," TNA, 69/63/20; NP AR 1950: 95.

72. Clarke, DC, MaD, to SPC, NP, 17 November 1950, TNA, 471/949/A/II.

73. Fraser-Smith, DC, MaD, to PC, NP, 10 September 1953, TNA, 471/D.3/2.

74. MDP (outline). The proposed expansion areas included the Losogonoi Plateau (approximately 900 square miles), the Simanjiro Plains, southeast Londergess, Kitwei, and Endulen.

75. See, for example, Revington, PC, NP, "Items for Discussion on Development of Masai," 20 April 1948, TNA, 471/949/A/I; Minutes, 28 March 1950, TNA, 471/949/A/II. See also "Note of a Discussion at Government House with Regard to the Future of the Masai and Masailand," April 1950, ATNA 289/II.

76. PC, NP, "Note regarding land policy in Masai District with particular reference to applications for alienations in the Essimingor and Lolkisale areas," 30 January 1954, TNA, 471/D.3/2.

77. SVO, NP, to PC, NP, 16 December 1948, TNA, 471/949/A/I; Meek, DC, MaD, to PC, NP, 29 April 1949, TNA, 471/949/A/I; PVO, NP, to DC, MaD, 18 July 1949, TNA, 471/949/A/I; Meek, DC, MaD, to Assistant Land Officer, MaD, 21 September 1949, TNA, 471/949/A/II; Clarke, DC, MaD, to SPC, NP, 17 November 1950, TNA, 471/949/A/II. See also documents in the file "300,000 Acre Ranching Project in the Masai District of Tanganyika," PRO, CO 822/225.

78. When the alienation was first proposed in the context of extending a water source to the area, District Commissioner Clarke tersely criticized it: "If anyone should benefit from this water supply it should surely be the people who put up the land and money for the ranching project." Clarke, DC, MaD, to PC, NP, 13 December 1948, TNA, 471/949/A/I.

79. "Mambo Yaliyozungumzwa Katika Olkiama ya December 1953" [Matters discussed at the Olkiama], ATNA 284/II.

80. See, for example, Maasai Olkiama to DC, MaD, 17 September 1950, ATNA 284/II; Engineering Hydrologist to Director, Water Development, 30 April 1952, TNA, 471/99/1/II.

81. DC, MaD, to DWD, Dar, 28 April 1953, TNA, 471/949/1/II (Estimates).

82. During the next decade, forest reserves were demarcated throughout Masai District, including the hills around Loliondo, Essimingor (15,000 acres), Burko, Lengoje, Mto-wa-Mbu, Gelai, Kitumbeine, Longido, Landekenya, and the Lemagrut Mountains (NP AR 1953: 86; NP AR 1954: 95; NP AR 1957: 92).

83. See Neumann (1995) for a history of the formation of the Serengeti National Park that is sensitive to the multiple and contradictory power interests and representations. Arhem (1985) provides a contemporary picture of how Maasai living in the Ngorongoro Conservation Area have been impoverished, and Homewood and Rodgers (1991) offer a comprehensive analysis of the complex history and relationships between pastoralists, livestock, wildlife, and ecology in the Ngorongoro Conservation Area.

84. NP AR 1950: 94; MaD AR 1952: 3; NP AR 1954: 98; NP AR 1955: 95; NP AR 1957: 95. See The Masai of [Serengeti] National Park, "Memorandum on the Serengeti National Park," 1957, Grant Papers, RHL, Mss. Afr. s. 1237(b) for a long response to the proposed eviction, including a detailed history of Maasai presence in the Serengeti area.

85. "Mambo Yaliyozungumzwa Katika Olkiama ya December 1953" [Matters discussed at the Olkiama], ATNA 284/II.

86. "Olkiama Address, August 1952," TNA, 471/L.5/1/4.

87. Oltimbau ole Masiaya, et al., to DC, MaD, 31 August 1952, TNA, 17/289/III.

88. "Extract from the Minutes of the 32nd Meeting of the N. P. L. U. C. held on 8th June 1956," TNA, 471/D.3/2/II.

89. Fraser-Smith, DC, MaD, "Memorandum: Land Utilization in Masailand," 20 November 1953, TNA, 471/D.3/2.

90. For example, in 1952, under pressure from administrators, the Monduli Division Development Sub-Committee decreed that "all 'Moran' warriors must undertake three months bush clearing work each year in order to assist in freeing the District from the tsetse fly." Despite the orders, the *ilmurran* only performed the work once the motorized police were called in, and they soon quit working completely (MaD AR 1952: 1; Stahl 1961: 52; NP AR 1953: 78).

91. Administrators claimed that part of the difference was that many of the Loliondo *ilmurran* lived in *manyattas* (*emanyata*, pl. *imanyat*: "warriors'" villages in which only *ilmurran* and their girlfriends and mothers resided) rather than dispersed in widely scattered homesteads (*enkang'*, pl. *inkang'itie*). Two other factors may account for the difference as well: many were in fact Maasai from Kenya and were accustomed to a different colonial regime, and the leaders from Loliondo were originally from Kenya and were extremely progressive and powerful. The *ilmurran* did such work as "cleaning dams, breaking stone for concrete drinking troughs, repair of furrows and the building of cattle markets" (NP AR 1951: 84–85).

92. It seemed no accident that the thefts were concentrated in the three areas—Engare Nanyuki, Engare Nairobi, and Oljoro—where long-term Maasai residents had been evicted in favor of European settlers. Claiming they were being "ruined" by the theft, the settlers organized public meetings to clamor for greater police presence and control of thefts. "Stock Thefts Mean Ruin to Farmers: Plans to Counter Increasing Threat," *The Tanganyika Standard*, Saturday, 26 June 1952, enclosure in TNA, 17/NR 35/I. See also Smeer (President, Oljoro Farmer's Association) to CS, Dar, 14 May 1957, TNA, 17/NR 35/II demanding, on behalf of settler "taxpayers," increased surveillance and punitive measures to deter stock thefts.

93. "Mambo Yaliyozungumzwa Katika Olkiama ya December 1953," ATNA 284/II.

94. Ibid.

95. *Ilmurran* who lived in the Kisongo area also refused to harvest or dry hay, forcing the Kisongo Pilot Scheme field officer to resort to mechanical methods. MDP (text).

96. "Mambo Yaliyozungumzwa Katika Olkiama ya December 1953," ATNA 284/II.

97. Parkes, Veterinary Officer, MaD, to Reg. Asst. Dir. of Vet. Services, Arusha, 21 November 1952, TNA, 471/949/II (Estimates).

98. "Minutes," 8 May 1952, TNA, 471/949/II (Estimates).

99. "Masai Local Native Council (Olkiama), 19 September 1950," ATNA 284/II.

100. See also Maasai Olkiama to DC, MaD, 17 September 1950, ATNA 284/II; SPC, NP, to CS, Dar, 7 October 1950, TNA, 471/949/A/II; NP AR 1950: 95. Clarke, DC, MaD, to PC, NP, 15 January 1951, ATNA 284/II.

101. See, for example, PC, NP, to Private Secretary, Dar, 4 March 1950, TNA, 471/949/A/II; "Minutes," 28 March 1950, TNA, 471/949/A/II. Veterinary officers were of course the most adamant about restricting Maasai to pastoralism. See, for example, Hornby, "Impressions of a Masailand Trypanosomiasis Problem," 18 September 1949, TNA, 471/949/A/II.

102. Masai District imported 200 tons of flour a month during 1949 (a bag of 200 pounds cost the "fantastic price" of 45 shillings at Loliondo) (NP AR 1949: 68).

103. Clarke, DC, MaD, "Notes for Provincial Annual Report, 1950, Masai District," TNA, 69/63/20. See also NP AR 1950: 89; MaD AR 1951: 7.

104. McGregor, Regional Assistant Director of Agriculture, Arusha, to Director of Agriculture, Dar, 6 December 1950, TNA, 471/949/A/II.

105. Clarke, MDP; MDP (outline).

106. "Majibu ya Wazee katika Olkiama" [Replies of Elders of the Olkiama], 19 September 1949, ATNA 284/II.

107. Quotation cited in Iliffe (1979: 493), see pp. 491–494 more generally. The Kilimanjaro Union was an offshoot of the African Association.

108. "Addressed to meeting of Masai headmen and elders at Ngorongoro on 11/1/51 by District Commissioner, Masai," ATNA 284/II.

109. Oltimbau, Ngorongoro Masai to Chairman, Olkiama, Monduli, 23 August 1952, ATNA 284/II.

110. "Mambo Yaliyozungumzwa Katika Olkiama ya December 1953," ATNA 284/II.

111. "Olkiama, Minutes of the Tanganyika Masai Council Meeting held from 6th to 10th October, 1954 at Monduli," ATNA 284/II.

112. Ibid.

113. Meek, DC, MaD, to PC, NP, 24 September 1949, ATNA 284/II.

114. See Chapter 15 in Iliffe (1979) for a detailed examination of the emergence of TANU. TANU was the new name given to the former Tanganyika African Association (TAA) at the famous "Saba Saba" [SW: *Seven Seven*] day meeting on July 7, 1954.

115. "Future Constitutional Development in the Colonies," Report by the Chairman of the Official Committee on Colonial Policy (Norman Brook), 6 September 1957, PRO, CPC (57) 30, CAB 134/1556. Cited in Cooper (1994: 8).

116. See Chapter 13 in Iliffe (1979) for a detailed history of the TAA.

117. For example, TANU membership in the Northern Province was reported as 3,531 in December 1956; it had jumped to 9,369 just a year later in December 1957 (NP AR 1956: 88; NP AR 1957: 80).

118. This figure probably included white settlers, Asians, and other non-Maasai living in the District. In his 1957 Annual Report, the provincial commissioner gives the breakdown as follows: 1) by composition: 3,889 Africans, 1,577 Asians, and 486 Europeans; 2) by "geographical distribution": 1,352 Arusha, 82 Masai, 866 Mbulu, and 3,652 Moshi (NP AR 1957: 73).

119. Recurrent expenditures on maintenance and upkeep of water installations in 1957 totaled £4,321 (NP AR 1956: 108).

120. A similar trip to the Konza Grazing Scheme in the Kajiado District of Kenya by a party of Maasai elders was reported in 1951; a second trip to the scheme was planned for February 1952 (MaD AR 1951: 8).

121. Murrells, DO, MaD, to PC, NP, re: proceedings of Masai Council, 16 September 1930, TNA, 69/47/MS.

122. Ibid.

123. Ibid.

124. Governor Symes (?), "Extract from Confidential Despatch 20/5/31 to S of S [Secretary of State], Original in M. P. 15165," 20 May 1931, TNA Secr/19951; see also A. E. Kitching (Secretary of Native Affairs), file notes, 22 April 1931, TNA, Secr/19951.

125. Browne, PC, NP, to CS, Dar, 15 March 1926, TNA, 17/37.

126. Sherwood, Acting Director of Education, Dar, to CS, Dar, 8 December 1931, TNA Secr/19951.

127. Ibid.

128. Kitching, file notes, 22 April 1933, TNA, Secr/19951.

129. Earlier, several elders had petitioned the Permanent Mandates Commission in June 1930 to educate their sons. Governor Symes (?), "Extract from Confidential Despatch 20/5/31 to S of S [Secretary of State], Original in M. P. 15165," 20 May 1931, TNA Secr/19951.

130. SVO, NP, to DO, MaD, 27 April 1938, TNA, 69/259/14. See also PC, NP, to Acting DO, MaD, 3 May 1938, TNA, 69/259/14.

131. Page-Jones, "Masai Native Authority Staff," 25 May 1944, MDB, 169.

132. "Minutes of Provincial Advisory Committee held in Arusha 22–23 May 1951," TNA, 17/45/II.

133. Revington, PC, NP, "Olkiama Address 25th August 1947," TNA, 17/252.

134. Clarke, DC, MaD, to PC, NP, 3 September 1947, TNA, 17/252.

135. "Minutes of Provincial Advisory Committee held in Arusha 22–23 May 1951," TNA, 17/45/II. Of course, such a broad provincial target conveniently masked the inequalities in school attendance among ethnic groups described above.

136. "Education," 1948–1951, MDB, 13; MaD AR 1950; MaD AR 1951.

137. "Minutes of Meeting of NP Provincial Departmental Heads and DCs, 26–27 November 51, Arusha," TNA, 17/45/II.

138. MaD AR 1952; Clarke, DC, MaD, to SPC, NP, 30 September 1951, TNA, 17/289/III.

139. Suggested sites included Kibaya, Longido, and Loliondo, for southern, central, and northern Maasailand respectively. "Education," 1948–1951, MDB, 13; Clarke, SPC, NP, to SPC, NP, 30 September 1951; MDP (outline); both in TNA, 17/289/III.

140. "Education," "Proposed Future Developments," 1951, MDB, 13.

141. "Minutes of Provincial Advisory Committee held in Arusha 22–23 May 1951," TNA, 17/45/II.

142. Ibid.

143. "Minutes of the First Meeting of the Executive Committee of the Masai Federal Council," 19–24 September 1958, TNA, 471/L.5/1/4.

144. In 1956, these communities were listed as Kijungu, Kibaya, Dossi Dossi, Lolkisale, Shambarai, Engaruka, and Loliondo. Furthermore, "each year sees more land put under the plough by Waarusha in the immediate neighborhood of Monduli" (NP AR 1956: 99).

145. P. H. Gulliver, "Interim Report on Land and Population in the Arusha Chiefdom," June 1957, Social Research, Provincial Administration, Tanganyika, EAC HCP/276; P. H. Gulliver, "Memorandum on the Arusha Chiefdom, Pop. 1948–1957," 1957, EAC HCP/277.

146. Clarke, DC, MaD, "Notes for Provincial Annual Report, 1950, Masai District," TNA, 69/63/20.

147. DC, MaD, "Food Shortage—Masai District Situation Report," January 1961, TNA, 17/A 3/5.

148. DC, MaD, to PC, NP, 27 January 1961, TNA, 17/A 3/5.

149. Edward Mbarnoti to DC, MaD, 13 February 1961, TNA, 17/A 35. In his letter, Mbarnoti outlined the reasons the Masai Council refused to allow TANU to use its vehicles anymore: 1) food was taken to areas that did not have hunger problems; 2) vehicles were used "at a complete loss"—in one example, a 5-ton lorry was sent to Moshi and returned with only ¼ ton of bananas; 3) much of the food consisted of items that the "real Maasai" (SW: *Maasai kwa asili*) did not eat, such as papayas, mangos, and "European fruit" (SW: *matunda ya Kizungu*); 4) TANU people did not want to follow the arrangements made by the Council.

150. Shelley, District Medical Officer, MaD, to Provincial Medical Officer, NP, 31 January 1961, TNA, 17/A 3/5.

151. DC, MaD, to Political, Same, 25 July 1961, TNA, 17/A 3/5/II.

152. DC, MaD, to PC, NP, 4 April 1961, TNA, 17/A 3/5.

153. DC, MaD, to PC, NP, 15 June 1961, TNA, 17/A 3/5.

154. Water Officer to PC, NP, 1 July 1961, TNA, 17/A 3/5.

155. DC, MaD, "Food Shortage—Situation Report," March or April 1961, TNA, 17/A 3/5.

156. Deputy PC, NP, "Famine Relief Report 1961—Northern Province," 24 January 1962, TNA, 17/A/3/5/II.

157. Sokoine, Executive Officer (hereafter EO), Masai District Council (hereafter MC), "Masai Movement to Other Districts," 2 April 1965, TNA, 471/L.5/1/4.

158. DC, MaD, to TANU Provincial Secretary, Arusha, 6 February 1962, TNA, 17/A 3/5/II.

Maasai Portrait 3: Thomas

1. The following information is based on two full days of interviews with Mzee Thomas Porokwa in his home on January 13th and 14th, 1997. All quotations are my translation from the Swahili original. Despite my offer to protect his anonymity, Mzee Porokwa did not want to mask his identity. Although few older Maasai know the exact year of their birth, Thomas has correlated certain events with their dates to figure out his birthdate.

4. Politics of the Postcolonial Periphery

1. *Daily News* (Tanzania), 8 October 1992, p. 1.

2. *Daily News* (Tanzania), 3 March 1992, p. 1.

3. Tanganyika changed its name to the United Republic of Tanzania in 1964 after its political merger with Zanzibar.

4. All of the above quotations are taken from "Ujamaa the Basis of Socialism," published as a TANU pamphlet in April 1962, reprinted in English in Nyerere (1968).

5. "The Arusha Declaration," 5 February 1967, reprinted in English in Nyerere (1968).

6. Ibid.

7. Ibid.

8. For an example of such avowed decentralization, see Presidential Circular 1 of 1968, "Decentralization of Rural Development Fund," ATNA D.3/3/III.

9. The contributions in Boesen et al. (1986) provide a good overview of the decline in manufacturing, agriculture, and provision of social services which occurred during this period of "crisis" in Tanzania. Maliyamkono and Bagachwa (1990) describe the emergence of the "second economy" as many Tanzanians struggled to survive financially through various "illegal" methods such as smuggling, over-invoicing, and bypassing official purchasing and distribution channels.

10. That is, did I want to "change" some of my foreign currency with them for a "good rate" (the other common "greeting").

11. See also TGNP (1994: 48). In 1984, 15/3 Tshs were worth 1 U.S. dollar; by 1984 the Tanzanian shilling had been devalued to 400 per 1 dollar, and in 1994 the rate was 500 Tshs per 1 dollar (TGNP 1994: 48).

12. Further divisions occurred in the 1990s, but Monduli, Kiteto, and Ngorongoro were the pertinent districts during the portion of the 1990s when most of the research for this book was completed.

13. Tenga (1992) provides a useful explanation of these and other overlapping land laws as they affect pastoral land rights.

14. Emphasis added. Administrative Secretary, Arusha Region (hereafter ARG), to Area Secretary (hereafter AS), Monduli District (hereafter MD), 31 March 1964, ATNA, AC/MON/D.1/4.

15. EO, MC, to Regional Commissioner (hereafter RC), ARG, 19 June 1964, ATNA, AC/MON/D.1/4.

16. Ibid.

17. Branagan, Range Management Officer (hereafter RMO), ARG, to EO, MC, 30 June 1964, ATNA, AC/MON/D.1/4.

18. Branagan, RMO, ARG, to AS, MD, 14 April 1964, ATNA, AC/MON/D.1/4.

19. See, for example, MC, Loliondo, to EO, MC, "Wenye Kutaka Mashamba Mapya Loliondo Division" [Those Requesting New Farms in Loliondo Division], 29 October 1964; Sokoine, EO, MC, to AC, MD, 3 September 1964; both in ATNA, AC/MON/D.1/4.

20. Sokoine, EO, MC, to RC, ARG, 17 November 1964, ATNA, AC/MON/D.1/4.

21. RC, ARG, to EO, MC, 2 December 1964, ATNA, AC/MON/D.1/4.

22. Sungura, Area Commissioner, Masai, Monduli, to Sokoine, MP, Dar, 31 March 1972; ATNA, AC/MON/D.3/6/IV. See, generally, documents in ATNA, AC/MON/D.3/6.

23. Schoolteachers who lived in the government teachers' houses near the school were not included in the census or survey since they were considered temporary residents.

24. Parkipuny reports that one team of administrators operating in the Loliondo area burned down houses and homestead fences and forced people to squeeze together in a narrow valley (1979: 155).

25. "Project Agreement USAID & TANGOV: Disaster Relief—Arusha Region Drought Project," 13 August 1975, MLDRMPA, Night Stops.

26. Kyamba to Maasailand Range Development Committee, 14 May 1969, ATNA D.3/6.

27. Tarafa ya Operation ya Kisongo [Report of the Operation in Kisongo], 30 October 1978, ATNA, AC/MON/D.3/6/II.

28. Kukamlisha Operation Mefereji, Arkatan, na Meserani [Completion of the Operation in Mfereji, Arkatan and Meserani], 24 February 1979, ATNA, AC/MON/DC/6/II.

29. Interview with John Lukumai, District Agricultural and Livestock Development Officer, Monduli District, 9 March 1992.

30. See Gulliver (1963, 1965, 1969) for ethnographic studies of Arusha which emphasize the distinctions between Arusha and Maasai.

31. Many Arusha do have a noticeable discoloration of their teeth. Doctors I spoke with attributed the difference to the high fluoride content of water in several predominantly Arusha areas and nutritional differences in consumption of milk, meat, and blood.

32. Four hundred twenty-one "families" comprised of 840 men, 1,075 women, 1,087 boys, and 1,075 girls (Hatfield 1975: 20).

33. See, generally, documents in ATNA, AC/MON/D.3/6.

34. Taarifa ya Kamati Ndogo ya Wilaya ya Vijiji vya Ujamaa Iliyotembelea Vijiji Vipya Toka 19–25/10/71 [Report of the District Ujamaa Village Committee on the New Villages it Visited from 19–25 of October, 1971], 8 November 1971, ATNA, AC/MON/D.3/6/IV.

35. Logolie, Ward Secretary, Monduli Juu, Taarifa ya Mwezi Machi 1981 [March 1981 Report], 30 March 1981, ATNA, AC/MON/D.3/6C.

36. For a brief report on cultivation activities throughout Masai District, see Van Voorthuizen (c. 1971).

37. Again, this increase is even higher, given the difference between Ndagala's definition of "household" (husband and wives) and my definition of "household" (each wife as separate household, husband included in own house or wife's house of his choosing). Acreages are based on self-reported totals, confirmed by random spot checks and observations.

38. The category "economically active" excludes those adults who are unable to work because of age or infirmity.

39. Pigg (1992, 1993) explores how schools and textbooks communicate national development ideals and ideologies in Nepal.

40. Beth Pratt, a graduate student in anthropology at Boston University, is completing a dissertation on children's education in Maasai areas based on field research at this school.

41. TANU became Chama Cha Mapinduzi (CCM) in 1977 when it merged with the Afro-Shirazi party of Zanzibar.

42. One of the primary NGOs that Molloimet worked with was the Arusha Diocesan Development Organization, ADDO, an NGO under the auspices of the Catholic Church that I worked with from March 1985–December 1987; I was coordinator from 1986–1987.

43. Maasai kill smallstock and cattle by suffocation rather than by slitting their throats.

44. Staff reporters, "More Poll Losers to Lodge Complaints," *Daily News* (Tanzania), 3 November 1990, p. 1.

Maasai Portrait 4: Edward Moringe Sokoine

1. *Marehemu* is a respectful Swahili word for naming a dead person.

2. Except where otherwise noted, the following information is taken from Halimoja's (1985) biography of Sokoine, which includes excerpts from his parliamentary speeches.

3. Sokoine to DC, MaD, 2 February 1961; Sokoine to DC, MaD, 18 February 1961; Sokoine to DC, MaD, 8 March 1961; Sokoine to DC, MaD, 14 April 1961; all in TNA, 17/A 3/5.

4. Sokoine to DC, MaD, 14 April 1961, TNA, 17/A3/5.

5. Sokoine, EO, MC, to RC, ARG, 17 November 1964, and other documents in TNA, 471/L.5/1/4.

6. Sokoine, EO, MDC, to Regional Mining Officer, 5 December 1964, TNA, 471/L.5/1/4.

7. Sokoine resigned as prime minister in 1980 for health reasons. After treatment in Yugoslavia, he studied at the University of Belgrade from 1981–1982, then returned to Tanzania in 1983 to resume his position as prime minister.

8. See, for example, Musendo (1990); Mwiliye (1989).

9. See Maliyamkono and Bagachwa (1990) for a vivid description of Sokoine's role in the 1985 "crackdown" against "economic saboteurs."

5. Poverty and Progress

1. See also Barclay's Bank (1958). Chapter 2 in Escobar (1995) provides an intriguing analysis of the first such World Bank mission to Colombia in 1949.

2. The Tanzanian government's request for assistance from the United States rather than Britain was a sign of both the displacement of Britain as a global political power with the collapse of colonialism and the rise of the economic and political hegemony of the United States in the "Third World," partly achieved by its expanding "development" interventions.

3. They consisted of the area commissioner, the chairman of the District Council and TANU, the regional water engineer, the conservator for Ngorongoro Game Reserve Station, the regional agricultural officer, and the Member of Parliament for the District (Deans, et al. 1968: 20).

4. Deans, et al. (1968: 55); Moris, Water Development Engineer, "Maasai Range Management Project Water Development Past—Present—Future," 27 January 1976, MLDRMPA. Primary materials from the MLDRMP Archives, which were found in the Regional Water Department (Arusha), are cited as MLDRMPA/file number or file name. Reuben ole Kunei, the Tanzanian "counterpart" sociologist trained by the project, kindly provided me with access to other project report documents. Other published documents consulted, but not cited, include Hatfield (1976, 1977a).

5. The "Livestock and Range Improvement in Masailand, Tanzania" survey illustrates well the rise of technocratic "experts" in designing, implementing, and evaluating development projects during this period. The survey was conducted by a livestock economist, a range management specialist, an agricultural engineer, a sociologist, and an agronomist seconded (temporarily transferred) from the U.S. Department of Agriculture by USAID (Deans, et al. 1968).

6. For other analyses of the MLDRMP, see Jacobs (1980), Bennett (1984), Arhem (1985), and Holland (1987). Official evaluations include Utah State University Team (1976), Hoben (1976), and DEVRES (1979).

7. The project also became integrally related to a major large-scale beef development scheme which the Tanzanian government initiated with International Development Association (IDA) loan financing, based on a comprehensive 1971 IDA Sector Analysis for livestock. Light, et al. (Evaluation Team), "Evaluation Report, Masai Range and Livestock Development Project," 4 February 1973, MLDRMPA.

8. Ibid.

9. Thomsen, Animal Production Specialist, "End of Tour Report, January 24 1977–January 24, 1979," MLDRMPA/55.

10. Engle, Range Management Specialist, "Evaluation Report for Range Management Activities of the Masai Range Project," 27 January 1976, MLDRMPA.

11. Ibid. Because of the influence of Sokoine (Maasai Portrait 4), the dry dam even prompted a much-publicized visit by President Nyerere (accompanied by Sokoine) in 1976 to examine the dam and discuss "the problem of its being empty" with the project's water engineer. USAID designed plans to repair the dam, but funding difficulties in 1977 (a 31 percent reduction in Monduli's allocation by the government treasury) put a halt to most water construction work and tsetse-clearing. But, spurred by Nyerere's visit and Sokoine's prodding, the 370 individuals (men) at Monduli Juu agreed to contribute Tshs 100/= each for the reconstruction of the Monduli Juu Dam. Eventually Tshs 1.1 million were appropriated in 1978 (from sources other than the MLDRMP) to repair the dam. Fisher, Chief of Party, to Kriegel, Project Manager, Arusha, 2 September 1976, MLDRMPA/62; Hatfield, Project Sociologist, to Fisher, 4 May 1977, MLDRMPA/Jim L. Fisher; Booth, Executive Engineer, to Vance, Chief of Party, 8 July 1978, MLDRMPA/52.

12. Salk, Veterinarian, "Evaluation Report on the Activities of the Veterinarian—

Masai Range Project," 1976, MLDRMPA/1975 and 1976 Project Agreements, with revisions.

13. Engle, Range Management Specialist, "Evaluation Report for Range Management Activities of the Masai Range Project," 27 January 1976, MLDRMPA.

14. "Project Writeup for the Taresaro Ujamaa Ranch, Monduli District, Arusha Region," 9 August 1975, MLDRMPA/46A.

15. "Project Agreement between the Dept. of State, AID an Agency of the Government of the United States of America and the Treasury and United Republic of Tanzania," 11 September 1975, MLDRMPA/Jim L. Fisher.

16. The terms were a repayment period of 40 years, with an annual interest rate as low as 2 percent for the first ten years, then rising to 3 percent on the balance of the outstanding interest and principal.

17. When the foreign exchange crisis in the 1980s prevented Tanzania's timely repayment of its debts, the United States was able to use these huge debts as leverage to pressure Tanzania to sign the Structural Adjustment Program agreement by invoking the Brooke Amendment to withdraw all U.S. aid except famine relief.

18. The "End of Tour" reports filed by American project team members are full of such complaints. See, for example, Esler, Heavy Equipment Specialist, "End of Tour Report, February 1, 1974–January 31, 1976," 10 November 1975; Vorhis, Hydrogeologist, "Hydrogeologic Work on the Maasai Project: End of Tour Report," 1979; both in MLDRMPA/loose.

19. Fisher, Chief of Party, MLDRMP, "Progress Report for Masai Livestock and Range Development Project: 621–0071, November 1976–April 1977," 30 June 1977, MLDRMPA/loose.

20. Vorhis, Hydrogeologist, "Hydrogeologic Work on the Maasai Project: End of Tour Report," 1979, MLDRMPA.

21. Thomsen, Animal Production Specialist, "End of Tour Report, January 24, 1977–January 24, 1979," MLDRMPA/55.

22. Ibid.

23. Lotasaruaki, Secretary Executive Officer, "Discussion between the Minister of Agriculture and Co-ops, Hon. D. C. Bryceson and Masai Range Commission Staff at Monduli on 30th July 1971," 6 September 1971, MLDRMPA, Ardai Ranch; also quoted in Jacobs (1980: 6) without citation.

24. Ibid.

25. Baluhi, District Development Director, "Confidential Letter re: Ujamaa Ranches," 21 November 1974, MLDRMPA/46A (my translation from Swahili original).

26. "Progress Report for Masai Livestock and Rangeland Development Project 621–11–130–093, July 1, 1977 through June 30, 1978," MLDRMPA/Progress Reports; Thomsen, Animal Production Specialist, "End of Tour Report," January 24, 1977–January 24, 1979," MLDRMPA/55.

27. Light, et al., Evaluation Team, "Evaluation Report, Masai Range and Livestock Development Project," 4 February 1973, MLDRMPA; Jacobs (1980: 7).

28. "Progress Report for Masai Livestock and Rangeland Development Project 621–11–130–093, July 1, 1977 through June 30, 1978," MLDRMPA/Progress Reports. Interestingly, Lazaro ole Parkipuny, the new Tanzanian project manager, was one of the project's greatest critics. His 1972 critical article in the national English-language newspaper "gained widespread attention and support from the national party" (Jacobs 1980: 7). Another article he wrote (1979), which I use in this chapter, is also very critical of the

MLDRMP. Parkipuny went on to become Member of Parliament for Ngorongoro District; he later started and ran one of the first "indigenous" Maasai development organizations, KIPOC.

29. Fisher, Chief of Party, MLDRMP, "Progress Report for Masai Livestock and Range Development Project: 621–0071, November 1976–April 1977," 30 June 1977, MLDRMPA/loose.

30. Fisher, Chief of Party, MLDRMP, "Progress Report for Masai Livestock and Range Development Project: 621–0071, November 1976–April 1977," 30 June 1977, MLDRMPA/loose.

31. Podol, Assistant Director, USAID, to Jacobs, 27 June 1977, attached to Jacobs (1978).

32. Worby (1988) describes a similarly antagonistic "development" relationship between Setswana pastoralists and the government of Botswana.

33. Thomsen, Animal Production Specialist, "End of Tour Report, January 24, 1977–January 24, 1979," MLDRMPA/55.

34. Ibid.

35. "Masai Livestock and Range Management Project" [typed list of "Return Participants," "Participants in Training," "Participants Scheduled to Go"], MLDRMPA/58C.

36. Salk, Veterinarian, "First Quarterly Report (May through July 1975)," July 1975, MLDRMPA/73.

37. That few Maasai leaders spoke (much less read) English or Swahili did not seem to be of concern. Thomsen, Animal Production Specialist, "End of Tour Report, January 24, 1977–January 24, 1979," MLDRMPA/55; "Masai Range and Development Project Annual Report January 78–January 79," MLDRMPA/Annual Reports.

38. Hatfield, Project Sociologist, to Fisher, Chief of Party, 19 April 1977; Fisher, Chief of Party, to Kriegel, 28 April 1977; both in MLDRMPA/Jim L. Fisher.

39. "Mradi wa Maziwa Wilaya ya Monduli" [Milk Project, Monduli District], no date, MLDRMPA/Milk Scheme; Dr. John Thomsen, Animal Production Specialist, "End of Tour Report," 1979, MLDRMPA/55.

40. Women use color combinations and jewelry styles to express multiple identities of clan, locality, and ethnicity (Klumpp and Kratz 1993; Klumpp 1987). They carefully study any beaded item to evaluate its craftsmanship, patterns, style, and identity statements. I always wore various beaded bangles and necklaces in the field which I had been given as gifts from women from numerous localities. Other women would carefully study each piece, then tell me whether they liked it or not. When prompted, they could explain the basis for their evaluation in great detail. Two non-Maasai beaded items that I had—a leather key chain purchased from Samburu in Kenya and a beaded Zulu "love-letter" necklace—elicited constant comments and praise.

41. As of November 1993, the line provided electricity to the wealthy widow's home, the complex housing Sokoine's widows in Enguiki, and the grinding machine. Plans to connect Emairete school and the surrounding teachers' houses were always being talked about but were never realized.

42. Resolution 45/164 of 18 December 1990; Resolution 48/163 of 21 December 1993; General Assembly of the United Nations.

43. The growth of IDOs in Africa and particularly in South and Central America has attracted increased scholarly attention, whether analyzed as "new social movements" (e.g., Escobar and Alvarez 1992; Smith 1994; Alvarez, Dagnino, and Escobar 1998),

"ethnodevelopment" (Stavenhagen 1987), "alternative development" (Alvarsson 1990), an example of the relationship between civil society and the state (Ndegwa 1996), a new form of identity politics (Mato 1996; Hale 1997), or in terms of issues of cultural and human rights (Greaves 1995). This literature draws on and informs important work on other local/global articulations, "globalization," and transnational processes and practices, such as Featherstone (1990), Appadurai (1991, 1996), Gupta (1992), Gupta and Ferguson (1992, 1997).

44. Although "indigenous" is most commonly used to refer to the first inhabitants of areas such as the Americas where subsequent colonizers eventually became the dominant majority population, the term has been used in Africa by distinct cultural minorities such as Maasai who have been historically repressed by majority populations of Africans in control of the state apparatus (Murumbi 1994). Despite these broad claims to represent all "indigenous" people in Tanzania, not just Maasai, KIPOC soon became identified with the interests of Ngorongoro Maasai, especially the Purko section.

45. These two projects are described and analyzed in great detail in Hodgson and Schroeder (n.d.). See also Inyuat e-Maa (1991a, 1991c, n.d.).

Maasai Portrait 5: Mary

1. Mary is a pseudonym. To protect her confidentiality, I have changed minor details in this narrative, but all the quotations are her own words.

6. The Gendered Contradictions of Modernity and Marginality

1. Other scholars have also examined spirit possession as a response to certain historical transformations which resulted in a decline in women's economic power or social prestige (see, for example, Harris 1957; Alpers 1984; and Vail and White 1991).

2. The following section is based on three studies of the phenomenon among Maasai in Tanzania. Briefly, the three studies were undertaken at approximately ten-year intervals: a set of twenty case studies based on interviews by David Peterson in 1971 when outbreaks of *orpeko* were sweeping through southern Maasailand, a 1984 study of *orpeko* by Arvi Hurskainen, commissioned by the Catholic and Lutheran churches as a means to settle their disputes over the diagnosis and cure of *orpeko*, and finally, my own data collected during field research from 1991 through 1993. I am grateful to David Peterson for permission to quote extensively from his unpublished paper.

3. Many scholars of spirit possession have supported I. M. Lewis's argument in *Ecstatic Religion* (1971) that possession is a mechanism used by women and other "oppressed" members of society to cope with difficult circumstances in their lives. But studies by Janice Boddy (1989) and Michael Lambek (1981, 1993), among others, have shown the value of exploring spirit possession in terms of its relationship to the cultural meanings, social relations, and historical context of the wider society.

4. According to Shorter (1970), the *migawo* spirit-possession cult and Christianity appeared at the same time in southern Ukimbu, but they were seen by Kimbu people as incompatible, and "the picture which the Kimbu have of the *migawo* differs radically from the traditional Christian concept of the Devil" (1970: 124).

5. In his paper, Peterson (1971) included summaries of his interviews with nineteen women and one man who had been possessed. References to Peterson's case studies are abbreviated as "DP/Informant #."

6. Out of the three communities, only one man was afflicted. He underwent in-

struction for baptism, was baptized and cured, and quit going to church. Male symptoms are reported to be different: during an acute attack, the man sits silently like a deaf and dumb person. Peterson discovered only two cases of possessed men out of hundreds of women (1971); Hurskainen found only two men among the eighty-three case studies of *orpeko* he collected (1985: 24). Other factors, including clan membership, number of children, economic status of household, and relationships with co-wives and husband, were not found to be significant indicators of which women became ill (Hurskainen 1985: 24–26).

7. Koritschoner discusses another kind of relation between naming and the symptoms: "The number of sheitani is almost countless, but it seems that the different names are merely the names for the different symptoms" (1936: 211).

8. For other discussions of spirit possession that consider embodiment, see Boddy 1989; Lambek 1993; and Stoller 1994.

9. Koritschoner reports that women possessed by the Ruhani *sheitani* dreamt about white turbans, figures of a white color (not Europeans) which alternately approached and receded (1936: 211).

10. The incidence of *ngomas* is decreasing as attendance at church increases.

11. Since Peterson presents only his English summary of his interviews, it is difficult to know whether the women spoke of *orpeko* as Satan, the devil, or demons. He infers that most perceived *orpeko* in terms of demon possession; this helps to explain the success of the church in exorcising the demons.

Bibliography

Primary Sources

Tanzania National Archives—Arusha (ATNA) (Arusha, Tanzania)

Accession MON: Monduli District
Accession District Commissioner's Office, Monduli District
Criminal Records

Tanzania National Archives—Dar es Salaam (TNA) (Dar es Salaam, Tanzania)

Native Affairs
Secretariat Files, Early Series (1919–1927)
Accession 4: Tanga Region
Accession 17: Monduli District
Accession 69: Northern Province
Accession 471: Masai District
Accession 472: Arusha District

East Africana Collection (EAC) (University of Dar es Salaam, Tanzania)

Hans Cory Papers (HCP)

Maasai Livestock Development and Range Management Project Archives (MLDRMPA) (Regional Water Department, Arusha, Tanzania)

The MLDRMP files are in complete disarray. Many documents are loose; others are mis-filed.

Rhodes House Library (RHL) (Oxford, England)

Mss. Afr. S. (Manuscripts—Africa)—various
Mss. Brit. Empire. S. (Manuscripts—British Empire)—various
Mss. Perham S. (Dame Margery Perham's Papers)

Public Records Office (PRO) (Kew Gardens, England)

CO 822 (East African Original Correspondence)
CO 892 (East African Royal Commission)

Bibliography

School Of Oriental And African Studies (SOAS) (London, England)

International Missionary Council/Conference of British Missionary Societies, East Africa—Tanganyika (Boxes 249, 250)

Miscellaneous Manuscripts—George Huntingford (PP. MS.17); C. D. Hamilton, n.d. (MS 297457 "Masai")

Cooperative Africana Microfilm Project (CAMP) (United States)

Arusha District Book (Reel 4)

Arusha Region Book (Reel 28)

Masai District Book (Reel 5)

Library of Congress (Washington, D.C., United States)

Tanganyika *Blue Books* (1926–1938, 1945–1948)

Annual Reports, Veterinary Department, Tanganyika (1921, 1924–1926, 1943–1960)

Annual Reports, Labour Department, Tanganyika (1927–1930, 1942–1943, 1951–1959)

Other Semi-Public/Private Collections

District Agricultural and Livestock Office, Monduli, Tanzania (Monthly village extension reports)

District Education Office, Monduli, Tanzania (Annual enrollment and attendance statistics, monthly primary school reports)

District Office, Monduli, Tanzania (Development plans and reports)

Enguiki Dispensary, Emairete/Enguiki Village, Tanzania (Monthly reports, Mother Child Health [MCH] project reports)

Henry Fosbrooke's Private Library (Lake Duluti, Tanzania)

Holy Ghost Fathers' Library, District House (Arusha, Tanzania)

Hodgson Census, 1992. In author's possession.

Monduli Catholic Mission (Journals, Baptismal Registers)

Monduli Hospital, Monduli, Tanzania (Annual patient statistics)

BOOKS AND ARTICLES

Akhtar, Sarah. 1989. "Masai Women Should Benefit from Changed Way of Life." Letter to the Editor. *The New York Times,* 12 November 1989, p. E22.

Alpers, Edward. 1984. "'Ordinary Household Chores': Ritual and Power in a 19th-Century Swahili Women's Spirit Possession Cult." *International Journal of African Historical Studies* 17 (4): 677–702.

Alvarez, Sonia E., Evelina Dagnino, and Arturo Escobar, eds. 1998. *Culture of Politics/Politics of Culture: Re-Visioning Latin American Social Movements.* Boulder: Westview.

Alvarsson, Jan-Åke, ed. 1990. *Alternative Development in Latin America: Indigenous Strategies for Cultural Continuity in Societal Change.* Uppsala, Sweden: Uppsala Research Reports in Cultural Anthropology.

Ambler, Charles. 1988. *Kenyan Communities in the Age of Imperialism.* New Haven: Yale University Press.

Amin, Mohamed, Duncan Willetts, and John Eames. 1987. *The Last of the Maasai.* London: The Bodley Head.

Anderson, Benedict. 1991. *Imagined Communities.* 2nd ed. London: Verso.

Anderson, David M. 1984. "Depression, Dust Bowl, Demography and Drought: The Colonial State and Soil Conservation in East Africa During the 1930s." *African Affairs* 82 (332): 321–343.

———. n.d. "Organising Ideas: British Colonialism and African Rural Development." Unpublished manuscript.

Anderson, David M., and Vigdis Broch-Due, eds. 1999. *The Poor Are Not Us: Poverty and Pastoralism in Eastern Africa.* Oxford: James Currey.

Appadurai, Arjun. 1991. "Global Ethnoscapes: Notes and Queries for a Transnational Anthropology." In *Recapturing Anthropology: Working in the Present,* ed. Richard Fox. Santa Fe, N.M.: School of American Research Press.

———. 1996. *Modernity at Large: Cultural Dimensions of Globalization.* Minneapolis: University of Minnesota Press.

Arhem, Kaj. 1985. *Pastoral Man in the Garden of Eden: The Maasai of the Ngorongoro Conservation Area, Tanzania.* Uppsala: Uppsala Research Reports in Cultural Anthropology.

———. 1987. *The Masai and the State: The Impact of Rural Development Policies on a Pastoral People in Tanzania.* Documentation Series paper 52. Denmark: International Working Group on Indigenous Affairs.

Author Unknown. 1949–1950. "Masai Initiation Ceremony" [photographic essay]. *East African Annual, 1949–1950:* 54–55.

Barclay's Bank D. C. O. 1958. *Tanganyika: An Economic Survey.* London: Barclay's Bank.

Baumann, Oscar. 1894. *Durch Massailand zur Nilquelle: Reisen und Forschungen der Massai-Expedition des deutschen Antisklaverei-Komite in den Jahren 1891–93.* Berlin: Dietrich Reimer.

Beaman, Anne. 1983. "Women's Participation in Pastoral Economy: Income Maximization among the Rendile." *Nomadic Peoples* 12: 20–25.

Beinart, William. 1984. "Soil Erosion, Conservationism and Ideas about Development: A Southern African Exploration." *Journal of Southern African Studies* 11 (1): 52–83.

Bennett, John. 1984. *Political Ecology and Development Projects Affecting Pastoralist Peoples in East Africa.* Madison: University of Wisconsin Land Tenure Center.

———. 1988. "Anthropology and Development: The Ambiguous Engagement." In *Production and Autonomy: Anthropological Studies and Critiques of Development,* ed. John W. Bennett and John R. Bowen. Monographs in Economic Anthropology, No. 5. New York: University Press of America.

Benson, Rev. Stanley. 1980. "The Conquering Sacrament: Baptism and Demon Possession among the Maasai of Tanzania." *Africa Theological Journal* (Lutheran Theological College, Makumira, Tanzania) 9: 52–61.

Berman, Bruce, and John Lonsdale. 1992. *Unhappy Valley.* London: James Currey.

Bernsten, John. 1976. "The Maasai and Their Neighbors: Variables of Interaction." *African Economic History* 2: 1–11.

———. 1979. "Pastoralism, Raiding and Prophets: Maasailand in the Nineteenth Century." Ph.D. diss., University of Wisconsin-Madison.

———. 1980. "The Enemy Is Us: Eponymy in the Historiography of the Maasai." *History in Africa* 7: 1–21.

Blackburn, Roderic. 1974. "The Okiek and Their History." *Azania* 9: 139–157.

———. 1976. "Okiek History." In *Kenya before 1900,* ed. B. A. Ogot. Nairobi: East African Publishing House.

Boddy, Janice. 1989. *Wombs and Alien Spirits.* Madison: University of Wisconsin Press.

Bodley, John H. 1975. *Victims of Progress.* Menlo Park, Calif.: Cummings Pub. Co.

Boesen, Jannik, Kjell J. Havnevik, Juhani Koponen, and Rie Odgaard, eds. 1986. *Tanza-*

nia: Crisis and Struggle for Survival. Uppsala: Scandinavian Institute of African Studies.

Bonner, Raymond. 1993. *At the Hand of Man: Peril and Hope for Africa's Wildlife.* New York: Vintage.

Brosius, J. Peter. 1999. "Locations and Representations: Writing in the Political Present in Sarawak, East Malaysia." *Identities* 6 (2–3): 345–386.

Bruner, Edward M., and Barbara Kirshenblatt-Gimblett. 1994. "Maasai on the Lawn: Tourist Realism in East Africa." *Cultural Anthropology* 9 (4): 435–470.

"Bwana Kongoni" [H. R. Tate]. 1956–1957. "Masailand: Its History, Its People." *East African Annual, 1956–1957:* 135–137.

Castells, Manuel. 1997. *The Power of Identity.* Oxford: Blackwell.

Chanock, Martin. 1982. "Making Customary Law: Men, Women, and Courts in Colonial Northern Rhodesia." In *African Women and the Law: Historical Perspectives,* ed. Margaret Jean Hay and Marcia Wright. Boston: Boston University Papers on Africa, VII.

———. 1985. *Law, Custom, and Social Order: The Colonial Experience in Malawi and Zambia.* Cambridge: Cambridge University Press.

Chieni, Telelia, and Paul Spencer. 1993. "The World of Telelia: Reflections of a Maasai Woman in Matapato." In *Being Maasai,* ed. Thomas Spear and Richard Waller. London: James Currey.

Cohen, David William, and E. S. Otieno Adhiambo. 1989. *Siaya: The Historical Anthropology of an African Landscape.* London: James Currey.

———. 1994. *Burying SM: The Politics of Knowledge and the Sociology of Power in Africa.* Portsmouth, N.H.: Heinemann.

Collett, David. 1987. "Pastoralists and Wildlife: Images and Reality in Kenya Maasailand." In *Conservation in Africa: Peoples, Policies and Practice,* ed. David Anderson and Richard Grove. Cambridge: Cambridge University Press.

Collier, Jane. 1988. *Marriage and Inequality in Classless Societies.* Stanford: Stanford University Press.

Collier, Jane, and Michelle Rosaldo. 1981. "Politics and Gender in Simple Societies." In *Sexual Meanings: The Cultural Construction of Gender and Sexuality,* ed. Sherry Ortner and Harriet Whitehead. Cambridge: Cambridge University Press.

Collier, Jane, and Sylvia Yanagisako, eds. 1987. *Gender and Kinship: Essays towards a Unified Analysis.* Stanford: Stanford University Press.

Conklin, Beth A., and Laura R. Graham. 1995. "The Shifting Middle Ground: Amazonian Indians and Eco-Politics." *American Anthropologist* 97 (4): 695–710.

Connell, R. W. 1987. *Gender and Power: Society, the Person and Sexual Politics.* Stanford: Stanford University Press.

Constantine, Stephen. 1984. *The Making of British Colonial Development Policy, 1914–1940.* London: Frank Cass.

Cooper, Frederick. 1994. "Conflict and Connection: Rethinking Colonial African History." *American Historical Review* 99 (5): 1516–1545.

———. 1997. "Modernizing Bureaucrats, Backward Africans, and the Development Concept." In *International Development and the Social Sciences: Essays on the History and Politics of Knowledge,* ed. Frederick Cooper and Randall Packard. Berkeley: University of California Press.

Cooper, Frederick, and Randall Packard, eds. 1997. *International Development and the So-*

cial Sciences: Essays on the History and Politics of Knowledge. Berkeley: University of California Press.

Cooper, Frederick, and Ann Stoler, eds. 1997. *Tensions of Empire: Colonial Cultures in a Bourgeois World.* Berkeley: University of California Press.

Cowen, M. P., and R. W. Shenton. 1996. *Doctrines of Development.* London and New York: Routledge.

Croll, Elizabeth. 1994. *From Heaven to Earth: Images and Experiences of Development in China.* New York: Routledge.

Crush, Jonathan, ed. 1995. *Power of Development.* New York: Routledge.

Curry, John, ed. 1996. *Gender and Livestock in Africa Production Systems.* Special Issue of *Human Ecology* 24 (2).

Dahl, Gudrun. 1979. *Suffering Grass: Subsistence and Society of Was Borana.* Stockholm: Stockholm Studies in Social Anthropology.

———. 1987. "Women in Pastoral Production: Some Theoretical Notes on Roles and Resources." *Ethnos* 52 (1–2): 246–279.

Davison, Jean. 1997. *Gender, Lineage and Ethnicity in Southern Africa.* Boulder, Colo.: Westview Press.

Deans, Robert, Clyde M. Teague, Lloyd G. Signell, Bruce M. John, and Melvin E. Knickerbocker. 1968. "Livestock and Range Improvement in Masailand: Tanzania Survey Report." Prepared for USAID and Ministry of Agriculture, Tanzania.

DEVRES. 1979. *Terminal Evaluation of the Masai Livestock and Range Management Project.* Prepared for USAID, Tanzania Mission, Dar es Salaam.

di Leonardo, Micaela, ed. 1991. *Gender at the Crossroads of Knowledge.* Berkeley: University of California Press.

Dirks, Nicholas, Geoff Eley, and Sherry B. Ortner, eds. 1994. *Culture/Power/History.* Princeton: Princeton University Press.

Driberg, J. H. 1932. "The Status of Women among Nilotics and Nilo-Hamitics." *Africa* 5 (5): 404–421.

Dupire, Margeurite. 1963. "The Position of Women in a Pastoral Society." In *Women of Tropical Africa,* ed. Denise Paulme. Berkeley: University of California Press.

East Africa Royal Commission (EARC). 1955. *Report, 1953–1955.* London: Her Majesty's Stationery Office.

Elam, Yitzchak. 1973. *The Social and Sexual Roles of Hima Women.* Manchester: Manchester University Press.

Ensminger, Jean. 1987. "Economic and Political Differentiation Among Galole Orma Women." *Ethnos* 52 (1–2): 26–49.

Escobar, Arturo. 1992. "Imagining a Post-Development Era? Critical Thought, Development and Social Movements." *Social Text* 31/32: 20–56.

———. 1995. *Encountering Development: The Making and Unmaking of the Third World.* Princeton: Princeton University Press.

Escobar, Arturo, and Sonia E. Alvarez, eds. 1992. *The Making of Social Movements in Latin America: Identity, Strategy and Democracy.* Boulder, Colo.: Westview.

Etienne, Mona, and Eleanor Leacock, eds. 1980. *Women and Colonization: Anthropological Perspectives.* New York: Praeger.

Evangelou, Phylo. 1984. *Livestock Development in Kenya's Maasailand.* Boulder, Colo.: Westview Press.

Evans-Pritchard, E. E. 1940. *The Nuer.* Oxford: Clarendon Press.

Farler, J. P. 1882. "Native Routes in East Africa from Pangani to the Masai Country and the Victoria Nyanza." *Proceedings of the Royal Geographical Society* 4 (12): 730–742, 776 (map).

Featherstone, Mike, ed. 1990. *Global Culture: Nationalism, Globalization and Modernity.* London: Sage Press.

Feierman, Steven. 1990. *Peasant Intellectuals: Anthropology and History in Tanzania.* Madison: University of Wisconsin Press.

Ferguson, James. 1990. *The Anti-Politics Machine: "Development," Depoliticization, and Bureaucratic Power in Lesotho.* Cambridge: Cambridge University Press.

Fosbrooke, Henry. 1948. "An Administrative Survey of the Masai Social System." *Tanganyika Notes and Records* 26: 1–50.

———. 1980. "Masai Motivation and Its Application: A Study of Maasai Organizational Ability as Applied to the Cattle Marketing System 1938–59." Consultancy Report submitted to Development Alternatives Inc., as part of the Arusha Integrated Regional Development Plan (copy in Fosbrooke's library).

Fosbrooke, Jane. 1944. "Masai Women and Their Work." *The Crown Colonist* 14 (150): 313–314, 332.

Foucault, Michel. 1972. *The Archaeology of Knowledge and the Discourse on Language.* Trans. A. M. Sheridan Smith. New York: Pantheon Books.

———. 1978 [1976]. *The History of Sexuality, Vol. I.* Trans. Robert Hurley. New York: Vintage Books.

———. 1979. *Discipline and Punish: The Birth of the Prison.* Trans. Alan Sheridan. New York: Vintage Books.

Fratkin, Elliot. 1991. *Surviving Drought and Development: Ariaal Pastoralists of Northern Kenya.* Boulder: Westview Press.

Fratkin, Elliot, Eric A. Roth, and Martha Nathan. 1999. "When Nomads Settle: The Effects of Commoditization, Nutritional Change and Formal Education among Ariaal Rendille Pastoralists of Kenya." *Current Anthropology* 40 (5): 729–735.

Fratkin, Elliot, and Kevin Smith. 1995. "Women's Changing Economic Roles with Pastoral Sedentarization." *Human Ecology* 23 (4): 433–454.

Friedman, Jonathan. 1994. *Cultural Identity and Global Process.* London: Sage Press.

Galaty, John. 1979. "Pollution and Pastoral Anti-Praxis: The Issue of Maasai Inequality." *American Ethnologist* 6 (4): 803–816.

———. 1980. "The Maasai Group-Ranch: Politics and Development in an African Pastoral Society." In *When Nomads Settle: Processes of Sedentarization as Adaptation and Response,* ed. Philip Carl Salzman. New York: Praeger.

———. 1981. "Land and Livestock among Kenyan Maasai." In *Change and Development in Nomadic and Pastoral Societies,* ed. John Galaty and Philip Salzman. Leiden: E. J. Brill.

———. 1982a. "Being 'Maasai'; Being 'People of the Cattle': Ethnic Shifters in East Africa." *American Ethnologist* 9 (1): 1–20.

———. 1982b. "Maasai Pastoral Ideology and Change." *Studies in Third World Societies* 17: 1–22.

———. 1983. "Ceremony and Society: The Poetics of Maasai Ritual." *Man* n. s. 18 (2): 361–382.

———. 1993a. "Maasai Expansion and the New East African Pastoralism." In *Being Maasai,* ed. Thomas Spear and Richard Waller. London: James Currey.

———. 1993b. "'The Eye That Wants a Person, Where Can It Not See?': Inclusion, Exclusion, and Boundary Shifters in Maasai Identity." In *Being Maasai,* ed. Thomas Spear and Richard Waller. London: James Currey.

Galaty, John, Dan Aronson, and Philip Salzman, eds. 1981. *The Future of Pastoralist Peoples: Research Priorities for the 1980s.* Ottawa: International Development Research Center.

Galaty, John, and Philip Salzman, eds. 1981. *Change and Development in Nomadic and Pastoral Societies.* Leiden: E. J. Brill.

Geiger, Susan. 1986. "Women's Life Histories: Method and Content." *Signs* 11 (2): 334–351.

———. 1997. *TANU Women: Gender and Culture in the Making of Tanganyikan Nationalism, 1955–1965.* Portsmouth: Heinemann.

Gewertz, Deborah, and Frederick Errington. 1991. *Twisted Histories, Altered Contexts: Representing the Chambri in a World System.* New York: Cambridge University Press.

Gluckman, Max. 1950. "Kinship and Marriage among the Lozi of Northern Rhodesia and the Zulu of Natal." In *African Systems of Kinship and Marriage,* ed. A. R. Radcliffe-Brown and Daryll Forde. London: Oxford University Press.

Gordon, Robert J., and Stuart Sholto Douglas. 2000. *The Bushman Myth.* 2nd ed. Boulder: Westview Press.

Great Britain Admiralty. c. 1915. *A Handbook of German East Africa.* London: His Majesty's Stationery Office.

Greaves, Thomas C. 1995. "Cultural Rights and Ethnography." *General Anthropology* (Bulletin of the General Anthropology Division) 1 (2): 1, 3–6.

Greene, Sandra. 1996. *Gender, Ethnicity and Social Change on the Upper Slave Coast: A History of Anlo-Ewe.* Portsmouth, N.H.: Heinemann.

Gregory, J. W. 1896. *The Great Rift Valley.* London: John Murray.

———. 1901. *The Foundation of British East Africa.* London: Horace Marshall & Son.

Griffiths, Mrs. J. E. 1938. "Masai Cattle Auction." *Tanganyika Notes and Records* 6: 99–101.

Grillo, R. D., and R. L. Stirrat, eds. 1997. *Discourses of Development: Anthropological Perspectives.* Oxford and New York: Berg Publishers.

Grosz-Ngate, Maria, and Omari Kokole, eds. 1997. *Gendered Encounters.* New York: Routledge.

Gulliver, Philip. 1963. *Social Control in an African Society.* London: Routledge and Kegan Paul.

———. 1965. "The Arusha—Economic and Social Change." In *Markets in Africa: Eight Subsistence Economies in Transition,* ed. Paul Bohannon and George Dalton. Garden City, N.Y.: Doubleday & Co.

———. 1969. "The Conservative Commitment in Northern Tanzania: The Arusha and Masai." In *Tradition and Transition in East Africa,* ed. Philip Gulliver. London: Routledge & Kegan Paul.

Gunder Frank, Andre. 1970 [1966]. "The Development of Underdevelopment." In *Imperialism and Underdevelopment: A Reader,* ed. Robert Rhodes. New York: Monthly Review Press.

Gupta, Akhil. 1992. "The Song of the Non-Aligned World: Transnational Identities and the Reinscription of Space in Late Capitalism." *Cultural Anthropology* 7 (1): 63–79.

———. 1998. *Postcolonial Developments: Agriculture in the Making of Modern India.* Durham: Duke University Press.

Gupta, Akhil, and James Ferguson. 1992. "Beyond Culture: Space, Identity, and the Politics of Difference." *Cultural Anthropology* 7 (1): 6–23.

———, eds. 1997. *Culture, Power, Place: Explorations in Critical Anthropology.* Durham: Duke University Press.

Hale, Charles R. 1997. "Cultural Politics of Identity in Latin America." *Annual Review of Anthropology* 26: 567–590.

Halimoja, Yusuf. 1985. *Sokoine: Mtu wa Watu* [Sokoine: Man of the People]. Dar es Salaam, Tanzania: Tanzania Publications.

Hall, C. L. 1956. "The Influence of the Social System and Environment on the Health of a Primitive People: A Study of the Masai Tribe in Tanganyika." Unpublished dissertation for Diploma in Public Health, London University (copy at RHL).

Hall, Stuart. 1992. "The West and the Rest: Discourse and Power." In *Formations of Modernity*, ed. Stuart Hall and Brian Gieben. Cambridge: Open University Press.

Hardin, Garret. 1968. "The Tragedy of the Commons." *Science* 162: 1243–1248.

Harman, Willis W. 1988. "Development—For What? Emerging Trends of Promise and Concern." In *Approaches that Work in Rural Development*, ed. John Burbidge. New York: K. G. Saur, Munchen.

Harris, Grace. 1957. "Possession 'Hysteria' in a Kenya Tribe." *American Anthropologist* 59 (6): 1046–1066.

Hatfield, Colby. 1975. "End of Tour Report of C. R. Hatfield, Jr., Sociologist, Masai Range Development Project (1973–1975)." Prepared for USAID. In author's possession.

———. 1976. "Current Trends in Masai Development: A Baseline Survey." Masai Project Evaluation Paper No. 3. Report Prepared for MLRMP/USAID. In author's possession.

———. 1977a. "End of Tour Report of C. R. Hatfield, Jr., Sociologist, Masai Range Development Project (1975–1977)." Prepared for USAID. In author's possession.

———. 1977b. "The Impact of Social and Technical Change in Masailand and Its Implications for Future Development." Report Prepared for Food and Agriculture Officer, USAID, Dar es Salaam. In author's possession.

Herskovits, Melville. 1926. "The Cattle Complex in East Africa." *American Anthropologist* 28: 230–272, 361–388, 494–528, 633–664.

Hess, Oleen. 1976. "The Establishment of Cattle Ranching Associations among the Maasai in Tanzania." Ithaca, N.Y.: Cornell University Rural Development Committee, Occasional Paper 7.

Hinde, Sidney Langford, and Hildegarde Hinde. 1901. *The Last of the Masai.* London: William Heinemann.

Hoben, Allan. 1976. "Social Soundness of the Maasai Livestock and Range Management Project." Unpublished manuscript prepared for USAID, Washington.

———. 1982. "Anthropologists and Development." *Annual Review of Anthropology* 11: 349–375.

Hodgson, Dorothy L. 1996. "'My Daughter . . . Belongs to the Government Now': Marriage, Maasai and the Tanzanian State." *Canadian Journal of African Studies* 30 (1): 106–123.

———. 1997. "Embodying the Contradictions of Modernity: Gender and Spirit Possession among Maasai in Tanzania." In *Gendered Encounters: Challenging Cultural Boundaries and Social Hierarchies in Africa*, ed. Maria Grosz-Ngate and Omari Kokole. New York: Routledge.

————. 1999a. "Pastoralism, Patriarchy and History: Changing Gender Relations among Maasai in Tanganyika, 1890–1940." *Journal of African History* 40 (1): 41–65.

————. 1999b. "Critical Interventions: Dilemmas of Accountability in Contemporary Ethnographic Research." *Identities* 6 (2–3): 201–224.

————. 1999c. "Once Intrepid Warriors: Modernity and the Production of Maasai Masculinities." *Ethnology* 38 (2): 121–150.

————. 1999d. "Images and Interventions: The Problems of Pastoralist Development." In *The Poor Are Not Us: Poverty and Pastoralism in Eastern Africa,* ed. David M. Anderson and Vigdis Broch-Due. Oxford: James Currey.

————. 1999e. Women as Children: Culture, Political Economy and Gender Inequality among Kisongo Maasai." *Nomadic Peoples* n. s. 3 (2): 115–130.

————. 2000a. "Engendered Encounters: Men of the Church and the 'Church of Women' in Maasailand, Tanzania, 1950–90." *Comparative Studies in Society and History* 41 (4): 758–783.

————, ed. 2000b. *Rethinking Pastoralism in Africa: Gender, Culture and the Myth of the Patriarchal Pastoralist.* London: James Currey; Athens: Ohio University Press.

————. 2000c. "Introduction: Gender, Culture and the Myth of the Patriarchal Pastoralist." In *Rethinking Pastoralism in Africa: Gender, Culture and the Myth of the Patriarchal Pastoralist,* ed. Dorothy L. Hodgson. London: James Currey; Athens: Ohio University Press.

————. 2000d. "Taking Stock: State Control, Ethnic Identity, and Pastoralist Development in Tanganyika, 1940–1961." *Journal of African History* 41 (1): 55–78.

Hodgson, Dorothy L., and Sheryl McCurdy, eds. 1996. *Wayward Wives, Misfit Mothers and Disobedient Daughters: "Wicked" Women and the Reconfiguration of Gender in Africa.* Special Issue of *Canadian Journal of African Studies* 30 (1).

————, eds. 2001. *"Wicked" Women and the Reconfiguration of Gender in Africa.* Portsmouth, N.H.: Heinemann; Oxford: James Currey; Cape Town: David Phillips.

Hodgson, Dorothy L., and Richard Schroeder. n.d. "Mapping the Maasai: Dilemmas of Counter-Mapping Community Resources in Tanzania." Unpublished manuscript under review.

Hogg, Richard. 1992. "NGOs, Pastoralists and the Myth of Community: Three Case Studies of Pastoral Development from East Africa." *Nomadic Peoples* 30: 122–146.

Holland, Killian. 1987. "On the Horns of a Dilemma: The Future of the Maasai." Montreal: Center for Developing Area Studies Discussion Paper Series 51, McGill University.

Hollis, Alfred C. 1905. *The Masai: Their Language and Folklore.* Freeport, N.Y.: Books for Libraries Press.

Homewood, Katherine, and William Rodgers. 1991. *Maasailand Ecology: Pastoralist Development and Wildlife Conservation in Ngorongoro, Tanzania.* Cambridge: Cambridge University Press.

Horowitz, Michael, and Forouz Jowkar. 1992. *Pastoral Women and Change in Africa, the Middle East, and Central Asia.* IDA Working Paper No. 91. Binghamton, N.Y.: Institute for Development Anthropology.

Hurskainen, Arvi. 1985. "Tatizo la Kushikwa na Pepo Umasaini Tanzania" [The Problem of Spirit Possession in Maasailand, Tanzania]. Helsinki. Privately circulated paper, commissioned by the Catholic and Lutheran churches, Tanzania.

————. 1989. "The Epidemiological Aspect of Spirit Possession among the Maasai of

Tanzania." In *Culture, Experience and Pluralism*, ed. Anita Jacobson-Widding and David Westerlund. Uppsala: Almqvist and Wiksell International.

Hutchinson, Sharon. 1996. *Nuer Dilemmas: Coping with Money, War and the State*. Berkeley: University of California Press.

Igoe, Jim. 1999. "Roadblocks to Community Conservation in Tanzania: A Case Study from Simanjiro District." Boston: Boston University African Studies Center Working Papers.

———. 2000. "Ethnicity, Civil Society and the Tanzanian Pastoral NGO Movement: The Continuities and Discontinuities of Liberalized Development." Ph.D. diss., Boston University.

Iliffe, John. 1969. *Tanganyika under German Rule 1905–1912*. Cambridge: Cambridge University Press.

———. 1979. *A Modern History of Tanganyika*. Cambridge: Cambridge University Press.

Imam, Ayesha, Amina Mama, and Fatou Sow, eds. 1997. *Engendering African Social Sciences*. Dakar: Council for the Development of Economic and Social Research in Africa.

International Bank for Reconstruction and Development (IBRD). 1961. *The Economic Development of Tanganyika*. Baltimore: Johns Hopkins University Press.

Inyuat e-Maa. 1991a. "Preliminary Report of a Conference (twice cancelled), First Maasai Conference on Culture and Development." Photocopy, Tanzania. In author's possession.

———. 1991b. "First Maasai Conference on Culture and Development: The Setting of the Maasai Community of Tanzania." Conference Report, Arusha Tanzania, 1–5 December 1991. In author's possession.

———. 1991c. "The Constitution and Rules of Inyuat e-Maa." Photocopy, Tanzania. In author's possession.

———. 1996. "First Maa Conference on Culture and Development: The Setting of the Maa Women of Tanzania." Conference Report, Arusha, Tanzania, 6–8 February 1996. In author's possession.

———. n.d. (ca. 1993). "Policy Document." Photocopy, Tanzania. In author's possession.

Jackson, Sir Frederick. 1969 [1930]. *Early Days in East Africa*. London: Dawsons of Pall Mall.

Jackson, Jean. 1995. "Culture, Genuine and Spurious: The Politics of Indianness in the Vaupes, Columbia." *American Ethnologist* 22 (1): 3–27.

Jacobs, Alan. 1965. "The Traditional Political Organization of the Pastoral Masai." D.Phil. thesis, Oxford University.

———. 1968. "A Chronology of the Pastoral Maasai." In *Hadith I*. Kenya: East African Publishing House.

———. 1971. "Traditional Home and Housing Among the Pastoral Maasai." *Plan East Africa* (Journal of the Architectural Association of Kenya) (January–February): 13–17, 33.

———. 1978. "Development in Tanzania Maasailand: The Perspective over 20 Years, 1957–1977." Final Report prepared for the USAID Mission in Tanzania. In author's possession.

———. 1980. "Pastoral Development in Tanzanian Maasailand." *Rural Africana* 7: 1–14.

Johnston, Harry. 1886. *The Kilima-Njaro Expedition: A Record of Scientific Exploration in Eastern Equatorial Africa*. London: Kegan Paul, Trench & Co.

———. 1902. *The Uganda Protectorate*. New York: Dodd, Mead & Co.

Jowkar, Forouz, and Michael M. Horowitz. 1991. *Gender Relations of Pastoral and Agro-pastoral Production: A Bibliography with Annotations.* IDA Working Paper No. 74. Binghamton, N.Y.: Institute for Development Anthropology.

Kametz, H. 1962. "Assessment of Known Water Sources and Suggestions for Future Development in Masailand." Prepared for the Government of Tanganyika (copy in ATNA).

Kettel, Bonnie. 1986. "The Commoditization of Women in Tugen (Kenya) Social Organization." In *Women and Class in Africa*, ed. Claire Robertson and Iris Berger. New York: Africana Publishing Company.

———. 1992. "Gender Distortions and Development Disasters: Women and Milk in African Herding Systems." *National Women's Studies Association Journal* 4 (1): 23–41.

"Kilusu." 1956–1957. "Masai and Their Finery." *East African Annual, 1956–1957:* 135–137.

Korongero Integrated People Oriented to Conservation (KIPOC). 1990. "The Constitution. Document No. 1." Photocopy, Tanzania. In author's possession.

———. 1991. "The Foundational Program: Background, Profile of Activities and Budget." Principal Document 2. Mimeo, Tanzania. In author's possession.

Kipuri, Naomi. 1978. "Engagement and Marriage among the Maasai." *Kenya Past and Present* 9: 38–42.

———. 1983. *Oral Literature of the Maasai.* Nairobi, Kenya: Heinemann Educational Book.

———. 1989. "Maasai Women in Transition: Class and Gender in the Transformation of a Pastoral Society." Ph.D. diss., Temple University.

Kituyi, Mukhisa. 1990. *Becoming Kenyans: Socio-Economic Transformation of the Pastoral Maasai.* Nairobi, Kenya: Acts Press.

Kjekshus, Helge. 1977. *Ecology Control and Economic Development in East African History: The Case of Tanganyika, 1850–1950.* London: Heinemann.

Klima, George. 1964. "Jural Relations between the Sexes among the Barabaig." *Africa* 34 (1): 9–20.

Klumpp, Donna. 1987. "Maasai Art and Society: Age and Sex, Time and Space, Cash and Cattle." Ph.D. diss., Columbia University.

Klumpp, Donna, and Corinne Kratz. 1993. "Aesthetics, Expertise, and Ethnicity: Okiek and Maasai Perspectives on Personal Ornament." In *Being Maasai*, ed. Thomas Spear and Richard Waller. London: James Currey.

Knowles, Joan, and David Collett. 1989. "Nature as Myth, Symbol and Action: Notes towards a Historical Understanding of Development and Conservation in Kenyan Maasailand." *Africa* 59 (4): 433–460.

Koponen, Juhani. 1994. *Development For Exploitation: German Colonial Policies in Mainland Tanzania, 1884–1914.* Helsinki: Finnish Historical Society Studia Historica 49.

———. 1996. "Population: A Dependent Variable." In *Custodians of the Land: Ecology and Culture in the History of Tanzania*, ed. Gregory Maddox, James Giblin, and Isaria Kimambo. London: James Currey.

Koritschoner, Hans [Hans Cory]. 1936. "Ngoma ya Sheitani: An East African Native Treatment for Psychical Disorder." *The Journal of the Royal Anthropological Institute* 66: 209–219.

Krapf, J. Lewis. 1968 [1860]. *Travels, Researches and Missionary Labours during an Eighteen Years' Residence in Eastern Africa.* 2nd ed. London: Frank Cass & Co.

Kratz, Corinne. 1980. "Are the Okiek Really Maasai? or Kipsigis? or Kikuyu?" *Cahiers d'Etudes Africaines* 79: 355–368.

Bibliography

———. 1994. *Affecting Performance: Meaning, Movement and Experience in Okiek Women's Initiation.* Washington, D.C.: Smithsonian Institution Press.

Lambek, Michael. 1981. *Human Spirits: A Cultural Account of Trance in Mayotte.* New York: Cambridge University Press.

———. 1993. *Knowledge and Practice in Mayotte: Local Discourses of Islam, Sorcery, and Spirit Possession.* Toronto: University of Toronto Press.

Last, J. T. 1882. "The Masai People and Country." *Proceedings of the Royal Geographical Society* 4 (4): 224–226.

———. 1883. "A Visit to the Masai People Living beyond the Borders of Nguru Country." *Proceedings of the Royal Geographical Society* 5 (9): 517–543, 568 (map)

Lewis, I. M. 1971. *Ecstatic Religion: An Anthropological Study of Spirit Possession and Shamanism.* Pelican: Middlesex.

Little, Peter. 1992. *The Elusive Granary: Herder, Farmer and State in Northern Kenya.* Cambridge: Cambridge University Press.

Llewelyn-Davies, Melissa. 1978. "Two Contexts of Solidarity among Pastoral Maasai Women." In *Women United, Women Divided,* ed. Patricia Caplan and Janet Bujra. London: Tavistock.

———. 1981. "Women, Warriors, and Patriarchs." In *Sexual Meanings,* ed. Sherry Ortner and Harriet Whitehead. Cambridge: Cambridge University Press.

MacCormack, Carol, and Marilyn Strathern, eds. 1980. *Nature, Culture and Gender.* Cambridge: Cambridge University Press.

Mafeje, Archie. 1971. "The Ideology of 'Tribalism.'" *Journal of Modern African Studies* 9 (2): 253–261.

Maguire, R. A. J. 1928. "The Masai Penal Code." *Journal of the African Society* 28 (109): 12–18.

Maliyamkono, T. L., and M. S. D. Bagachwa. 1990. *The Second Economy in Tanzania.* London: James Currey.

Mallet, Marguerite. 1923. *A White Woman among the Masai.* London: T. Fisher Unwin.

Mato, Daniel. 1996. "On the Theory, Epistemology, and Politics of the Social Construction of 'Cultural Identities' in the Age of Globalization: Introductory Remarks to Ongoing Debates." *Identities* 3 (102): 61–72.

Mbilinyi, Marjorie. 1988. "Runaway Wives: Forced Labour and Forced Marriage in Colonial Rungwe." *International Journal of Sociology of Law* 16 (1): 1–29.

Mbise, Ismael R. 1974. *Blood on Our Land.* Dar es Salaam: Tanzania Publishing House.

Meena, Ruth. 1991. "The Impact of Structural Adjustment Programs on Rural Women in Tanzania." In *Structural Adjustment and African Women Farmers,* ed. Christina Gladwin. Gainesville: University of Florida Press.

Merker, Moritz. 1910 [1904]. *Die Masai. Ethnographische Monographie eines ostafrikanischen Semitenvolkes.* 2nd ed. Berlin: Dietrich Reimer.

Mol, Frans. 1977. *Maa: A Dictionary of the Maasai Language and Folklore.* Nairobi: Marketing and Publishing.

———. 1996. *Maasai Language and Culture Dictionary.* Narok: Maasai Centre Lemek.

Moore, Henrietta. 1986. *Space, Text, and Gender: An Anthropological Study of the Marakwet of Kenya.* Cambridge: Cambridge University Press.

———. 1988. *Feminism and Anthropology.* Minneapolis: University of Minnesota Press.

Moore, Sally Falk. 1986. *Social Facts and Fabrications: "Customary" Law on Kilimanjaro, 1880–1980.* Cambridge: Cambridge University Press.

Morgan, D. J. 1980. *The Official History of Colonial Development.* 5 vols. Atlantic Highlands, N.J.: Humanities Press.

Murumbi, D. 1994. "The Concept of Indigenous." *Indigenous Affairs* 1: 52–57.

Musendo, Zephania. 1990. "Sokoine: Man of the People." *Daily News* (Tanzania), 12 April 1990, p. 4.

Mwapachu, Juma Volter. 1979. "Operation Planned Villages in Rural Tanzania: A Revolutionary Strategy for Development." In *African Socialism in Practice,* ed. Andrew Coulson. Nottingham: Spokesman.

Mwiliye, Mgala Satiel. 1989. "The Best Monument for Sokoine." Letter to the People's Forum. *Daily News* (Tanzania), 25 April 1989, p. 9.

Nathan, Martha, Elliot Fratkin, and Eric Roth. 1996. "Sedentism and Child Health among Rendille Pastoralists of Northern Kenya." *Social Science and Medicine* 43 (4): 503–515.

Ndagala, Daniel. 1982. "Operation Imparnati: The Sedentarization of the Pastoral Maasai in Tanzania." *Nomadic Peoples* 10: 28–39.

———. 1990. "Territory, Pastoralists, and Livestock: Resource Control among the Kisongo Maasai." Ph.D. thesis, Uppsala University.

Ndegwa, Stephen. 1996. *The Two Faces of Civil Society: NGOs and Politics in Africa.* West Hartford, Conn.: Kumarian Press.

Neumann, Roderick P. 1995a. "Ways of Seeing Africa: Colonial Recasting of African Society and Landscape in Serengeti National Park." *Ecumene* 2 (2): 149–169.

———. 1995b. "Local Challenges to Global Agendas: Conservation, Economic Liberalization and the Pastoralists' Rights Movement in Tanzania." *Antipode* 27 (4): 363–382.

Nyerere, Julius. 1968. *Ujamaa: Essays on Socialism.* Dar es Salaam: Oxford University Press.

Oboler, Regina. 1985. *Women, Power and Economic Change: The Nandi of Kenya.* Stanford: Stanford University Press.

———. 1996. "Whose Cows Are They Anyway? Ideology and Behavior in Nandi Cattle 'Ownership' and Control." *Human Ecology* 24 (2): 255–272.

Okeyo, Achola Pala. 1980. "Daughters of the Lakes and Rivers: Colonization and the Land Rights of Luo Women." In *Women and Colonization: Anthropological Perspectives,* ed. Mona Etienne and Eleanor Leacock. New York: Praeger.

Ortner, Sherry, and Harriet Whitehead, eds. 1981. *Sexual Meanings.* Cambridge: Cambridge University Press.

Page-Jones, F. H. 1944. "Maasailand Comprehensive Report." In Masai District Book (copies in CAMP and TNA).

———. 1948. "Water in Masailand." *Tanganyika Notes and Records* 26: 51–59.

Parkipuny, Lazaro ole. 1975. "Maasai Predicament beyond Pastoralism: A Case Study in the Socio-Economic Transformation of Pastoralism." M. A. thesis, Development Studies, University of Dar es Salaam.

———. 1979. "Some Crucial Aspects of the Maasai Predicament." In *African Socialism in Practice,* ed. Andrew Coulson. Nottingham: Spokesman.

Pastoralist Network in Tanzania (PANET). 1993. *Newsletter of the Pastoral Network of Tanzania.* Issue 4.

———. 1994. *Newsletter of the Pastoral Network of Tanzania.* Issue 5.

Perham, Margery. 1976. *East African Journey: Kenya and Tanganyika 1929–30.* London: Faber & Faber.

Bibliography

Perlez, Jane. 1989. "The Proud Masai's Fate: Finally, to Be Fenced In?" *The New York Times,* 16 October 1989, p. A4.

Peters, Pauline. 1994. *Dividing the Commons: Politics, Policy and Culture in Botswana.* Charlottesville: University Press of Virginia.

Peterson, David. 1971. "Devil Possession among the Masai." Unpublished paper.

Pigg, Stacy Leigh. 1992. "Inventing Social Categories through Place: Social Representations and Development in Nepal." *Comparative Studies in Society and History* 34 (3): 491–513.

———. 1993. "Unintended Consequences: The Ideological Impact of Development in Nepal." *South Asia Bulletin* 13 (1–2): 45–58.

Potkanski, Tomasz. 1994. *Property Concepts, Herding Patterns and Management of Natural Resources among the Ngorongoro and Salei Masai of Tanzania.* London: International Institute for Environment and Development.

Raikes, Philip. 1981. *Livestock, Development and Policy in East Africa.* Uppsala: Scandinavian Institute of African Studies.

Ranger, Terence. 1983. "The Invention of Tradition in Colonial Africa." In *The Invention of Tradition,* ed. Eric Hobsbawm and Terence Ranger. Cambridge: Cambridge University Press.

Presidential Commission of Inquiry into Land Matters. 1994. *Report of the Presidential Land Commission of Inquiry into Land Matters.* Vol. I. *Land Policy and Land Tenure Structure.* Dar es Salaam: The Ministry of Lands, Housing and Urban Development, Government of the United Republic of Tanzania.

Presidential Land Commission of Inquiry into Land Matters. 1994. *Report of the Presidential Land Commission of Inquiry into Land Matters.* Vol. II. *Selected Land Disputes and Recommendations.* Dar es Salaam: The Ministry of Lands, Housing and Urban Development, Government of the United Republic of Tanzania.

Rigby, Peter. 1985. *Persistent Pastoralists: Nomadic Societies in Transition.* London: Zed Books.

———. 1992. *Cattle, Capitalism, and Class: Ilparakuyo Maasai Transformations.* Philadelphia: Temple University Press.

Rocheleau, Dianne, Barbara Thomas-Slayter, and David Edmunds. 1995. "Gendered Resource Mapping: Focusing on Women's Spaces in the Landscape." *Cultural Survival Quarterly* 18 (4): 62–68.

Rocheleau, Dianne, Barbara Thomas-Slayter, and Esther Wangari, eds. 1996. *Feminist Political Ecology: Global Issues and Local Experiences.* New York: Routledge.

Rosaldo, Michelle. 1980. "The Use and Abuse of Anthropology: Reflections on Feminism and Cross-Cultural Understanding." *Signs* 5 (3): 389–417.

Rosaldo, Michelle, and Louise Lamphere, eds. 1974. *Women, Culture and Society.* Stanford: Stanford University Press.

Rostow, Walt Whitman. 1960. *The Stages of Economic Growth: A Non-Communist Manifesto.* Cambridge: Cambridge University Press.

Sachs, Wolfgang, ed. 1992. *The Development Dictionary.* London: Zed Books.

Sacks, Karen. 1979. *Sisters and Wives: The Past and Future of Sexual Equality.* Westport, Conn.: Greenwood Press.

Saitoti, Tepilit ole. 1986. *The Worlds of a Maasai Warrior: An Autobiography.* Berkeley: University of California Press.

Saitoti, Tepilit ole, and Carol Beckwith. 1980. *Maasai.* New York: Harry N. Abrams.

Sandford, G. R. 1919. *An Administrative and Political History of the Maasai Reserve.* London.

Saul, John. 1979. "The Dialectic of Class and Tribe." In *The State and Revolution in Eastern Africa.* New York: Monthly Review Press.

Scharfman, Susan. 1989. "Tanzania Must Not Fence in the Proud, Cattle-Herding Maasai." Letter to the Editor. The *New York Times,* 3 November 1989, p. A34.

Schmidt, Elizabeth. 1991. "Patriarchy, Capitalism and the Colonial State in Zimbabwe." *Signs* 16 (4): 732–756.

Schneider, Harold K. 1979. *Livestock and Equality in East Africa: The Economic Bases for Social Structure.* Bloomington: Indiana University Press.

Schrire, Carmel, ed. 1984. *Past and Present in Hunter-Gatherer Studies.* Orlando, Fla.: Academic Press.

Scott, James C. 1998. *Seeing Like a State.* New Haven: Yale University Press.

Scott, Joan. 1988. *Gender and the Politics of History.* New York: Columbia University Press.

Shorter, Aylward. 1970. "The *Migawo:* Peripheral Spirit Possession and Christian Prejudice." *Anthropos* 65 (1–2): 100–126.

Shostak, Marjorie. 1981. *Nisa: The Life and Words of a !Kung Woman.* New York: Vintage Books.

Smith, Michael Peter. 1994. "Can You Imagine? Transnational Migration and the Globalization of Grassroots Politics." *Social Text* 39 (Summer): 15–33.

Sommer, Gabriele, and Rainer Vossen. 1993. "Dialects, Sectiolects, or Simply Lects? The Maa Language in Time Perspective." In *Being Maasai,* ed. Thomas Spear and Richard Waller. London: James Currey.

Spear, Thomas. 1993. "Being 'Maasai,' but Not 'People of the Cattle': Arusha Agricultural Maasai in the Nineteenth Century." In *Being Maasai,* ed. Thomas Spear and Richard Waller. London: James Currey.

———. 1997. *Mountain Farmers.* Oxford: James Currey.

Spear, Thomas, and Derek Nurse. 1992. "Maasai Farmers: The Evolution of Arusha Agriculture." *The International Journal of African Historical Studies* 25 (3): 481–503.

Spear, Thomas, and Richard Waller, eds. 1993. *Being Maasai: Ethnicity and Identity in East Africa.* London: James Currey.

Spencer, Paul. 1988. *The Maasai of Matapato: A Study of Rituals of Rebellion.* Bloomington: Indiana University Press.

Stahl, Kathleen. 1961. *Tanganyika: Sail in the Wilderness.* The Hague: Mouton & Co.

Stavenhagen, Rudolfo. 1987. "Ethnocide or Ethnodevelopment: The New Challenge." *Development: Seeds of Change—Village through Global Order* 1: 74–78.

Steady, Filomina. 1987. "African Feminism: A Worldwide Perspective." In *Women in Africa and the African Diaspora,* ed. Rosalyn Terborg-Penn, Sharon Harley, and Andrea Benton Rushing. Trenton, N.J.: Africa World Press.

Stichter, Sharon, and Jane Parpart. 1988. "Introduction: Towards a Materialist Perspective on African Women." In *Patriarchy and Class: African Women in the Home and the Workforce,* ed. Sharon Stichter and Jane Parpart. Boulder, Colo.: Westview Press.

Stoller, Paul. 1994. "Embodying Colonial Memories." *American Anthropologist* 96 (3): 634–648.

Sudarkasa, Niara. 1987. "The Status of Women in Indigenous African Societies." In *Women in Africa and the African Diaspora,* ed. Rosalyn Terborg-Penn, Sharon Harley, and Andrea Benton Rushing. Trenton: Africa World Press.

Sutton, John. 1990. *A Thousand Years in East Africa.* Nairobi: British Institute in Eastern Africa.

———. 1993. "Becoming Maasailand." In *Being Maasai,* ed. Thomas Spear and Richard Waller. London: James Currey.

Talle, Aud. 1987. "Women as Heads of Houses: The Organization of Production and the Role of Women among the Pastoral Maasai in Kenya." *Ethnos* 52 (1–2): 50–80.

———. 1988. *Women at a Loss: Changes in Maasai Pastoralism and Their Effects on Gender Relations.* Stockholm: Stockholm Studies in Social Anthropology.

Tanganyika Territory. *Blue Books.* Dar es Salaam: The Government Printer (annual report, 1926–1938, 1945–1948).

Tanzania Gender Networking Programme (TGNP). 1994. "Structural Adjustment and Gender Empowerment or Disempowerment." Symposium report, Dar es Salaam. In author's possession.

Tate, H. R. 1949–1950. "Three East Africans of Mark." *East African Annual, 1949–1950:* 44–48.

Tenga, R. W. 1992. "Pastoral Land Rights in Tanzania: A Review." In *Drylands Programme: Pastoral Land Tenure Series.* London: International Institute for Environment and Development.

Thomson, Joseph. 1968 [1885]. *Through Masai Land.* London: Frank Cass.

Tidrick, Kathryn. 1990. "The Masai and Their Masters." In *Empire and the English Character.* London: I. B. Tauris & Co.

Tsing, Anna. 1993. *In the Realm of the Diamond Queen: Marginality in an Out-of-the-Way Place.* Princeton: Princeton University Press.

Turner, Terence. 1991. "Representing, Resisting, Rethinking: Historical Transformations of Kayapo Culture and Anthropological Consciousness." In *Colonial Situations: Essays on the Contextualization of Ethnographic Knowledge,* ed. George Stocking. Madison: University of Wisconsin Press.

Udvardy, Monica, and Maria Cattell. 1992. "Gender, Aging and Power in Sub-Saharan Africa." *Journal of Cross-Cultural Gerontology* 7: 275–288.

Utah State University Team. 1976. *Evaluation of the Maasai Livestock and Range Management Project.* Logan, Utah: Utah State University.

Vail, Leroy, ed. 1991. *The Creation of Tribalism in Southern Africa.* Berkeley: University of California Press.

Vail, Leroy, and Landeg White. 1991. "The Possession of the Dispossessed: Song as History among Tumbuka Women." In *Power and the Praise Poem: Southern African Voices in History.* Charlottesville: University Press of Virginia.

Van Beusekom, Monica, and Dorothy L. Hodgson, eds. 2000. *Lessons Learned? Development Experiences in the Late Colonial Period.* Special Issue of *Journal of African History* 41 (1).

Van Binsbergen, W. 1981. "The Unit of Study and the Interpretation of Ethnicity." *Journal of Southern African Studies* 8 (1): 51–81.

Van Voorthuizen, E. G. c. 1971. "Report on Cultivation Activities in Masai District." Prepared for Masai Livestock and Range Management Project, USAID. In author's possession.

Veterinary Department. 1926. Annual Report of the Veterinary Department, Tanganyika Territory.

von Freyhold, Michaela. 1979. *Ujamaa Villages in Tanzania: Analysis of a Social Experiment.* New York: Monthly Review Press.

Voshaar, Jan. 1979. "Tracing God's Walking Stick in Maa: A Study of Maasai Society, Culture and Religion." Doktorale scriptie. Nijmegen, The Netherlands: Catholic University of Nijmegen.

W., E. H. 1943–1944. "Masailand: Tradition and Progress." *East African Annual* 1943–1944: 89–96.

Wakefield, Rev. Thomas. 1870. "Routes of Native Caravans from the Coast to the Interior of Eastern Africa." *Journal of the Royal Geographical Society* 40: 303–339.

———. 1882. "Native Routes through the Masai Country." *Proceedings of the Royal Geographical Society* 4 (12): 742–747.

———. 1883. "The Wakwafi Raid on the District near Mombassa." *Proceedings of the Royal Geographical Society* 5 (5): 289–290.

Walby, Sylvia. 1990. *Theorizing Patriarchy.* Oxford: Basil Blackwell.

Waller, Richard. 1976. "The Maasai and the British 1895–1905: The Origins of an Alliance." *Journal of African History* 17 (4): 529–553.

———. 1978. "Lords of East Africa: The Maasai in the Mid-Nineteenth Century (c. 1840–c. 1885)." Ph.D. thesis, Cambridge University.

———. 1984. "Interaction and Identity on the Periphery: The Trans-Mara Maasai." *The International Journal of African Historical Studies* 17 (2): 243–284.

———. 1985a. "Ecology, Migration and Expansion in East Africa." *African Affairs* 84 (336): 347–370.

———. 1985b. "Economic and Social Relations in the Central Rift Valley: The Maa-Speakers and Their Neighbours in the Nineteenth Century." In *Kenya in the Nineteenth Century,* ed. Bethwel Ogot. Nairobi: Anyange Press.

———. 1988. "Emutai: Crisis and Response in Maasailand 1883–1902." In *The Ecology of Survival: Case Studies from Northeast African History,* ed. Douglas Johnson and David Anderson. Boulder, Colo.: Westview Press.

———. 1993a. "Acceptees and Aliens: Kikuyu Settlement in Maasailand." In *Being Maasai,* ed. Thomas Spear and Richard Waller. London: James Currey.

———. 1993b. "Conclusions." In *Being Maasai,* ed. Thomas Spear and Richard Waller. London: James Currey.

Waller, Richard, and Kathy Homewood. 1997. "Elders and Experts: Contesting Veterinary Knowledge in a Pastoral Community." In *Western Medicine as Contested Knowledge,* ed. Andrew Cunningham and B. Andrews. Manchester: Manchester University Press.

Wallerstein, Immanuel. 1974. *The Modern World-System: Capitalist Agriculture and the Origins of the European World Economy in the 16th Century.* New York: Academic Press.

Watts, Michael. 1993. "Development I: Power, Knowledge, Discursive Practice." *Progress in Human Geography* 17 (2): 257–272.

White, Luise. 1990. *The Comforts of Home: Prostitution in Colonial Nairobi.* Chicago: University of Chicago Press.

Wienpahl, J. 1984. "Women's Roles in Livestock Production among the Turkana of Kenya." *Research in Economic Anthropology* 6: 193–215.

Williams, Raymond. 1977. *Marxism and Literature.* Oxford: Oxford University Press.

Wilmsen, Edwin. 1989. *Land Filled with Flies: A Political Economy of the Kalahari.* Chicago: University of Chicago Press.

Worby, Eric. 1988. "Livestock Policy and Development in Botswana." In *Power and Poverty: Development and Development Projects in the Third World,* ed. Donald W. Attwood, Thomas C. Bruneau, and John G. Galaty. Boulder, Colo.: Westview Press.

Bibliography

———. 1994. "Maps, Names and Ethnic Games: The Epistemology and Iconography of Colonial Power in Northwestern Zimbabwe." *Journal of Southern African Studies* 20 (3): 371–392.

Yanagisako, Sylvia Junko. 1979. "Family and Household: The Analysis of Domestic Groups." *Annual Review of Anthropology* 8: 161–205.

Index

Index

commoditization, 67–72, 91–92, 221–27
culture: and development, 7–8, 108–109, 199–200, 213–14, 216–17, 258, 270–76; and "modernity," 250–69
curses, 65
customary law, 12, 65

dances, 42, 47, 247–48, 263–64; photo, 32
decolonization, 119–24
descent, 98–99, 252
development: questionable impact, 4–5; competing visions, 5, 7–8; paradoxes, 6; and pastoralists, 6; anthropologists and, 7–9; and cultural change, 7, 108–109, 145, 199–200, 213–14, 216–17, 250–69, 270–76; cultural politics of, 7–10; as a transnational process, 9–10; issues of scale, 10; and state control, 10, 87, 88–91, 101, 109–10; and bureaucracies, 10, 82, 102; colonial legacies, 10–11; and ethnicity, 11–13; and gender, 13–16, 86–87, 118–19, 218–20, 234–39, 274–75; in precolonial period, 36; in early colonial periods, 74–91; Maasai financing of projects, 74–80, 103, 107, 109, 124, 137, 214; integrated vision, 89–90, 102; in late colonial period, 100–38; Maasai attitudes toward, 105, 198, 258; women's projects, 141, 147, 227–28; in postcolonial period, 142–43, 148–49, 202–40. *See also* agriculture; economic diversification; education; grinding machines; livestock; Masai Development Plan; Masai Livestock Development and Range Management Project; Masai Water Loan; medical; Monduli Juu Dairy Project; water; World Bank
disasters: epidemics of 1883–92, 36–37, 38–39; rinderpest and drought of 1934–35, 87–89
disease: venereal, 35, 38, 109; smallpox, 36; cholera, 167. *See also orpeko*
divorce, 27. *See also kirtala*
domestic sphere, relation to political sphere, 32–33, 66–67, 92, 284n11
dress: customary, 30, 43, 47; changes in, 43, 45–46, 246–47, 254–55, 257; state campaigns against, 149
drought: of 1929, 59; of 1934–35, 87–89; of 1960–62, 136–37; of 1983–84, 221

East Africa Royal Commission, 119
East African Governors Conference (1932), 85–86
East Coast fever, 220–21

economic diversification, 173, 242; and polygyny, 180. *See also* agriculture; labor; shops
education: Maasai attitudes toward, 46, 97, 126–34 passim, 140, 141–42, 147, 183–84, 186, 199, 241, 248, 251; colonial experiences, 97, 126–34, 140, 198; gender differences, 97, 133–34, 187–88, 241; postcolonial experiences, 97, 141–42, 144–45, 182–88; nationalization of schools, 97, 142; debates over curriculum, 126–28; enrollment figures, 185; and "indigenous" development, 233. *See also* Catholic church; Lutheran church; Masai School
elaitin tree, 246, 247
elections, 191–93, 199, 201
electricity, 306n41
Eluwai, 163
Emairete, 17, 40, 96, 135, 162, 163–65, 167–95 passim, 196–99 passim, 220–21, 225–27, 227–30; map, 164. *See also* Komolonik mountain; Monduli Juu; Monduli Juu Dairy Project
emanyata, 27, 256, 298n91
Embopong', 166–67, 167–95 passim; map, 164. *See also* Mfereji
Eng'ai, 23, 33, 94, 97, 168, 265, 269, 284n12
Engarenaibor, 4, 5
Engitau (Maasai elder), 64
enkaji: photo, 28, 173; spatial layout, 32, 34; changes in, 172–73, 241
enkang': 27, 30; photo, 28; changes in, 171–72
enkanyit, 4, 18–19, 26–27, 31, 39, 66, 94, 99, 119, 273, 276
enyorrata, 39, 43–44, 99
Escobar, Arturo, 8–9
Essimingor, 113, 162
ethnicity: and development, 11–13, 100–22, 270–76; contemporary salience, 12–13; colonial concept of "tribes," 12, 48–49, 51, 54, 62, 73; and gender, 14–16, 72–73, 276; relationships between Maasai and Arusha, 35, 58, 72, 73, 135, 167–71; racialized differences, 73; and national identity, 201; and "indigenous" identity, 230–39; and beadwork, 306n40
Eunoto ritual, 34, 54, 56

farming implements, 178, 179
Ferguson, James, 11
fire-stick elders. *See ilpiron*
First Maasai Conference on Culture and Development (1991), 234–36, 239
food: preferences/restrictions, 30, 41, 44, 136,

Index

Komolonik Ranching Association, 160–61, 171, 177, 205–208, 209–11, 215; map, 207

Korongoro Integrated People Oriented to Conservation (KIPOC), 231–39. *See also* Parkipuny, Lazaro

Kotokai (Laigwenan), 111

Kuiya, 64

Kwavi, 24, 54, 73, 282*n4*

labor: colonial demands, 77, 115–116, 136–37; Maasai as wage-laborers, 95, 134; Maasai employment of, 114, 115–16, 117, 180, 242; by children, 184–86

land alienation, 52–54, 56–59, 111–16, 121, 142–43, 162, 199, 217, 296*n67;* and development, 80–81, 103, 113, 198, 236–39

land allocation, 177–78, 220, 237–38

Lekisaka (Laigwenan), 114, 121

Lemisigie stream, 52–53, 57

Lenana (Laibon), 61

Lendikenya, 135, 162, 165, 186

Lengijabe, 77

livestock: production, 29–30, 174–76, 180–81; rights in, 29, 44–45, 143, 222–24; exchange, 30, 44–45; diseases, 36, 80–81, 82, 84, 87, 291*n146;* sales, 44, 70–72, 84–87, 95, 107–108, 146–47, 213, 222–24, 294*n41*, 295*n44;* "trespassing," 55, 137; thefts, 37, 65, 115, 298*n92;* permits, 55, 82–84; "overstocking," 71, 84–86; development projects, 80–87; quarantines, 82–84; as a national asset, 85, 87, 107; deaths, 87–88, 146; census of holdings, 101, 174–76; "voluntary" sales quotas, 103; and stratification, 174–76; chickens, 175; dips, 209–10, 220; "improved" bulls, 211; slaughter, 244, 303*n43. See also* Masai Development Plan; Masai Livestock Development and Range Management Project; milk; Monduli Juu Dairy Project; range management; veterinary department; veterinary guards

Llewelyn-Davies, Melissa, 15

Lolbene, 78

Loliondo, 4, 130, 150, 160

Lolkisale, 112

Lossimingor, 215

Lutheran church, 163; schools, 126, 130; and development, 221; and *orpeko,* 259–69 passim

Maa language, 144–45

Maasai: stereotypes, 1–3, 6, 49, 80, 91, 108–109, 119, 148, 150–51, 208, 232, 250–51, 270, 277–78; as masculine identity, 2, 14, 72–73, 134; attitudes toward development, 3, 105, 197–98, 214, 272–75; relationship to nation-state, 3, 272–73; early history, 22–26; origin myths, 23; relations with other ethnic groups, 23–25, 51, 120–21; and Swahili traders, 25–26; and early travelers, 25–26; early gender relations, 26–36; and social stratification, 29; consolidation in Reserve, 50–59; relationship to Arusha ethnic group, 72, 73, 120–21, 135, 167–71; financing of development projects, 74–80, 103, 107, 109, 124, 137, 214; relationship to colonial state, 90–91, 119, 120–21; perceptions of Europeans, 95, 98, 138, 273, 287*n55;* population census, 101; as "indigenous" people, 230–39; and "modernity," 250–69

Maasai Women's Conference (1996), 236

Maasai Women's Cultural Exhibit (1991), 234–35

Maasailand. *See* Masai District; Masai Reserve

Maguire, 90

marriage, 38, 43–44, 292*n1;* elopement, 38, 99, 258; role of women, 98–99, 143; intermarriage between Maasai and Arusha, 135; as strategy of economic diversification, 180–81; and *ormeek,* 252, 258. *See also* bridewealth; *kirtala* (divorce)

"Mary," 223, 241–49

Masai. *See* Maasai

Masai Council, 64, 88, 90, 103, 124, 133, 159–60, 198, 200, 300*n149. See also* Masai Native Authority; Olkiama

Masai Development Plan (1951–1955), 100–22, 124–26, 142

Masai District, 56–59, 90, 158; map, 207. *See also* Masai Livestock Development and Range Management Project

Masai Livestock Development and Range Management Project (MLDRP) (1970s), 143, 165, 166, 202–21

Masai Native Authority, 58, 61–67, 90. *See also* Masai Council; Olkiama

Masai Reserve, 38, 51–59, 109, 285*n8;* map of, 53

Masai School, 57, 126–33

Masai Water Loan, 68, 74–80

"Masaiitis," 112

Masailand Comprehensive Report (1944), 129, 289*n104. See also* Page-Jones

Mbarnoti, Edward, 199, 300*n149*

Index

Poyoni, Morani ole, 18–19
pregnancy, 263; and miscarriage, 264
propaganda campaigns, 125
prophets. *See iloibonok*

quarantines. *See* livestock, quarantines

radios, 193–94, 257
ranching associations, 124–25, 205–208, 209–
    11, 214–15, 217. *See also* Komolonik
    Ranching Association; Masai Livestock
    Development and Range Management
    Project
range management: Maasai system, 96, 116–17,
    158–59; implementation of grazing con-
    trols, 104; changes in, 238
Range Management and Development Act of
    1964, 158–60, 205, 215
Ranger, Terrence, 12
research methods and sources, 14, 16–19, 22,
    105, 194, 222, 276
respect. See *enkanyit*
rinderpest, 36, 80–81, 82, 87
rituals, 33, 145, 243–49
roads, demands for, 5
Rowe, 90

Sanya Corridor, 112
Schneider, Harold, 15
Serengeti National Park, 112, 113–14, 162,
    297*n83*
Sherwood, 130–31
shops, 146–47; picture, 181
sickness, and *orpeko*, 258–69
Simanjiro, 4, 99, 141, 143, 160
Sinya, 191
Sirowei (headman), 132
Small Industries Development Organization
    (SIDO), 229–30
social stratification, 29, 173–76, 186
socialism. *See* Ujamaa
Sokoine, Edward, 98, 149, 162, 183, 184, 186,
    188, 191, 196–201, 272, 304*n11*
songs, 245, 247–48, 263–64
Spencer, Paul, 15
spirit possession. *See orpeko*
state control, and development, 10, 87, 88–91,
    101, 109–10
Structural Adjustment Program (SAP), 155,
    156–57, 305*n17*
Swahili language, 45, 128, 153, 183–84, 251,
    254–55, 259

Swahili people, 3, 46, 244. *See also ormeek*
Symes, Governor, 85–86

Talamai Ranching Association, 209–11, 212,
    213; map, 207. *See also* Kijungu; Masai
    Livestock Development and Range Man-
    agement Project
Tanganyika Africa National Union (TANU),
    122–24, 136, 142, 188–89, 198, 300*n149*
Tanganyika African Association (TAA). *See*
    Tanganyika Africa National Union
Tanzania Breweries, 162, 225–27
Tanzanian administrators: local government, 97;
    Maasai experiences of, 144–45, 194, 217–
    18, 272–73; attitudes toward Maasai, 148–
    50, 162, 217; and political affiliation, 188;
    members of Parliament, 191–93, 199–201;
    relations with USAID personnel, 214–16.
    See also specific names
Tarangire National Park, 162
Taresaro Ujamaa Ranch, 210–11. *See also* Komo-
    lonik Ranching Association
taxation, 55, 63, 68–70, 76, 80, 95, 103, 107,
    143, 293*n18*
Terrat, 146
Thomas, Mama Joseph, 141
Thomson, Joseph, 35
tobacco, 30
Toure, Dr. Salash, 191–93
Toure, President Sekou (of Guinea), 192
tourism, 150, 227–28
trade, formalization of, 70–72
traders: Swahili caravans, 25–26, 30; "itinerant,"
    55, 70, 71. *See also* women, as traders
travelers: accounts, 25–26; interactions with
    women, 35
"tribes." *See* ethnicity
tsetse eradication efforts, 102, 104, 116–17,
    292*n9*. *See also* Masai Development Plan
Twining, Governor, 123

Ugandan War, 154, 201
Ujamaa, 151–55, 182–83, 214–15, 241. *See also*
    Operation Imparnati
Ujamaa Corporate Ranch Livestock Credit Proj-
    ect, 212
umbrellas, 30
Umoja wa Wanawake wa Tanzania (UWT),
    189, 228
United States Agency for International De-
    velopment (USAID), 159, 205–20, 234,
    304*n11*. *See also* Masai Livestock De-

DOROTHY L. HODGSON

teaches anthropology at Rutgers University, New Brunswick, New Jersey, where she is affiliated with the Center for African Studies and the Women's Studies Department. She is the editor of *Rethinking Pastoralism in Africa: Gender, Culture, and the Myth of the Patriarchal Pastoralist; Gendered Modernities: Ethnographic Perspectives;* and co-editor of *"Wicked" Women and the Reconfiguration of Gender in Africa.*